New
Testament
Ethics

The Legacies of Jesus and Paul

New Testament Ethics

FRANK J. MATERA

Westminster John Knox Press
Louisville, Kentucky

Some of the material in chapter 1 appeared in another form in F. J. Matera, "Ethics for the Kingdom of God: The Gospel according to Mark," *Louvain Studies* 20 (1995) 187–200.

Book design by Jennifer K. Cox
Cover design by Vickie Arrowood

First edition

Published by Westminster John Knox Press
Louisville, Kentucky

This book is printed on acid-free paper that meets the American National Standards Institute Z39.48 standard. ∞

PRINTED IN THE UNITED STATES OF AMERICA

96 97 98 99 00 01 02 03 04 05 — 10 9 8 7 6 5 4 3 2 1

Library of Congress Cataloging-in-Publication Data
Matera, Frank J.
    New Testament ethics : the legacies of Jesus and Paul / Frank J. Matera — 1st ed.
        p.   cm.
    Includes bibliographical references and index.
    ISBN 0-664-22069-X (alk. paper)
    1. Ethics in the Bible.   2. Bible. N.T.—Criticism, interpretation, etc.   I. Title.
BS2545.E8M38   1996
241.5—dc20   96-16563

Contents

Preface   vii

Introduction
    The Task of New Testament Ethics   1

PART ONE: The Legacy of Jesus   **11**

1. Ethics for the Kingdom of God
    The Gospel according to Mark   13

2. Doing the Greater Righteousness
    The Gospel according to Matthew   36

3. Ethics in an Age of Salvation
    The Gospel according to Luke   64

4. Ethics Becomes Christology
    The Gospel according to John   92

PART TWO: The Legacy of Paul   **119**

5. An Ethic of Election
    The Letters to the Thessalonians   123

6. Ethics for the Sanctified Community
    The Letters to the Corinthians   138

7. Walking by the Spirit
    The Letter to the Galatians   161

8. An Ethic of Imitation and Example
    The Letter to the Philippians   174

9. The Obedience of Faith
    The Letter to the Romans   184

10. Ethics for a New Creation
    The Letters to the Colossians and the Ephesians   207

11. Reliable Moral Guides
    The Pastoral Epistles   229

Conclusion
    The Ethical Legacy of Jesus and Paul   248
Abbreviations   256
Notes   258
Select Bibliography   301
Scripture Index   311
Subject Index   321

Preface

*N*ow that this work has been brought to completion, it is my pleasure to acknowledge the help and assistance I received from others. First and foremost is the help and encouragement of my colleagues in the School of Religious Studies at the Catholic University of America, Christopher Begg, Raymond Collins, John Meier, and John Galvin, all of whom undertook the laborious task of reading this manuscript. In doing so, they provided me with numerous suggestions for improvement and saved me from embarrassing errors. Thanks to their careful attention to detail, this manuscript is much improved.

Second, I wish to acknowledge the assistance I received from students at the Catholic University of America, especially Pamela Hamilton, my research assistant during the Fall semester of 1994. In large measure, this book is the result of a dialogue with students who heard its content in class and responded with constructive suggestions for improvement.

Third, I wish to acknowledge the assistance and encouragement of my editor, Jon L. Berquist of Westminster John Knox Press. He enthusiastically supported this project when I first proposed it to him, and ever since he has offered sound advice.

Finally, I wish to acknowledge the friendship of Monsignor Francis A. Fries: pastor, educator, and friend. He has continually encouraged my academic endeavors and been a constant source of friendship and support. In recognition of that support and friendship, this book is dedicated to him.

The Task of New Testament Ethics

The New Testament is immensely important for the moral or ethical life of the church, and its writings are continually employed for preaching, teaching, and nurturing the Christian community.[1] The stories and parables it tells, the moral exhortations and guidance it gives, the lists of virtues and vices it presents have influenced and formed the moral life of believers. That the church should turn to the New Testament for moral guidance is not surprising since it contains the ethical teaching of Jesus, Paul, and others. Thus the church holds that these writings, in conjunction with those of the Old Testament, are a sure and reliable guide to the moral life.

When one inquires about the ethical teaching of the New Testament with a view to organizing this teaching in a systematic fashion, however, it is important to take into consideration the following facts. First, the New Testament consists of several diverse writings: four Gospels that are essentially narrative in structure; a popular history of the early church and its great missionary, Paul (Acts); thirteen letters attributed to Paul; seven letters ascribed to James, John, Peter, and Jude; a homiletic letter-essay (Hebrews); and a book of prophecy (Revelation). Second, the writings within these categories, for example, the Synoptic Gospels and the Gospel of John, are often strikingly different from one another. Third, the diverse writings of the New Testament were occasioned by historical circumstances that greatly influenced their literary shape and the manner in which they proclaimed their religious message. While this is most evident in the letters of the New Testament, it is also true for its narrative writings since they were written with particular communities of believers in view. Fourth, while the New Testament's writings are concerned with moral or ethical behavior, they are not ethical treatises or discussions of the moral life as are the essays and letters of Seneca and other popular Greco-

1

Roman moral philosophers of the time. The moral teaching of the New Testament is part of a religious message that proclaims salvation, and it is best understood in light of that message.

Because the New Testament mediates moral teaching through a diverse body of religious literature that is historically and culturally conditioned, those engaged in the task of New Testament ethics cannot summarize the New Testament's moral teaching in the same way that they might condense or systematize the ethical teaching of an individual moral philosopher such as Aristotle or Epictetus. Accordingly, one might well ask about the legitimacy of this enterprise called New Testament ethics. Inasmuch as the New Testament was not written by a single author, is it proper to speak of New Testament ethics? Perhaps it would be better to discuss the many and diverse ethical writings in the New Testament. In a word, the literary character of the New Testament as a collection of diverse writings raises a series of questions about the discipline traditionally called New Testament ethics. It is important, therefore, to clarify the purpose and method of the present work. But before doing so, it is necessary to see how others have viewed the task.

APPROACHES TO NEW TESTAMENT ETHICS

Overall, specialists have approached New Testament ethics in one of two ways: either diachronically or synchronically.[2] In what follows, I will summarize representative works of each approach.[3]

A Book of Many Writings

The diachronic method assumes that the New Testament is a collection of diverse writings composed by different authors for varying circumstances, and that many of these writings, such as the Gospels, are the products of a complex tradition history. Consequently, in order to hear the many and distinct voices of the New Testament, as well as the submerged voices embedded in its writings,[4] this approach views the New Testament as if it were an archaeological mound that must be excavated layer by layer. Chronological and historical considerations, therefore, play an important role in the diachronic approach, and most studies of this type move from (1) the moral teaching of the historical Jesus, to (2) the teaching of the early church, to (3) the individual writings of the New Testament.

The diachronic method has been employed by Wolfgang Schrage, Allen Verhey, Siegfried Schulz, and Rudolf Schnackenburg. Before describing the ethical teaching of the New Testament writings, each of these authors considers the moral teaching of Jesus and the early church. For example, the first chapter of Verhey's *The Great Reversal: Ethics of the New Testament*[5] is titled "The Ethics of Jesus," and the second, "The Beginnings of a Moral Tradition," by which Verhey means the tradition of Jesus' words and deeds as it was used in the early church, and the paraenetic tradition (moral exhortation or encouragement) handed down by the church for "instructing inquirers about their responsibilities within the believing community."[6] Only after this extended prolegomenon does Verhey turn to "Ethics in the New Testament," and then in the following order: "The Synoptic Gospels," "Paul and His Interpreters," "The Catholic Epistles and Hebrews," "The Johannine Literature."

Schrage, in *The Ethics of the New Testament*,[7] places less emphasis upon the period between Jesus and the New Testament writings, but he follows a somewhat similar outline. Beginning with a consideration of "Jesus' Eschatological Ethics," he moves to a brief treatment of the "Ethical Beginnings in the Earliest Congregations," and then studies the New Testament writings in the following order: "Ethical Accents in the Synoptic Gospels," "The Christological Ethics of Paul," "The Ethics of Responsibility in the Deutero-Pauline Epistles," "Paraenesis in the Epistle of James," "The Commandment of Brotherly Love in the Johannine Writings," "Exhortations Addressed to the Pilgrim People in the Epistle to the Hebrews," and "Eschatological Exhortations in the Book of Revelation."

In contrast to these authors, Schulz develops an overarching thesis about the status of the Mosaic law within early Christianity in his *Neutestamentliche Ethik*.[8] He argues that Jesus heightened the moral demands of the law and diminished its ritual aspects, but without abolishing the latter. The earliest communities of the Jesus movement, according to Schulz, remained faithful to their master in this regard. An important change, however, occurred within the Hellenistic church, which affirmed the moral and salvific aspect of the law but finally did away with its ritual aspects. This, in turn, was followed by early Gnosticism, which abandoned the law entirely. The "earlier Paul," represented by 1 Thessalonians, followed the Hellenistic church in affirming the salvific value of the moral aspects of the law, according to Schulz, but controversies with Jewish Christians of a legalistic persuasion and Gnostics of a libertine bent led Paul to a change of mind. Consequently, the "later Paul" no longer considered the moral aspect of the Mosaic law as salvific. In his examination of other New Testament writings such as the Deutero-Pauline letters, Schulz continually returns to this theme of the law. In his view, these writings do away with the ritual law but uphold the moral aspects of the Mosaic law as salvific. In a word, their authors do not see a conflict between faith and works as did the "later Paul."

Schulz's work proceeds chronologically, and his view of New Testament ethics flows from his reconstruction of early Christianity. It has the advantage of reading the New Testament from a single focal point: how its writings view the Mosaic law. But in my judgment, it is dependent upon a questionable reconstruction of Christian origins and makes too great a distinction between an "earlier" and "later" Paul.

Schnackenburg's *Die sittliche Botschaft des Neuen Testaments*[9] is more akin to the works of Verhey and Schrage. He moves from the moral teaching of

Jesus to the appropriation of that teaching by the early church. In doing so, he maintains that the church adapted Jesus' teaching to new circumstances while remaining essentially faithful to him. In volume one, titled "From Jesus to the Early Church," Schnackenburg argues that the presupposition of Jesus' moral teaching is the in-breaking rule of God, and that it was on the basis of the kingdom of God that he called people to repentance and faith. A true Israelite, Jesus remained faithful to the moral traditions of his people. But in light of God's in-breaking kingdom, he emphasized God's original will and called people to live by the commandment of love. The dominant experience of the early church, according to Schnackenburg, was the outpouring of the Holy Spirit, which led to a consciousness of being God's people and heirs of the promises to Israel. Schnackenburg maintains that even though the church adapted Jesus' teaching regarding the law, discipleship, and the love commandment—as the gospel moved into the Gentile world— there is an essential continuity between the teaching of Jesus and that of the early church.

In volume two, "The Early Christian Preachers," Schnackenburg considers the writings of the New Testament in the following order: Paul; the inheritors of the Pauline tradition; the Synoptic evangelists; John; James; and other early christian preachers (the authors of 1 Peter, Hebrews, Jude, 2 Peter, Revelation). Schnackenburg listens to the many voices of the New Testament; he does not suggest that there is a decline in the moral teaching of the New Testament's later writings. Overall, his two-volume work makes a significant advance over earlier editions of his work by introducing new chapters on the moral teaching of the Synoptic Evangelists and the Deutero-Pauline epistles. Nevertheless, the section on the theology of the Synoptic Gospels is not fully developed since Schnackenburg's major interest seems to be the historical Jesus. Thus, after devoting a substantial section of volume one to the moral teaching of the historical Jesus, his treatment of the Synoptic Evangelists is necessarily brief since he has already dealt with much of the material in discussing Jesus' own ethics.[10]

A common feature of these authors is the manner in which they begin by considering the moral teaching of Jesus and the early church. As a result, their chapters on the moral teaching of the Gospels are not as developed as one might expect since central themes such as the kingdom of God and the Sermon on the Mount are treated when considering Jesus' ethical teaching. Finally, as regards the organization of their works, they tend to treat the Gospel of John in isolation from the Synoptic Gospels, and the Deutero-Pauline letters separately from Paul's undisputed correspondence.

The diachronic approach allows one to hear the distinctive voices within the New Testament and to observe a growth or trajectory in its writings. But there are disadvantages, the most serious of which is a fragmentation of the New Testament witness. Moreover, this procedure often leads to a judgment that the theological content of some later writings, such as the pastoral epistles, represents a decline from earlier writings.

Viewing the Whole

Standing over and against the diachronic method is the more synthetic approach of the synchronic method. Instead of viewing the New Testament as an archaeological mound with layers of tradition to be excavated layer by layer, it attempts to view it as a unified work in order to hear its singular witness to the moral life. Those who adopt this approach usually arrange their studies around a number of themes that, they believe, summarize this singular vision. As a result, this method has the advantage of treating the New Testament as a whole, but in a way that often mutes the individual voices of its writings. The most important works exemplifying this approach are those of Ceslas Spicq and Karl H. Schelkle.

Spicq is aware of the levels of tradition and redaction that are present in the New Testament, but in *Théologie morale du Nouveau Testament*[11] he chooses to examine the canonical text rather than the stages of redaction behind it. Consequently, his study does not discuss source questions, nor are issues of authorship and dating of primary concern to him. Moreover, while he is aware that there are different theologies in the New Testament, he does not highlight them. Spicq is convinced that there is a fundamental coherency in the New Testament that allows him to view its moral teaching as a unity. Therefore, instead of examining its individual writings, he gathers the New Testament's moral teaching under a number of themes: "New Being and New Life," "Grace and Glory," "Justification, Sin, Sanctification," "Faith and Fidelity," "Perspectives on the Future: Waiting, Hope, Fear," "Love of God and Love of Neighbor," "Pastoral Instructions, the Formation of Conscience," "Freedom of the Children of God," "From the Image of God to Eschatological Transformation."[12]

As he explores these themes, Spicq writes with a mastery of the biblical material that allows him to marshal a multitude of texts from diverse writings in order to flesh out his chosen categories. Convinced that the New Testament is the Word of God, he treats it as a unified book that speaks with a single voice. While Spicq's work is an admirable achievement, it never offers an adequate explanation for its organizational categories.[13]

Schelkle, in his *Theology of the New Testament*,[14] organizes his treatment of New Testament ethics around what he calls "Basic Concepts," "Basic Attitudes," "Objectives," and "Various Areas for Consideration."[15] But unlike Spicq, he also listens to the different voices of the New Testament, distinguishing what writers say about the concepts, attitudes, and objectives mentioned above. His approach, however, subordinates the unity of the individual New Testament writings to his chosen categories. Consequently, Schelkle never presents the reader with the full message of any New Testament writing.

A synchronic study of New Testament ethics that could synthesize its diverse ethical patterns would be of extraordinary value, especially if it were based upon a thorough study of the New Testament's diverse writings.

But in this regard, the history of scholarship presents something of a puzzle since Spicq's and Schelkle's synchronic studies were written *before* the diachronic works discussed above. One wonders then how Spicq and Schelkle might have structured their works if they had had the advantage of reading Schnackenburg,[16] Schrage, Schulz, and Verhey.

Other Approaches

Before completing this review, it is necessary to mention two authors whose works do not fit either the diachronic or the synchronic approaches described above: Jean-François Collange and Eduard Lohse.

Although Collange's *De Jésus à Paul* is subtitled "The Ethic of the New Testament," it is in fact a study of the relationship between the ethical teaching of Jesus and that of Paul. Collange notes that the world of the epistles is not that of the Gospels.[18] The language of the epistles, as well as the cultural and social universe they reflect, is different from that of the Gospels. But the differences, in Collange's view, only heighten the profound analogies that characterize the ethics of Jesus and Paul. For both, the ethical life involves freedom and attention to what is concrete and real.[19] Jesus' ethic is inscribed in what he does as well as in his preaching, while Paul's ethic is born from an event: the saving justice of God made manifest in the Christ event. In Collange's view, it was the Hellenists who established the bridge between Jesus and Paul that allowed the apostle to adapt Jesus' ethical teaching in a faithful manner.

The moral teaching of the New Testament, then, is not an ethical system but an account of how the kingdom of God (Jesus' ethical horizon) and the saving justice of God (Paul's ethical horizon) released the ethical forces of freedom, love, and faith. Jesus channeled these forces into the life of discipleship lived in a company of disciples for whom he interpreted the law in terms of love. Paul channeled the same forces in a life of imitation of himself and Christ within a community for whom Christ had put an end to the law.

Collange's work is characterized by careful exegesis and has the advantage of synthesizing the ethical teaching of Jesus and Paul under the themes of freedom, love, and faith. Its primary focus, however, is Jesus and Paul rather than the writings of the New Testament.

Like Collange, Lohse, in his *Theological Ethics of the New Testament*,[20] seeks a middle ground between the diachronic and synchronic methods. Aware that a diachronic approach is unable to clarify "the extensive common character of early Christian instruction and the systematic motifs that determined the development of that ethical content," and that a synchronic approach overlooks "the distinctive contours of the individual early Christian witness,"[21] he attempts a mediating solution. Choosing major themes that characterize New Testament ethics, Lohse illustrates them in terms of various New Testament writings. For example, under "The Worldliness of Faith" he considers Romans 13 and the household codes of the Deutero-Pauline writings, while under "Law and Commandment" he deals with the law in Galatians and Romans, the commandment of love in Paul and the Johannine literature, and the epistle of James. In this regard, his approach is similar to that of Schelkle, although not as systematic. It has the advantage of bridging the diachronic and synchronic methods, but it also fragments the New Testament writings, not one of which is heard in its entirety.

There is little doubt that New Testament ethics has been a lively and fruitful area of research. There is also a sense that the task needs to be done again and again since our understanding of the text and the questions that we bring to it inevitably change.

APPROACHING THE TASK ANEW

This book proceeds on the assumption that the *primary* object of New Testament ethics should be the writings of the New Testament rather than a historical reconstruction of the ethical teaching of Jesus, the early church, Paul, and so on. Consequently, it does not begin with a discussion of the moral teaching of Jesus and the early church, nor does it synthesize the ethical teaching of Paul. This procedure does not imply a negative judgment on these endeavors. To the contrary! Renewed interest in the historical Jesus, as well as new perspectives in Pauline studies, suggest that this may be an opportune time to reassess cherished assumptions about the ethical teaching of Jesus, the early church, and Paul. But the work of historical reconstruction is not the primary object of New Testament ethics. Indeed, it is not even the proper prolegomenon to this discipline.

Since the New Testament is a collection of writings, in my view the primary subject of *New Testament* ethics is the ethical teaching of these writings. For example, what does a particular Gospel tell the church about the moral teaching of Jesus? How does a Pauline letter exhort the church so that believers will live a life worthy of the gospel to which they have been called? Such questions demand a method that is primarily literary and rhetorical in nature; that is, a method that will seriously deal with the rhetorical and literary aspects of these writings in order to determine how they persuaded, and continue to persuade, audiences to live a moral and ethical life.

Historical reconstruction necessarily deals with these writings in a different way. In the case of the Sermon on the Mount, for example, historians want to know what Jesus actually taught. To answer this question, they must deconstruct the text in order to determine its earliest sources and then, on the basis of various criteria of historicity, evaluate what comes from Jesus and what derives from the early church and the editorial activity of the Evangelist. Such a procedure is especially necessary when the Gospels report similar incidents in different ways. In Matthew's Gospel, for example, Jesus' Sermon on the Mount focuses on the theme of righteousness within the context of the Mosaic law, as interpreted by Jesus. In the Gospel of Luke, Jesus' Sermon on the Plain deals with enemy love but says nothing of righteousness or the law. Although it is possible that Jesus delivered two different sermons (one that focused on righteousness and the law, and one that did not), it is more probable that Matthew and Luke are responsible for the final form and theological orientation of the Sermon on the Mount and the Sermon on the Plain, respectively. Each sermon now proposes a distinctive and sophisticated ethic that must be respected and listened to. And each is indebted to Jesus, albeit in different ways.

To speak of New Testament ethics, then, is to speak of the moral teaching of its writings rather than of a reconstruction of what Jesus said or taught. The latter discipline is necessarily hypothetical, always open to revision and correction, whereas the writings of the New Testament are literary records whose content can be verified (even though their interpretation is open to revision and correction).

While most works of New Testament ethics begin with the teaching of Jesus and the early church, I submit that historical reconstructions should be undertaken only after one has thoroughly investigated the redactional and theological tendencies present in the various New Testament writings. An example will clarify what I mean. Archaeologists do not start their excavations with the earliest stratum of the excavation site but with the most recent stratum and then work back to what is earlier. Many works of New Testament ethics, however, begin with the earliest and most difficult stratum to uncover (Jesus and the early church), and then move to the most recent stratum, the writings of the New Testament. Should they not have proceeded instead by considering these writings in their present literary form, moved back by means of form criticism to the early church, and only then speculated about the ethical teaching of the historical Jesus?[22]

For the reasons listed above, this book does not begin with Jesus and the early church but with the writings of the New Testament. As I have said, its approach is primarily literary and rhetorical, although this book will also make use of the historical-critical method.[23] The task at hand is primarily descriptive inasmuch as this work seeks to describe as accurately as possible the moral and ethical vision that a given writing proposes. In the case of the Gospels, this entails attention to the narrative structure of each Gospel and the manner in which the narrative communicates its ethical teaching. In the case of the Pauline letters, it entails attention to the circumstances that necessitated the letters, their epistolary genre, and the rhetorical strategies these letters employ to persuade their audiences.[24]

As the subtitle of this work indicates, its focus is the ethical legacies of Jesus and Paul, that is, the moral teaching ascribed to them. Thus it does not deal with every writing in the New Testament and, to that extent, it is not a comprehensive study of New Testament ethics. The reasons for this choice are practical and theoretical. On the one hand, by limiting this work to the legacies of Jesus and Paul, I have obviously excused myself from dealing with a number of daunting New Testament writings. On the other hand, this decision has enabled me to bring a certain unity to this project by grounding it in the persons of Jesus and Paul.

In the first part of this work, I deal with the four Gospels. In doing so, I have tried to draw the reader's attention to the person of Jesus *as found in each of the Gospels* rather than to the Evangelists, since Jesus is the focal point of these writings. To put it another way, while many speak of Markan, Matthean, Lukan, and Johannine ethics, I prefer to speak of Jesus' ethics as mediated by these writers. To be sure, each of the Evangelists brings a distinctive ethical vision to his work, but I doubt that any one of the Gospel writers would have identified the moral teaching of his Gospel as *his* ethic. Would they not have argued rather that the moral teaching they propose truly reflects the ethical teaching of Jesus? Would they not have been shocked by the notion of a "Markan" or "Lukan" ethic? The ethic they propose is the legacy of Jesus, which each Evangelist mediates in a distinctive manner.

As regards the Pauline letters, the situation is notably different, since at least seven, and perhaps more, of these letters come from Paul himself.[25] Thus we have *direct* literary access to Paul's ethics whereas Jesus' teaching is mediated through the Gospels. But a problem still arises with the Deutero-Pauline correspondence. How are these letters to be treated? Should 2 Thessalonians be separated from 1 Thessalonians? Should we refrain from using Paul's name when dealing with Ephesians, Colossians, and the Pastorals? What should be our primary concern when dealing with the Deutero-Pauline correspondence: to compare them with Paul's undisputed correspondence in order to trace a trajectory from Paul to his successors, or to read them in their own right, and not as a fall from Pauline grace? Once more, I have tried to find a middle ground. Instead of synthesizing Paul's teaching on the basis of his undisputed correspondence through the prism of Romans, I have taken the occasional nature of these letters seriously and treated each in its own right. As a result, the second part of this work is not dominated by Romans and Galatians, although both are heard. They are heard, however, in conjunction with other voices that are too often submerged by an excessive concern for Paul's theology of justification as presented in Romans and Galatians. The person of Paul will serve as the focal point of this section: the Paul who wrote Romans, 1 and 2 Corinthians, Galatians, Philippians, 1 Thessalonians, and Philemon, as well as the Paul whose legacy is reflected in Ephesians, Colossians, 2 Thessalonians, and the pastoral epistles.

Two final points need to be made. First, because this is primarily a descriptive work, it was not written with a particular thesis in view. But as the work unfolded, several "minor theses" about New Testament ethics emerged from the text. These are summarized at various points throughout this book and then synthesized in the concluding chapter, "The Ethical Legacy of Jesus and Paul."

Second, generally speaking, this work does not engage in hermeneutical questions about the normative value of the moral teaching in the writings of the New Testament. While recognizing that it is not easy to apply individual sayings or teachings of the New Testament, such as the household codes, to contemporary life, I assume that the ethical vision of the New Testament is normative for the community of saints, that is, the church. This ethical vision is rooted in Jesus' proclamation of the kingdom and Paul's announcement of God's saving justice in Christ. It is also, as we shall see, an ethical vision with specific demands made within very concrete historical circumstances. While I find this vision persuasive and compelling, in my view it is not to be *imposed* upon those outside of the community. This statement is not made in a spirit of political correctness but from a conviction that the moral teaching of the New Testament should not be separated from the message of salvation that it proclaims. While outsiders will inevitably admire certain aspects of the moral teaching of Jesus and Paul and dispute others, I do not believe that they can fully appreciate this ethic since they do not participate in the faith life of the believing community. In this respect, the moral vision of the New Testament is primarily for the church.

This does not mean that the church cannot or should not speak to the contemporary world, or that the ethical life of the church should become purely sectarian in the moral or ethical stance that it takes. Contemporary Christians must engage in the ongoing process of ethical reflection and establish bridges of communication between themselves and the wider society. In doing so, they will communicate to others what they believe. The moral vision of the believer, however, must ultimately be rooted in the New Testament.

PART ONE
THE LEGACY OF JESUS

1

Ethics for
the Kingdom of God

The Gospel according to Mark

On first appearance the Gospel according to Mark, the oldest of the four Gospels, is an unlikely source for moral or ethical instruction.[1] An episodic narrative that rapidly moves from one incident to another, Mark's Gospel does not contain extended blocks of Jesus' moral instruction. Most importantly, it lacks anything comparable to Jesus' great sermon as reported by Matthew and Luke. Sermons and explicit moral instruction, however, are not the only ways to communicate moral teaching. Moral and ethical traditions can also be transmitted through narrative.[2] Indeed, one of the functions of national epics—and of the Bible—is to communicate an ethos, or a way of life lived in accordance with specific ideals. For better or for worse, people are shaped by the stories they hear, and narratives create a moral universe in which characters must choose between good and evil.

Biblical narratives are no exception. The parable of the good Samaritan, for example, has taught countless generations how to act as Christians by being a neighbor to those in need. The account of Peter's denial vividly portrays what it means to fail as a disciple. In a word, biblical narratives communicate moral meaning. Indeed, they often make their points more effectively than explicitly moral instruction would do. For example, while Christians know that Jesus delivered a great sermon, few recall the explicit content of that sermon. Most, however, remember the story of Jesus, and it is that story which functions as a "narrative norm" for them.[3] Consequently, although the Gospel of Mark may appear to be an unlikely source for ethical instruction, its engaging narrative has shaped the moral and ethical life of believers.

HOW A NARRATIVE WORKS

Stories with engaging plots and strong characterization have a hypnotic effect upon listeners, readers, and viewers. Once the

13

audience accepts the presuppositions of the narrative and enters the world the narrator creates, it is not satisfied until it discovers how the plot unfolds.[4] Even when audiences know the plot line, as is the case when contemporary Christians read the Gospels, narratives remain engaging because audiences want to know what events lead to the final unfolding of the plot and how various characters respond to these events.[5]

The spell an engaging narrative casts upon its audience has a further effect: listeners, readers, and viewers make themselves vulnerable to being persuaded by the moral logic of the narrative. In the case of the four Gospels, for example, each presents Jesus as upright and accredited by God, whereas the religious leaders are portrayed as hypocritical and self-serving. Consequently, readers are encouraged to identify with the behavior of Jesus and to disassociate themselves from that of the religious leaders.[6] What is happening is more than passively reading or listening to the narrative. Whether the audience realizes it or not, the narrative voice that tells the story is guiding it to a predetermined goal in a variety of ways: the manner in which the material is ordered, the omission of certain details, narrative asides, and so on.

Consider this narrative comment in Mark: "Thus he declared all foods clean" (7:19). This narrative aside occurs in a private instruction to Jesus' disciples, after a dispute with the religious leaders about the ethical importance of hand washing and other "traditions of the elders." Immediately after the dispute, Jesus tells the crowd that nothing that enters a person from outside can defile a person. Rather, only those things which come out of a person defile a person. When the disciples question Jesus about this, he responds: "Do you not see that whatever goes into a person from outside cannot defile, since it enters, not the heart but the stomach, and goes out into the sewer?" (7:18–19). It is at this point that Mark introduces his narrative comment: "Thus he declared all foods clean." Most readers would not have deduced such a conclusion from Jesus' response, since food laws play little if any role in Mark's narrative. But by this narrative aside the Markan narrator makes explicit what is implicit. In doing so, he has Jesus make a major ethical statement[7] and guides the audience to embrace a particular kind of conduct. To put the matter simply, narratives are seductive, and they are always trying to persuade their audiences to adopt a particular point of view. This point of view inevitably has moral or ethical implications. Thus narratives invite their readers to enter a moral universe in which characters and readers must choose between good and evil. Whether they are aware of it or not, audiences are being encouraged to adopt moral and ethical standards.

THE KINGDOM OF GOD
AS MARK'S MORAL UNIVERSE

If my observations about narrative are correct, what is the moral universe created by the Gospel according to Mark? What is the moral premise of this Gospel? Why does the Markan Jesus behave as he does and make moral and ethical demands upon others? The beginning of Jesus' public ministry, as presented in Mark's Gospel, offers an answer.

The Gospel according to Mark begins with a brief introduction (1:1–13) that can be structured as follows: the beginning of the gospel about Jesus Christ as foretold by the prophet Isaiah (Mark 1:1–3); the appearance of John the Baptist (1:4–8); the baptism of Jesus (1:9–11); the testing of Jesus in the wilderness (1:12–13).[8] By the conclusion of this introduction, the Markan audience has learned that Jesus is the spirit-endowed Son of God who successfully endures Satan's testing in the wilderness. And although Jesus' mission has not yet begun, the reader already knows that it will be the fulfillment of prophecy as spoken by Isaiah. The beginning of Jesus' ministry, then, is 1:14–15.

> Now after John was arrested, Jesus came to Galilee, proclaiming the gospel[9] of God, and saying, "The time is fulfilled, and the kingdom of God has come near [or: "is at hand"]; repent, and believe in the gospel."

This beginning, moreover, is not one scene among others; it is programmatic for all that will happen in Mark's narrative. In this scene, the Markan Evangelist identifies the essential content of Jesus' proclamation and the ethical response it requires. To be more specific, the content of Jesus' preaching here, and in the rest of the Gospel, is the kingdom of God, and the moral response he seeks is twofold: to repent and to believe in the gospel. This "gospel" in which one must believe is God's good news (*euaggelion*) that the time is fulfilled and his kingdom has drawn near, or is at hand.[10] Thus those who hear Jesus' proclamation and listen to his teaching in the rest of the narrative are faced with a moral challenge: to repent and believe that the kingdom of God has truly drawn near, indeed, is already present in some fashion. Exactly what repentance and faith entail is not yet clear but will become so as the narrative unfolds, just as will the nature of the kingdom of God. The moral universe of Mark's Gospel can be diagramed as follows:

God's gospel	The time is fulfilled
	The kingdom of God has drawn near
Response	Repent
	Believe in God's gospel

The Kingship of God

When the Markan Jesus proclaims that the kingdom of God has come near, he introduces a concept that can only be fully understood after one has listened to the entire Gospel. The notion of the kingdom of God, however, is not an entirely new concept, since it is rooted in the rich notion of

God's kingship as found in the Old Testament. In order to grasp the meaning of Jesus' proclamation, therefore, it is necessary to summarize some of this Old Testament background pertinent to the kingdom of God.[11]

Although the kingdom of God is a foundational notion for the New Testament, especially the Synoptic Gospels, the phrase only occurs once in the writings of the Hebrew Bible (1 Chron. 28:5, where "kingdom of Yahweh" is employed) and once in the deuterocanonical writings (Wisd. Sol. 10:10, where "kingdom of God" is used). Moreover, neither occurrence is especially helpful for decoding the New Testament concept. More helpful is the Hebrew expression YHWH *malak* which can be rendered "The Lord reigns," "The Lord is king," or "The Lord has become king." Chronologically, the earliest occurrence of the expression is found in the final verse of the song sung by Moses and the Israelites in response to God's delivering Israel from the Egyptians at the Reed Sea (Ex. 15:1–18): "The LORD will reign forever and ever." Thus Moses and the Israelites proclaim God's kingship in light of their deliverance from Egypt: The God who saved Israel and destroyed her enemies is king.

The theme of God's kingship, however, finds its fullest expression in the psalms, especially the so-called enthronement psalms (Psalms 47, 93, 95–99). Whether or not these psalms were employed on a festal occasion when God was thought to be enthroned as king is disputed. They do, however, clearly announce God's kingship over creation, Israel, and Israel's enemies, as the following examples show.[12]

> *The LORD is king*, he is robed in majesty; the LORD is robed, he is girded with strength (93:1).

> For the LORD is a great God, and *a great King* above all gods (95:3).

> Say among the nations, "*The LORD is king*! The world is firmly established; it shall never be moved. He will judge the peoples with equity (96:10).

> *The LORD is king*! Let the earth rejoice; let the many coastlands be glad! (97:1).

> With trumpets and the sound of the horn make a joyful noise before *the King, the LORD* (98:6).

> *The LORD is king*; let the peoples tremble! He sits enthroned upon the cherubim; let the earth quake (99:1)!

In some cases, the psalms relate God's kingship to his victory over chaos: God rules over the world he created by subduing chaos.

> The LORD sits *enthroned* over the flood; the LORD sits *enthroned as king* forever (Ps. 29:10).

16

In other instances, the psalms relate God's kingship to his victory over the nations, on behalf of Israel. Thus the God of creation also rules over history, especially Israel's history. Psalm 47 is especially instructive in this regard.

> Clap your hands, all you peoples; shout to God with loud songs of joy. For the LORD, the Most High, is awesome, *a great king over all the earth.* He subdued peoples under us, and nations under our feet. He chose our heritage for us, the pride of Jacob whom he loves (Ps. 47:1–4).

In still other instances, the above two themes are united, as in the lament of Psalm 74. The psalmist begins with a plea for help during a period of national disaster. In the midst of the lament, God is addressed as king because of his work of creation.

> Yet *God my King* is from of old, working salvation in the earth. You divided the sea by your might; you broke the heads of the dragons in the waters (Ps. 74:12–13).

Thus the king of creation is the Lord of history: Israel's God reigns over creation and history, over Israel and her enemies.

God's kingship is also proclaimed in Deutero-Isaiah, an important work for understanding the introduction to Mark's Gospel.[13]

> I am the LORD, your Holy One, the Creator of Israel, *your King* (Isa. 43:15).

> Thus says the LORD, *the King of Israel,* and his Redeemer, the LORD of hosts: I am the first and I am the last; besides me there is no god (44:6).

In Isa. 52:7, the "good news" the prophet brings is directly related to God's kingship.

> How beautiful upon the mountains are the feet of the messenger who announces peace, who brings good news, who announces salvation, who says to Zion, *"Your God reigns."*

The parallelism of the last two relative clauses here ("who announces salvation, who says to Zion, 'your God reigns'") shows that God's kingship *is* salvation for Israel. Thus the prophet is already alluding to God's kingship when he writes, "'Here is your God!' See, the Lord GOD comes with might" (Isa. 40:9–10). As in Israel's past, God's kingship is salvation for his people. The "good news" of Deutero-Isaiah is God's kingship, what the Gospel of Mark calls the "kingdom of God."

God's kingship, however, is also an eschatological reality; that is, at the end of the ages God's rule will be manifested in a public way for all the nations to see and acknowledge. This dimension of God's kingship finds expression in apocalyptic writings. In the book of Daniel, for example, when Daniel decodes the dream of Nebuchadnezzar (2:24–45), he explains that the stone that struck and destroyed the statue Nebuchadnezzar saw in his dream symbolizes the kingdom that God will establish once all human kingdoms have been destroyed: "a kingdom that shall never be destroyed, nor shall this kingdom be left to another people" (2:44). Later, in a night vision, Daniel sees this kingship given to one like a "son of man" (7:13), who is identified as "the holy ones of the Most High" (7:18).[14] The kingdom that they receive is God's kingdom, "an everlasting kingdom, and all dominions shall serve and obey them" (7:27).

To summarize, although the expression "the kingdom of God" does not occur with any frequency in the Old Testament, the notion of God's kingship does. Israel acknowledges God's kingship now: God is the Creator God who rules over creation and the Savior God who rules over Israel and Israel's enemies. Although the nations do not acknowledge this kingship, they will do so when God establishes his definitive kingship at the end of the ages. It is this notion of kingship, present in a hidden way but soon to be revealed in power, that informs Jesus' proclamation of the kingdom of God. God's kingdom is his kingship, a powerful and dynamic reality by which God rules over creation and the nations. The Old Testament concept of God's kingship provides a helpful background for understanding what Jesus means when he proclaims the kingdom of God: he is announcing God's kingship over creation and history. This kingship is a dynamic reality, and even when Jesus speaks of entering "the kingdom of God" (Mark 9:47; 10:23–25), he means entering the realm or sphere of God's rule, reign, or kingship. Thus there is much to be said for translating *hē basileia tou theou* as "the reign of God" since "the kingdom of God" suggests a spatial reality rather than God's dynamic and salvific rule.[15] To understand fully what the Markan Jesus means by the kingdom of God, however, it is necessary to explore how the concept is developed within the Gospel narrative.

The Kingdom of God
in Mark's Gospel

Although the phrase "the kingdom of God" occurs only fourteen times in Mark's Gospel,[16] it underlies everything that Jesus says and does. As I have already noted, Jesus' ministry begins with a proclamation of the kingdom which serves as the leitmotiv of his ministry. Returning to Galilee after the imprisonment of John, he announces that the time is fulfilled (*peplērōtai*) and the kingdom of God "has come near," or "is at hand" (1:15). The precise sense of the Greek verb *ēggiken*, used here, is difficult to determine. On the one hand, it can mean that the kingdom has drawn near but has not yet arrived. On the other, it can mean that the kingdom has made its initial appearance, even though it has not fully arrived. The parallel structure of Jesus' proclamation (the time is *peplērōtai* . . . the kingdom of God *ēggiken*), however, favors the latter interpretation, for if the time is fulfilled, then the kingdom of God is at hand. In other words, God's reign is making its appearance because the God-determined time for its arrival has been completed.[17] The new aspect of Jesus' preaching, then, is the proclamation that God's eschatological kingship, promised in the Old Testament, is already making its appearance. The time of waiting is past, and the time of fulfillment has arrived. This proclamation is good news (*euaggelion*) for Jesus' audience, but it also requires those who hear him to make a crucial moral choice: to repent and to believe in God's gospel.

But how is the kingdom of God present? The Markan Gospel answers this question in two ways. First, the kingdom of God is already present in Jesus' powerful deeds of healing, feeding, rescue at sea, and exorcism, which dominate the first part of Mark's narrative.[18] His miracles are concrete manifestations of God's kingly power, which is already present in Jesus' ministry. Second, in a series of parables found in chapter 4, Jesus explains that the kingdom of God is already present in a hidden way to those who believe.[19] Therefore, when the disciples ask Jesus the meaning of the parable of the sower, he responds that the mystery of the kingdom of God is given to them, while to those "outside," everything is given in parables: a mysterious speech that must be decoded (4:10–12). The "mystery of the kingdom of God," as the rest of the parable discourse reveals, is *the present but hidden aspect of the kingdom of God*. The sower (Jesus) has sown the seed (the proclamation of the kingdom of God), which is already taking root and bearing fruit even though, for a variety of reasons, much of the seed has not found fertile ground among Jesus' audience (4:13–20). The kingdom of God is a present but hidden reality similar to the situation of a farmer who sows seed and then continues with his daily life. The earth produces fruit of its own accord (*automatē*) until the time of harvest. How this happens, the farmer does not know (4:26–29). So it is with the kingdom of God. Jesus has sown the word of the kingdom, and the kingdom of God is already present, secretly growing of its own accord until the day of harvest. At the present moment, the kingdom is like a small and insignificant mustard seed, but one day it will become the largest plant so that all the birds of the sky can dwell in its shade (4:30–32).[20]

The moral universe of Mark's Gospel, then, is divided between insiders and outsiders. The first group consists of those who believe in Jesus' proclamation of the kingdom—that God's rule has made its appearance with Jesus' ministry, even though the kingdom is currently hidden from their eyes. Mark's second group consists of those who do not believe in Jesus' proclamation because they do not see the presence of the kingdom. In this moral universe, the first group believes in order to see, whereas the second seeks to see in order to believe (see 15:32). For the Markan Evangelist, however, only those who believe can see and understand, while those who seek to see in order to believe are blind and without comprehension.

In addition to Jesus' initial proclamation that the kingdom of God is at hand, albeit in a hidden way that can only be perceived by those who believe, Jesus speaks several times of "entering the kingdom of God." As I have already noted, this expression refers to the sphere of God's rule rather than to a spatial realm. To enter the kingdom of God is to live under God's rule, be it in the present or in the future. For example, Jesus warns his disciples that "it is better for you to enter the kingdom of God with one eye than to have two eyes and to be thrown into hell" (9:47). Here, entering the kingdom clearly refers to a future reality that is equated with life and contrasted with Gehenna (see 9:43, 45). In other sayings it is more difficult to determine if Jesus has the present or the future in view. For example, he speaks of the need to receive the kingdom of God like a child (presumably with the faith of a child) in order to enter it (10:15), and he tells his disciples how difficult it is for those with riches to enter the kingdom of God (10:23–25).[21] In every case, however, entering the kingdom means to live or dwell in the sphere of God's rule, be it now or in the future.

In a number of other sayings, the future reality of the kingdom of God is clearly in view. For example, after predicting his passion and resurrection, Jesus says that "there are some standing here who will not taste death until they see that the kingdom of God has come with power" (9:1). Here the kingdom is viewed as a reality whose powerful manifestation is imminent, either at Jesus' resurrection or at his parousia.[22] At the Last Supper, Jesus tells his disciples that he will no longer drink of the fruit of the vine (the Passover cup) until he drinks it anew in the kingdom of God (14:25). Here Jesus once more seems to anticipate the imminent arrival of God's kingdom in power. Finally, the Markan narrator describes Joseph of Arimathea as someone "waiting expectantly for the kingdom of God" (15:43). The Markan narrator does not tell his readers whether Joseph's hope was disappointed by Jesus' death, but his hope for the kingdom suggests there is a future dimension to the kingdom that is yet to be fulfilled.

In light of the above, it is apparent that Jesus' preaching of the kingdom of God, as presented by Mark's Gospel, has many dimensions. In continuity with the Old Testament concept of God's kingship, it refers to God's dynamic and salvific rule over creation and history. The distinctive aspect of Jesus' preaching, however, is the present aspect of the kingdom: God's rule is already making its appearance in his life and ministry. At present, the kingdom is hidden and can only be perceived by faith. The hidden kingdom, however, will be revealed in power, and on that day everyone will acknowledge God's rule. To enter the sphere of God's kingdom one must receive the kingdom with childlike faith and guard against temptations and attachment to possessions that distract one from God's rule. The ethical challenge presented by Jesus' proclamation is to repent and believe because the hidden kingdom, already present in Jesus' ministry, will soon be made manifest in power. It is to these concepts of repentance and faith that I now turn.

The Call to Repent
and Believe

The proclamation that the reign of God is at hand requires a response from those who hear the gospel of God. Faced with God's in-breaking rule, people must repent and believe in the gospel; that is, they must believe in God's good news that his rule, his reign, his kingship has made its appearance and will soon be manifested in power. The two elements of this response, repentance and faith, should not be separated. In the Gospel according to Mark, "The response of faith presupposes the comprehensive break with the past and that reorientation of life in both its ethical and religious dimensions connoted by *metanoein* [to repent; to change one's ways]."[23] Put another way, faith completes the work begun by repentance, for faith is "repentant faith."[24]

Repentance. At the beginning of the Gospel, John the Baptist preaches "a baptism of repentance for the forgiveness of sins" (Mark 1:4). Soon afterward, Jesus proclaims the kingdom of God and calls people to repent and believe in the gospel (1:15).[25] When he explains why he speaks to the crowds in parables, Jesus quotes from Isa. 6:9–10, which says in part, "lest they *turn* (*epistrepsōsin*) and be forgiven" (4:12).[26] Finally, when Jesus sends the Twelve on mission, the Markan narrator explains: "So they went out and proclaimed that all should repent" (6:12). Given Jesus' initial proclamation of the kingdom, it is clear that the disciples also call people to repentance because God's reign is making its appearance.

Although the specific vocabulary of repentance does not occur frequently in Mark's Gospel, the need for people to repent is central to his narrative. As I have already noted, Jesus' initial proclamation of the kingdom is not one event among others; it is a foundational event that is paradigmatic for everything that follows. It represents the *constant* theme of his preaching, and it is the reason for his ministry of healing and expelling demons. Consequently, when Jesus tells his disciples, "Let us go on to the neighboring towns, so that I may proclaim the message there also for that is what I came out to do" (1:38), *the message* is the proclamation of the kingdom in 1:15. Or when Mark informs his audience, upon Jesus' return to Capernaum, that Jesus "was speaking the word (*ton logon*) to them" (2:2), readers and listeners are meant to understand that this is the word about the kingdom with its summons to repent and believe in the gospel that Jesus announced in 1:15. Put simply, Jesus' initial proclamation of the kingdom is the key to unlocking all that he says and does. His ministry is a constant call to repent and believe in God's good news that the kingdom of God has made its initial appearance.

To understand what Jesus means by repentance it is necessary to situate his call for people to repent within its narrative context. Immediately after his initial call for repentance and faith (1:15), Jesus summons his first disciples (1:16–20). Like Jesus' initial preaching of the kingdom, this scene is paradigmatic inasmuch as it portrays the proper response to Jesus' preaching that the kingdom of God is at hand. As Christopher Marshall notes, the response of the four fisherman, leaving their nets and following Jesus, corresponds to Jesus' call to repent and believe in the gospel.

JESUS' PREACHING		FISHERMEN'S RESPONSE
repent	=	leave behind livelihood
believe in gospel	=	follow Jesus

21

The repentance of Jesus' first disciples consists in leaving behind one way of life in order to embrace another way of life lived under the in-breaking rule of God's kingdom. The literary juxtaposition of these two episodes, Jesus' preaching and the call of the fishermen, suggests that the fishermen have heard and accepted Jesus' initial proclamation of the kingdom. How real their repentance is becomes apparent when Peter says to Jesus, "Look, we have left everything and followed you" (10:28). At the beginning of the Markan narrative, then, the disciples function as examples of what it means to repent; they leave behind family, livelihood, and possessions to follow Jesus because they perceive the presence of God's kingdom in his ministry.[27]

The repentance of the disciples, as the rest of the Gospel makes clear, is not complete. The Markan disciples can be cowardly (4:40), lacking in comprehension (8:14–21), concerned for social status (9:33–34; 10:35–41), and disloyal to Jesus (14:50). Nevertheless, their initial response to him provides a paradigm for understanding what repentance involves: a break with the past in order to embrace the kingdom of God.

Embracing the kingdom of God entails a new way of thinking that often contradicts the values and standards of this age.[28] In Mark's Gospel, Jesus teaches and challenges his disciples to adopt this new way of evaluating what is good and important. For example, on three occasions, after teaching them that he must suffer, be rejected, and rise from the dead, Jesus explains what it means to follow him. After his first prediction, he says that those who wish to follow him must deny themselves and take up their cross, for those who try to save their life will lose it, whereas those who lose their life for the sake of Jesus *and the gospel* will save it (8:35). After the second prediction, Jesus tells the Twelve that those who wish to be first must be last of all and servant of all (9:35). Finally, after the third prediction, Jesus instructs the Twelve that whoever wishes to become great and first among the disciples must become the servant and slave of all (10:43–44).

The key to unlocking this paradoxical reasoning is found in Jesus' rebuke of Peter (8:33). When Peter rebukes Jesus for speaking of rejection and suffering (8:32), Jesus rebukes Peter for judging the fate of the Messiah from a merely human point of view (*ta tōn anthrōpōn*) rather than from God's point of view (*ta tou theou*). The difference between these two evaluative points of view can be illustrated as follows:

THE WORLD'S POINT OF VIEW	GOD'S POINT OF VIEW
save one's own life	surrender one's life
be first of all	be last of all
be great	be the servant of all
	be the slave of all

Within Mark's Gospel, the call to repent means aligning one's point of view with God's point of view as manifested in the ministry of Jesus.

Adopting God's point of view results in living under his kingship by "entering the kingdom of God," which has made its appearance with Jesus. Repentance, however, is not an end in itself. Those who repent must believe in the gospel.[29]

Faith. Faith, in Mark's Gospel, is not merely one virtue among others. In the Markan narrative, it is the all-embracing term that describes the moral and ethical life of those who embrace the kingdom of God. Faith is perceiving and understanding, whereas the lack of faith is blindness and incomprehension. Those who believe, perceive, and understand what Jesus says and does can see the presence of God's kingdom in his ministry even though the manifestation of the kingdom is presently hidden and seemingly insignificant. Convinced that the kingdom of God is present, although not yet in power, such people live lives of discipleship in a community of disciples gathered around Jesus. Within Mark's Gospel, people believe in order to see.

When Jesus makes his initial proclamation of the kingdom, he specifies the object of this faith: believe *in the gospel* (Mark 1:15). This gospel is God's good news (1:14) that the time is fulfilled and God's rule is making its appearance. People of faith believe in the hidden presence of God's reign and are confident that this rule will soon be manifested in power.

Faith in the gospel is intimately associated with the person of Jesus because in the post-resurrection church the proclamation *about* Jesus has become part of the gospel. Thus the opening verse of Mark's narrative, "The beginning of the gospel of Jesus Christ, the Son of God," means the good news *about* Jesus Christ as well as the good news of the kingdom of God proclaimed *by* Jesus. It is not surprising, then, that on two occasions Jesus closely connects his person with the gospel.

> . . . And those who lose their life *for my sake,* and *for the sake of the gospel,* will save it . . . (8:35).

> . . . There is no one who has left house or brothers or sisters or mother or father or children or fields, *for my sake* and *for the sake of the gospel,* who will not receive a hundredfold now in this age . . . (10:29).

In the post-resurrection church, to dedicate one's life to the risen Lord is to dedicate oneself to the gospel, that is, to the good news of the kingdom of God. Conversely, to believe in this gospel is to believe the message of Jesus and dedicate oneself to him.

Because of the relationship between Jesus and the gospel, people express their faith in the gospel by responding positively to his ministry, especially his miracles. Within Mark's narrative, miracles are not isolated phenomena but "are signs of the presence of God's kingly power in Jesus."[30] They are manifestations of God's power over those forces which would return creation to chaos: sickness, death, and Satan.

The prominence of miracles in the first half of Mark's Gospel is hardly a chance occurrence.[31] After Jesus' initial proclamation of the kingdom, his miracles and exorcisms *are* his proclamation of the kingdom. This activity effects what it proclaims: the end of Satan's rule, the recovery of health, the restoration of the sick to the human community, and deliverance from chaos, hunger, and even death. Moreover, one could say that Jesus' miracles possess an ethical dimension since they are powerful protests against the suffering caused by hunger, sickness, chaos, and Satan.[32]

Of themselves, however, miracles are ambiguous. The Jerusalem scribes, for example, accuse Jesus of casting out demons by the prince of demons (3:22), and Jesus' compatriots do not understand that the powerful deeds he effects are manifestations of the presence of the kingdom of God (6:1–6). In effect, Jesus' miracles are like his parables: they reveal the mystery of the kingdom to those who believe God's good news that the kingdom has made its appearance. Those who believe in this good news see and understand that Jesus' powerful deeds are manifestations of God's kingly reign.

Examples of faith and unbelief. Several of the minor characters of Mark's Gospel are examples of people who believe. For example, Jesus forgives the sins of a paralytic and heals him because he sees the faith of the paralytic and those who bring him to be healed (Mark 2:5). Jesus tells the woman with hemorrhages that her faith has saved her (5:34). He encourages Jairus not to fear but to believe (5:36) and then raises his daughter from the dead. The father of a boy possessed by a demon cries out to Jesus, "I believe; help my unbelief!" (9:24), and Jesus heals his son. Finally, after restoring the sight of Bartimaeus, Jesus tells him, "Go; your faith has made you well" (10:52). In every case those healed by Jesus overcome obstacles in order to approach him: the paralytic must be lowered through a roof; the woman with hemorrhages must overcome the crowd to touch Jesus; Jairus must overcome fear; the father must overcome unbelief; and Bartimaeus must approach Jesus even though the crowd tries to silence him. But in every instance, these people persevere in their faith because they perceive that the power of God's kingdom is present in Jesus' ministry.

The disciples of Mark's Gospel are more complicated than those minor characters, and Mark clearly uses the disciples to teach important lessons about discipleship and the need for faith.[33] On the one hand, they are clearly generous people who have left everything in order to follow Jesus (10:28); they are among the first to believe in the gospel of God. But on several occasions their faith falters. When Jesus rescues them from a storm on the lake of Galilee, for example, he asks, "Why are you afraid? Have you still no faith?" (4:40). After Jesus feeds the five thousand in the wilderness, and then a crowd of four thousand, the disciples still do not perceive the messianic significance of these miracles, leading Jesus to ask if their hearts are hardened (8:17) and if they still do not understand (8:21).[34] And when the disciples fail to exorcise an unclean spirit from a young boy, Jesus seems to associate them with this "faithless generation" (9:19).

The faith of Jesus' disciples is weak at best. Although they have repented and believed in the gospel (1:16–20), they must continue to repent by adopting God's point of view as espoused by Jesus, especially as embodied in his fate as the suffering and rising Son of Man (8:31; 9:31; 10:33–34). The disciples' pursuit of honor and prestige, however, prevents them from adopting this viewpoint (9:34; 10:41). In effect, they present Mark's audience with an example of how even generous disciples who welcome the kingdom with joy and enthusiasm can fail because of Satan (4:15), trouble, or persecution on account of the word (4:17), the cares of the world, the lure of wealth, and the desire for other things that lead one astray (4:19).[35]

If the disciples provide an example of faltering faith, the religious leaders exemplify nonbelief.[36] Rather than believe that Jesus' ministry inaugurates the kingdom of God, they seek a sign from him that will dispense them from faith (8:11). They mock the crucified Jesus, "Let the Messiah, the King of Israel, come down from the cross now, *so that we may see and believe*" (15:32). Instead of believing in order to see, the religious leaders want to see in order to believe. In effect they are the mirror image of those minor characters who, because they believe, see the hidden presence of the kingdom of God in Jesus' ministry.

To summarize, there is an important ethical dimension to faith in Mark's Gospel. Faith in the gospel of God leads people to see the hidden presence of God's kingdom already active in Jesus' ministry. In light of the kingdom, those who believe find the power to adopt God's evaluative point of view. They live as a community of disciples in which the greatest is the servant and slave of all.

JESUS AND THE LAW

One of the most important ethical issues the early church faced was its relationship to the Mosaic law. How should those who believe in Jesus as the Messiah and Son of God observe the law? The issue is complicated for modern readers since they approach texts such as the Gospels with a prior understanding of law, for example, the moral law, the natural law. Within the New Testament, however, "the law" normally refers to the Mosaic law, which contains rules and regulations governing every aspect of life from cultic and purity regulations to the Decalogue.[37] Observance of this law was the means by which the Jewish people maintained its covenant status.[38] Graciously chosen by God, Israel stood in the proper covenant relationship to God by observing the prescriptions of the law.

On face value, therefore, it would seem that Jesus' disciples should continue to observe the Mosaic law.[39] This solution, however, was not to be. The influx of Gentiles presented the church with a problem: Should Gentiles be required to observe all aspects of a law whose customs and practices, such as dietary prescriptions and circumcision, identified its adherents as Jewish? To be sure, Jesus came into conflict with the religious leaders of his day over the observance of the law, but did he abolish part or all of the law?

Jesus' teaching about the law does not play as great a role in Mark's Gospel as it does in the Gospel of Matthew, nor does the Markan Jesus ever discuss the law in the manner that Paul does. Indeed, the word for law (*nomos*) does not even occur in this Gospel, and the original audience of Mark's Gospel seems to have been composed of Gentiles who had little understanding of the Mosaic law and did not practice its many ritual prescriptions (see 7:3–4). At no point in Mark's Gospel, however, does Jesus explicitly abolish the Mosaic law, although Mark does note that Jesus declared all foods clean. For the Markan Jesus, the law is equated with the commandments of God, which clearly remain in force. Thus, Mark presents Jesus as upholding God's commandments in the face of the religious leaders, who nullify God's law for the sake of their human traditions. The Gospel of Mark belongs to a tradition that distinguishes between the moral and cultic aspects of the law. While the former remain in effect, the latter are no longer incumbent upon Jesus' disciples.[40]

The Gospel of Mark portrays Jesus as being in conflict with the religious authorities throughout his ministry: in Galilee, on the way to Jerusalem, and in the city of Jerusalem.[41] In what follows, I examine the controversies between Jesus and the religious leaders that deal with Jesus' attitude toward, or observance of, the law. In doing so, I will pay close attention to the narrative setting of each controversy.

Controversies in Galilee

The first confrontation between Jesus and the religious leaders occurs in Galilee (Mark 2:1–3:6), shortly after Jesus' initial proclamation of the kingdom of God. It consists of five controversy stories and represents the first explicit opposition to Jesus' ministry. Prior to these controversies, Jesus preaches the kingdom of God in word and deed throughout the whole of Galilee with such success that people even seek him in the wilderness (1:35–37, 45). Moreover, immediately following these controversies, Mark provides his audience with a summary statement that highlights the initial success of Jesus' ministry (3:7–12). The opposition of the religious leaders to Jesus, therefore, stands in sharp contrast to the response of the crowds. While the crowds manifest an initial enthusiasm for Jesus' proclamation of the kingdom, the religious leaders clearly reject it.

The Galilean controversies are highly stylized, and Mark undoubtedly received much of his material from earlier traditions that reflect the controversies between the post-Easter church and the synagogue.[42] Within Mark's narrative, however, the focus of the material is upon Jesus and the religious leaders who view his message with skepticism. As we shall see, the controversies grow in hostility, beginning with the private thoughts of the religious leaders that Jesus has blasphemed (2:7) and concluding with an explicit decision on their part to destroy him (3:6).

In the first controversy, there is no public opposition to Jesus. The Markan narrator merely relates what the scribes were thinking: that Jesus blasphemes by assuming God's prerogative to forgive sins (2:6–7).[43] Jesus, however, knows their thoughts and shows by healing the paralytic that he truly has the power to forgive sins. In the second controversy, the scribes and Pharisees complain to the disciples that Jesus eats with sinners and tax collectors (2:16). Once more their opposition to Jesus is indirect since the religious leaders do not speak to Jesus. But when Jesus hears of their objection, he explains his behavior in light of his mission to call sinners (2:17). In the third controversy, Jesus is approached directly[44] and asked why his disciples do not fast while those of John the Baptist and the Pharisees do (2:18). He explains that his disciples cannot fast because the Bridegroom (Jesus) is with them (2:20). The last two controversies concern the Sabbath and conclude with the Pharisees and Herodians plotting to destroy Jesus. First, the Pharisees ask Jesus why his disciples do what is not "lawful" (*ho ouk exestin*) on the Sabbath by picking grain (2:24). Then they watch Jesus to see if he will violate the Sabbath by curing a man with a withered hand. Before acting, therefore, Jesus asks if it is "lawful" (*exestin*) to do good on the Sabbath by saving a life (3:4), echoing the earlier accusation of the Pharisees that the disciples did what was not "lawful" on the Sabbath (2:24). When the Pharisees do not respond, Jesus heals the man.

There is no explicit mention of the law in any of these controversies, but the question of the law and Jesus' interpretation of it underlie the entire section. The religious leaders accuse him or his disciples of blasphemy, violating laws of purity by associating with sinners, not fasting, and most importantly, breaking the Sabbath.

From the point of view of Mark's Gospel, however, neither Jesus nor his disciples have violated the law. In every instance, Jesus and his disciples are conducting themselves in the light of God's gospel about the kingdom of God. Jesus forgives sins and shares table fellowship with sinners because the in-breaking kingdom of God requires him to call sinners to repentance. Jesus' disciples do not fast, and he is Lord of the Sabbath, because he is the Bridegroom of the kingdom of God. Jesus acts in light of the in-breaking kingdom of God; he does not blatantly disregard the law. The real controversy, then, is about the kingdom of God rather than the law. The religious leaders do not understand Jesus' attitude toward sinners, fasting, and the Sabbath because they have not believed in his initial proclamation of the kingdom.

Clean and Unclean

In Mark 7 the Pharisees and scribes observe Jesus' disciples eating without first washing their hands. Consequently, they ask why his disciples violate the tradition of the elders by eating with defiled hands (7:5). In response, Jesus accuses the Pharisees and scribes of abandoning the commandment of God (*entolēn tou theou*) for the sake of human tradition (*tēn paradosin tōn anthrōpōn*; 7:8). Next, Jesus explains how the religious leaders nullify God's commandment to honor mother and father (Ex. 20:12; Deut. 5:16) for the sake of their human tradition (7:9–13). Throughout the controversy there is a clear opposition between the commandment or word of

God upheld by Jesus (7:8, 9, 10, 13) and the tradition of the elders upheld by the religious leaders (7:3, 4, 5, 7, 8, 9, 13).

After this controversy, Jesus tells the crowd that nothing that enters a person from outside is able to defile a person, but rather it is what comes out of a person that defiles (7:15). When the disciples do not understand this saying, Jesus explains that externals do not defile because they do not enter one's heart (7:19), but things that come from within a person defile because they originate in the heart (7:20). Two points need to be made here. First, Jesus' parabolic saying (7:15) functions as a further critique of the Pharisees and scribes who hold to the tradition of the elders. Jesus declares that the traditions of the elders, in addition to being secondary to God's commandment, are matters of indifference: they do not cleanse, nor does violating them make one unclean. Second, lest the reader miss the point, the Markan Evangelist explains that Jesus declared all foods clean by this pronouncement (7:19). In doing so the Markan Jesus has clearly gone beyond the prescriptions of the Mosaic law, which requires the observance of a variety of purity laws.[45] From the point of view of the Markan Gospel, however, it is Jesus who upholds the law and the religious leaders who nullify it. What allows Mark to present Jesus in this manner?

Once more, the answer is to be found in Jesus' initial proclamation of the kingdom of God. Jesus declares all foods clean because the kingdom of God has made its appearance and is in the process of uniting Jew and Gentile. It is not coincidental, therefore, that this controversy occurs between the feeding of the five thousand in the wilderness (6:30–44) and the feeding of the four thousand in the wilderness (8:1–10). As many have indicated, the feedings occur on opposite sides of the Sea of Galilee, the first in Jewish territory and the second in Gentile territory.[46] By commenting that Jesus declared all foods clean, Mark makes explicit what is implicit in the feeding narratives: Jew and Gentile may now share table fellowship because Jesus, the Shepherd Messiah, has fed both. The kingdom of God is establishing a new reality that requires the rethinking of old traditions.[47]

Divorce and Possessions

As Jesus journeys to Jerusalem, some Pharisees "test" him by asking if a man is allowed (*ei exestin*) to divorce his wife (Mark 10:2).[48] The question is somewhat puzzling since divorce was in fact clearly allowed by the Old Testament (Deut. 24:1–4). Thus it is not surprising that Matthew edits Mark's Gospel so that the question concerns the reason for granting a divorce ("Is it lawful for a man to divorce his wife *for any cause*?" Matt. 19:3). In Mark's narrative, then, the question is more fundamental: It concerns divorce itself rather than the grounds for it.[49]

Although the law allowed divorce, Mark again presents Jesus as one who upholds God's law rather than abolishes it. First, Jesus asks the Pharisees what Moses *commanded* (10:3). When they respond that Moses *allowed* a husband to write a bill of divorce (10:4), Jesus attributes Moses' commandment to write a bill of divorce to their hardness of heart.[50] Turning to

scripture (Gen 1:27; 2:24), he explains that divorce contravenes God's original will that husband and wife should become and remain one flesh.
Moses allowed divorce and commanded a bill of divorce because the hearts
of people were hardened, but now in the time of the kingdom disciples
must return to God's original will.

As in chapter 7, the disciples require further instruction. "In the
house,"[51] therefore, Jesus tells them that if a man divorces his wife and marries another, he commits adultery against her, and if a woman divorces her
husband and marries another she does the same. In effect, the Markan Jesus
develops his teaching further here. Not only is divorce forbidden by God's
will, but those who divorce and remarry commit adultery.

To understand Jesus' teaching about divorce, one must pay attention
to the wider context. The text we have been discussing belongs to a unit
(10:1–31) that provides the audience of Mark's Gospel with instruction on
the subjects of marriage (vv. 1–12), children (vv. 13–16), and possessions
(vv. 17–31). Thus, after his teaching on divorce, Jesus instructs his disciples
to welcome little children since the kingdom of God consists of those who
are like children, and he challenges a rich man to sell his possessions, give
the proceeds to the poor, and follow him. In this unit, the Markan Jesus
does not legislate a new law, nor does he abolish the old law. Indeed, when
the rich man asks what he must do to inherit eternal life, Jesus reminds him
of the commandments (10:19). But in light of God's kingly rule, Jesus makes
extraordinary demands upon disciples: They must not divorce their
spouses; they must welcome children because the kingdom consists of
those who are like little children in their attitude of faith toward God; they
must be willing to sacrifice all their possessions for the sake of the kingdom.

Controversies in Jerusalem

When Jesus reaches Jerusalem, his ministry is marked by controversy
once more. After he cleanses the Temple, the chief priests, the scribes, and
the elders ask by what authority he does such things and who gave him the
authority to do these things (Mark 11:28). After Jesus responds with the
parable of the vineyard, Mark reports a series of controversies between
Jesus and the religious leaders concerning the payment of taxes to Caesar,
the resurrection of the dead, and the most important commandment
(12:13–34).[52] In the first of these, the Pharisees ask if it is "lawful" (*exestin*)
to pay taxes to the emperor (12:14), the same type of question they asked
earlier (10:2). Although Jesus' answer is *not* the foundation for a doctrine of
church and state, as is often thought, it does put one's relationship to authority in a new perspective. In light of God's coming rule, everything belongs to God. Disciples may give Caesar the coin that bears his image, but
kingship belongs to God alone.

Later, a friendly scribe asks Jesus which commandment is first of all
(12:28). Given the multiplicity of commandments in the law (613 by some
reckonings), the question is not frivolous. In his response, Jesus draws
upon Deut. 6:4–5 and Lev. 19:18. The most important commandment is to

love God; the second is to love one's neighbor as oneself. The scribe concurs and repeats Jesus' response, adding that these two commandments are more important than all whole burnt offerings and sacrifices (12:33). The scribe's final remark is especially apropos since Jesus has recently cleansed the Temple, which, he says, has become a den of thieves rather than a house of prayer for all the nations (11:17). For Jesus' disciples, living after the destruction of the Temple of Jerusalem, keeping the commandments, especially love of God and love of neighbor, has replaced temple sacrifice.

We will return to this episode again when we study it in Matthew and Luke. For now, it is important to note that Jesus does not reduce the commandments to love of God and neighbor. Nor does he equate the two. The other commandments remain in force, but these two are the most important, with the love of God holding primacy of place. Jesus' response to the scribe—that he is not far from the kingdom of God—suggests that there is a relationship between doing God's commandments and entering God's kingdom. The kingship of God makes the love of God and neighbor more urgent than ever, and in a time when there will be no temple cult, observing God's commandments will be the perfect sacrifice. The Markan Jesus is far from being an antinomian. Although he declares all food clean, he does not abolish the law or lessen its importance: the commandments of God remain in effect. Indeed, they take on new importance. But later additions to the law, such as the traditions of the elders, are merely human traditions. In the time of the kingdom they are no longer in force.

REWARD AND PUNISHMENT

If one were to ask the Markan Jesus why disciples should live a moral life, the answer would be simple: God wills such behavior. Thus Jesus defines his family as those who do God's will (Mark 3:35). Jesus does not add new commandments to God's law, much less replace the old law with a new moral code. Rather, in light of God's in-breaking kingdom he calls disciples to do God's will by repenting and believing in the gospel. Thus the ultimate motivation for moral conduct is doing God's will. In this regard, Jesus stands squarely in the great traditions of Israel. Mark's Gospel, however, provides its audience with powerful motives for doing God's will; namely, the hope of reward and the fear of punishment. Thus the behavior of disciples in the present will have profound consequences for the future: those who are ashamed of Jesus now, Jesus will be ashamed of when he returns as the glorious Son of Man at his parousia (8:38).

Reward, in Mark's Gospel, is equated with entrance into the kingdom of God, which is eternal life, while punishment involves exclusion from the kingdom and its life. For example, when Jesus warns his disciples to avoid temptations to sin, he says that it would be better to enter life maimed than to be cast into Gehenna (9:43–48). In this same section, Jesus equates life (vv. 43, 45) with entering the kingdom of God (v. 47). The same happens when a rich man asks Jesus what he must do to inherit eternal life (10:17).

Jesus tells the man to sell his possessions, give the proceeds to the poor, and follow him; then he will have treasure in heaven (10:21). When the rich man turns away sad, Jesus laments to his disciples how hard it is for the rich to enter the kingdom of God (10:23, 24), thereby equating the eternal life sought by the rich man with entrance into God's kingdom. Finally, when Peter says that the disciples have left everything in order to follow Jesus, Jesus promises the disciples rewards in the present age, accompanied by persecution, "and in the age to come eternal life" (10:30).

While Jesus promises rewards in the present age (10:29–30), the ultimate reward or punishment will come at his parousia. On that day the Son of Man (Jesus) will send the angels to gather the elect from every corner of the earth (13:27). On the basis of what Jesus has said earlier, one can presume that the elect will be gathered into God's kingdom where they will enjoy eternal life while all others will be excluded.

Overall, the Markan Jesus, unlike the Matthean Jesus, is more concerned with describing the reward of those who are saved than the fate of those who are lost. As we shall see, the Jesus of Matthew's Gospel describes in greater detail the fate that awaits sinners. The little that is said on the matter in Mark's Gospel, however, is sufficient to warn its audience of the punishment that awaits those who do not enter the kingdom of God. Those who blaspheme against the Holy Spirit, by attributing Jesus' exorcisms to Satan, will never be forgiven (3:29). Those who try to save their lives will lose them (8:35). Those who are ashamed of the Son of Man will find that the Son of Man is ashamed of them (8:38). Those who fall from faith (are scandalized) will be cast into Gehenna, a place of unending fire (9:48). And those who extort widows and act hypocritically will receive "the greater condemnation" (12:40).

Inasmuch as Jesus' ethic is oriented toward the future, it is teleological: it calls people to act in view of a specific goal or end. Disciples who do God's will now will be saved; they will enter the kingdom and inherit eternal life. Those who do not do God's will now will be excluded from the kingdom. Excluded from the kingdom, they will not inherit eternal life. Indeed, the very life they sought to save will be lost. If, as many have suggested, this Gospel was written in a period when the Markan community was threatened by imminent persecution, these promises of reward and threats of punishment would have been powerful reasons for persevering in the life of discipleship. But even in more tranquil times they serve as a promise and warning that the present and the future are intimately intertwined.

JESUS A MODEL FOR MORAL BEHAVIOR

Thus far I have focused on Jesus' ethical teaching as presented in Mark's Gospel. But the story about Jesus and how he acts within that story also provide a fertile ground for moral reflection. Those who read or listen to the Gospel story observe and learn from Jesus' conduct. Like Jesus' first disciples, they are taught by what he does as well as by what he teaches. To some extent I have already pointed to important aspects of Jesus' conduct. For example, in my discussion of the law, I noted that Mark presents Jesus as one who upholds God's commandments and calls his disciples to observe God's original will as expressed in scripture. In this section I pursue this line of investigation in terms of Jesus' desire to do God's will, his faithfulness to God, and his compassion for others.

Doing the Will of God

The essence of Jesus' moral teaching is doing God's will. Those who do the will of God are brother, and sister, and mother to Jesus (Mark 3:35); they are members of a new family united by a common desire to do God's will, and not simply by blood. As the central figure of this new family, Jesus does the will of God in an exemplary fashion. For example, when Peter and the other disciples want him to remain in Capernaum, because everyone is looking for him, Jesus responds that he must go to other villages in order to preach the message of the kingdom, because it was for this that he came (1:38). Jesus' desire to do God's will, however, is most clearly expressed when he teaches his disciples his fate as the Son of Man.[53] In the first of these teachings (8:32), he says that the Son of Man must (*dei*) suffer; be rejected by the elders, the chief priests, and the scribes; and rise from the dead after three days. In the second (9:31), he teaches his disciples that the Son of Man will be handed over to sinful men who will kill him. And in the third (10:33–34), Jesus gives a detailed description of what will happen to him in Jerusalem. Throughout his ministry, therefore, Jesus knows God's will for him: to proclaim the good news of the kingdom of God, and to suffer, be rejected, die, and rise from the dead.

But the Markan Jesus is not a wooden figure who simply does God's will without struggle or pain. In the garden of Gethsemane (14:33–42) he undergoes a great agony that a modern writer might call a crisis of faith.[54] Although he knows God's will for the messiah, Jesus is utterly dismayed and distressed at the prospect of his fate (14:33). He goes so far as to ask his Father, if it is possible, to let this hour of testing pass and to remove the cup of suffering he must endure (14:35–36). Mark's portrayal of Jesus' prayer should not be overlooked. In Gethsemane, the Markan Jesus faces a crisis of resolve. Although he knows God's will for the messiah, he asks his Father to deliver him from it. Only through persevering in prayer is Jesus able to say, "but yet, not what I want, but what you want" (14:36). Only after Jesus has undergone an intense struggle and crisis of resolve does he face his hour of testing with a renewed determination to do God's will. When his agonized prayer is completed, he tells his disciples the hour has come for the Son of Man to be handed over into the hands of sinful men (14:41), echoing his earlier teaching about the fate of the Son of Man who will be handed over to sinful men (9:31). Having finally determined to persist in doing God's will, Jesus can fulfill his destiny as the Son of Man.

In contrast to Jesus, the disciples do not watch and pray (14:38, 40, 41).

Having failed to do so, they flee when Jesus is arrested (14:50). Thus there is a sharp contrast between their behavior and that of Jesus. He is the one who watches and prays at the crucial moment and resolves to do God's will after an intense agony. The disciples, however, do not do God's will because they do not watch and pray at the critical hour. Mark's portrayal of Jesus' behavior provides all would-be disciples with an example to follow and warns that knowing God's will may not be sufficient. One must also watch and pray in order to do God's will, often in intense pain and struggle.

The Faithfulness of Jesus

Jesus' proclamation of the gospel calls people to repent and believe in the gospel. Moreover, Mark's Gospel provides numerous examples of faith and unbelief. But what of Jesus? Having summoned others to believe, does he also believe? This may seem a strange question, since the Gospel of Mark never explicitly speaks of Jesus' faith or of Jesus believing. Nevertheless, there are indications that Mark thinks of Jesus as someone who believes. For example, when Peter points to the withered fig tree that Jesus had earlier cursed (Mark 11:21), Jesus responds: "Have faith in God (*echete pistin theou*) . . . and if you do not doubt in your heart, but believe that what you say will come to pass, it will be done for you" (11:22–23). Jesus' response to Peter is rightly understood as an exhortation to disciples that if they believe in the power of God to do all things, they will be capable of performing miraculous deeds as did Jesus. But is Jesus also disclosing something about his own miraculous powers? That is, when doing his mighty deeds, does he also believe in the power of God? Could it be that Jesus' own faith in the gospel, that God's kingdom is breaking in, empowers him to heal and cast out demons?

Faith in God entails faithfulness to God, and in the Passion Narrative Mark portrays Jesus as one who is faithful, even when he no longer experiences God's presence. For example, at his crucifixion Jesus is mocked and ridiculed by those who pass by, by the chief priests and scribes, and by the violent criminals crucified with him. The first group blasphemes him as a temple destroyer and challenges him to save himself by coming down from the cross (15:29–30). The second ridicules him by saying that he saved others but cannot save himself. They challenge Jesus to prove that he is the Messiah, the king of Israel, by descending from the cross so that they can see and believe (15:31–32a). Finally, those crucified with Jesus taunt him in the same way (15:32b). In the face of this threefold mocking call to save himself by miraculously descending from the cross, Jesus remains silent. Why? Earlier, after announcing his fate as the Son of Man, Jesus instructed the crowd and his disciples that "those who want to save their life will lose it, and those who lose their life for my sake, and for the sake of the gospel, will save it"(8:35). At the moment of his crucifixion, Jesus must himself trust in the power of God to save him, for if he tries to save his life he will surely lose it. Thus Jesus' silence upon the cross is the perfect expression of his faithfulness to God: his faith that God will save him.

Jesus' faithfulness to God, however, is not without anguish. As was the case with his resolve to do God's will, Jesus' determination to remain faithful to God is born of anguish and suffering. At the moment of his death, he cries out the opening words of Psalm 22, "My God, my God, why have you forsaken me?" (Mark 15:34). The Markan Jesus has not despaired of God's help, but neither are his last words a peaceful cry of submission. At the last moment of his life, Jesus experiences the absence of the God whose kingship he has proclaimed. Nevertheless, like the suffering righteous one portrayed in Psalm 22, he trusts in the God whose comforting presence is withdrawn from him. Jesus never says "I believe," but his conduct proves that he is a man of profound faith.

Jesus' Compassion

The Jesus of Mark's Gospel exhibits a variety of emotions. He looks at the Pharisees with anger and is saddened by their hardness of heart (3:5). He becomes indignant when the disciples forbid little children to approach him (10:14). And when the rich man tells Jesus that he has kept all the commandments, Mark says that Jesus looked at him and loved him (10:21). But in addition to these emotions, Mark describes Jesus as someone moved with compassion at the suffering of others. When a leper begs Jesus to cleanse him, for example, Jesus is moved with compassion (1:41). When Jesus sees the great crowd in the wilderness, the Markan narrator tells us that Jesus was moved with compassion because the people were like sheep without a shepherd (6:34). And before Jesus feeds the crowd of four thousand in the wilderness, he tells his disciples, "I have compassion for the crowd" (8:2). But Mark's description of Jesus as compassionate need not be limited to these instances. All of Jesus' mighty deeds are acts of compassion for those afflicted by demons and disease. Thus, on more than one occasion, Mark summarizes Jesus' miraculous activity, explaining how large crowds of people brought the sick and demon-possessed to be healed by him (1:32–33; 3:7–12; 6:53–56). The Jesus of Mark's Gospel is a powerful miracle worker capable of not only anger and indignation but compassion as well. The Jesus who calls others to be the slave and servant of all presents himself as the Son of Man who came not to be served but to serve and give his life as a ransom for the many (10:45).

JESUS' MORAL TEACHING:
A SUMMARY STATEMENT

The Markan Jesus does not offer a new ethical code, much less abolish the old. He supposes that all people, and especially his disciples, will follow the "commandments" of God, which he clearly distinguishes from "human traditions." There is nothing more important than doing God's will. Of these commandments the first is to love God, and the second is to love one's neighbor as oneself. The other commandments are not abrogated, but they are subservient to these two. Normally, the observance of the commandments leads to eternal life, but in some instances it may be necessary to forsake all of one's possessions in order to follow Jesus.

The most distinctive aspect of Jesus' moral teaching is the kingdom of God. He calls people to repent and believe in the gospel of God because the God-appointed time for waiting has been completed, and the kingdom of God has made its appearance, albeit in a hidden way. To repent means turning away from one's former way of life in order to embrace a new way of life under God's kingship. In this new way of life, faith in God's gospel about the kingdom plays a central role. This faith, however, is not one virtue among others; it is the all-embracing virtue by which people perceive the hidden presence of God's rule. People believe in order to see.

Those who accept Jesus' message of the kingdom live in a community of disciples instructed by Jesus. They judge the world from the point of view of God rather than from a merely human vantage point. They surrender their life in order to save it; they become the servants and slaves of one another, knowing that the greatest among them is the servant of all. Aware of the hidden presence of the kingdom, disciples wait in faith for the kingdom's manifestation in power. Then those who have been faithful will enter the kingdom, that is, eternal life. Those who have not believed, or who have fallen from faith, will be excluded.

Discipleship, however, is a difficult vocation, and even the strongest disciples are liable to fail. Consequently, they must constantly watch and pray as Jesus did in Gethsemane. They must remain faithful, even when they no longer experience God's presence, as did Jesus at the moment of his death. They must be compassionate, as was Jesus, who came not to be served but to serve.

The ethics of Jesus in Mark's Gospel are necessarily bound up with the story of Jesus. To know that story is to be shaped by a new ethical vision whose horizon is none other than the in-breaking kingdom of God.

2

Doing the
Greater Righteousness

The Gospel according to Matthew

Although the Gospel according to Matthew is the first Gospel in the canonical collection of the New Testament writings, most scholars maintain that it was written after Mark's Gospel, and that its author revised the Gospel according to Mark to respond to the needs of the Jewish-Gentile community that he was addressing.[1] In addition to Mark's Gospel, Matthew made use of other sources as well: a collection of Jesus' sayings and teachings, usually designated "Q," and special material found only in Matthew's Gospel, designated "M."[2] Consequently, in addition to having much in common with Mark's Gospel, the Gospel of Matthew contains a significant amount of material, much of it ethical and moral in nature, not found in Mark. For example, a good part of the Sermon on the Mount comes from Q, while many of Matthew's parables— such as the parable of the ten virgins (25:1–13)—as well as his prophetic description of what will take place when the Son of Man comes to judge the nations (25:31–46) are peculiar to him. In a word, Matthew offers a revised and expanded version of Mark's Gospel that is more explicitly ethical in character.

As in my study of Mark's Gospel, the focus of this chapter will be upon the ethical teaching of Jesus as presented by the Evangelist Matthew rather than upon the historical Jesus.[3] By focusing upon the Matthean Jesus, I intend to highlight the distinctive way in which Matthew presents Jesus' moral teaching. This investigation, however, will not result in an entirely different view of Jesus since Matthew's primary source is Mark's Gospel. As we shall see, the Markan and Matthean presentations of Jesus' ethics agree on major issues such as the importance of the kingdom of God, the need to do God's will as expressed in the commandments, the threat of judgment, the promise of reward, and the moral example of Jesus. However, since Matthew had access to material unavailable to or not used by Mark, his portrait of Jesus' ethics is greatly enhanced. Moreover, the altered circumstances in which Matthew wrote led him to emphasize new aspects of Jesus' moral teaching. For example, there is general agreement that the community of Christians that Matthew addressed faced a different situation than did the Markan community. Whereas Mark's Gospel appears to have been written in Rome for a community of Gentile Christians facing a crisis of discipleship because of impending persecution, Matthew's Gospel was probably written for a group of Jewish and Gentile Christians, perhaps in Antioch of Syria, who were in a bitter debate with the Jewish synagogue over the observance of the Mosaic law.[4] Consequently, Matthew is at pains to show that Jesus did not abolish the law, and that his disciples continue to observe the law and practice a righteousness in accordance with God's will.

Since the kingdom of God (usually referred to as the kingdom of heaven in Matthew's Gospel) remains the primary ethical horizon for the Matthean Jesus, I begin with a discussion of its ethical implications in Matthew. From a discussion of the kingdom of heaven, I turn to Jesus' great sermon, the Sermon on the Mount, which functions as a compendium of ethical instruction for those who seek to enter the kingdom. Next, I turn to Matthew's portraits of Jesus and the religious leaders since they function as positive and negative examples of righteous behavior, respectively. Then I consider the themes of judgment and reward, which play a prominent role in Matthew and are more fully developed than in Mark's Gospel. Finally, I will discuss the relationship between human ethical conduct and God's saving action. Does the ethic of this Gospel, with its strong emphasis upon doing good works, leave any room for God's grace? While there will be some overlap with what has already been said in my chapter on Mark, the Gospel of Matthew will provide us with a fuller presentation of what it means to be a disciple.

THE KINGDOM OF HEAVEN
AS ETHICAL HORIZON

As was the case in Mark's Gospel, in Matthew's Gospel Jesus' ethical teaching presupposes that the kingdom of God has drawn near (Matt. 4:17). Matthew, however, has greatly expanded upon the theme of the kingdom, providing readers and listeners with a more detailed ethical horizon against which to situate Jesus' moral teaching about the law, righteousness, judgment, and reward. Whereas Mark has 14 references to the kingdom of God, Matthew has 50 references to the kingdom of God/heaven, 32 of which are peculiar to him.[5] Of these 50, Matthew shares with Luke 9 sayings about the kingdom that are not found in Mark's Gospel.[6] Moreover, many of Matthew's references to the kingdom of heaven are found in, or explained by, parables of the kingdom. These parables provide readers with an insight into the moral universe, created by the kingdom of heaven, in which Jesus' disciples live. In effect, they describe what it means to live in light of the kingdom of heaven.

37

While Matthew usually speaks of the kingdom of heaven,[7] he also employs the expression "the kingdom of God" (12:28; 19:24; 21:31, 43). At other times, he simply speaks of "the kingdom" (6:10; 25:34), "your kingdom," referring to God's kingdom (6:33); "his kingdom," referring to the kingdom of the Son of Man (13:41; 16:28); "your kingdom," referring to Jesus' kingdom (20:21); "the sons of the kingdom" (8:12; 13:38); "the kingdom of their Father" (13:43); "the word of the kingdom" (13:19); "the gospel of the kingdom" (4:23; 9:35), and "this gospel of the kingdom" (24:14). Matthew's fundamental understanding of the kingdom, however, is comparable to that found in Mark's Gospel, and so there is no need to repeat what I have already discussed there: that the kingdom of God, or of heaven, is a dynamic reality that refers to the rule or reign of God.[8] As we shall see, Matthew views the kingdom as both present and to come. Consequently, he follows the basic line of thought developed in Mark's Gospel. He has, however, developed Jesus' teaching about the kingdom more fully, especially as this teaching touches upon the subject of moral instruction.[9]

The Preaching of John, Jesus, and Jesus' Disciples

In Matthew's Gospel, the first reference to the kingdom of heaven is found in the preaching of John the Baptist: "Repent, for the kingdom of heaven has come near" (3:2). When the Pharisees and Sadducees approach John, he warns them to produce fruit that is worthy of repentance rather than to rely upon their descent from Abraham (3:7–9), if they wish to escape God's eschatological wrath. Employing an image that will be repeated several times in this Gospel, John the Baptist says that every tree that does not produce good fruit will be cut down and thrown into the fire (3:10). The kingdom of heaven, therefore, requires a radical change of mind (*metanoia*) that must express itself in concrete deeds comparable to good fruit produced by sound trees, if one hopes to escape the wrath of God (3:7).

Jesus' initial proclamation of the kingdom repeats the preaching of John, showing that he and John stand in the same prophetic tradition. After describing the events of Jesus' infancy, baptism, and temptation in the wilderness (1:1–4:16), Matthew introduces Jesus' public ministry: "From that time Jesus began to proclaim, 'Repent, for the kingdom of heaven has come near'" (4:17).[10] Subsequently, on two other occasions, Matthew employs summary statements to inform his readers that the essential content of Jesus' ministry is to teach, to preach the gospel of the kingdom, and to heal the sick (4:23; 9:35). Matthew's initial presentation of Jesus' public ministry, therefore, is similar to Mark 1:14–15. But there are important differences.

In Mark's Gospel, Jesus' initial proclamation is, "The time is fulfilled, and the kingdom of God has come near; repent, and believe in the gospel" (Mark 1:15). In Matthew's Gospel this proclamation has been edited in three ways. First, there is no reference to the fulfillment of time. Second, the call to repent comes before the announcement of the kingdom. Third, there is no mention of the need to believe in the gospel. Matthew's editorial work is purposeful. The omission of any reference to the fulfillment of time clarifies the meaning of the verb *ēggiken* ("has drawn near"), suggesting that the kingdom of heaven has drawn near but has not yet broken in.[11] This emphasis upon the imminent dawning of the kingdom, in turn, explains why Matthew places the announcement of the kingdom after the call to repent. Repentance, as the Baptist has already warned, is the necessary preparation for receiving God's kingdom.[12] Therefore, Jesus' initial announcement of the kingdom is preceded by a call to repentance. However, whereas John simply tells the religious leaders to produce fruit worthy of repentance, Jesus will show his disciples how to produce fruit worthy of repentance in the Sermon on the Mount (Matthew 5—7) with its several references to the kingdom of heaven (5:3, 10, 19, 20; 6:10, 33; 7:21) and righteousness (5:6, 10, 20; 6:1, 33).

After his great sermon, and after performing a series of mighty deeds, Jesus summons his twelve disciples and sends them on mission to the lost sheep of the house of Israel to announce that "the kingdom of heaven has come near" (10:7). Thus the disciples stand in the tradition of John and Jesus. They are to preach the gospel of the kingdom, a task that will last until the end of time: "And this gospel of the kingdom will be proclaimed throughout the world, as a testimony to all the nations; and then the end will come" (24:14).

Although his Gospel focuses upon the kingdom of heaven as a future reality, Matthew is aware that the kingdom has made its appearance in Jesus' ministry, especially in his exorcisms. For example, when people wonder if Jesus is the son of David because he expels demons and cures the sick, the Pharisees say that Jesus casts out demons by the power of Beelzebub, the prince of demons. But Jesus responds that if he expels demons by the power of Satan, then Satan's house is divided and cannot stand. If he casts out demons by the spirit of God, however, "then the kingdom of God has come to you" (12:28; *ephthasen*). This strong verb leaves little doubt that there is a present dimension to the kingdom.[13] To be sure, the fullness of the kingdom is not yet here; disciples must pray for its arrival (6:10); and Jesus himself looks forward to its eschatological manifestation (26:29). But when Jesus casts out demons, God's kingly rule invades human history. As in the Gospel of Mark, then, there is a hidden aspect of the kingdom that will only be revealed at Jesus' parousia.

The Kingdom in Jesus' Parables

Some of the most distinctive aspects of the Matthean Jesus' teaching about the kingdom of heaven are presented in parables, many of which provide a rich source of ethical instruction.[14] These parables describe a world in which ethical decisions must be made in light of the kingdom of heaven. In the moral world they create, the norm for good and evil is how one acts when faced with the prospect of God's in-breaking rule. I turn to these parables of the kingdom in order to see how they function as sources of ethical instruction.

Chapter 13. The midpoint of Matthew's Gospel is chapter 13. Previous to this chapter Israel receives Jesus favorably, except for the response of the religious leaders. In chapters 11 and 12, however, Jesus encounters opposition from all sides, causing him to speak to Israel in parables about the kingdom, a speech that Israel cannot understand. Jesus does, however, explain the meaning of the parables to his own disciples (Matt. 13:10–17). As a result, by the end of the discourse they understand everything, thus assuming the status of scribes trained for the kingdom of heaven (13:51–52). The parables of chapter 13 create a moral universe of good and evil that shows disciples how to live as "children of the kingdom."

In the parable of the sower (13:1–9, decoded by Jesus in vv. 18–23), Jesus reveals that the word about the kingdom can be impeded by a lack of understanding, tribulation, persecution, anxiety, and the lure of riches. An essential quality for disciples, therefore, is understanding: an ability to perceive how God's kingdom is at work. In the parable of the weeds and wheat (13:24–30, decoded by Jesus in vv. 36–43), Jesus explains that at the present time the "children of the kingdom" find themselves side by side with the "children of the evil one." While the "children of the kingdom" might be tempted to resolve the situation for themselves by expelling the "children of the evil one," Jesus tells his disciples that this situation is to be resolved at the end of the ages when the Son of Man sends his angels to expel from his kingdom all those who practice sin and evil (*panta ta skandala kai tous poiountas tēn anomian;* 13:41). Then the righteous will be revealed (13:43). The parable of the weeds and wheat, therefore, warns that the present composition of the church is a mixture of good and bad, and it is not always possible to tell who is righteous and who is not. A similar point is made in the parable of the net (13:47–50). Like a great net, the kingdom takes in all kinds of people, but at the end of the ages the angels will separate those who are evil from those who are righteous (13:49). In the parables of the mustard seed and the leaven (13:31–33), the kingdom of heaven is presented as a reality whose beginnings are insignificant and hidden but whose final manifestation will be beyond all expectation. Therefore, one should be prepared to sacrifice everything for the sake of the kingdom, just as does the person who finds a treasure hidden in a field (13:44), or the merchant who finds one pearl of exceedingly great price (13:45–46).

To summarize, one needs to hear the word about the kingdom with understanding because appearances are deceiving. The final manifestation of the kingdom will effect a separation of good and evil, and many will be surprised when the righteous are revealed. Therefore, one must pursue the kingdom of heaven with total commitment because it is the greatest good.

God's gracious mercy. Two parables describe the mercy and grace the kingdom of heaven brings. The parable of the unforgiving servant (Matt. 18:23–35) begins, "For this reason the kingdom of heaven may be compared to a king . . . ," and then explains why disciples must not set any limits to their forgiveness: just as the king forgave the debt of his servant who could not pay, so God has forgiven the debt of his servants, the disciples. Having received mercy through the kingdom, disciples must extend mercy to one another. In the parable of the vineyard (20:1–16), which begins, "For the kingdom of heaven is like a landowner . . . ," Jesus teaches that although one must produce good fruit, one's work does not result in a claim upon God. The God of the kingdom of heaven is generous and chooses to give the last the same as he gives to the first (20:14). Here we find Matthew at his Pauline best!

Doing God's will. In three parables addressed to the religious leaders, Jesus stresses the need to do God's will. In the first (Matt. 21:28–32), he contrasts the behavior of two sons: one who says he will work in his father's vineyard but does not, and another who at first refuses to work but eventually does. The second son represents the tax collectors and prostitutes who are entering the kingdom of God because they have repented of their former disobedience and are now doing God's will, while the first son represents the religious leaders who did not believe and repent even when John the Baptist showed them a "way of righteousness" (21:32). In the parable of the vineyard (21:33–43), Jesus warns the religious leaders that the kingdom of God will be taken from them and be given to a nation that will produce fruit that is worthy of it, namely, doing God's will. Finally, in the parable of the marriage feast (22:1–14), Jesus explains that God's gracious invitation to the kingdom requires a positive response, otherwise the invitation will be withdrawn and offered to others. Once more the parable is allegorical. The original guests represent Israel, while those invited later stand for the Gentiles. This great reversal, however, ends with yet another reversal (22:11–14). When the king discovers that one of the guests (who had been invited as a replacement for the original guests) does not have a wedding garment, he expels the man from the banquet. The context of this parable suggests that the wedding garment represents the deeds of righteousness that must clothe all who enter God's kingdom. One must do God's will by deeds of righteousness.

Parousia and judgment. In a series of parables about the kingdom of heaven found in his final great discourse (Matthew 24—25), Jesus explains how disciples must behave in the period between his resurrection and the parousia, when he will return as the royal Son of Man to judge the nations. In the parable of the ten virgins (25:1–13), he instructs his disciples that the kingdom of heaven is similar to the situation of ten virgins (disciples) waiting for a bridegroom (Jesus, the Son of man). Not only must they be vigilant, they must also be prepared with oil in their lamps (deeds of righteousness).[15] Again, the kingdom of heaven is like the situation of a man (Jesus, the Son of Man) who entrusts different amounts of money to various servants (disciples) and goes on a journey (25:14–30). Good and faithful disciples will be enterprising so that they can produce a profit for their master when he returns after a long time (25:19), a profit of righteous deeds. Finally, in Jesus' description of the last judgment (25:31–46), the criterion by which the Son of Man judges the nations is merciful and compassionate conduct. Those who do not act with compassion will be cast into eternal fire, while the righteous will enter the kingdom prepared for them from the foundation of the world (25:34).

To summarize, Jesus' parables of the kingdom of heaven present his audience with a moral universe in which the kingdom is viewed as God's gracious gift. To enter it one must do God's will, produce the fruit of righteousness worthy of the kingdom, be vigilant, enterprising, compassionate, and merciful. At the end of the ages, when Jesus returns as the royal Son of Man, he will reveal who is righteous and who is not. In the meantime, disciples must endure an outrageous situation in which evil and righteousness dwell alongside each other. In the moral universe created by Jesus' parables, the kingdom of heaven is the greatest good and one must pursue it at all costs. The norm for moral living is conduct that corresponds to the kingdom: compassion, mercy, and vigilance. In this moral universe, there is no moral discourse apart from the kingdom of heaven. God's will, righteousness, mercy, and compassion are to be done in light of the kingdom of heaven. Because the kingdom of heaven has made its appearance in Jesus' ministry, and because the kingdom will come in complete power at the end of the ages, one must live in its light even now. Jesus' ethics are not autonomous or self-authenticating; they are rooted in God's will and rule. A key concept for understanding Jesus' ethics in Matthew's Gospel, therefore, is righteous conduct: conduct done in light of God's will and the kingdom of heaven.

THE SERMON ON THE MOUNT:
A GREATER RIGHTEOUSNESS

The Gospels of Mark and Matthew offer a combined witness that God's kingly rule is foundational to Jesus' understanding of the moral life. People must repent and turn from their former way of life because the kingdom of heaven is at hand and, indeed, has already made its initial appearance in Jesus' ministry. In our study of Mark's Gospel, however, we did not find any extensive ethical instruction given by Jesus. The Markan Jesus requires people to obey God's commandments, especially the love of God and the love of neighbor, and he calls them to a life of discipleship that is lived from the point of view of God rather than of human beings. In the Gospel of Matthew, however, Jesus gives extensive ethical teaching that deals with the law and righteousness (*dikaiosynē*). Moreover, promises of reward and threats of punishment are more central to the moral teaching of the Matthean Jesus than to that of the Markan Jesus. The outstanding example of Jesus' ethical teaching is his Sermon on the Mount. In what follows, I focus upon righteousness as the organizing theme of the sermon rather than provide a detailed commentary on the Sermon.[16]

Context and Structure

Before proceeding to the sermon, it is necessary to say something about its context and structure within Matthew's Gospel. I begin with the question of context.

Jesus' Sermon on the Mount occurs shortly after his initial proclamation that the kingdom of heaven has come near (Matt. 4:17). Following this proclamation, he calls his first disciples (4:18–22), after which Matthew provides a summary of Jesus' ministry of teaching, preaching, and healing (4:23–25). This summary, in turn, provides the setting for the sermon, for, when Jesus sees the great crowds mentioned in the summary, he ascends the mountain and sits down. His disciples come to him, and he begins to teach (5:1–2). Jesus' Sermon on the Mount, therefore, occurs at the beginning of his public ministry, shortly after his proclamation of the kingdom of heaven. Addressed to the disciples in the hearing of the crowds (7:28–29), it offers a systematic presentation of how disciples must conduct themselves in light of the kingdom of heaven. Put another way, the sermon presents an ethic for the kingdom of heaven.

Immediately following his great sermon, Jesus performs a number of mighty deeds (8:1–9:34), after which Matthew provides his readers with yet another summary statement on Jesus' teaching, preaching, and healing (9:35). Filled with compassion for the crowds because they were troubled like sheep without a shepherd (9:36), Jesus sends the disciples on a mission to the lost sheep of the house of Israel (10:1–42) to announce that the kingdom of heaven is at hand (10:7). Having heard Jesus' great sermon and witnessed his mighty deeds, the disciples are prepared for their initial missionary activity. The beginning of Jesus' ministry according to Matthew can be outlined as follows.

Initial preaching of the kingdom of heaven
    Disciples called
        Summary
        Sermon
            Mighty deeds
        Summary
    Disciples sent on mission

A comparison of Jesus' public ministry as presented by Mark and Matthew discloses that in both Gospels Jesus begins his ministry with an announcement of the kingdom (Mark 1:15; Matt. 4:17) that is foundational for all that he will say and do. However, whereas in Mark's Gospel Jesus' initial proclamation of the kingdom is undergirded by his mighty deeds, in Matthew the emphasis is upon his authoritative word, which is followed by his mighty deeds. The Sermon on the Mount becomes a blueprint for life within the kingdom, and its teaching should not be separated from Jesus' initial proclamation that the kingdom of heaven has come near.

Jesus' sermon is carefully structured. After its introduction (5:3–16), there follows an important statement on the abiding validity of the law and the prophets (5:17–20). What Jesus means by this statement is explained in the body of the sermon (5:21–7:11), which can be divided into three parts (5:21–48; 6:1–18; 6:19–7:11), each dealing with the theme of righteousness. After a summary statement that identifies the essence of the law and the prophets in terms of the Golden Rule (7:12), the sermon concludes with a series of warnings (7:13–27). Hence the sermon may be outlined as follows.

Introduction to the sermon
    The law and prophets remain in force
        First teaching on righteousness
        Second teaching on righteousness
        Third teaching on righteousness
    The law and prophets fulfilled by Golden Rule
Conclusion of the sermon

The Sermon on the Mount

The central theme of Jesus' sermon is righteousness, an important concept that occurs seven times in Matthew's Gospel (3:15; 5:6, 10, 20; 6:1, 33; 21:32). The meaning of this term within Matthew's Gospel has been disputed, in large part because righteousness also plays an important role in Pauline theology, where it refers to God's salvific activity (God's righteousness), an eschatological gift of God (the righteousness that comes from God), as well as the status of someone who stands in the correct and proper relationship to God. While many scholars have tried to import the Pauline notion of righteousness as gift into Matthew's Gospel,[17] I am convinced by those who argue that righteousness in Matthew's Gospel refers to conduct in conformity with God's will as expressed in the law.[18] Therefore, when I speak of righteousness, I am referring primarily to conduct. But what kind of conduct does God demand in light of the kingdom of heaven? The Sermon on the Mount provides an answer: conduct that observes the law and prophets as interpreted by Jesus Messiah.

Introduction to the sermon. The sermon begins with nine beatitudes and two metaphors that call disciples to live their lives in light of the kingdom of heaven (Matt. 5:3–16). While the beatitudes pronounce a blessing, the manner in which Jesus frames the first eight of them, in the third-person plural, gives each an ethical content as well. For example, the beatitude pronounced upon the poor in spirit is an invitation to become totally dependent upon God as well as a pronouncement of blessing. In contrast to the first eight beatitudes, the ninth is framed in the second-person plural, as are all the Lukan beatitudes, and primarily proclaims a blessing: the despised and persecuted will receive a great reward because God will reverse the intolerable situation in which they now find themselves. Although the beatitudes describe various kinds of individuals as blessed and promise different rewards, their structure suggests that righteousness is the conduct that is described in every instance, and that the kingdom of heaven is the ultimate blessing for those who are righteous. It is not by chance, therefore, that the first and eighth beatitudes are enclosed by references to the kingdom of heaven. Thus the poor in spirit will inherit the kingdom (5:3), and the kingdom belongs to those persecuted on account of their righteous conduct (5:10). Moreover, the first four beatitudes conclude with a reference to those who hunger and thirst for righteousness (5:6), and the last four with a mention of those persecuted because of righteousness (5:10), suggesting that Jesus sets off the first four beatitudes (more passive in nature) from the second four (more active in nature).

1. Blessed are the poor in spirit, for theirs is *the kingdom of heaven.*
2. Blessed are those who mourn . . .
3. Blessed are the meek . . .
4. Blessed are those who hunger and thirst *for righteousness,* for they will be filled.

5. Blessed are the merciful . . .
6. Blessed are the pure in heart . . .
7. Blessed are the peacemakers . . .
8. Blessed are those who are persecuted *for righteousness'* sake, for theirs is *the kingdom of heaven.*

At the outset of the sermon, therefore, it is clear that the righteous are the blessed who will inherit the kingdom of God if they are poor in spirit, meek, merciful, pure in heart, and so on.

Following the beatitudes, Jesus applies two metaphors to his disciples. They are to the earth what salt is to food, and they are to the world what a lamp is to a room: the light of the world (5:13–16). If disciples no longer act as disciples, they will lose their value, and if they conceal their light, the world will be deprived of light. Therefore they must let their light shine so that others will see their good works (*ta kala erga*) and praise God. These good works are the deeds of righteousness that Jesus has already announced in the beatitudes, and which he describes in greater detail in the body of the sermon.

The law and the prophets. Having established a relationship between righteousness and the kingdom of heaven, Jesus next makes a programmatic statement that clarifies his relationship to the law and the prophets (Matt. 5:17–20). These verses are among the most disputed texts of the New Testament, and I do not pretend to solve the many exegetical problems they pose. I will, however, try to summarize the major thrust of Jesus' message.

First, the Matthean Jesus makes a clear statement that he has not come to destroy the law or the prophets but to fulfill them, by which I understand the following: Jesus both obeys the law and brings it to fulfillment by explaining God's original intention and the law's inner meaning. In Jesus the law and the prophets have found their fulfillment.[19] Second, the law remains in effect "until all is accomplished." While the meaning of this phrase is disputed, I understand it to be a further explanation of Jesus' earlier statement that "until heaven and earth pass away, not one letter, not one stroke of a letter, will pass away." Third, observance of the law will determine one's status in the kingdom of heaven: those who break the least commandments will be called least in the kingdom of heaven, while those who do and teach them will be called greatest in the kingdom.[20] Finally, Jesus warns his disciples that if their righteousness does not surpass that of the scribes and Pharisees, they will not enter the kingdom of heaven. Exactly what Jesus means by a righteousness that surpasses that of the religious leaders will become clear in the body of the sermon. For the moment I note that the law and prophets remain valid for the Matthean Jesus. Jesus is not an antinomian. He clearly calls disciples to a righteousness in which observance of the law plays a central role.

Jesus' first teaching on righteousness. Having called his disciples to practice a righteousness that surpasses that of the scribes and Pharisees, Jesus begins the main part of his sermon in which he gives three teachings on what he means by a more abundant righteousness. The first of these teachings consists of six antitheses in which Jesus presents his interpretation of the law (Matt. 5:21–48). The basic form of each antithesis is essentially the same. First, Jesus introduces a portion of the law with a formula such as, "you have heard that it was said to those of ancient times," or "you have heard that it was said," or "it was also said." Then he introduces his interpretation of the law with a strong counterstatement, "but I say to you." While some commentators argue that Jesus actually abrogates certain laws, for example, the taking of oaths and the law of retribution, Jesus' strong statement about the abiding validity of the law (5:17–20) convinces me that the antitheses are intended rather as his interpretation of the law.[21] For example, the deeper meaning of the commandment not to commit murder includes a prohibition against anger or calling another a fool (5:21–26). The commandment against adultery must be observed by avoiding even lustful thoughts (5:27–30). The commandment to give a bill of divorce, when divorcing one's wife, only applies to *porneia* (adultery or certain unlawful marriages); in all other cases divorce is forbidden.[22] The commandment to fulfill one's oaths to the Lord becomes a call to an honesty that makes oath taking superfluous (5:33–37). The law of retaliation, which set limits to the retribution that one could inflict upon another, becomes a call to nonviolence (5:38–42). And the commandment to love one's neighbor becomes a call to love one's enemies as well (5:43–47).[23] The Matthean Jesus does not challenge the authority of Moses, nor does he abrogate the law. Rather, he summons his disciples to live God's original will by interpreting the true meaning of the law.[24]

At the conclusion of these antitheses, Jesus tells his disciples to be *teleios* (perfect) as their heavenly Father is *teleios*. Once more Jesus' precise meaning is disputed. Benno Przybylski thinks that Jesus intends "an extremely meticulous observance of the law" which is strongly influenced by the principle of "making a fence around Torah."[25] Thus, Jesus is telling disciples to do more than the law requires so that they will not violate God's commandments. Others argue that the Hebrew word *tamin* lies behind *teleios*, with the meaning that one must be wholehearted, complete, and single-minded in one's devotion to God. To be *teleios* is to serve God with an undivided heart and not to act like hypocrites, whom Jesus will describe in the next section. The two interpretations of *teleios* are not contradictory, since meticulous observance of the law requires single-minded devotion to God.

The radical demands of the antitheses are not a new set of commandments, as if Jesus were giving a new law, or official legal rulings.[26] The fact that they deal with only a small portion of the law suggests that they are examples of how Jesus interpreted the law—by returning to God's original will. The antitheses are invitations for disciples to do the same: to seek the deepest meaning of God's law in order to produce a more abundant righteousness. Disciples trained for the kingdom of heaven will interpret the law as Jesus has taught them.

Jesus' second teaching on righteousness. Having told disciples that they must be *teleios* in their observance of the law, Jesus warns them not to practice their righteousness in order for others to see, as do the hypocrites whose hearts are divided. Jesus' second teaching on righteousness is more practical and warns that "even if one knows the nature of true righteousness, one will not receive a reward unless one adheres to the proper practice of righteousness."[27] Therefore, Jesus explains how disciples are to practice the righteous deeds of almsgiving, prayer, and fasting. Once more the form of Jesus' instruction is highly stylized. First, in every instance he begins with an example of what not to do, based on the behavior of the hypocrites who seek human approval. For example, when they give alms they sound the trumpet in the synagogue and streets.[28] Second, a refrain is repeated in each example: "Truly, I tell you, they have received their reward." Third, Jesus instructs his disciples to give alms, pray, and fast in secret, Finally, another refrain is repeated in each example: ". . . and your Father who sees in secret will reward you." From these examples, it is clear that hypocrites are not *teleios* because their hearts are divided; while trying to please God they also seek human approval. The surpassing righteousness of the kingdom must seek only God's approval.

At the center of Jesus' second teaching about righteousness, and at the center of the Sermon on the Mount, stands the Lord's Prayer.[29]

6:2–4	Almsgiving	
6:5–6	Prayer	
	6:7–8	Introduction to the Lord's Prayer
	6:9–13	The Lord's Prayer
	6:14–15	Conclusion to the Lord's Prayer
6:16–18	Fasting	

Matthew's decision to place the Lord's Prayer within the sermon, rather than at some other place in Jesus' ministry,[30] suggests that for him the prayer may have an ethical as well as an eschatological dimension.[31] For example, when disciples pray that God's name be sanctified and that God's will be done, they are enunciating ethical tasks as well as an eschatological hope.[32] They must do God's will in order to be righteous, and they must sanctify his name. Likewise, if they are to receive God's forgiveness, they must forgive others. In effect, Matthew's literary setting for the Lord's Prayer gives it an ethical dimension that should not be overlooked.

To summarize, Jesus' second teaching on righteousness is more practical than is the first, but not unrelated to it. Disciples who have been taught the greater righteousness by Jesus must practice that righteousness in a way different from that of the hypocrites. They must remember that the heart of this righteousness is the kingdom of heaven and doing God's will.

Jesus' third teaching on righteousness. The material in Jesus' third teaching on righteousness (Matt. 6:19–7:11) is not as clearly organized as is that of the first two teachings, in which he proposes six antitheses and then discusses three works of righteousness. The section consists of seven units: an exhortation for the disciples to store up treasure for themselves in heaven (6:19–21); a saying about the eye as the lamp of one's body (6:22–23); a warning that one cannot serve two masters (6:24); an extended exhortation not to be anxious (6:25–34), with its climax, "But strive first for the kingdom of God[33] and his righteousness, and all these things will be given to you as well" (6:33); a warning not to judge others (7:1–5); a further warning not to cast one's pearls before swine (7:6); an exhortation to be persistent in prayer (7:7–11).

In my view this section is loosely organized around Jesus' extended exhortation not to be anxious for one's life but to seek the kingdom of God and its righteousness (6:25–34). The material that precedes this unit speaks of the kingdom and its righteousness. That righteousness is the treasure that can neither decay nor be destroyed. Those who pursue the righteousness of the kingdom see clearly because they are filled with light.[34] Such people serve a single master. The material that follows Jesus' extended exhortation describes people who seek the kingdom of God and its righteousness. They do not judge each other; they do not squander the treasures of the kingdom;[35] and they are persistent in prayer. The central theme of the entire section, then, is the urgency of seeking the kingdom of God and the righteous behavior that is appropriate to it. While Jesus' first teaching on righteousness provided examples of how he interprets the law, and the second offered concrete examples of how one should practice righteousness, this final section explains what it means to seek the righteousness of the kingdom.

The law and the prophets once more. We have seen that the body of Jesus' sermon is prefaced by an important statement about the law and the prophets: Jesus did not come to destroy them but to fulfill them (Matt. 5:17). After his three teachings on righteousness, he summarizes all that he has said thus far: "In everything do to others as you would have them do to you; for this is the law and the prophets" (7:12).[36] The final phrase, "for this is the law and the prophets," clearly echoes Jesus' earlier statement about fulfilling the law and the prophets (5:17), thereby forming a bracket around the body of the sermon and summarizing Jesus' message. As we shall see, the love of God and the love of neighbor are the hermeneutical keys that unlock Jesus' interpretation of the law and the prophets (22:40). Here, Jesus does not mention the love of God but does focus upon the need to do good to others. This is the righteousness required by the kingdom of heaven.

Conclusion. Jesus' sermon concludes with a series of warnings that threaten those who hear him with severe judgment if they do not act upon the words of this sermon. In language reminiscent of the "Two Ways" such as is found in Psalm 1, he exhorts disciples to enter by the narrow gate since the gate is wide and the road is broad that leads to destruction (Matt. 7:13–14).

Next he issues a warning against false prophets who come in sheep's clothing but underneath are ravenous wolves (7:15–20). The false prophets that Jesus has in view are people who present themselves as disciples but are not. In the period before the return of the Son of Man they will arise and deceive many (24:11) by their signs and wonders (24:24). True disciples, however, will be able to recognize them by their fruits, since good trees bear good fruit and rotten trees bear rotten fruit (7:17). The good fruit to which Jesus refers is the fruit of righteousness; the rotten fruit is lawlessness (*anomia*).

The false prophets do not understand that doing the will of God is more important than calling Jesus "Lord." Therefore, Jesus warns that it is not those who call him "Lord" who will enter the kingdom of heaven but those who do the will of his heavenly Father. Here is another correlation between the moral universe of Jesus' parables and the Sermon on the Mount. The false prophets are like the son who said he would go into his father's vineyard but did not (21:30). They say they will obey, but they do not do God's will. Therefore, at the eschatological judgment Jesus will disown them as "workers of lawlessness" (*hoi ergazomenoi tēn anomian;* 7:23).

In a concluding parable (7:24–27) Jesus draws a comparison between those who listen to his words and do them and those who hear his words but do not do them. The first group is like a wise man who built his house on a firm foundation, the second like a foolish man who built his house on sand. When the floods came, the house of the wise man withstood them, while the house of the fool was completely destroyed. Again, there is a correlation with the moral universe of Jesus' parables. The five foolish virgins are excluded from the wedding banquet because they were not vigilant and did not have oil in their lamps (25:1–13). To be wise is to *do* Jesus' words; that is, to produce the fruit of righteousness.

Jesus' Sermon on the Mount is not a new ethical code in the sense that it replaces the Mosaic law, nor is it an ethical ideal that can never be realized. Rather, it represents Jesus' interpretation of the law in light of the kingdom of heaven. The sermon teaches disciples to practice a righteousness that surpasses that of the scribes and Pharisees by doing God's will. Doing God's will is the essence of the righteousness that Jesus proposes (6:10; 7:21), and those who do the will of God will be brother, and sister, and mother to him (12:50).[37] In effect, the Gospel of Matthew has taken a central notion from Mark's Gospel, doing the will of God, and expanded it in terms of the traditional Jewish concept of doing righteousness.

Jesus' Sermon on the Mount is intended for disciples who live in light of the coming kingdom of heaven, which has already made an initial appearance in the ministry of Jesus Messiah. For such people, living in a community of like-minded disciples, the strenuous commands of the sermon are neither unreasonable nor impossible to fulfill. The sermon is how disciples live. It only becomes an impossible ideal when Christians forget the ethical horizon of the kingdom of heaven, or when they no longer live in a community of like-minded disciples. The Matthean Jesus intends that his words be observed within the horizon of the kingdom of heaven and the community of his disciples. Apart from these, the sermon is reduced to strenuous commands, impossible to fulfill.

JESUS AND THE RELIGIOUS LEADERS

By placing Jesus' Sermon on the Mount at the beginning of the Gospel, Matthew presents his audience with a comprehensive teaching on the kind of righteousness for which disciples must strive if they wish to enter the kingdom of heaven. But in addition to providing his audience with an extended teaching on righteousness, Matthew presents Jesus' own conduct as an example of the righteousness that surpasses that of the scribes and Pharisees. Moreover, his Gospel portrays the religious leaders as examples of people who have failed to attain a greater righteousness because they are fundamentally hypocritical, seeking the approval of human beings as well as of God. The conduct of Jesus and the religious leaders, therefore, affords us yet another opportunity to learn what the Matthean Gospel means by righteousness.

Jesus a Model
of Righteous Behavior

Throughout his Gospel, Matthew portrays Jesus as the righteous and obedient Son of God, filled with mercy and compassion for his people Israel. Thus, when Pilate's wife warns her husband not to have anything to do with that righteous man (27:19; *mēden soi kai tō dikaiō ekeinō*), she says more than she realizes. Not only is Jesus "innocent" of the false charges that have been brought against him, he is "righteous" in the full religious sense of *dikaios* because, having done God's will, he, not his accusers, stands in the proper covenental relationship to God. As those familiar with Matthew's Gospel have learned, Jesus has lived the life of righteousness to which he calls disciples in the Sermon on the Mount. To illustrate these remarks, I turn to three episodes that exemplify Jesus' righteous behavior: his baptism, his testing in the wilderness, and his final testing upon the cross. Then I will highlight a series of texts that portray Jesus as merciful, compassionate, and law-observant. I will conclude with a brief reflection on Jesus as one who exemplifies the Beatitudes.

The righteous and obedient Son of God. In the first major portion of his Gospel (1:1–4:16), Matthew identifies Jesus as the messianic Son of God in a variety of ways.[38] But in addition to identifying the person of Jesus, this section begins to explain what it means to call Jesus the Son of God. First comes the account of Jesus' birth, which establishes that he was conceived through the power of the Spirit. Then in the accounts of Jesus' baptism (3:13–17) and testing in the wilderness (4:1–11) Matthew provides further insight into Jesus' sonship: Jesus is the obedient Son of God who trusts in his Father. For example, when Jesus presents himself for John's baptism, the Baptist immediately recognizes who Jesus is and protests that he should be baptized by Jesus rather than baptize him. In response to John's protest, Jesus insists that it is fitting for him and John to fulfill all righteousness (*plērōsai pasan dikaiosynēn;* 3:15). These are the *first* words spoken by Jesus, and they establish the leitmotiv for all that will follow: Jesus the Son of God comes to fulfill God's righteous decrees; he comes to do God's will.[39] Consequently, when God publicly proclaims that Jesus is his beloved Son in whom he is well pleased (3:17), the Matthean audience understands why God is pleased with his Son: Jesus does God's will.

Immediately after God declares that Jesus is his beloved Son, the Spirit leads Jesus into the wilderness where he is tested by the devil. In testing him, the devil seeks to determine if Jesus is truly the Son of God.[40] Accordingly, his first two temptations begin, "If you are the Son of God . . . (4:3, 6)." Jesus' trial in the wilderness recalls the testing of the people of Israel in the wilderness; Israel was also called God's son (Ex. 4:22; Hos. 11:1). When the people of Israel were hungry in the wilderness of Sin, they complained against Moses and Aaron (Ex. 16:1–36), and when they were thirsty at Rephidim (Ex. 17:1–7), they quarreled with Moses. In both instances Israel proved to be a disobedient son that did not trust in God's salvific power. In contrast to Israel, Jesus shows that he is truly God's Son by his obedience to the Father. Unlike Israel of old, he heeds the words of Deuteronomy (Deut. 8:3 is quoted in response to the first test, and Deut. 6:3 to the second test). Thus the temptation narrative presents him as the obedient Son of God who trusts in God's power to save him.

The third episode that portrays Jesus as righteous occurs immediately before his death. At his crucifixion, Jesus endures a series of insults by the passersby, by the chief priests, and by those crucified with him (Matt. 27:39–44).[41] While this episode is a mockery scene, it is also the final testing of God's Son. The passersby use the same language as did the devil in the wilderness: "If you are the Son of God . . . (27:40)." The mockery of the chief priests is similar. They taunt Jesus, "He trusts in God; let God deliver him now, if he wants to; for he said, 'I am God's Son'" (27:43). These strong allusions to Ps. 22:8 and Wisd. Sol. 2:18–20 are filled with irony, for as was the case with Pilate's wife, the chief priests do not comprehend the full sense of what they are saying. Jesus *is* manifesting his sonship by obediently trusting in God rather than miraculously descending from the cross. At the end of his life, as at the beginning of his ministry, he shows that he is God's righteous Son by his trusting obedience. The righteous behavior of Jesus at his baptism and during his times of testing is a model for disciples.

51

The merciful, compassionate, law-observant Son of God. The testing of Jesus in the wilderness and on the cross stand like two pillars at the beginning and close of his ministry. Between them, however, are other texts in Matthew that also point to Jesus' righteousness. For example, compassion and mercy are central components in Matthew's portrait of Jesus. Consequently, on several occasions the Evangelist notes that Jesus healed every disease and all who were sick or possessed (4:23, 24; 8:16; 9:35; 12:15; 14:14; 15:30). On two occasions, Matthew employs quotations from Isaiah to show that Jesus' healing is the fulfillment of scripture. Thus the messianic Son of God is God's servant who takes on the infirmities of his people and bears their diseases (Matt. 8:17, which quotes Isa. 53:4). He is the servant of God who deflects attention from himself by commanding those whom he heals not to make him known (Matt. 12:16–21, which quotes Isa. 42:1–4).

The motivation for Jesus' activity is compassion. For example, when he sees the crowds like sheep without a shepherd, he has compassion on them (Matt. 9:36) and then sends his disciples on a mission exclusively to the lost sheep of the house of Israel (10:5–6). Likewise, before the feeding of the five thousand, Jesus has compassion on the crowd and heals their sick (14:14). Later, his compassion leads him to feed a crowd of four thousand in the wilderness (15:32). The compassionate Jesus responds to cries for mercy from a Canaanite woman (15:22–25), the father of an epileptic boy (17:15), and the blind (9:27; 20:30, 31). His mighty deeds point to his compassion, especially for those at the margin of society: lepers, demoniacs, paralytics, the blind, and so on.

The centrality of mercy and compassion in Jesus' understanding of his mission can be seen in his use of Hos. 6:6, "I desire mercy, not sacrifice." When he explains his behavior toward sinners (Matt. 9:13) and when he defends his disciples from accusations of violating the Sabbath (12:7), he makes use of this text. It is not surprising, then, that Jesus describes himself as meek (*praüs*) and humble of heart (11:28–30), and that Matthew should employ the text of Zech. 9:9 ("Look, your king . . . meek (*praüs*), and mounted on a donkey . . . ") to show that Jesus is the humble king prophesied by Zechariah (21:5).

Jesus' compassion and mercy do not stand in opposition to God's law. After cleansing a leper, he instructs the man to show himself to the priests and to bring the offering prescribed by Moses (8:4). Before Jesus heals on the Sabbath, he first determines that it is allowed to heal on the Sabbath in order to do good (12:12). In his debate with the Pharisees about the tradition of the elders (15:1–20), he subordinates their traditions to the commandment of God, but there is no parenthetical comment by Matthew, as in Mark, that by doing so, Jesus declared all foods clean (compare Matt. 15:17 with Mark 7:19). Perhaps, then, the food laws were still in force in the Matthean community.[42] Before delivering his woes against the hypocrisy of the scribes and Pharisees (23:1–36), Jesus instructs his disciples to do all that the scribes and Pharisees say because they sit on the chair of Moses (23:2). It is their behavior that should not be imitated. Finally, when describing the great tribulation that will precede the destruction of the Temple, Jesus instructs his disciples to pray that their flight will not be in the winter or on the Sabbath (24:20), perhaps because travel on the Sabbath would be prohibited by the law.[43] The absence of any reference to the Sabbath in the parallel passage of Mark (13:18) highlights Matthew's concern for the Sabbath, which, like the food laws, was probably still observed by his community of Jewish and Gentile Christians. The Matthean Jesus, as should be clear from the Sermon on the Mount, is law-observant. How could it be otherwise since the law is an expression of God's will, and Jesus has come to form a new family called to do God's will (12:50)? Consequently, when the rich man asks him what he must do to gain eternal life, Jesus responds, "keep the commandments" (19:17), adding Lev. 19:18 ("You shall love your neighbor as yourself") to the Decalogue.[44] Any judgment that Jesus blatantly contravenes the law is misguided. As in the Sermon on the Mount, he requires a greater righteousness in observing the law. When the rich man responds that he has kept all of the commandments, therefore, Jesus says that if he would be perfect (*teleios*) he must sell his possessions, give the proceeds to the poor, and follow him (19:21).

Jesus' response to the lawyer's question about the greatest commandment of the law (22:34–40) reveals that mercy, compassion, and love are the hermeneutical keys he employs to interpret the law.[45] In his response, Jesus says that the whole law hangs (*krematai*) on these two commandments, and the prophets as well: to love God with all one's heart, soul and mind, and to love one's neighbor as oneself (22:40). The manner in which he frames his answer suggests that all the other commandments are to be interpreted in light of these two.[46]

Jesus and the Beatitudes. The Matthean Jesus exemplifies the Beatitudes in his life. Poor in spirit, he utterly trusts and relies upon God, especially at the hour of his testing (27:39–44). Humble, he is meek and humble of heart (11:29), the meek king prophesied by Zechariah (21:5). Hungering and thirsting for righteousness, he comes to fulfill God's righteous commands (3:15). Merciful, he has compassion on his people, especially on those of no account (9:13; 12:7). Pure of heart, he is single-minded in his desire to please God; he is perfect (16:23; 26:42). He tells his disciples that he did not come to bring peace (10:34), but by shedding his blood for the forgiveness of sins he reconciles humanity to God (1:21; 20:28; 26:28). Finally, because of his righteous behavior, he is unjustly accused and put to death (26:66; 27:15–26). In sum, the Matthean Jesus exemplifies the righteousness proclaimed in the Sermon on the Mount, thereby providing an example of ethical behavior that is pleasing to God.

The Religious Leaders
as Examples of Hypocrisy

Whereas Matthew portrays Jesus as an example of perfect righteousness, he presents the religious leaders as the archetypes of hypocrisy. Divided in their loyalties, they seek human esteem as well as the approval of God. Therefore they are hypocrites.[47] The historical religious leaders, of course, were a much more diverse group than the one-dimensional literary figures portrayed in Matthew's narrative. Pharisees and Sadducees held different religious views, and it is unlikely that they formed a unified block opposed to Jesus of Nazareth, or that all of them were divided in their allegiance to God. Within his Gospel, however, Matthew presents them as a hypocritical lot, uniformly opposed to Jesus. One must approach Matthew's Gospel, therefore, with caution. My own remarks should not be taken as an indictment of the religious leaders of Jesus' day. What follows refers to Matthew's literary portrait of the religious leaders. As a group within his narrative, they represent a particular response to Jesus that can best be described as hypocrisy.[48]

John and the religious leaders. The first appearance of the religious leaders after the infancy narrative comes in Matthew's account of John the Baptist (3:7–12). When John sees the Pharisees and Sadducees coming for his baptism, he calls them a brood of vipers and challenges them to produce fruit worthy of repentance. Matthew does not report the outcome of John's sermon to the Pharisees and Sadducees, leaving his audience to wonder if the religious leaders did repent. But later, when Jesus tells the parable of the two sons (21:28–30), he indirectly refers to this incident. Comparing the religious leaders to a son who says that he will work in his father's vineyard but does not, Jesus says that tax collectors and prostitutes are entering the kingdom of God before them, for although John showed them a "way of righteousness" they did not believe him. And even when the tax collectors and prostitutes believed, the religious leaders refused to change their minds and believe (21:31–32). In light of the Baptist's sermon, there can be little doubt that the "way of righteousness" (21:32) is conduct in accord with God's will, what John calls "fruit worthy of repentance" (3:8). In Matthew's view, the religious leaders have failed because, as in the case of the elder son, their words do not correspond to their deeds. They do not practice what they preach (23:3).

Jesus and the religious leaders. During his ministry the Matthean Jesus has several encounters with the religious leaders. Three of these encounters are especially significant for understanding why the religious leaders fail to lead lives of righteousness. In the first, the Pharisees come into conflict with Jesus over the Sabbath (Matt. 12:1–14) and then accuse him of casting out demons by the prince of demons (12:22–32). In response to these attacks, Jesus takes up language reminiscent of the Baptist's sermon. He describes the religious leaders as a brood of vipers who are essentially evil; they are like rotten trees that produce bad fruit (12:33–37). Ultimately, the problem has to do with the heart, the seat of morality, "For out of the abundance of the heart the mouth speaks" (12:34). In the case of the Pharisees, they are like evil persons who bring forth evil from their treasury of evil (12:35).

In the second example Matthew recounts a major dispute between Jesus and the Pharisees and scribes over the tradition of the elders (15:1–20). The religious leaders accuse Jesus' disciples of transgressing the traditions of the elders,[49] causing Jesus to accuse them of transgressing the commandment of God (15:2–3). Next, Jesus juxtaposes what God says to what

54

the scribes and Pharisees say (15:4). Finally, he accuses them of breaking God's word for the sake of their tradition (15:6). Thus the Matthean Jesus claims a fundamental difference between himself and the Pharisees and scribes. Whereas they observe the tradition of the elders, he observes God's word and commandment. Employing a quotation from Isa. 29:13, he calls the religious leaders "hypocrites" for the first time within the narrative since they honor God with their tongues but their hearts are far from him.[50] As in Matthew 12, the root problem has to do with the heart; the religious leaders are not "pure in heart" (5:8) because they are not single-minded in their devotion to God. They teach human precepts as doctrines (15:9). Consequently, they are more concerned with the appearance of things than with reality. They do not understand that what issues from the heart defiles a person, not unwashed hands (15:17–20). In effect, Matthew draws a relationship between the hypocritical behavior that Jesus described in the Sermon on the Mount (6:1–18) and the behavior of the religious leaders. The Pharisees and scribes are hypocrites because of their divided loyalty.

Having identified the scribes and Pharisees as hypocrites in chapter 15, Jesus launches a full-scale attack against them by pronouncing a series of seven woes in chapter 23.[51] He prefaces these woes by instructing his disciples to do all that the Pharisees and scribes say but not to act according to their works since they do not practice what they preach (23:3). They do all of their works in order to be seen by others (23:5) rather than in secret before their heavenly Father (6:4, 6, 18). Each woe, except the third, begins in the same way, "Woe to you, scribes and Pharisees, hypocrites! For you . . . " (23:13, 15, 23, 25, 27, 29). The third woe begins, "Woe to you, blind guides . . . " (23:16), recalling Jesus' earlier description of the scribes and Pharisees as blind guides (15:14), and establishing a literary connection between chapters 15 and 23.

All of the woes echo themes introduced earlier, especially in the Sermon on the Mount. Like the first beatitude, the first woe concerns the kingdom of heaven. Jesus promises the kingdom of heaven to the poor in spirit, but the scribes and Pharisees lock people out of the kingdom of heaven and do not go in themselves (23:13). Jesus makes his disciples sons of his heavenly Father, but the scribes and Pharisees make their converts children of Gehenna (23:15). Jesus warns his disciples against taking oaths at all, but the scribes and Pharisees studiously differentiate between grades of oath taking (23:16–22). Jesus promises that the merciful will receive mercy, and is himself a perfect example of compassion, but the scribes and Pharisees neglect judgment, mercy, and fidelity (23:23–24). Jesus points to the importance of behavior that comes from the heart, but the scribes and Pharisees concern themselves with externals (23:25). Jesus demands a righteousness rooted in the heart, but the scribes and Pharisees merely appear righteous; inwardly they are filled with hypocrisy and lawlessness (23:27–28). Jesus promises the kingdom to those persecuted for the sake of righteousness and reminds his disciples that the prophets were persecuted before them, but the scribes and Pharisees are the descendants of those who murdered the prophets (23:29–32).

It is not surprising, then, that at the conclusion of these woes, Jesus identifies the scribes and Pharisees as a brood of vipers as did John the Baptist (23:33, see 3:7). Matthew sees the behavior of the religious leaders as a mirror image of that practiced by Jesus. They are hypocritical and guilty of lawlessness (*anomia*); Jesus is single-minded in his devotion to God and practices righteousness (*dikaiosynē*). The hypocritical behavior of the religious leaders merits condemnation, whereas Jesus' righteous behavior will result in eschatological vindication.

JUDGMENT AND REWARD

Moral behavior does not occur in a vacuum. People act in a particular way because they are motivated to do so. In Matthew's Gospel, Jesus motivates his audience by constantly holding before his listeners the fearful prospect of judgment and the promise of eschatological reward.[52] For some this is disappointing, an indication of an immature morality that depends upon reward and punishment for motivation. For others it suggests that the ethic of the Matthean Jesus borders on a righteousness attained by works and leaves little room for God's grace. I will deal with the second of these points in the next section. For the moment, however, I remind the reader that the Matthean Jesus—and I dare say the historical Jesus—is not a philosopher who reasons to what is good and exhorts his followers to do the good for its own sake. Conduct, for Jesus, is good because it is in accord with God's will in light of the kingdom of heaven, and it is evil because it opposes God's will and his kingly rule. Promises of eschatological reward and punishment, therefore, must be viewed within the horizon of God's will and rule. Those who do the will of God by living righteous lives will enter the kingdom of heaven, while those who oppose the will of God will be excluded.

The threat of judgment and the promise of reward play a prominent role in the ethics of the Matthean Jesus. Robert Mohrlang notes: "Matthew has more material relating to rewards and punishment than any of the other evangelists."[53] There are frequent references to judgment (5:21–23; 12:41–42; 23:33), the day of judgment (10:15; 11:22, 24; 12:36), Gehenna (5:22, 29, 30; 10:28; 18:9; 23:33), and reward (5:12, 46; 6:2, 5, 16; 10:41–42). Moreover, Jesus' description of exclusion from the kingdom as being consigned to a place "where there will be weeping and gnashing of teeth" (8:12; 13:42, 50; 22:13; 24:51; 25:30) and being cast "into the outer darkness" (8:12; 22:13; 25:30) echoes throughout this Gospel.

Although the threat of judgment and the promise of reward are most prominent in Jesus' eschatological discourse (24:1–25:46), they occur in other parts of the Gospel as well. For example, when the Pharisees and Sadducees come to John's baptism, John threatens them with the coming wrath (*tēs mellousēs orgēs*) of God that will consume the unrepentant like an unquenchable fire (3:7–12). At the conclusion of the Sermon on the Mount, Jesus warns that the gate is wide and the road broad that leads to destruction (7:13), that false prophets will be cut down like rotten trees and thrown into the fire (7:19), that he will disown all those who practice lawlessness (7:23), and that the foolish man who does not listen to his words will suffer total ruin (7:27). But it is not only at the conclusion of the sermon that Jesus refers to judgment and reward. There are frequent references within the body of the sermon as well. The Beatitudes promise eschatological rewards (5:3–12); disciples who do not practice a greater righteousness will not enter the kingdom of heaven (5:19–20); the one who is angry with his brother will be liable to judgment; and one who calls his brother a fool will be liable to Gehenna (5:22–23). Those who do acts of righteousness secretly will be rewarded by God (6:3, 6, 18), and those who forgive will be forgiven, whereas those who do not will not receive God's forgiveness (6:14–15).

When sending his disciples on mission (10:1–42), Jesus assures them that it will go easier for the land of Sodom and Gomorrah on the day of judgment than for those who reject them (10:15). He promises that disciples who persevere to the end will be saved (10:22), and whoever loses his life for his sake will save it (10:39). Therefore, disciples should acknowledge Jesus before others, otherwise he will deny them before his heavenly Father (10:32–33). Finally, he warns them to fear the one who is able to destroy body and soul in Gehenna (10:28) and promises that those who receive them as his emissaries will not lose their reward (10:40–42).

In his parable discourse (13:1–53) Jesus refers to the end of the ages (*en tē synteleia tou aiōnos;* 13:40, 49), when the Son of Man will dispatch his angels to "collect out of his kingdom all causes of sin (*panta ta skandala*) and all evildoers (*tous poiountas tēn anomian*)." These will be thrown into the fiery furnace, while the righteous will shine like the sun in their Father's kingdom (13:41–43, also see 13:49–50). In his discourse on church life (18:1–35), he warns disciples that unless they "change" (*straphēte*) and become like children, they will not enter the kingdom of heaven, where the greatest is like a child (18:3–4). Disciples who cause other disciples to sin will suffer a fate worse than death (18:6). One must avoid all sin, therefore, for it is better to enter life maimed than to be cast into Gehenna (18:7–9). Finally, Jesus reminds his disciples, who have experienced the forgiveness of God, that if they do not forgive each other they will receive a fearsome punishment from God (18:35).

In his final discourse (24:1–25:46) the Matthean Jesus admonishes disciples to watch and prepare for the return of the Son of Man. Judgment will come swiftly and unexpectedly as it did in the days of Noah (24:37–41); therefore they must be as prepared as a householder who anticipates the arrival of a burglar (24:42–44). In a series of parables, Jesus contrasts faithful and unfaithful servants (24:45–51), wise and foolish virgins (25:1–13), and good and evil servants (25:14–30) in order to reinforce the importance of being watchful and industrious. While these parables tell different stories, the scenario of each is similar. A period of delay on the part of the returning master or bridegroom (the Son of Man) leads to an ethical crisis: what will the servants or virgins do during this time? Foolish servants and virgins abuse their status, take their rest, or become paralyzed with fear, whereas wise servants and virgins are vigilant and industrious. During the period before Jesus' return, especially when it appears that the parousia of the Son of Man has been delayed, disciples must be vigilant, industriously "doing" righteousness.

Matthew concludes his eschatological discourse with a description of the royal Son of Man sitting upon his glorious throne, judging the nations on the basis of six actions: feeding the hungry, giving drink to the thirsty, offering hospitality to strangers, clothing the naked, caring for the sick, and visiting the imprisoned (25:31–46). Jesus' final words before his passion complement those of the Sermon on the Mount, for the criterion of judgment will be the mercy and compassion described in that sermon and exemplified in Jesus' behavior. But whereas the sermon presents a more traditionally Jewish ethic that focuses upon Jesus' interpretation of the law, the ethical demands of the final judgment are not explicitly related to the law. The central concern is for a mercy and compassion that has no boundaries because it extends to all, especially the least significant, with whom the Son of Man identifies himself.[54]

The themes of reward and punishment pervade the rest of Matthew's narrative as well. Jesus warns that while many from the east and the west will recline with Abraham, Isaac, and Jacob in the kingdom of heaven, the heirs of the kingdom[55] will be expelled into the exterior darkness (8:11–12). It will be more tolerable on the day of judgment for the cities of Tyre and Sidon than for the unrepentant cities of Galilee where Jesus performed his mighty deeds (11:20–24). Jesus warns the Pharisees that on the day of judgment people will be required to render an account for every careless word they uttered, and that they will be acquitted or condemned by the words that they spoke (12:36–37). On the day of judgment, the people of Nineveh will condemn "this generation" because it has not repented (12:41). Again, Jesus tells the Pharisees and scribes that plants that his heavenly Father has not planted will be uprooted (15:13). On the other hand, disciples who have left everything and followed him will be seated on twelve thrones judging the twelve tribes of Israel in the new age, and everyone who has left family or land for his sake will receive a hundredfold and inherit eternal life (19:25–30). Most importantly, when the Son of Man comes with his angels, he will repay each one according to his conduct (*hekastō kata tēn praxin autou*; 16:27), a phrase that is absent from the parallel text in Mark 9:38.

To summarize, the threat of judgment and the prospect of eschatological salvation in the kingdom of heaven play a major role in Jesus' teaching in Matthew. These themes provide disciples with a powerful motivation for doing God's will by practicing deeds of righteousness. In addition, Jesus' preaching about eschatological judgment assures the church that the present situation, wherein the righteous and unrighteous dwell alongside each other, will not endure. The Son of Man will put an end to the outrageous persecution and slander directed against the righteous when he returns to reward and punish each one according to his or her deeds. This confident hope of the elect, however, presents a further problem. Does the teaching of the Matthean Jesus about reward and punishment leave any room for God's grace?

HUMAN ETHICAL ACTION
AND GOD'S SAVING ACTION

In Matthew's Gospel, Jesus places a premium upon doing God's will by practicing righteousness. He says that when he returns as the exalted Son of Man, he will judge each one according to his or her deeds (16:27). Actions are more important than words (7:21), and what a person does or fails to do will be decisive at the final judgment (25:31–46). In light of this emphasis on doing good and producing the fruit of righteousness, the question arises: What is the relationship between human ethical action and God's saving work?

I raise the question, in part, because of the important role that God's grace plays in Paul's ethics and anthropology. As we shall see, Paul's theology of law and righteousness is different from that found in Matthew's Gospel. According to Paul's understanding of the human situation, apart from Christ humankind is under the sway of a powerful force called *hamartia* (sin) that continually frustrates those who seek to do the just requirements of God's law. Whereas the Matthean Jesus focuses on righteousness as conduct, Paul presents righteousness as a gift made possible by the death and resurrection of Christ. Thus he writes, "Christ is the end of the law" (Rom. 10:4), and "if a law had been given that could make alive, then righteousness would indeed come through the law" (Gal. 3:21). In Paul's view the law was never intended to make people righteous, otherwise Christ died in vain (Gal. 2:21). Later, it will be necessary to discuss Paul's understanding of righteousness and law in detail. For the moment, however, these examples are sufficient to show that Matthew and Paul approach the law and righteousness from different perspectives.[56]

The Gospel of Matthew does not contain the sophisticated understanding of the human predicament found in Paul's letters. The Matthean Jesus never questions the innate power of a person to do what God commands. He seems to presuppose that human beings can do God's will as expressed in the law. The problem is not "indwelling sin," as in Paul's letters, but a stubborn and impenitent refusal to do God's will. Thus the following questions arise. What is the relationship between the indicative of salvation and the imperative of moral action? Does the salvation that God effects in Jesus enable moral action? Or does God's salvation presuppose moral action? Or are the indicative and imperative related in some other way?

Robert Mohrlang, in a comparative study of ethics in the Gospel of Matthew and the letters of Paul, to which I am indebted, argues that despite Matthew's emphasis upon doing and producing the fruit of righteousness, there is an underlying structure of grace in this Gospel.[57] In what follows, I discuss four indications of God's saving activity in Matthew's

Gospel: the soteriological significance of Jesus' death; the portrait of Jesus' disciples as chosen and elected; Jesus' saving presence to the church and those in need; and two parables that present the gracious aspect of the kingdom.

Because Matthew's Gospel is primarily a narrative about Jesus' ministry, which culminates in his death and resurrection, it does not present a theological reflection on the meaning of Jesus' death comparable to that found in Paul's letters. Nevertheless, Matthew points to the salvific dimension of Jesus' life and death. At the beginning of the Gospel, for example, the angel instructs Joseph to name the child "Jesus" because "he will save his people from their sins" (1:21). When instructing his disciples on the need for humble service, Jesus describes his life as the life of one who comes "not to be served but to serve, and to give his life a ransom for many" (20:28). Finally, at the Last Supper, Jesus takes a cup of wine and says that it is the "blood of the covenant, which is poured out for many *for the forgiveness of sins*" (26:28). The italicized words are absent from the parallel passage in Mark (14:26), suggesting that Matthew purposely emphasized this aspect of Jesus' death. These programmatic statements, then, indicate that Jesus' life and death are salvific because they lead to the forgiveness of sins.[58] Consequently, even if Matthew is more optimistic about a person's ability to do righteousness, he has not forgotten that the forgiveness of sins is God's gracious work.

In this study of Matthew, I have been discussing the nature of discipleship, even though I have not dealt with the topic under a separate heading. Jesus' sermon, discourses, and parables are teachings about discipleship. What I have not previously discussed is the manner in which Matthew presents the disciples as chosen and elected by Jesus.[59] Thus, at the beginning of Matthew's Gospel, as in Mark's Gospel, Jesus "calls" his first disciples (4:18–22). The importance of this call becomes apparent when one contrasts this narrative with the story of the eager scribe who volunteers to be a disciple (8:18–20), proclaiming, "Teacher, I will follow you wherever you go."[60] Not only does this would-be follower lack an understanding of what he is seeking ("Foxes have holes, and birds of the air have nests; but the Son of Man has nowhere to lay his head"), but Jesus has not called him to discipleship.

In Matthew's view, Jesus' disciples are in a privileged position because the Father has revealed to them what he has hidden from the wise and the learned, and because Jesus has revealed the Father to his disciples (11:25–27). The disciples are those to whom the mysteries of the kingdom have been given (13:11); they are the good seed sown by the Son of Man (13:38). Faithful disciples are the elect who will be gathered by the angels at the parousia of the Son of Man (24:31; also see 24:22, 24). The disciples whom Jesus requires to do and practice righteousness, then, are those chosen and elected by God.

There are other texts that present Jesus as one who saves, responds to cries of mercy, and is present to his church as the exalted Lord. When the disciples find themselves in distress upon the Sea of Galilee, for example, they cry to Jesus, "Lord, save us! We are perishing" (8:25).[61] When Peter begins to sink into the deep, he cries out "Lord, save me!" (14:30). And on several occasions, Jesus responds to cries for mercy from people in need: the blind (9:27; 20:30–31), a Canaanite woman (15:22), the father of a possessed boy (17:15). In every instance Jesus acts as the Savior, even though Matthew never employs the title. Moreover, Jesus' salvific presence continues after his resurrection. In the discourse on church life, he tells his disciples that where two or three are gathered in his name, he will be present (18:20). Most importantly, the final words of the Gospel are the risen Lord's promise to be present to the church to the end of the ages (28:20), echoing the angel's words at the beginning of the Gospel that Jesus is "Emmanuel," "God is with us" (1:23). Again, the Jesus who requires his disciples to do works of righteousness is the exalted Lord, ever present to save his church in time of need.

Finally, in two parables to which I have already alluded, Jesus emphasizes the gracious aspect of God's rule. In the parable of the workers in the vineyard (20:1–16), the owner of the vineyard pays a full day's wage to every worker, even though some have borne the heat of the entire day while others were hired at the last hour. All work in the vineyard producing the fruit of righteousness, but their wages depend upon the owner's generosity rather than upon the work they do. In the parable of the wedding banquet (22:1–14), when the original guests refuse the invitation, the king invites everyone to the banquet. But when he finds a guest who does not have a wedding garment, he expels the man to the outer darkness where there is weeping and gnashing of teeth. The invitation to the kingdom is a gracious gift that does not depend upon prior works, but once invited, guests must clothe themselves with the righteous deeds appropriate to the kingdom of heaven.

This brief survey has been selective, but it is sufficient to show that there is an underlying structure of grace that is fundamental to Matthew's Gospel. God accomplishes the work of salvation in Christ, but human beings must respond to that salvation by lives of righteousness. The Sermon on the Mount is not merely a call to ethical conduct; it is a summons to a more abundant righteousness in light of the kingdom of heaven. Separated from Jesus' proclamation of the kingdom, the sermon becomes an irrational and impossible ethic. In light of the kingdom, and within the community of the church, it is the blueprint for a life of discipleship.

Like Paul, Matthew understands that the ethical imperative is related to the salvific indicative, for the call to a greater righteousness is part of Jesus' proclamation about the kingdom of heaven. But the relationship between the ethical imperative and the salvific indicative in Matthew's Gospel is different from that found in Paul's letters. Whereas Paul emphasizes that the indicative makes the imperative possible, Matthew stresses that "the fulfillment of the imperative is a prerequisite for the ultimate, full and final expression of the indicative."[62] The Matthean Jesus comes to save his people from their sins, and by his death and resurrection he effects redemption for the many. Human beings must affirm what God has already done for them by producing a greater righteousness. Such ethical conduct does not accomplish salvation, but without it the personal appropriation of salvation is impossible.

JESUS' MORAL TEACHING:
A SUMMARY STATEMENT

As one might expect, the moral teaching of Jesus, according to Matthew, has much in common with Mark's Gospel. Once more the presupposition of Jesus' ethical imperative is the kingdom of heaven with its attendant call to repentance. Jesus summons people to repent because the kingdom of heaven is at hand. As in Mark's Gospel, doing God's will and observing the commandments remain central concepts; the Matthean Jesus is not an antinomian. In both Gospels, too, those who sin by violating God's law will be excluded from God's kingdom at the judgment, whereas those who do the will of God will enter the kingdom. Finally, for both Matthew and Mark, Jesus serves as a model for ethical conduct. Compassionate and righteous, he does the will of God. Nevertheless, there are a number of ways in which the moral teaching of Matthew's Gospel goes beyond that of Mark's Gospel.

On the other hand, the Matthean Gospel has, first of all, greatly expanded the moral vision of its Markan source, in part because it was written to respond to a new situation and in part because its author had access to traditions apparently unknown to Mark. Matthew has developed Mark's notion of the kingdom of God with a number of sayings and parables, many of which focus upon the future coming of the kingdom. The ethical universe created by Matthew's parables provides important ethical instruction. The parables instruct disciples about the present situation in which good and evil dwell side by side, and they point to the importance of being vigilant and industrious while awaiting the parousia of the Son of Man. In developing his notion of the kingdom of God, Matthew points to the importance of producing fruit, by which he means good deeds and works of righteousness. Faith is not absent from Matthew's Gospel, even though I have not discussed it in this chapter. Matthew, however, appears to emphasize doing and producing works of righteousness more than faith.

Second, as in Mark's Gospel, doing God's will and keeping the commandments are central to the moral teaching of the Matthean Jesus, but in Matthew's Gospel these concepts are complemented by the traditional Jewish notions of law and righteousness. Mark presents Jesus as keeping God's commandments, but he never uses the word "law." In Matthew's Gospel, however, the fulfillment of the law and prophets is a major theme. Jesus Messiah, the Son of God, is the supreme interpreter of the law for his church; he does not come to destroy the law but to fulfill it. Consequently doing God's will, by practicing righteousness as taught by Jesus, is a major ethical category in Matthew's Gospel. Disciples must produce a righteousness that surpasses that of the scribes and Pharisees if they wish to enter the kingdom of God. This Gospel appears to have been written for Jewish and Gentile Christians who practiced the law as interpreted by Jesus Messiah. The Sabbath and the dietary prescriptions of the law were probably still in effect for them. One suspects that those who opposed Paul at Galatia would have felt at home in the community for which Matthew wrote.

Third, in Matthew's Gospel Jesus provides an example of the righteousness he requires of others. He comes to fulfill all righteousness, and in his life he exemplifies the beatitudes that preface his great sermon. The obedient Son of God, he utterly trusts in the power of God. Compassionate, humble, and merciful, he extends mercy to others. In a word, Jesus is "perfect" because he is totally dedicated to doing God's will. In contrast to him, the religious leaders are hypocritical because of their divided allegiance. They crave human approval even as they seek to please God. Therefore, although Jesus tells his disciples to do and obey all that the scribes and Pharisees say because they sit on the chair of Moses, he cautions the disciples not to act as they do, since their actions do not correspond to their speech. Such people will bear the greater judgment.

Fourth, judgment and reward play a major role in the ethical teaching of Jesus according to Matthew. Matthew's Jesus describes the fearful fate that awaits those whom he calls workers of lawlessness (*hoi ergazomenoi tēn anomian*). The iniquity of such people will be uncovered at the parousia of the Son of Man when the righteous will be revealed. On that day, the Son of Man will repay people according to their deeds. All will be judged in light of the forgiveness and compassion that they extended, or refused to extend, to others. Those excluded from the kingdom will be cast into the exterior darkness where there will be the weeping and gnashing of teeth.

Fifth, more than any of the other Gospels, Matthew's Gospel stresses the need to do good deeds, to produce the fruit of righteousness. Jesus' disciples must be like good trees that produce the good fruit of righteousness, otherwise they will be cut down and cast into the fire to be destroyed. For all of its emphasis upon doing and producing fruit, however, the Gospel of Matthew proclaims that salvation and the forgiveness of sins come from God alone.

At the conclusion of the Gospel, the risen Lord commands his disciples, "Go therefore and make disciples of all nations, baptizing them in the name of the Father and of the Son and of the Holy Spirit, and teaching them to obey *everything* that I have commanded you" (28:19–20). Jesus commanded his disciples to do the will of God by producing a righteousness that surpasses that of the scribes and Pharisees. His disciples can confidently obey this commission because they know that he has received full authority from God and, as the risen Lord, he is present to the church until the end of the ages.

3

Ethics in an
Age of Salvation

The Gospel according to Luke

*L*ike Matthew, Luke makes use of Mark's Gospel as his primary source in writing his Gospel. Consequently, there is considerable overlap in the ethical vision of the three Synoptic Gospels. In all of them, for example, Jesus' moral teaching is firmly rooted in his proclamation about the kingdom of God. As in the case of Matthew's Gospel, however, the Gospel according to Luke presents a slightly different portrait of Jesus when compared to its Markan source. Three reasons account for this: First, Luke had access to the source known as "Q," with its extensive ethical teaching, as did Matthew, although Luke makes use of it in a different way.[1] Second, in addition to Q, Luke had access to material, usually called "L," that is peculiar to his Gospel.[2] Much of this material consists of parables and stories that provide examples of moral behavior. Third, the Gospel of Luke addresses a new situation in which Gentiles play a dominant role in the church.[3] As newcomers, Luke's Gentile audience needed assurance about the faith that it had embraced. Consequently, he provides them with an orderly account of what has come to fulfillment in the Christian community through Jesus of Nazareth.[4]

Because he writes for Gentiles, Luke is not as interested in the Mosaic law and its interpretation as is Matthew.[5] Nor does the concept of righteousness play a central role in his description of the moral life. He is, however, concerned to show the continuity between faith in Christ and the faith of Israel. Luke's infancy narrative, for example, presents a series of pious Israelites who walk blamelessly in the ordinances of the law (1:6; 2:25, 36–37). Moreover, he notes that Jesus' parents presented him in the Temple according to the law of Moses (2:22), and each year they went to Jerusalem for the festival of Passover (2:41). In the Acts of the Apostles, Luke finally explains the relationship of Gentile converts to the law (Acts 15). With Paul and Barnabas in attendance, the church at Jerusalem solemnly declares that Gentile Christians need not observe all of the prescriptions of the Mosaic law. It is sufficient for them to "abstain from what has been sacrificed to idols and from blood and from what is strangled and from fornication" (Acts 15:29).[6]

In studying the ethics of Jesus as presented in the Gospel according to Luke, therefore, one must take into consideration the manner in which Luke has edited his Markan source, his use of material from Q and L, and the new situation for which he writes. Most importantly, one must heed the manner in which Luke has shaped this material to form a new narrative that is distinctively his own. In what follows, I begin with a consideration of Jesus' preaching about the kingdom of God since it underlies all that he teaches about the moral life. Second, I will discuss Jesus' preaching about repentance, which plays a greater role in this Gospel than in those of Matthew and Mark. Third, I will turn to Luke's version of Jesus' great sermon, the Sermon on the Plain (6:20–49). Fourth, I will consider how Jesus presents the life of discipleship as he journeys to Jerusalem (9:51–19:46), focusing upon themes such as the cost of discipleship, vigilance, prayer, and the proper use of possessions. Fifth, I will conclude with some reflections on Jesus as a model of the ethical life that he proposes. While my primary focus will be on Luke's Gospel, I will also draw on the Acts of the Apostles since Acts often completes Luke's treatment of important themes begun in the Gospel.[7]

THE KINGDOM OF GOD

In Luke's Gospel, as in the Gospels of Matthew and Mark, the kingdom of God is the horizon against which Jesus makes his ethical demands. With the in-breaking of God's kingdom, a new age of salvation has begun in which God is effecting a reversal of fortunes.[8] Those who wish to be exalted by God in this age of salvation must humble themselves now.

The Kingdom in Luke-Acts

Luke's presentation of the kingdom of God "is richer than Mark's but less nuanced than Matthew's."[9] Whereas Mark refers to "the kingdom" or "the kingdom of God" 14 times, and Matthew 50 times, these phrases occur in Luke's Gospel 39 times, 21 of which are peculiar to him.[10] Luke also shares 9 sayings from Q with Matthew.[11] In addition to these sayings, one should note the 8 occurrences of the term in the Acts of the Apostles.[12] As was the case with Matthew, Luke seems to understand the term in much the same way as does Mark, from whom he derives 9 sayings about the kingdom:[13] It is the dynamic and powerful reign of God.

The sayings about the kingdom of God that Luke inherited from Mark's Gospel repeat the major themes found in that Gospel: the mysterious and hidden aspect of the kingdom (Luke 8:10; 13:18), its future coming (9:27; 22:18; 23:51), the need to become like a child in order to enter the kingdom (18:16–17), and the difficulty for those with riches to enter the kingdom of God (18:24–25). However, whereas the Markan Jesus promises that some of his contemporaries will see the kingdom "come with power" (Mark 9:1), this phrase is absent from the lips of the Lukan Jesus (see 9:27).

In a series of sayings that Luke has in common with Matthew, Jesus presents the kingdom of God as an eschatological reality for whose coming disciples must pray (Luke 11:2), but which has already come upon (*ephthasen*) people through the power of Jesus' exorcisms (11:20).[14] The period up until John the Baptist was that of the law and the prophets, but from that time on (from the appearance of John; see 3:1–17) the kingdom of God is being preached, and everyone is being pressed (*biazetai*) to enter it (16:16).[15] Jesus says that although there was none greater than John, the least in the kingdom of God is greater than John (7:28).[16] Jesus sends the Twelve to preach the kingdom of God (9:2) and assures his disciples that if they seek God's kingdom, all things will be given to them besides (12:31).[17] This kingdom is like yeast, he says, whose hidden presence leavens flour (13:21). At its final appearance, people will come from the four corners of the earth to sit at its banquet (13:29). Most importantly, the kingdom of God belongs to the poor (6:20).

In a series of sayings found only in his Gospel, Luke presents Jesus as one who constantly preaches about the kingdom of God (4:43; 8:1; 9:11). The pressing need to preach the kingdom leads Jesus to make extraordinary demands upon disciples and would-be disciples (9:60, 62). Their preaching about the kingdom becomes a warning to those who hear them that the kingdom of God has drawn near (*ēggiken eph' hymas hē basileia tou theou;* 10:11). Consequently, people will have no excuse on the day of judgment.

Not everybody, however, understands the nature of God's rule. When a dinner guest says, "Blessed is anyone who will eat bread in the kingdom of God!" (14:15), Jesus tells the parable of the great banquet (14:16–24), warning that the appearance of God's kingdom will effect an unexpected reversal of fortunes for many. When the Pharisees ask about the coming of the kingdom (17:20), Jesus responds that it does not come in a way that can be empirically observed, for the kingdom of God is among them (*entos hymōn estin;* 17:20–21), presumably in Jesus' own ministry.[18] Then, as he approaches Jerusalem, some suppose that the kingdom of God is to appear immediately (19:11). Therefore, Jesus tells the parable of the pounds (19:12–27) to teach that the kingdom will only come after a period of time during which disciples must act as industrious servants.[19] Jesus' continues to instruct the Twelve about the kingdom during the period after his resurrection (Acts 1:3), and before Pentecost the disciples still look for the restoration of the kingdom to Israel (Acts 1:6). After Pentecost, Philip preaches about the kingdom of God (Acts 8:12) as does Paul (Acts 14:22; 19:8; 20:25). Indeed, the Acts of the Apostles concludes with Paul preaching and teaching about the kingdom of God, unhindered, in Rome (Acts 28:23, 31).

An Age of Salvation

Understanding Jesus' preaching of the kingdom of God within Luke's Gospel requires some knowledge of the infancy narrative in which the kingdom's salvation is foreshadowed.

The dominant theme of the infancy narrative is that a new age of salvation has begun.[20] When Mary visits her cousin Elizabeth, for example, Mary proclaims the power of God her "savior" (*sōtēr*), who has looked upon her lowliness (Luke 1:47–48). At the birth of his son, Zechariah praises God for this new age of salvation, proclaiming that God has visited and effected redemption (*lytrōsin*) for his people by raising up a savior (*keras sōtērias*; literally "a horn of salvation") from the lineage of David (1:68–69). God has granted Israel salvation from its enemies (1:71); thus Israel can serve the Savior God in holiness and righteousness (1:74–75). Turning to his son, Zechariah says that John will give knowledge of salvation to his people by the forgiveness of sins (1:77).[21] At Jesus' birth, the angel of the Lord tells the shepherds that a savior (*sōtēr*), the Lord Messiah, has been born this day (2:11). Finally, when Jesus is presented in the Temple of Jerusalem, Simeon praises God because his eyes have seen God's salvation, a light for Gentiles and glory for God's people Israel (2:29–32). The aged Anna too speaks of the child to all who were awaiting the redemption of Israel (2:38). From start to finish, then, the infancy narrative proclaims that an age of salvation and redemption has begun.

This age of salvation brings with it a reversal of fortunes, already announced in Mary's Magnificat (1:47–55). The Savior God has effected power (*epoiēsen kratos*); he has scattered (*dieskorpisen*) the arrogant; he has pulled down (*katheilen*) the powerful from their thrones; he has exalted (*hypsōsen*) the lowly; he has filled (*eneplēsen*) the hungry with good things; he has sent away (*exapesteilen*) the rich empty; and he has cared for (*antelabeto*) his servant Israel (1:51–54). But Mary is not merely celebrating the past deeds of the Savior God and anticipating what is yet to come. The reversal of fortunes that she proclaims has already begun with her and Elizabeth.[22] The Savior God has taken away Elizabeth's shame (*oneidos*; 1:25). Looking upon the lowliness (*tapeinōsin*) of Mary, he has exalted her for all generations (1:48). In effect, Elizabeth and Mary exemplify the reversal of fortunes that the Savior God is effecting by the birth of his Son.

The Lukan infancy narrative has three important implications for understanding Jesus' proclamation of the kingdom of God. First, the births of John and Jesus inaugurate an age of salvation that finds its fulfillment in the kingdom of God.[23] Second, this age of salvation will effect a reversal of fortunes whereby the rich and powerful will be humbled, while the poor and the weak will be exalted. Third, only those who humble themselves before God will be exalted, whereas those who exalt themselves will be brought low.

Salvation Today

Although the kingdom of God is the centerpiece of Jesus' teaching in Luke's Gospel, there is no explicit proclamation of the kingdom or call to repentance at the opening of Jesus' ministry as there is in the Gospels of Matthew (4:17) and Mark (1:14–15). The ministry of the Lukan Jesus begins with an inaugural sermon at Nazareth (4:16–30) that has Isa. 61:1–2 as its focal text. It is only some verses after this episode that we hear of the kingdom of God for the first time and realize that Jesus' sermon was indeed a proclamation of the kingdom.

> But he said to them, "I must proclaim the good news of *the kingdom of God* to the other cities also; for I was sent for this purpose." So he continued proclaiming the message in the synagogues of Judea (4:43–44).

Luke's account of Jesus' inaugural sermon[24] begins with his reading from a text of Isaiah (a combination of Isa. 61:1–2 and 58:6). The spirit-endowed Jesus (Luke 4:14) proclaims:

> The Spirit of the Lord is upon me,
>   because he has anointed me
>   to bring good news to the poor.
> He has sent me to proclaim release to captives
>   and recovery of sight to the blind,
>   to let the oppressed go free,
> to proclaim the year of the Lord's favor.
> (Luke 4:18–19)

Then he begins his sermon, "Today this scripture has been fulfilled in your hearing" (4:21).[25] The sermon goes no further because the text of Isaiah is the program for Jesus' ministry, and the point of the sermon is that the age of salvation announced by the prophet is being fulfilled in Jesus' ministry. Later in the Gospel, therefore, when messengers from John the Baptist ask Jesus if he is the Coming One (7:20), he responds, "Go and tell John what you have seen and heard: the blind receive their sight, the lame walk, the lepers are cleansed, the deaf hear, the dead are raised, the poor have good news brought to them" (7:22). Jesus' answer summarizes what he has done thus far[26] and recalls his inaugural sermon with its promise to bring good news to the poor, release to captives, sight to the blind, freedom to the oppressed, and to proclaim a year of the Lord's favor.[27]

As was the case in the infancy narrative, Jesus' inaugural sermon fore-shadows a reversal of fortunes that unfolds in his ministry. In the Sermon on the Plain, for example, his four blessings upon the poor and the oppressed (6:20–23) will be followed by four woes upon the rich and the powerful (6:24–25). Throughout his ministry, he will be faulted for eating and drinking with sinners (5:30; 7:34; 15:1–2; 19:7), but in doing so, he calls sinners to repentance (5:32) and searches for those who have gone astray (19:10). The result of Jesus' ministry, then, is a reversal of fortunes: while sinners and those of no account respond to him, the self-righteous and honored members of society refuse to change their way of thinking and behaving, even though a new age of salvation has dawned.

To summarize, the presupposition of Jesus' ethics in Luke's Gospel remains the kingdom of God. The Lukan Gospel, however, has enhanced its Markan source as well as Q by more explicitly showing that the kingdom brings a new age of salvation that is effecting a reversal of fortunes. This reversal of fortune theme, which appears throughout Luke's narrative,[28] has important ethical implications. It shows that the age of salvation calls for a corresponding reversal of behavior and thought. The kingdom requires repentance (*metanoia*) and conversion (*epistrophē*).

THE CALL TO REPENTANCE
AND CONVERSION

The Lukan Jesus' inaugural sermon does not include a call to repentance as does his initial proclamation of the kingdom according to Matthew (4:17) and Mark (1:14–15). Repentance, however, plays a more important role in Luke's Gospel—as well as in the Acts of the Apostles—than in the Gospels of Matthew or Mark. Moreover, when speaking of repentance Luke employs the verb *epistrephō* (to turn back, to return) and the noun *epistrophē* (conversion) as well as the verb *metanoeō* (to repent, to regret, to have a change of heart) and the noun *metanoia* (repentance). With the first two words there is an emphasis upon turning toward God, whereas with the second two the accent falls upon the need for a radically new way of thinking about reality that involves a profound change of mind. In what follows, I trace the theme of repentance in the ministries of John, Jesus, and the early church.[29]

Repentance in the Ministry
of John the Baptist

In the infancy narrative, the angel Gabriel defines John's ministry as one of turning (*epistrepsai*)[30] the children of Israel to the Lord their God to prepare a people fit for the Lord (Luke 1:16–17). When John makes his initial appearance, Luke describes him as preaching a baptism of repentance which leads to the forgiveness of sins (3:8), and John challenges the people to produce fruit worthy of repentance rather than to rely upon their status as physical descendants of Abraham (3:8). When the crowds (3:10), the tax collectors (3:12), and the soldiers (3:14) ask what they must do (*ti poiē-sōmen*), John provides each with specific ethical instructions. The crowds must share their clothing and food with those in need; the tax collectors must not defraud others; and the soldiers are not to extort money or accuse others falsely and be satisfied with their wages. Here John's ethical teaching foreshadows a major theme of Jesus' preaching: the correct use of possessions. Moreover, the question asked by the crowds, tax collectors, and soldiers ("What shall we do?") will appear throughout Luke-Acts (Luke 10:25; 12:17; 16:3; 18:18; Acts 2:37; 16:30; 22:10).

Although John himself soon disappears from the scene, Luke utilizes retrospective references to his ministry to remind his audience that John preached a baptism of repentance. Thus we are informed that whereas the people and tax collectors accepted John's baptism, the Pharisees and lawyers did not (7:29–30). At Antioch in Pisidia (Acts 13:24), Paul tells his audience that John proclaimed a baptism of repentance for all the people of Israel. When Paul encounters some of John's disciples at Ephesus, he tells them that John baptized with a baptism of repentance, instructing people to believe in the one who was to come after him, that is, in Jesus (Acts 19:4). Repentance from sins, therefore, is necessary for faith in Christ.[31]

Repentance in the Ministry of Jesus

Although the Lukan Jesus' inaugural sermon at Nazareth does not include a call to repentance, nonetheless repentance plays a major role in his ministry. When the Pharisees and scribes ask his disciples why he eats and drinks with tax collectors and sinners, Jesus replies with a statement that is programmatic for his ministry: "I have come to call not the righteous but sinners to repentance" (5:32).[32] Jesus' call to repentance, however, is not as successful as one might imagine. In a retrospective statement, while on his great journey to Jerusalem, he complains that the Galilean cities of Chorazin, Bethsaida, and Capernaum did not repent despite the mighty works performed in their midst (10:13–15). Soon afterward, he calls the crowd "an evil generation" because it has not repented (11:29–32). Still later he warns that if the crowd does not repent it will be destroyed (13:3, 5). The parable of a fig tree that has not borne fruit for three years (13:6–9) suggests that Jesus' call to repentance has fallen upon deaf ears. Nonetheless, he continues to call sinners to repentance, and in response to the Pharisees and scribes who complain that he welcomes and eats with sinners (15:1–2), he tells three parables that exemplify the joy in heaven at the repentance of a single sinner: the lost sheep, the lost coin, and the lost son (15:3–32). At the conclusion of his parable of Lazarus and the rich man (16:19–31), spoken in the presence of the religious leaders, the rich man tells Abraham that his brothers will repent if someone from the dead appears to them, but Abraham replies that if they do not listen to Moses and the prophets, they will not be convinced even by someone who rises from the dead (16:31). Here, the Lukan Jesus clearly has the religious leaders in view who, if they really listened to Moses and the prophets, would have repented at his preaching.

Finally, at the end of the Gospel, the risen Lord appears to the eleven apostles in Jerusalem and says:

> Thus it is written, that the Messiah is to suffer and to rise from the dead on the third day, and that repentance and forgiveness of sins is to be proclaimed in his name to all nations, beginning from Jerusalem. You are witnesses of these things (24:46–48).

These words of the risen Lord summarize what has been most central to Jesus' ministry and foreshadow what will happen in the Acts of the Apostles. Israel will receive a second opportunity to repent when the apostles proclaim the Lord's resurrection.[33]

In addition to these explicit references to repentance, one should note the stories of repentant individuals and the parables of repentance that occur in this Gospel and are peculiar to Luke: the woman who anoints Jesus' feet (7:36–50), the parable of the prodigal son (15:11–32), the parable of the pharisee and the publican (18:9–14), and the criminal crucified with Jesus (23:40–43). The sinful woman, the prodigal son, the publican, and the condemned criminal are people on the margin of society, but in each case they repent because they experience or trust in the love and forgiveness of God. Because they humble themselves by acknowledging their sinfulness, God effects a reversal of their fortunes by exalting them. In contrast to these people stand those who see no need to repent and so do not experience the kingdom's salvation: Simon the Pharisee, the elder son, the Pharisee who goes up to the temple to pray, those who grumble that Jesus receives Zacchaeus, and the unrepentant criminal who mocks Jesus.

Like John, Jesus preaches the need for repentance. However, whereas John called people to repentance in order to prepare Israel for the coming of the Messiah, Jesus summons Israel to repentance because the age of salvation inaugurated by the kingdom of God has begun. To enter this kingdom and be exalted by God, one must humble oneself. Acknowledgment of a person's true status before God is at the core of the repentance that Jesus requires.

Repentance in the Acts of the Apostles

In the Acts of the Apostles, the early church carries out the task that the risen Lord assigned to it: to preach repentance and the forgiveness of sins in his name to all the nations (24:47). Consequently the theme of repentance, begun in the Gospel, finds its completion in Acts, where Luke presents the major figures of his second volume, Peter and Paul, as spirit-filled men who preach repentance.

The first part of Acts recounts several occasions when Peter calls Israel to repentance. For example, after his speech on Pentecost, in which he accuses his fellow Israelites of having rejected God's Messiah, the people ask him and the other apostles the same question that the crowds asked John the Baptist: "Brothers, what should we do?" In response, Peter tells them: "Repent, and be baptized every one of you in the name of Jesus Christ so that your sins may be forgiven; and you will receive the gift of the Holy Spirit" (Acts 2:38). Shortly after this, when he heals a crippled man at the Temple, Peter gives a second speech in which he accuses the people of rejecting and killing the Holy and Righteous One, the Author of Life (3:14–15).[34] Acknowledging that they acted out of ignorance, Peter says,

"Repent therefore, and turn to God (*metanoēsate oun kai epistrepsate*) so that your sins may be wiped out" (3:19). Still later, he and the apostles defend themselves before the Sanhedrin, saying, "God exalted him at his right hand as Leader and Savior that he might give repentance to Israel and forgiveness of sins. And we are witnesses to these things, and so is the Holy Spirit whom God has given to those who obey him" (5:31–32).[35] Thus in his portrait of the early church at Jerusalem, Luke presents God as offering Israel a second opportunity through the preaching of the apostles to repent and receive the forgiveness of their sins.[36]

An opportunity to repent and turn to God is also extended to Gentiles. For example, after Peter explains why he went to the household of Cornelius, the church at Jerusalem says, "Then God has given even to the Gentiles the repentance that leads to life" (Acts 11:18). After the persecution at Jerusalem, believers from Cyprus and Cyrene proclaim the new faith in Antioch, and "a great number became believers and turned (*epestrepsen*) to the Lord" (11:21). In Lystra, Barnabas and Paul say, "we bring you good news, that you should turn (*epistrephein*) from these worthless things to the living God, who made the heaven and the earth and the sea and all that is in them" (14:15). Finally, at Jerusalem, James declares that he has "reached the decision that we should not trouble those Gentiles who are turning (*epistrephousin*) to God" (15:19). In a word, the death and resurrection of Jesus provide the Gentiles with an opportunity to turn from idols to the living God who will grant them life.

In the latter part of Acts, Luke also portrays Paul as calling people to repentance. For example, he tells the Athenians, God "commands all people everywhere to repent" (17:30) because he has appointed a day on which the world will be judged in righteousness by the risen Lord. In reviewing the course of his ministry, Paul reminds the elders of Ephesus that he has testified to Jews and Greeks about repentance toward God and faith toward Jesus Christ (20:21). Likewise, in his defense speech before Festus and Agrippa, he reports that the risen Lord commissioned him, saying:

> I will rescue you from your people and from the Gentiles—to whom I am sending you to open their eyes so that they may turn (*epistrepsai*) from darkness to light and from the power of Satan to God, so that they may receive forgiveness of sins and a place among those who are sanctified by faith in me (26:17–18).

Paul goes on to say that, faithful to the vision, he has preached in Damascus, in Jerusalem, in the countryside of Judea, and to the Gentiles that they should repent and turn to God (*metanoein kai epistrephein*) and do deeds worthy of repentance (26:20). Thus he follows in the footsteps of John, Jesus, Peter, and the other apostles who preached repentance.[37]

To summarize, repentance plays a major role in Luke's two-volume work covering the period from the ministry of John to the preaching of Paul. John prepares Israel by preaching a baptism of repentance that leads to the forgiveness of sins. When Jesus appears, he eats and associates with sinners in order to call them to repentance. After Jesus' death and resurrection, God offers Israel a new opportunity to repent and extends life-giving repentance to the Gentiles as well.

While repentance entails a turning away from sin, and in the case of those Gentiles who do not know God a turning away from idols, there are a variety of reasons to repent in Luke-Acts. John calls Israel to repent so that the people will be prepared when the messiah comes. Jesus calls the people of Israel to repent because the kingdom of God has drawn near and, in his exorcisms, has come upon them. The church calls Israel to repent because Israel rejected God's Anointed One. Paul calls Gentiles to repentance because the living God has set a day on which the world will be judged by righteousness. For John repentance entails a baptism for the forgiveness of sins and doing concrete deeds of repentance. For Jesus it requires a positive response to his preaching about the kingdom and humbling oneself before the Savior God. In Acts repentance manifests itself by baptism into Jesus' name and faith in the God who raised him from the dead.

Those who repent become part of a reestablished Israel. John prepares such a people for the messiah. Jesus restores sinners and outcasts such as Zacchaeus to the people of Israel (Luke 19:9). Those who repent at the preaching of the apostles and Paul become the nucleus of a reestablished Israel upon whom God bestows the forgiveness of sins and the eschatological gift of the Spirit. Repentance is central to the Lukan vision of the moral life for those who live in the time of the church, just as it was for those who lived during the period of John and Jesus. In the time of the church repentance leads to baptism in Jesus' name, the forgiveness of sins, and the gift of the Spirit. Those who share in these gifts are Jesus' disciples.

JESUS' GREAT SERMON ON THE PLAIN

As in the Gospel of Matthew, the Lukan Jesus delivers a great sermon to his disciples. But whereas the Matthean version of this sermon occurs at the beginning of Jesus' ministry and serves as a compendium of his teaching about righteousness and the law, the Lukan version, which is commonly called the Sermon on the Plain,[38] occurs after Jesus' Galilean ministry is well under way and, unlike the Sermon on the Mount, discusses neither righteousness nor the law. A briefer sermon, its principal themes are the need for Jesus' disciples to love their enemies and to refrain from judging each other. As such, it is more accessible to Luke's Gentile audience than would be the Sermon on the Mount with its distinctively Jewish concerns.[39]

In their present forms, the Sermon on the Mount and the Sermon on the Plain are literary creations of the Evangelists, who in turn were indebted to an earlier version, or versions, of a sermon derived from their Q source. I say version or versions because it is difficult to determine if Matthew and Luke had access to the same sermon from Q or different versions of it. For example, is the Sermon on the Mount longer because

Matthew incorporates more material from Q into the original form of the Q sermon? Is the Sermon on the Plain briefer because Luke omitted material from the original form of the Q sermon? Or did the Evangelists have access to slightly different versions of the sermon, which they edited in light of their own needs? While there is no agreement on this matter, it is apparent that the present form of each sermon has been carefully edited by each Evangelist.[40] Moreover, while the Sermon on the Plain is briefer than the Sermon on the Mount, much of the material absent from the Lukan version can be found in Luke's other literary masterpiece, Jesus' great journey to Jerusalem (9:51–19:46).[41] In what follows, I begin with a brief discussion of the context and structure of the sermon. Then I focus upon four topics: the reversal of fortunes that God is effecting; Jesus' teaching on loving one's enemies; his injunction not to judge others; and the importance of doing what is good.

Context and Structure

I have already noted that in Luke's Gospel Jesus' ministry begins with an inaugural sermon at Nazareth in which he proclaims that the Spirit of the Lord is upon him, and that he has been anointed to proclaim good news to the poor (4:18). Thus the inaugural sermon at Nazareth provides the program for his ministry to Israel. In contrast to this sermon, the Sermon on the Plain occurs after Jesus' ministry is well under way, and is an example of the good news that Jesus brings to the poor (compare 4:18 with 6:20). In the period between the sermon at Nazareth and the Sermon on the Plain Jesus heals and casts out demons; teaches, preaches, and proclaims the good news of the kingdom; and gathers disciples. Eventually he ascends a mountain and, after praying throughout the night, chooses twelve apostles from the many disciples who have begun to follow him.[42] Coming down from the mountain with the Twelve, he encounters a great crowd of his disciples and a great multitude of people from Jerusalem and all Judea, and the coastal region of Tyre and Sidon, who have come to hear him and be cured of their afflictions (6:17–19). After healing many, Jesus delivers a sermon to his disciples (6:20) in the hearing of the great crowd of people (7:1).

The context of the sermon shows that its teaching is intended for disciples. Having gathered a multitude of disciples, Jesus gives them specific ethical instruction. Unlike the Sermon on the Mount with its focus upon righteousness, the central theme of the Sermon on the Plain is the need to love one's enemies. In this regard, the Sermon on the Plain appears to offer a more distinctively Christian ethic.

The sermon begins with four beatitudes and four woes that exemplify the reversal of fortunes that has already begun with Jesus' preaching of the kingdom (6:20–26). In the body of the sermon (6:27–42), Jesus teaches his disciples to love their enemies (vv. 27–36) and not to judge one another (vv. 37–42). In its conclusion he points to the necessity of producing good fruit by acting upon his words (6:43–49). The sermon may be outlined as follows:[43]

Introduction: Blessings and woes (6:20–26)
    Blessings (6:20–23)
    Woes (6:24–26)
Body of the sermon: Love and judgment (6:27–42)
    Love for enemies (6:27–36)
    Judging others (6:37–42)
Conclusion: Doing Jesus' words (6:43–49)
    A tree known by its fruit (6:43–45)
    Two foundations (6:46–49)

The Reversal of Fortunes

In his inaugural sermon Jesus announced that he had been anointed to bring good news to the poor (Luke 4:18). It is not surprising then that his Sermon on the Plain begins with a series of blessings and woes that vividly portray the reversal of fortunes that will occur in favor of the poor.[44] While the poor are called blessed because the kingdom of God is theirs (6:20), Jesus pronounces a woe upon the rich because they have already received their consolation (6:24). Indeed, all the beatitudes have a corresponding woe that vividly portrays the reversal of fortunes that is about to occur. Those who are hungry now will be satisfied (6:21); those who are filled now will be hungry (6:25). Those who are weeping now will laugh (6:21); those who laugh now will grieve and weep (6:25). Those who will be hated and excluded on account of their allegiance to Jesus have cause to rejoice since they stand in the tradition of the prophets (6:22–23); those who are spoken well of are doomed since they stand in the tradition of the false prophets (6:26).

The Lukan beatitudes, cast in the second person ("Blessed are *you* . . . "), are a proclamation of God's grace. The kingdom of God does not belong to the poor because of something they have done but because a gracious God is reversing their fortunes. The first eight Matthean beatitudes, cast in the third person ("Blessed are the . . . "), while hardly devoid of grace, imply a certain kind of moral behavior. For example, according to Matthew, the kingdom of God belongs to those who are, or become, poor *in spirit*. This does not mean, however, that there are no moral implications in the beatitudes the Lukan Jesus pronounces. After all, Jesus pronounces these beatitudes over disciples who will be persecuted because they live as his followers.

The woes stand as severe warnings to those who find themselves in the circumstances described by Jesus. Those who are rich, well fed, laughing, and well spoken of must assess their situation. If they do not humble themselves now, the Savior God will humble them later.

The reversal of fortunes theme, first announced in Mary's Magnificat and now repeated in Jesus' beatitudes and woes, is a constant motif of his teaching.[45] When invited to the home of a Pharisee, Jesus tells a parable to the other guests about the importance of taking the lowest place if they wish to be raised to a higher place (14:8–10). Then he advises his host to invite the poor, crippled, lame, and blind when giving a dinner, rather than friends, relatives, or wealthy neighbors who can repay the favor. Only then will one be repaid at the resurrection of the righteous (14:12–14). Finally, when a guest proclaims that those who will eat bread in the kingdom of God are blessed, Jesus tells the parable of the great banquet (14:16–24) in which a startling reversal of fortunes occurs: the poor, crippled, blind, and lame replace the invited guests. So it will be in the kingdom of God.

Other expressions of this theme occur in the parables of the rich man and Lazarus (16:19–31) and the Pharisee and the publican (18:9–14). But the essential message remains the same. Those who exalt themselves will be humbled, while those who humble themselves will be exalted by God (14:11). In the kingdom that Jesus preaches one saves one's life by losing it (9:24; 17:33), and the last will be first while the first will be last (13:30). The announcement of the reversal of fortunes that the kingdom of God brings, therefore, is good news to the poor and a warning to the rich and powerful to reassess their ethical conduct.

Loving One's Enemies

Having told his disciples that they are the beneficiaries of a coming reversal of fortunes, Jesus exhorts them to love their enemies (Luke 6:27–36). The section can be outlined as follows.

Theme: Love for enemies (6:27–28)
    Doing good to those who hate you
    Blessing those who curse you
    Praying for those who mistreat you
Four examples of nonretaliation (6:29–30)
    Offering the other cheek
    Not withholding one's tunic
    Giving to everyone who asks
    Not seeking restitution
Summary statement: The Golden Rule (6:31)
Criticism of the principle of reciprocity (6:32–34)
    If you love those who love you
    If you do good to those who do good to you
    If you lend expecting repayment
Theme: Loving your enemies (6:35)
Summary statement: Being merciful (6:36)

Jesus' central theme is expressed by a simple imperative: his disciples should love their enemies,[46] namely, those mentioned in the fourth beatitude as hating, excluding, insulting, and denouncing them because of the Son of Man. Jesus' imperative is then reinforced by three other imperatives that explain what he means by love. It requires disciples to do good to those who hate them, to bless those who curse them, and to pray for those who mistreat them.

Having told his disciples to do good to those who hate them, Jesus develops his theme from yet another perspective: disciples must not retaliate when enemies inflict evil upon them. Once more, he provides examples to illustrate what he means. The first envisions an insulting blow to one's cheek; the second, the theft of one's outer garment; the third, the request for money, perhaps from a beggar; the fourth, the theft of one's possessions. In each case, Jesus' admonition is the same: do not retaliate or resist. Rather than resist or retaliate, disciples must offer the other cheek, give their tunic (*chitōna*) as well,[47] give to everyone who asks, and not seek restitution.

Jesus summarizes the first part of his teaching on love with a positive statement of the Golden Rule[48] that the Matthean Jesus employed to summarize the law and the prophets. Disciples must treat others as they would have others treat them. This teaching, however, could lead disciples to live by the principle of reciprocity, as sinners do.[49] Therefore, lest the disciples only do good to those from whom they expect to receive some benefit, Jesus asks four rhetorical questions to show that the principle of reciprocity is insufficient for his disciples. Each question begins with a conditional clause, "if you do such and such," and concludes with the phrase, "what credit is that to you?" Finally, he explains why such behavior is not sufficient: sinners act in the same way in the hope of reciprocity. Thus Jesus calls his disciples to a greater generosity that does away with the principle of reciprocity.

Having explained the true meaning of the Golden Rule by his criticism of the principle of reciprocity, Jesus repeats the theme "love your enemies" and adds two clarifying examples: do good to the enemy and lend without expecting any return. If the disciples love their enemies in this way, they will truly be "children of the Most High."[50] In a second summary, which also serves as a transition to the next section, Jesus calls his disciples to be merciful as God is merciful (6:36; *oiktirmones*),[51] an expression that would be more comprehensible to a Gentile audience than "be perfect" (Matt. 5:48). The essence of the love that Jesus requires is a compassion that leads disciples to do good even to their enemies.

On Not Judging Others

Having instructed his disciples to love their enemies (Luke 6:27–36), Jesus turns to the question of how disciples should deal with one another (6:37–42). In doing so, he focuses on a single theme that he develops in a variety of ways: disciples should refrain from judging one another. The section can be outlined as follows.

Theme: On not judging others (6:37–38)
    Two negative imperatives (6:37)
    Two positive imperatives (6:38)
    Parable about the blind leading the blind (6:39)
    Comments on the parable (6:40–42)

A disciple not greater than his teacher (6:40)
The splinter and the beam (6:41–42)

This part of the sermon begins with four imperatives, each of which contains a promise. The first two imperatives state the theme negatively: if the disciples do not judge or condemn one another, they will not be judged or condemned. The last two present the theme positively: if the disciples forgive and give to one another, they will be forgiven, and a superabundance will be given to them.[52] Whereas Jesus rejected the principle of reciprocity in his instruction on love, now he employs it in his teaching on not judging others. God will deal with disciples just as they deal with one another. If they do not judge one another, and if they forgive one another, God will forgive them, and they will not be judged.

Next, Jesus tells a brief parable (6:39) that exemplifies the foolishness of disciples trying to judge one another. Just as one blind man cannot lead another blind man without both falling into a pit, so one disciple cannot judge another disciple without disastrous consequences when both are blind to their own faults. The material that follows (6:40–42) provides further commentary on this parable. First, disciples are learners; they are not superior to their teacher. But when they are fully trained, then they will be like their teacher (6:40). Since disciples are not yet fully like their teacher, however, they are not in a position to judge one another. Second, it is hypocritical for disciples to notice the tiny splinter of wood in the eye of a fellow disciple (that is, to criticize a fellow disciple) while not taking note of the beam of wood in their own eye (that is, without acknowledging their own much larger faults; 6:41–42). The first task of disciples, then, is not to judge or condemn one another, but to remove those things from their lives that blind them from seeing their own faults.

This section is not as tightly knit as is Jesus' teaching on loving one's enemies, but its central point is clear enough: disciples must not judge or condemn one another.

The Importance of Doing Good

As was the case in his Sermon on the Mount, Jesus' Sermon on the Plain concludes with a strong warning that emphasizes the importance of "doing" in the moral life of disciples. First, he employs the familiar metaphor of a tree and its fruit to show that what proceeds from a person indicates that person's character (Luke 6:43–45). Just as good trees produce good fruit, so good persons bring forth good from the store of goodness in their hearts. Conversely, evil proceeds from evil. True morality is rooted in the heart, so that good and evil proceed from the abundance of good or evil within a person. Second, Jesus warns disciples that if they simply call him "Lord, Lord," without doing his words, they are no different from the person who builds a house without digging a foundation. When the river bursts against it, the house collapses and is completely destroyed (6:46–49). Thus, the sermon ends on a note of judgment and warning. Jesus has promised his disciples that they will be the beneficiaries of a reversal of fortunes, but if they do not act upon his words they will experience God's judgment. There is an intimate connection, then, in Jesus' preaching between the reversal of fortunes that the kingdom of God is effecting and the ethical life. God graciously extends salvation to Jesus' disciples who, in turn, must act upon Jesus' word.

The Sermon on the Plain relates moral conduct to God's mercy and to Jesus' words. Because God is merciful and compassionate, disciples must extend mercy and compassion to their enemies and to one another. In speaking of the first group, Jesus insists that the principle of reciprocity is not sufficient; disciples must love their enemies, even if there is no hope that their enemies will love or do good to them in return. When speaking of disciples, Jesus employs the principle of reciprocity in a positive way; if disciples do not judge and condemn one another, God will not condemn or judge them.

Jesus' sermon does not relate morality to the Mosaic law, and to that extent it is more accessible to Luke's Gentile audience. Yet, while the Gentile world understood the importance of doing good for others, Jesus' teaching on loving one's enemies is an explicit criticism of any morality that bases itself upon a principle of reciprocity. Jesus does not exhort his disciples to love others because it will ultimately benefit them, or because it is the best way to live in an evil world. He commends the love of enemies because it imitates God's compassion.

Jesus' injunctions to refrain from retaliation and to love one's enemies are also found in the fifth (Matt. 5:38–42) and sixth (Matt. 5:43–47) antitheses of the Sermon on the Mount where the Matthean Jesus employs them to interpret the law: "You have heard that it was said, . . . but I say to you." In the Sermon on the Plain, however, these injunctions are no longer employed as examples of how Jesus interprets the law. Rather, they are Jesus' own teaching, spoken without reference to the law. To that extent, the moral injunctions of the Sermon on the Plain are more accessible to Gentiles.

Jesus' Sermon on the Plain is his first explicit moral instruction to disciples in Luke. This sermon, however, does not present the whole of his ethical teaching. As he journeys to Jerusalem (9:51–19:46), he continues to instruct his disciples how to live in light of the kingdom of God.

FURTHER INSTRUCTIONS FOR DISCIPLES

One of the most distinctive aspects of Luke's Gospel is his account of Jesus' great journey to Jerusalem.[53] Whereas Mark narrates this journey in a single chapter (Mark 10), and Matthew in two (Matthew 19—20), Luke's account consists of nearly nine chapters (9:51–19:46).[54] More importantly, Jesus' decision to go to Jerusalem is a major turning point in his ministry, which Luke announces with this majestic sentence: "When the days drew near for him to be taken up, he set his face to go to Jerusalem" (9:51).[55] Jesus' determination to go to Jerusalem signals the end of his Galilean ministry (4:14–9:50) and the beginning of a period of intense teaching and controversy as he journeys to Jerusalem (9:51–19:46), where he will teach daily in the Temple (19:47–21:38) before his passion, death, resurrection, and ascension into heaven (22:1–24:53).[56]

Nearly all commentators recognize that the present form of the journey narrative is a Lukan literary construction that makes extensive use of material from the Evangelist's Q and L sources, as well as Mark's Gospel. There is less agreement, however, about Luke's purpose.[57] The problem arises because of the manner in which he narrates this section. On the one hand, Jesus is ostensibly on his way to Jerusalem but, when one examines the narrative closely, there are relatively few geographical indications of his progress toward the city.[58] Instead, one finds him in constant conversation with his disciples, with the crowds that accompany him, and with the religious leaders, especially the Pharisees. In effect, Jesus' journey to Jerusalem becomes an occasion for Luke to present extensive blocks of Jesus' teaching. For example, much of the material from Matthew's Sermon on the Mount that is absent from Luke's Sermon on the Plain is found in this section, as are most of the parables that are peculiar to Luke. Much of this material has been cast by Luke into a series of speeches spoken to the disciples, the crowds, and the religious leaders.[59]

In these speeches, the Lukan Jesus touches upon topics that have ethical implications for the life of his disciples: the cost of discipleship, the need for prayer and vigilance, the need to humble oneself before God, the proper use of possessions, the nature of the kingdom of God, and the need for repentance. Since I have already discussed the nature of the kingdom of God, repentance, and the need to humble oneself because of the coming reversal of fortunes, I will focus upon Jesus' teaching on the cost of discipleship, the need for prayer and vigilance, and the proper use of possessions.

The Cost of Discipleship

Because of the urgency of preaching the kingdom of God, the Lukan Jesus makes harsh demands upon his disciples and those who would be his disciples. In most instances, discipleship entails leaving "everything" behind and following Jesus (Luke 5:11, 28; 18:28). At the beginning of the journey narrative, for example, Jesus encounters three would-be disciples, two of whom volunteer their services, and one of whom Jesus calls directly (9:57–62). In each case these would-be disciples do not understand the cost of discipleship. The first does not realize that Jesus is an itinerant and homeless preacher (9:58). The second and third do not comprehend that the need to proclaim the kingdom of God is so urgent that it supersedes the most serious family obligations (9:60) as well as all family ties (9:62). Luke never tells his readers how these would-be disciples respond, but by placing this episode at the beginning of the journey section he issues a challenge to all who read or hear his narrative: those who wish to make the journey of discipleship with Jesus must be willing to forsake all else.

Later, midway through the journey, Luke narrates a second episode that highlights the demands of discipleship (14:25–33). When Jesus notices that great crowds of people are traveling with him, he turns and says: "Whoever comes to me and does not hate father and mother, wife and children, brothers and sisters, yes, and even life itself, cannot be my disciple. Whoever does not carry the cross and follow me cannot be my disciple" (14:26–27). The first of these sayings (14:26) echoes what Jesus told the three would-be disciples at the beginning of the journey about the need to leave family behind (9:59–62), while the second (14:27) echoes a demand Jesus made previous to the journey to take up one's cross daily and follow him (9:23).[60] Next he tells the crowd two parables that indicate the importance of calculating the cost of discipleship. Before undertaking the life of discipleship, one must calculate what it will cost, just as a person who is about to build a tower estimates its costs (14:28–30), or as a king marching to war determines the strength of his army relative to that of his enemy (14:31–32). Finally, Jesus tells the crowd exactly what discipleship demands: "So therefore, none of you can become my disciple if you do not give up all your possessions" (14:33).

Toward the end of the journey, a rich official asks Jesus what he must do to inherit eternal life (18:18). When Jesus reminds the official of the commandments, the man responds that he has observed all of them from his youth, to which Jesus replies, "there is still one thing lacking. Sell all that you own and distribute the money to the poor, and you will have treasure in heaven; then come, follow me" (18:22). As in the previous episode, Jesus' call to discipleship requires the complete surrender of possessions.

To summarize, in the journey narrative the demands of discipleship require those who would follow Jesus to forsake family and possessions because of the pressing need to preach the kingdom of God. This picture of discipleship, however, should be read in light of Luke's second volume, the Acts of the Apostles. There, after the resurrection of its Lord, the Christian community adjusts the radical demands of Jesus to its new situation. All who repent and are baptized into his name are disciples. In Jerusalem these disciples share their possessions and no one is in need (Acts 2:42–47), but it is no longer necessary for all disciples to forsake family or to sell all their possessions; this suggests that Luke sees a distinction between the time of Jesus and the time of the church.[61]

In the time of Jesus, the urgency of preaching the kingdom requires disciples to forsake family and possessions in order to live and travel with him. In the time of the church, there is still need for itinerant disciples such as Paul and Barnabas, but other disciples such as Philip (Acts 21:8) continue to live with their families. Thus we should distinguish between those disciples who actually followed Jesus day by day because he summoned them to preach the in-breaking kingdom of God and others who adhered to his teaching but did not actually follow him, because they were not summoned to preach the kingdom as were the Twelve (Luke 9:1–6) or the Seventy-two (10:1–12). Note, for example, Martha and Mary (10:38–42) and Zacchaeus (19:1–10), all of whom live lives of discipleship but remain at home. Jesus' radical demands primarily concern the first group, and yet they are not without effect upon the second as well, reminding all disciples that at any moment they may be summoned to an even more generous form of discipleship, as was the rich official.

Vigilant Servants
Persistent in Prayer

The relationship between Jesus and his disciples is one of master to servants. He is the Lord; they are his servant-slaves. Employing the master-servant imagery, Jesus describes the qualities required of a disciple as being similar to those expected of a servant: vigilance, preparedness, faithfulness, and prudence. Speaking to his disciples, he exhorts them to be as vigilant as servants who await the return of their master from a wedding feast (Luke 12:35–40). Then, in a remarkable description of a reversal of fortunes, he promises that the master himself will wait on those servants whom he finds prepared (12:37).

In a further teaching (12:41–48), when Peter asks if this teaching is for the disciples alone, Jesus changes the imagery slightly. The faithful and prudent manager, whom the master puts in charge of his servants, does not abuse fellow servants during the master's absence.[62] In return, the master places that servant in charge of all his property (12:44). Faithless and imprudent managers, however, who abuse their fellow servants during the period of their master's delay, will be punished accordingly. In both instances, Jesus' teaching clearly has the parousia of the Son of Man in view. He is the master who will return to reward or punish his servant-disciples.

The hope of reward and the fear of punishment at the parousia, however, are not the primary motivating factors for doing what is commanded. In a parable peculiar to Luke's Gospel, Jesus shows disciples what their attitude should be (17:7–10). Just as servants do not expect that their master will be grateful when they have done all that is commanded of them, neither should disciples expect rewards for doing what has been required of them. The proper attitude of disciples is to acknowledge that they have merely done their duty: "We are worthless slaves; we have done only what we ought to have done!" (17:10).

In two other instances in the journey narrative Jesus relates the theme of the parousia to the life of discipleship. First, he warns disciples that the day of the Son of Man will come unexpectedly (17:22–37). At the very moment that people are carrying out the ordinary affairs of life, without any thought of God's judgment, the Son of Man will appear. Second, with the parable of the pounds (19:11–27), Jesus instructs disciples to be enterprising servants in the period between his death and the parousia, for when he comes he will require an accounting from each of them.

As vigilant servants who await their Lord's parousia, the disciples must be persistent in prayer. At the beginning of the journey, therefore, Jesus provides them with an instruction on prayer (11:2–13) in which he teaches disciples how to pray (11:2–4), encourages them to be as persistent as a rude friend who troubles another at midnight for three loaves of bread because a guest has arrived unexpectedly (11:5–8), and to be as confident in prayer as children who ask their father for good gifts (11:9–13). Later, after warning that the parousia will come unexpectedly (17:22–37), Jesus instructs the disciples to pray with the persistence of a widow who badgers a judge into rendering a decision against her adversary (18:1–6). If a corrupt judge hears and answers such cries, how much more will God hear the prayers of his chosen ones and vindicate them on the day of the Son of Man (18:7–8)?

To summarize, disciples are servants who must be persistent in prayer. As servants they must be faithful, vigilant, prudent, and industrious as they await the parousia of the Son of Man.

The Correct Use
of Possessions

I have already dealt with the question of possessions in Luke. For example, in the theme of the reversal of fortunes, we have seen that the age of salvation is good news for the poor and judgment upon the rich if they do not reform their lives. In the preaching of John the Baptist, I noted that his ethical instructions to the crowds, tax collectors, and soldiers foreshadow one of Luke's favorite themes, the correct use of possessions. Above, I noted that Jesus' disciples must forsake everything in order to follow him. It is now time to complete this theme.[63]

As he journeys to Jerusalem, an important topic in Jesus' conversation with the religious leaders, crowds, and disciples is the correct use of possessions. Moreover, at the end of the journey, Jesus shows that one rich man, despised by others as an outcast, is truly a descendant of Abraham because he shares his possessions with the poor.

The religious leaders. Throughout the journey narrative and throughout Luke's Gospel the religious leaders function as a foil to Jesus' teaching about the kingdom of God and his behavior toward sinners. In Luke's view, they are examples of people who are greedy and do not use possessions correctly.[64] Thus Luke, and Luke alone among the Evangelists, describes the Pharisees as those who love money (*philargyroi hyparchontes*; 16:14).

Jesus' first encounter with the religious leaders in the journey section occurs when a Pharisee invites him to dine at his home (11:37). The Pharisee is amazed to see Jesus eat without washing first. Aware of this, Jesus says:

> Now you Pharisees clean the outside of the cup and of the dish, but inside you are full of greed and wickedness. You fools! Did not the one who made the outside make the inside also? So give for alms those things that are within;[65] and see, everything will be clean for you (11:39–41).

Having accused the Pharisees of being filled with greed and wickedness, the Lukan Jesus tells them that if they give alms they will be truly clean. In effect, he provides them with a solution for purifying themselves of their wickedness and greed. The Lukan Pharisees, however, are more concerned with external appearances than with the interior reality of their lives. They pay tithes on the smallest vegetables but ignore judgment and the love of God. In his criticism of them Jesus does not abolish their customs, but he does put things in proper perspective (11:42). If the Pharisees practice justice and the love of God, and if they give alms, they will be clean in God's eyes. At the outset of the journey, then, Jesus teaches his adversaries a new way to purify themselves: by giving alms.

Toward the middle of the journey, Jesus tells his disciples the parable of the dishonest steward (16:1–8) and warns them that they cannot serve both God and money. The Pharisees hear Jesus' warning and sneer (*exemyktērizon*) because, in Luke's estimation, they are lovers of money (16:14). In response, Jesus criticizes them as those who justify themselves in the sight of others (16:15). He then tells the parable of the rich man and Lazarus (16:19–31). The parable is an another example of the reversal of fortunes that awaits rich and poor as announced in Mary's Magnificat (1:53) and Jesus' beatitudes and woes (6:20, 24).[66] Spoken as a response to the Pharisees who have just sneered at Jesus, it stands as a warning to them. They will experience the same reversal of fortune as did the rich man of the parable if they neglect to give alms to the poor. To remedy their situation, they must listen to Moses and the prophets (16:29).

To summarize, Luke presents the Pharisees as lovers of money who are more concerned with external appearances than with the inner reality of their lives. However, he provides them with a way to avoid judgment: obey Moses and the prophets, and give alms.

The crowd. It is not only the religious leaders who are tempted by money. When someone from the crowd asks him to settle an inheritance dispute, Jesus warns the crowd to guard against greed (*pleonexia*) in all its forms since possessions do not guarantee life (12:13–15). Next he tells the parable of the rich fool, which, like the parable of the rich man and Lazarus, is peculiar to Luke's Gospel. As in many of Luke's special parables, Jesus provides his audience with an insight to the inner struggle of the main character, who asks, "What should I do?" (12:17). It is, of course, the same question raised by the crowds, tax collectors, and the soldiers who came for John's baptism (3:10–14), as well as the lawyer (10:25) and the rich official (18:18) who inquire what they must do to inherit eternal life. In this case, however, the rich man chooses the wrong course of action. Instead of sharing his wealth with those in need, he proposes to store it in still larger barns. The man is not foolish because he is rich; he is foolish because he does not share his possessions.

The disciples. Disciples are not exempt from the danger of misusing possessions or becoming anxious about acquiring them. Therefore, Jesus speaks to them about the proper use of wealth. After warning the Pharisees to give alms, and exhorting the crowd to avoid greed, Jesus calls on his disciples not to be anxious about their lives (12:22–34). Instead of worrying about what they will eat or wear, they are to seek God's kingdom (12:31), sell their possessions, and give alms (12:33), for where their treasure is, there will their heart be.

Still later, Jesus tells his disciples the parable of the dishonest steward (16:1–8). Again, the parable discloses the thoughts of its main character, who asks, "What will I do?" Unlike the rich fool, however, the dishonest steward answers the question correctly: he will make prudent use of his master's wealth while he still has access to it in order to make friends for the future. Jesus employs the parable to provide his disciples with an example of prudent conduct in the use of wealth, not to approve of the steward's dishonest actions. The disciples should be as prudent in their use of wealth as are the children of this age (12:8b–9); that is, they should share their possessions so that they will have treasure in heaven. The Lukan Jesus then draws two further lessons from this parable. First, if the disciples cannot act as faithful servants when dealing with this world's wealth, they will not be entrusted with true riches (16:11–12). Second, disciples cannot simultaneously serve God and wealth any more than a slave can serve two masters (16:13). Although these last two applications are not as directly related to the parable as is the first (12:8b–9), they continue to focus upon Luke's central theme: the correct use of possessions. In this Gospel a disciple's use of possessions is a barometer of his or her discipleship.

In his encounter with a rich official, Jesus exhorts the man to sell his possessions and give the proceeds to the poor (18:22), just as he told his disciples to sell their belongings and give alms (12:33). In contrast to the rich official, Jesus' own disciples have given up everything to follow him (5:11, 28; 18:28). It is not impossible for the rich to enter the kingdom of God, since all things are possible with God (18:27), but the accumulation of possessions makes it more difficult.

Zacchaeus. The story of Zacchaeus, a chief tax collector, occurs shortly after the incident of the rich official and provides an example of a rich man who is inheriting eternal life because he uses possessions wisely. When Zacchaeus approaches Jesus, the crowds grumble (19:7), as did the religious leaders when Jesus welcomed and ate with sinners (5:30; 15:2). In their view, Zacchaeus's profession makes him a sinner. But in Jesus' eyes, he is a descendant of Abraham (19:9) since he gives half of his possessions to the poor, and if he extorts anything from anyone he repays it fourfold (19:8). While some believe that Zacchaeus's statement is an act of repentance, it is more probable that he is simply stating a fact of which the crowds are not aware.[67] Jesus calls him a descendant of Abraham precisely because he shares his possessions with others. Thus, at the end of the journey narrative, Luke provides his audience with another example of a reversal of fortunes: a tax collector is called a descendant of Abraham because he shares his wealth with those in need.

The correct use of possessions is a central theme of Jesus' teaching and, as we have seen, is related to two other themes: the reversal of fortunes and the cost of discipleship. Those with wealth must share their possessions with the poor, or they will experience a reversal of fortunes. Those who actually follow Jesus on the way of discipleship, proclaiming the kingdom of God, must give up everything to do so. Other disciples, who do not actually follow him on the way to Jerusalem, must use their wealth prudently for the good of others.

JESUS A MODEL FOR ETHICAL CONDUCT

As in the Gospels of Mark and Matthew, Jesus also functions as a model for ethical behavior within the narrative that Luke has created. In many instances the portraits of Jesus presented by the Synoptic Evangelists overlap since Matthew and Luke make use of Mark. In other instances there is an overlap between Matthew and Luke because they rely upon another common source, the Q material. But in still other cases, Luke brings something distinctive to his ethical portrait of Jesus since he has access to still other material, which he employs in the composition of his narrative in addition to Mark and Q.

Doing God's Will

As in the other Synoptic Gospels, Luke's Jesus has a clear understanding of God's will. He knows that he has come to preach the kingdom of God (4:43) and to call sinners to repentance (5:32). At his transfiguration he speaks with Moses and Elijah about the "exodus" he is about to accomplish in Jerusalem (9:30–31).[68] When the time comes for him to go to Jerusalem, he resolutely sets his face toward the city (9:51). He understands that his journey will end in judgment for all and in testing for himself. Therefore, he says that he has come to bring fire upon the earth and that a baptism awaits him (12:49–50). The fire that he brings is a judgment that will divide families (12:51–53), and the baptism with which he must be baptized will be his final testing at the Passion. Thus, when some Pharisees caution him to flee because Herod is trying to kill him, Jesus responds that he will not flee; he will go to Jerusalem at the God-appointed hour, for it is impossible for a prophet to be killed outside of that city (13:31–33).

Jesus' passion is the moment of his final testing by Satan. After Jesus' trial in the wilderness, the devil departs for a time (4:13), only to return at the hour of the Passion (22:3, 31, 53) to make a final assault upon him. At the Mount of Olives, however, Jesus prays that God's will be done (22:42). Consequently, he is victorious when tested at his crucifixion (23:35–38), and at the moment of his death he prays, "Father, into your hands I commend my spirit" (23:46). After his resurrection, the risen Lord teaches his disciples what they failed to understand during his earthly ministry (9:45; 18:34), that it was necessary for the Messiah to suffer and die in order to enter into his glory (24:26, 46). Thus the life of Jesus provides disciples with a model of what it means to take up their cross daily and follow him (9:23).

Jesus at Prayer

In addition to teaching his disciples how to pray (Luke 11:2–13) and exhorting them to pray unceasingly without becoming weary (18:1), Jesus is a model of one who prays constantly, especially at the significant moments of his ministry. Luke says that Jesus was praying after his baptism, when the heavens opened and God declared that Jesus is his beloved Son (3:21–22). After great crowds come to hear him and be cured of their ailments, Jesus withdraws to the wilderness to pray (5:16). Before choosing twelve apostles from his many disciples, Jesus spends the entire night absorbed in prayer to God (6:12). Before asking his disciples who the crowds say that he is, Jesus prays in solitude (9:18). Eight days later, he climbs a mountain with Peter, John, and James in order to pray (9:28). While praying, he is transfigured (9:29), and he speaks to Moses and Elijah about his coming "exodus" in Jerusalem. Later, during his journey to Jerusalem, the example of Jesus at prayer becomes the occasion for the disciples to ask him to teach them to pray as John taught his disciples to pray (11:1). Finally, before undergoing his passion, Jesus goes to the Mount of Olives, as was his custom, and instructs his disciples to pray lest they undergo the great eschatological test that the Passion will bring (22:40). In his own prayer, Jesus asks to do God's will (22:42). Consequently, he is ready when the time comes for his baptism of suffering and testing.

From the beginning to the end of his narrative, Luke presents Jesus as one who constantly prays. Therefore, it is not surprising that his dying words are those of Ps. 31:5. Having done God's will, he commends his spirit to his heavenly Father (23:46). The example of the Lukan Jesus teaches disciples the necessity for prayer in their own lives, for unless they pray with constancy and determination, they will fail when Satan tests them at the final hour.

Jesus and the Law

The Lukan Jesus does not give any extended teaching about the law. And although he makes a distinction between the period of the law and the prophets and the time of the kingdom of God (Luke 16:18), the law remains valid even in the time of the kingdom (16:17). Consequently when a lawyer inquires what he must do to inherit eternal life, Jesus asks him what is written in the law (10:26). When the rich official asks the same question, Jesus reminds him of the commandments (18:20). Likewise, in the parable of the rich man and Lazarus, Abraham tells the rich man that there is no need to send Lazarus to warn the rich man's five brothers because they have Moses and the prophets (16:29). As S. G. Wilson notes, "The demands of the Law are an accurate expression of the will of God and a reliable guide to piety.[69]

Nonetheless, Jesus comes into conflict with the religious rulers over those aspects of the law which deal with Sabbath observance and ritual cleansing. Two of these controversies are drawn from Mark (Luke 6:1–11; see Mark 2:23–3:6) and will not be addressed here;[70] the other two occur during the course of Jesus' journey to Jerusalem. In the first, he cures a crippled woman on the Sabbath (13:10–17), and in the second a man with dropsy (14:1–6). In both instances, Jesus employs a similar line of argument to justify his behavior. If one unties an ox or an ass on the Sabbath to lead it to water, should he (Jesus) not loosen a daughter of Abraham from the bonds of Satan on the Sabbath (13:15–16)? And if one rescues a son or an ox who falls into a pit on the Sabbath, is it unlawful to cure on the Sabbath (14:5)? Jesus does not criticize the Sabbath institution. Doing good, however, takes precedence over the legalities devised by the religious leaders to protect its observance.

As for purity laws, Luke omits the debate and discussion found in Mark 7:1–23 about the tradition of the elders and Mark's comment that Jesus declared all foods clean (7:19). But as we have seen, Jesus accuses the Pharisees of being more concerned with external cleansing than with internal purity (11:39–40). Without abolishing the traditions of the Pharisees (11:42), he indicates that the way to real purity is giving alms (11:41).

S. G. Wilson notes that there is a certain ambiguity in the attitude of the Lukan Jesus toward the law.[71] There is no explicit criticism of the law, and at no point does Jesus deliberately violate it. But there is an implicit criticism of how the Pharisees and lawyers interpret the law. Moreover, at least in the incident of the rich man, the law is supplemented by further demands (18:22).

The essence of the law for Jesus is love. Thus, when he asks the scribe what is written in the law, the scribe responds as if the love commandment were a single commandment of the law rather than a composite of two texts: "You shall love the Lord your God with all your heart, and with all your soul, and with all your strength, and with all your mind; and your neighbor as yourself" (10:27). When the scribe tries to justify himself by asking who is his neighbor (10:29), Jesus tells the parable of the good Samaritan (10:30–37) and explains that it is more important to be a neighbor to one in need (10:36) than to ask who is my neighbor (10:29), as did the scribe. A Gentile audience, unfamiliar with the Mosaic law, would surely have concluded that love was the essence of the law that Jesus upheld. Moreover, Gentiles would have made a connection between Jesus' Sermon on the Plain, in which he required disciples to love their enemies, and the behavior of the Samaritan. And surely a Gentile audience would have noted the ironic twist to Jesus' parable: a despised Samaritan, rather than an Israelite, helps the man in need (presumably an Israelite), thereby fulfilling Jesus' injunction to love one's enemies.

The Company He Keeps

One of the most distinctive aspects of the Lukan Jesus is the company he keeps. He welcomes and eats with sinners (5:30–32; 7:33–34, 39; 15:1–2); he allows lepers to approach him even though they are unclean (5:12–16; 17:11–19); he embraces children (18:15–17) and heals a blind beggar (18:35–42), even though they are considered to be of no account; and he stays in the home of Zacchaeus, a chief tax collector (19:5). Women also play a prominent role in Jesus' ministry.[72] A group of them accompany him and the Twelve, providing for them from their own means (8:1–3). On his journey to Jerusalem, Jesus is welcomed into the home of Martha and Mary (10:38–42). While Martha prepares the meal, Mary assumes the role of a disciple by sitting at Jesus' feet and listening to his word (10:39). During his ministry, Jesus extends care to women in need. He restores to life the son of a widow at Nain (7:11–15); he tells the woman who anoints his feet that her sins are forgiven (7:48); he heals a woman with a hemorrhage and raises Jairus's daughter (8:40–56); and he heals a crippled woman on the Sabbath (13:10–17). By associating freely with sinners, lepers, women, and those on the margin of society, Jesus acts out the reversal of fortunes that the kingdom of God is effecting in his ministry.

The Lukan Jesus also associates with his adversaries even though this inevitably leads to conflict. He dines in the house of Simon the Pharisee (7:36) and shares meals with other Pharisees as he journeys to Jerusalem (11:37; 14:1). In effect, he does not exclude anyone from his company. He brings good news to the poor and comes to call sinners, but he also dines with the rich and those who view themselves as righteous, inviting them to the kingdom as well. Jesus' example foreshadows the inclusive nature of the church in the Acts of the Apostles, a community of believers consisting of Gentiles as well as Jews.

Jesus and the Sermon
on the Plain

As was the case in Matthew's Gospel, Jesus exemplifies the sermon that he preaches. Homeless, he has nowhere to lay his head (Luke 9:58), and so he must depend upon the generosity of others for his sustenance (8:1–3). When a Samaritan village refuses to receive him, he rebukes James and John, who want to destroy it (9:52–55). When arrested, he refuses to resist, even though he is innocent (22:47–53). And when one of his disciples strikes the servant of the high priest, cutting off his ear, Jesus forbids any further resistance and even heals the servant's ear. Brought to trial, Jesus is condemned to death even though he is innocent, as Pilate and Herod (23:4, 14–15, 22), the repentant criminal (23:41), the centurion (23:47), and the crowd recognize (23:48). In a word, Jesus practices what he preaches. Homeless, he is numbered among the poor. Hated by his enemies and persecuted like the prophets of old, he does not resist. Indeed, even at the moment of his arrest he does good to one who would harm him (22:51). Although the text of 23:34 is not found in all manuscripts, it captures the essence of the Lukan Jesus, who prays for his enemies in accordance with his sermon: "Father, forgive them; for they do not know what they are doing."[73]

In summary, Jesus' actions give those who read and hear this Gospel an important source of ethical instruction. Jesus' behavior teaches disciples to seek God's will, to pray constantly, to listen to Moses and the prophets, to form a community that excludes none, and to overcome evil by doing good to one's enemies.

THE MORAL TEACHING OF JESUS:
A SUMMARY STATEMENT

Jesus' moral teaching, as presented in Luke's Gospel, repeats and, in most cases, enhances the important ethical themes enunciated by the Markan Jesus: the appearance of the kingdom of God and its ethical consequences, the need for repentance, the life of discipleship, and Jesus as a model of the ethical life that he proposes. The one exception to this statement is the Markan emphasis upon faith. The Lukan Jesus speaks approvingly of the need for faith, but there is little development in the concept beyond what is already found in Mark's Gospel.[74] More importantly, Luke has not chosen to repeat the summons of the Markan Jesus to believe in the gospel (Mark 1:15).[75]

For the Lukan Jesus the kingdom of God inaugurates a time of salvation in which the Savior God is effecting a reversal of fortunes on behalf of the poor and oppressed. While the fullness of the kingdom and its salvation lies in the future, there is a sense in which the kingdom of God has come upon people (Luke 11:20) and is in their midst (17:21) through Jesus' ministry. The most important moral imperative, resulting from the appearance of the kingdom of God, is for people to repent. Those who repent believe in Jesus' proclamation about the kingdom of God and the salvation it brings. Aware that God is effecting a reversal of fortunes, they humble themselves before God so that they may be exalted by God. Because they are profoundly aware that much has been forgiven them, they show great love in return (7:47).

Repentance results in following Jesus as his disciple. Those who embrace a life of discipleship, however, must calculate the cost carefully to determine if they can finish what they begin. They must be vigilant, like servants awaiting the return of their master, and persistent in prayer, even if it appears that the parousia of the Son of Man has been delayed. Most importantly, disciples must use their possessions prudently. Those who actually follow Jesus as disciples must be willing to leave family behind and surrender their possessions. Others not called to this radical form of discipleship must share their possessions with one another and with those in need. The manner in which disciples use possessions, then, becomes a barometer of their discipleship. The more disciples are willing to surrender their possessions, give alms, and share with the poor, the greater their commitment to their Lord.

One of the most distinctive aspects of discipleship as presented in Luke's Gospel, however, is Jesus' insistence upon love for one's enemies.[76] In his Sermon on the Plain, he emphasizes the importance of loving others, especially those who cannot, or will not, return such love in kind. But if the principle of reciprocity is criticized in Jesus' summons to love others, it is invoked in his imperative not to judge or condemn fellow disciples. As disciples forgive and judge, so they will be judged and forgiven.

Jesus is a model of the moral life that he proposes for others. A man of prayer, he honors God's law and seeks to do God's will. Realizing that the kingdom of God is already effecting a reversal of fortunes, he shares table fellowship with sinners and outcasts and freely associates with women and other people considered to be of little or no account. But Jesus also dines with the rich and self-righteous because none who repent will be excluded from the kingdom of God.

The Gospel of Luke has taken the basic elements of Jesus' moral teaching in Mark's Gospel and enhanced them by (1) emphasizing the reversal of fortunes effected by the kingdom of God, (2) developing the theme of repentance, (3) accentuating the importance of using possessions correctly, (4) focusing upon the centrality of loving one's neighbor, and (5) presenting Jesus as one who actively sought out and associated with sinners and those of no account. The seeds of these themes are already in Mark's Gospel, but it is the Lukan Gospel that brings them to fruition.

Similar themes can be found in Matthew's Gospel, but there is a significant difference between the Gospels of Matthew and Luke. While the Gospel of Matthew presents Jesus as the interpreter of the law, the Gospel of Luke focuses upon his teaching on love, especially love for one's enemies. While these two approaches should not be harmonized, neither should they be viewed as irreconcilable and contradictory. The Lukan Jesus upholds the law (16:17), even if he does not provide extensive interpretation of it as does the Matthean Jesus. The Matthean Jesus commands love of enemies, but in the context of the law (Matt. 5:43–47). Upon closer examination, however, it becomes apparent that Matthew is more interested in the moral law than in ritual laws or the tradition of the elders. Thus there may not be as much difference as first appears between the two Evangelists. Writing for a more Jewish community, Matthew adapts Jesus' teaching to its needs. Writing for a Gentile audience, Luke does the same.

4

Ethics
Becomes Christology

The Gospel according to John

*F*or anyone interested in the study of New Testament ethics, the Gospel according to John is a major challenge. On the one hand, this Gospel and the letters associated with it contain some of the most sublime statements about love found in the writings of the New Testament, leading many to identify the author (or authors) of these writings as the theologian of love par excellence.[1] On the other hand, there are remarkably few references to moral conduct in the Fourth Gospel. Many of the ethical debates found in the Synoptic Gospels concerning Jesus' observance or interpretation of the Mosaic law and the Sabbath, for example, are absent from John's Gospel. Moreover, the most explicitly ethical teaching of the Fourth Gospel—that Jesus' disciples should love one another as he has loved them—raises a series of questions. What is the content of this love? How do disciples exercise this love in real-life situations? Whom does this love include? Is this a universal love such as is found in the Gospel of Luke, or has love become exclusive and sectarian in the Fourth Gospel? In a word, there appears to be remarkably little ethical content in the Gospel according to John, and its most explicit ethical teaching raises a host of questions.

JOHN AMONG THE GOSPELS

A further difficulty for New Testament ethics concerns the relationship of the Fourth Gospel to the Synoptic Gospels. In our study of the Synoptics, we saw that the kingdom of God plays a central role in Jesus' ethics. In the Gospel according to Mark, for example, Jesus calls people to repent and believe in God's good news that the time is fulfilled and the kingdom of God is at hand. Those who respond positively to Jesus lead lives of discipleship in which the cross and service to others play a central role. In Matthew's Gospel the threat of eschatological judgment and a call to practice a greater righteousness supplement these themes, while the Gospel according to Luke emphasizes the reversal of fortunes that the kingdom of God effects and its attendant demands to love one's enemies and share one's possessions. When we come to the Gospel of John, however, nearly all of these themes seem absent. The Johannine Jesus does not proclaim the kingdom of God or call people to repentance.[2] When he speaks of faith, the object of this faith is the Son of God whom the Father sent into the world rather than the good news about the kingdom. Discipleship remains a central theme but receives a new emphasis: abiding and dwelling in Jesus. There are controversies about Jesus' behavior on the Sabbath (5:1–47; 9:1–41), but they are primarily occasions for christological discourses rather than examples of how he interprets the law. Finally, although future judgment is not excluded, the theme of judgment tends to focus upon the present rather than upon the coming eschatological judgment that will take place at the parousia of the Son of Man. People judge themselves now by either believing or refusing to believe in Jesus as the one sent by the Father into the world. In a word, the Gospel of John exemplifies a christological implosion so that ethics becomes Christology.

The presence of John among the Gospels, then, presents a problem. What is the relationship between the ethical teaching of the Synoptic Jesus and that of the Johannine Jesus? Does the Johannine Jesus represent a new ethical tradition, unrelated to that found in the Synoptics? Or has the Fourth Gospel interpreted the Jesus tradition in a new way? These questions, of course, are related to the complicated literary problem of the relationship between John and the Synoptics. Was John aware of the Synoptic tradition or does he represent a new tradition unrelated to it? In this chapter, I proceed on the assumption that although John may have been aware of the Synoptic tradition, he was not literally dependent upon one or more of the Synoptic Gospels.[3] As for the relationship between the ethics of the Johannine Jesus and the Synoptic Jesus, I will briefly compare the ethics found in John and the Synoptics at the end of this chapter and argue that many of the themes found in the Synoptic Gospels are present in the Fourth Gospel, albeit in a new and transformed way.

Akin to the question of the relationship of John to the Synoptics is that of this Gospel's relationship to the Johannine letters. These letters have a close literary relationship to the Gospel, even if they were not composed by the same author. Thus, while noting the differences between the theological motifs of the Gospel and the letters, scholars often treat them with the Gospel. This approach makes eminent sense if one is examining the theology of the Johannine literature.[4] However, since my concern is the ethical teaching of the Johannine Jesus, I will not consider the teaching of the letters in this chapter.[5] My primary focus remains the ethical instruction of Jesus as found in the Gospel.

Except for the love commandment found in Jesus' farewell discourse (John 13:31–17:26), explicit ethical teaching does not play as prominent a role in the Fourth Gospel as in the Synoptics. For example, there is no discussion about the correct use of possessions, righteousness, observance of the law, the greatest commandment of the law, or divorce. Paradoxically, however, because everything collapses into Christology, the Fourth Gospel presents the most distinctive ethical teaching of all the Gospels. More clearly than in any other Gospel, ethical conduct is related to the person of Jesus. Whereas observance of the law continues to play an important role in the Synoptic Gospels, in the Fourth Gospel the norm of morality is one's relationship to Jesus. In the words of the Johannine Jesus, "This is the work of God, that you believe in him whom he has sent" (6:29). Moreover, the Fourth Evangelist provides his audience with a profound theological reflection of humanity's plight and need for salvation. In this regard, John's Gospel is similar to an exposition of fundamental moral theology, which explains the foundations of the moral life.

Apart from its prologue (1:1–18) and epilogue (21:1–15), the Gospel of John can be divided into two major sections: a Book of Signs (1:19–12:50) and a Book of Glory (13:1–20:31).[6] In the first section, Jesus performs a number of signs before the world that manifest his glory and testify that he comes from God.[7] Despite the many signs that he performs, the world does not believe in him (12:37). Therefore, in the Book of Glory, Jesus turns to his disciples. Knowing that the hour has come for him to depart from the world and return to the Father (13:1), he delivers a farewell discourse to his disciples (13:31–17:26) in which he gives them a new commandment: love one another (13:34–35). In the last part of the Book of Glory (18:1–19:42) Jesus is glorified by being lifted upon the cross (cf. 3:14; 8:28; 12:34).

In the Book of Signs the focus is upon Jesus and the world. Sent by the Father, he comes into the world to bear witness to the truth. Those who hear and believe in him escape judgment and receive eternal life, while those who refuse to believe condemn themselves to live in the darkness that is sin. The fundamental ethical demand of the Book of Signs consists of faith *in* Jesus and faith *that* Jesus comes from God. In the Book of Glory, however, the focus is upon Jesus' disciples and their life in the world after his departure. Jesus gives them a new commandment by which the world will recognize that they are his disciples, promises them the assistance of the Paraclete, and prays for them and those who will believe in him because of their word. The fundamental ethical demand of the Book of Glory is Jesus' new commandment that his disciples should love one another as he has loved them. Faith and love are the ethical poles of John's Gospel, but understanding these themes requires an understanding of the human plight according to the Fourth Gospel.[8]

THE HUMAN PLIGHT

The concept of "the world" (*ho kosmos*) plays a central role in John's Gospel and is crucial for understanding what this Gospel views as humanity's plight. The concept, however, is not easily explained, since the world can refer to the totality of all that is created as well as to humankind. For example, the prologue of the Gospel says that the *Logos* was "in the *world,* and the *world* came into being through him; yet the *world* did not know him" (John 1:10). In this one verse "world" is used three times but with varying shades of meaning. In the first two instances one is inclined to think of the created world, and in the last of the world of humanity. The world is the sphere into which the Son of God comes as opposed to the realm from which he came. Thus Jesus tells the Jews: "You are from below, I am from above; you are of this world, I am not of this world" (8:23). Here the world is one pole of a vertical contrast. It is "below" while the realm of God is "above."[9] Humanity, often represented by "the Jews" in the Fourth Gospel, belongs to the realm that is "below"; Jesus, because he comes from heaven, belongs to what is "above." Thus the world can refer to the realm of humanity as distinguished from the realm of God. In other instances, the Fourth Evangelist clearly refers to the world as the world of human beings, as when Jesus' brothers tell him to manifest himself to the world (7:4), leading him to respond, "The world cannot hate you, but it hates me because I testify against it that its works are evil" (7:7). To summarize, "the world" has many shades of meaning in John's Gospel, and while there are times when one or the other predominates, these meanings often overlap. The world is both God's creation and the world of human beings. Human beings dwell in the world; they belong to what is below as opposed to what is above.

Overall, the Fourth Evangelist views the world as hostile to God. Even though the world came to be through the *Logos,* the world did not know him, and when he came to his own it did not receive him (1:10–11). The Johannine narrator echoes these sentiments of the prologue, explaining that the light came into the world but people preferred the darkness because their works were evil (3:19). At no point, however, does the Fourth Evangelist or Jesus say that the world is intrinsically evil or incapable of redemption. The world is and remains God's creation. "For God so loved the world that he gave his only Son, so that everyone who believes in him may not perish but may have eternal life. Indeed, God did not send the Son into the world to condemn the world, but in order that the world might be saved through him" (3:16–17). The world is in need of redemption, however, because it is under the power of the "ruler of this world" who must be cast out (12:31; 14:30). There is a "sin of the world" which only the Lamb of God can take away (1:29).

Among the images and concepts that the Fourth Evangelist employs to describe the situation of the world are darkness, blindness, sin, slavery, falsehood, and judgment. When Jesus says that whoever follows him does not walk in darkness (8:12), he implies that apart from him the world of humanity is in darkness. And when, at the end of the Book of Signs, he proclaims that he came into the world as light so that everyone who believes in him might not remain in the darkness (12:46), he reveals that darkness is the condition of humanity apart from God.

Akin to darkness is the image of blindness, which plays a major role in the narrative of the man born blind (9:1–41). More than a miracle in which a blind man receives sight, this episode is a sign that points to the salvation that the Son of God brings to the world.[10] Thus, in his final encounter with the man born blind, Jesus says that he came into the world for judgment "so that those who do not see may see, and those who do see may become blind" (9:39). From the point of view of the Johannine Gospel, the world of humanity does not see. Indeed, like the man born blind, it has never seen. The world, however, does not recognize its own blindness. Like the Pharisees—to whom Jesus says, "If you were blind, you would not have sin. But now that you say, 'We see,' your sin remains" (9:41)—the world denies its own blindness. When the world does not acknowledge its blindness, it is condemned to remain in the darkness. Only when it acknowledges its blindness will the world receive its sight.

Darkness and blindness, of course, are Johannine images for sin, which in turn leads to slavery and judgment. The sinless Jesus (8:46) comes into the world as the Lamb of God who takes away the "sin of the world" (1:29), and as the risen Lord he grants his disciples the power to forgive sins (20:23).[11] He comes as the light of the world so that those who follow him will not walk in darkness but in the light which is life (8:12). Jesus is in the world as the light of the world for only a little while, however. Consequently, the world must walk while it still has the light, lest the darkness overcome it (12:35). But this is precisely what the world, which refuses to believe in Jesus, does not do. Thus Jesus tells the Jews (the unbelieving world in John's Gospel) that he is going away and that if they do not believe that he is who he says he is, they will die in their sin (8:21). Shortly after this, he promises those Jews who believe in him that if they remain in his word they will truly be his disciples, and they will know the truth and the truth will make them free (8:31–32). In return, they retort that they are already free because they are Abraham's descendants (8:33). Jesus responds that everyone who commits sin is a slave of sin (8:34), implying that even these believing Jews are still enslaved to sin because, although they believe in him, they do not yet dwell in his word.

In one of the harshest exchanges between Jesus and the Jews (8:39–47), he accuses them of doing the works of their father, the devil, the father of lies (8:41, 44).[12] Jesus' statement does not mean that the Jewish race is physically or spiritually descended from Satan. Were that the case, it would be impossible to explain why he continues to speak with the Jews. But it does identify them as part of the unbelieving world that walks in darkness.[13] The ultimate judgment (*krisis*) is this: although the light came into the world, human beings preferred darkness to light (3:19). The appearance of Jesus is a time of judgment for the world, when the ruler of this world will be cast out (12:31; 16:11). Those who hear Jesus' word, however, and believe that he has been sent by the Father have eternal life and do not come to judgment; they pass from death to life (5:24).

What then is the plight of the world according to the Johannine Jesus? Most simply put, the world dwells in a darkness of which it is not even aware. The world is like a man born blind who has never seen the light. Ignorant of the light, it does not recognize its own blindness and need for salvation. The darkness in which the world dwells is the sin of the world, which leads to slavery, judgment, and death. If the world is to be freed from its plight, its salvation must come from above. Jesus' mission to the world, therefore, is supremely important. Sent by the Father as the light of the world to give eternal life to all who believe in him, Jesus reveals that the world dwells in the darkness of sin. To believe in him as the one sent by God is the ethical challenge of the Fourth Gospel.

BELIEVING IN THE ONE GOD
SENT INTO THE WORLD

Because the world is unaware that it dwells in darkness, it can only be saved "from above," and this is precisely what God has done by sending his Son into the world as the light of the world (John 8:12; 9:5). Although the Johannine Jesus never calls people to repentance, as in the Synoptic Gospels, all who believe in him must undergo a profound change in the way they perceive life and the world in which they live. The sending of the Son into the world is the hour of judgment (*krisis*) when the world must decide whether it will continue to live in darkness and sin or believe in the one sent by the Father. Thus when the crowds ask Jesus what they must do to accomplish the works of God, it is not surprising that he responds that they need only perform a single work: "This is the work of God, that you believe in him whom he has sent" (6:29). Likewise, at the conclusion of the Gospel, the Evangelist writes: "But these are written so that you may come to believe that Jesus is the Messiah, the Son of God, and that through believing you may have life in his name" (20:31).[14] Those who believe in Jesus as the one sent by the Father undergo a profound "conversion" that fundamentally alters their understanding of, and their relationship to, the world.[15] Like the man born blind, their eyes are opened to a new reality in which truth and life are defined in terms of the one sent by the Father, Jesus the Son of God.

The One Sent
into the World

The sending of God's Son into the world is the Johannine equivalent of the Synoptic proclamation that the kingdom of God is at hand. The appearance of Jesus as the light of the world, proclaiming what he has seen and heard in the Father's presence, is salvation for those believe in him.[16] Thus, the Gospel constantly refers to Jesus as the one sent by the Father into the world,[17] just as the Synoptic Gospels present him as the herald of the kingdom of God.

The central affirmation of the Gospel is that God sent his Son into the world in order to save the world (John 3:17). As the one sent by the Father, Jesus speaks the words of God (3:34). To honor the Son is to honor the

Father who sent him into the world (5:24). As the one sent by the Father, he does not do his own will but the will of the one who sent him (6:38). His teaching is not his own but the teaching of the one who sent him (7:16). When some of the Jerusalemites claim to know Jesus' origin, he responds: "You know me, and you know where I am from. I have not come on my own. But the one who sent me is true, and you do not know him. I know him, because I am from him, and he sent me" (7:28–29). In fact, then, the Jerusalemites do not know who Jesus is because they do not know that he comes from God. In contrast to them, Jesus knows who God is because it is the Father who sent him into the world and testifies on his behalf (8:18). Jesus' mission to the world, then, is to tell the world what he has heard from the Father (8:26). At the close of the Book of Signs, Jesus summarizes his mission to the world by saying that whoever believes in him believes not only in him but in the one who sent him, and whoever sees him sees the one who sent him (12:44–45). To see Jesus is to see the Father (14:8–9).

In his farewell discourse Jesus reminds his disciples that he is the one sent into the world by the Father. The words that they hear are the words of the Father who sent Jesus (14:24). The disciples believe that the Father sent Jesus into the world (17:8), and after his return to the Father, the world will persecute them because it did not know the one who sent Jesus (15:21). Despite the world's lack of faith, Jesus continues to pray for the world that it will believe "that you sent me" (17:21). Thus, the risen Lord sends his disciples just as the Father sent him: "As the Father has sent me, so I send you" (20:21). Abiding in Jesus' word, and believing that he was sent by the Father, the disciples continue Jesus' mission to the world.

The sending of God's Son into the world is salvific because the Son reveals the Father to the world. The very revelation of the Father is redemptive since it discloses what the world does not know: that it dwells in darkness and sin, in bondage to the ruler of this world. The sending of the Son is light, truth, and life.

Light, Truth, and Life

We have already met the theme of light several times, and so there is no need to repeat all that has been said thus far. Within John's Gospel, light and darkness are two poles of a moral and ethical dualism that is announced in the prologue (1:5). Light is a metaphor for the illumination Jesus brings to human existence. When people walk in the light, they judge everything "from above," that is, from God's point of view. The presence of the light makes them aware of the darkness in which the world dwells and their profound need for the salvation that only God can give. On the other hand, when people live in darkness, they live "from below," that is, from a purely human point of view. Ignorant of God, they do not realize they are living in darkness. The appearance of the light, then, presents people with a profound choice: to continue to dwell in the darkness or to come into the light.

In the view of the Johannine Evangelist, the majority of people prefer darkness to light because their works are evil (3:19). Fearful that the corruptness of their lives will be exposed by the light, they refuse to come to the light. On the other hand, those who do the truth willingly come to the light so that their works may be clearly seen as done by God (3:21).

Jesus makes his first and most explicit announcement that he is the light of the world during the feast of Tabernacles: "I am the light of the world. Whoever follows me will never walk in darkness but will have the light of life" (8:12). Since light played a prominent role in the feast of Tabernacles, Jesus suggests that he, rather than the ancient feast, provides light for those seeking salvation.[18] When this proclamation leads the Pharisees to accuse him of testifying on his own behalf, Jesus responds that his testimony is true because he comes from, and will return to, God (8:14). Because the one who has come from God must return to God, however, the light is only in the world for a limited time. Therefore it is crucial that people walk in the light while the light is still with them, lest the darkness overcome them. To become children of the light they must believe in the light (12:35–36).[19]

In addition to proclaiming that he is the light of the world, the Johannine Jesus says that he is "the way, and the truth, and the life" (14:6). Because he *is* the truth (*alētheia*), Jesus is the source of "grace and truth" (1:14, 17), allowing people to worship the Father in "spirit and truth" (4:23). As the one sent into the world by God, he bears witness to the truth (5:33; 18:37) and speaks the truth that he has heard from God (8:40). Thus people are not to confuse the truth with an intellectual or philosophical concept, as Pilate appears to do when he asks, "What is truth?" (18:38).[20] The truth is God's own self-revelation incarnate in the one whom he has sent into the world. This is why Jesus can say that he *is* the truth. Moreover, when he tells the Jews that he has spoken the truth (8:45), he is not merely affirming that he has not lied. Speaking the truth means that Jesus has told the world who he is: the one sent by God into the world. Jesus reveals himself to the world, and in so doing reveals the Father to the world.

Because the truth reveals the authentic nature of God to the world, it has an ethical dimension. Those who do the truth come to the light so that their works may be seen as done in God (3:21). Everyone who is of the truth hears the voice of Jesus, the Good Shepherd (18:37). Before he departs from the world, therefore, Jesus promises to send his disciples the "Spirit of truth" (16:13) and prays that the Father will consecrate them in the truth; that is, in his (the Father's) word (17:17). Because the disciples are consecrated in the truth, which is God's word, Jesus is able to send them into the world to speak the truth to the world, just as the Father sent him into the world (17:18).

The all-encompassing term for the salvation that Jesus brings is life (*zōē*).[21] Jesus is "the bread of life" (6:35), "the resurrection and the life" (11:25), "the way, and the truth, and the life" (14:6). Eternal life is to know the Father, and the one he has sent into the world, Jesus Christ (17:3). Thus the Fourth Evangelist writes in order that people will believe that Jesus is the Messiah, the Son of God, and so have life in his name (20:31).

The terms "life" and "eternal life" do not refer to two different realities, that is, life before and life after death.[22] The life that believers enjoy by faith in Jesus *is* eternal life. Thus, although believers must still face death, death does not mean a final separation from God and no longer controls their life in this world. Eternal life is a present reality because the light and truth that Jesus reveals transcend death. So he can say, "anyone who hears my word and believes him who sent me *has* eternal life, and does not come under judgment, but has passed from death to life" (5:24), and "whoever believes *has* eternal life" (6:47). Jesus, however, is not unaware of the reality of death. He knows that believers will die, even though they presently enjoy eternal life. He says that an hour is coming when the dead will hear the voice of the Son of God, "and those who hear will live" (5:25). He tells Martha that "those who believe in me, even though they die, will live, and everyone who lives and believes in me will never die" (11:25–26). Eternal life has both a present and future dimension, but in the Fourth Gospel the present reality of this life enjoys a primacy of place. Those who dwell in the light and hear the truth that the Son of God reveals share in a life that transcends death. Just as their lives are no longer determined by a world that dwells in darkness and sin because they have come to the truth and the light, so their lives are no longer determined by death.

To summarize, because the world does not know the darkness in which it dwells, God sends his Son into the world as the light of the world, to reveal the truth so that the world might have eternal life.

Believing *in* and Believing *That*

For the world to move from darkness to light, it must believe *in* Jesus as the Son of God, the one sent by the Father into the world. In this respect, the Fourth Gospel develops the notion of faith differently than do the Synoptic Gospels, which demand faith in the gospel or in Jesus' miracles as signs of the kingdom. In John's Gospel, as in Paul's letters, the person of Jesus is the object of faith.

While I will make use of the noun "faith," the Greek noun *pistis* (faith or belief) which occurs 24 times in the Synoptics, does not appear in John's Gospel. In its place stands the verb *pisteuein* (to believe; used 98 times in John's Gospel, 34 times in the Synoptics), which is employed in four ways. First, it is most frequently used with the proposition *eis* (in) plus the accusative.[23] With a single exception (John 14:1), the one in whom people believe is Jesus. Second, the verb is sometimes used absolutely. The context, however, often suggests a claim on the part of Jesus that people are to believe in the fullest sense of the term (1:7; 3:15, 18; 4:41, 53; 6:47; 9:38; 11:40).[24] Third, "to believe" is used with the dative case. Here, there can be a variety of objects: Jesus, his word, the Father who sent Jesus, the scriptures, Moses or his writings, and the works of Jesus.[25] Finally, "to believe" is sometimes followed by *hoti* ("that"), indicating that faith *in* Jesus has a definite content.[26] The frequency of the verb "to believe" and the different ways in which it is employed suggest that this concept plays a central role in John's Gospel.

The importance of faith. The central role of faith in John's Gospel can be seen from three strategically placed texts that occur in the prologue, at the end of the Book of Signs, and at the end of the Book of Glory. In the prologue, the narrator says that those who received the Word and believed *in* his name were given the power to become children of God through the power of God (1:12–13). At the end of the Book of Signs, summarizing his mission to the world, Jesus reveals that he came into the world so that those who believe *in* him might not remain (*meinē*) in darkness (12:46). Finally, in describing the purpose of his Gospel, the Evangelist affirms that he has written these things so that readers and listeners might believe *that* Jesus is the Christ, the Son of God, and so that by believing they might have life in his name (20:31). These texts, which summarize the main themes of the Gospel, indicate that believing *in* Jesus and believing *that* he is the Christ, the Son of God, have a salvific value: believers are rescued from the darkness, made children of God, and given eternal life.

The salvific value of this faith is expressed in other ways. Those believing *in* Jesus are not judged, whereas those who do not believe are already judged for refusing to believe *in* the name of the only begotten Son of God (3:18).[27] Those hearing Jesus' word and believing in the one who sent him have eternal life and do not come to judgment because they have passed from death to life. While the Fourth Gospel knows of an eschatological judgment in which those who do what is good and those who practice evil will be rewarded and punished, respectively (5:29), a person's faith or lack of faith in Jesus anticipates this judgment. The Gospel supposes that those who believe in him will do what is good, while those who do not will practice evil because they love the darkness (3:20–21). Consequently, the decision people make now about Jesus foreshadows God's eschatological judgment. For the Johannine believer, the eschatological judgment holds no surprise as does the last judgment described in Matthew 25. Those believing in Jesus can be confident that they will not be condemned.

Because believers have passed from death to life (5:24), the fear of death no longer controls their lives. Those believing *in* Jesus will live even if they die since death is not eternal for those who believe (11:25–26). The source of believers' lives is a river of life-giving water that quenches their thirst; it is the Spirit that Jesus gives by his death and resurrection (7:38–39; 19:30; 20:22). But those who refuse to believe that Jesus is "I Am"[28] will die in their sins (8:24).

The many images that the Johannine Jesus employs, however, culminate in the promise of eternal life, which is often associated with believing in Jesus. For example, Jesus tells Nicodemus that the Son of Man must be lifted up so that everyone who believes *in* him may have eternal life (3:15). The Johannine narrator relates that the one believing *in* the Son has eternal life, while those who disobey the Son will not see life, for the "wrath of God" remains upon them (3:36). Here, lack of faith is equated with disobedience, and the "wrath of God" (the only occurrence of the term in the

101

Gospel) is viewed as a present reality already experienced by those who do not believe.[29] In the Bread of Life discourse, Jesus says that God's will is that everyone who sees and believes in the Son might have eternal life, and that Jesus might raise them up on the last day (6:40).[30] In a word, those believing in Jesus already have eternal life because they believe in the one who has seen God (6:46–47). It is little wonder, then, that Jesus identifies faith as the one work that God requires (6:29).

As for the nature of faith, two elements predominate. First, people must believe in Jesus as the one sent into the world by the Father. By faith in him, believers affirm that Jesus is the Revealer, the only-begotten Son of God who has seen and revealed the Father (1:18). Second, those who believe *in* Jesus as the one sent by the Father believe *that* Jesus is the Savior of the world (4:42); the Holy One of God who has the words of everlasting life (6:68–69); the Son of Man who has descended from, and will return to, heaven (1:51; 9:35–38); the Christ, the Son of God (11:27; 20:31). It is inadequate, therefore, to describe Johannine faith as merely trust in Jesus. Believing in Jesus includes knowing who he is and where he comes from. So Peter, in the name of the Twelve, responds: "We have come to believe and know (*pepisteukamen kai egnōkamen*) that you are the Holy One of God" (6:69). The parallelism of believing and knowing indicates a single reality: a believing faith that knows who Jesus is.

Examples of faith and unbelief. Since faith is so central to the Fourth Gospel, the Gospel presents several examples of faith and unbelief, all of which have profound ethical implications. Among those who believe in Jesus are the disciples, the Samaritan woman and many of the citizens of the city in which she lives, a royal official whose son is at the point of death, the man born blind, Martha and Mary, the crowds who witness the raising of Lazarus, and eventually Nicodemus. Jesus' disciples believe in him when they witness his first sign at Cana of Galilee (2:11), and although some of them abandon him after the Bread of Life discourse (6:60, 66), the Twelve do not. The Samaritan woman is led to faith over the course of a lengthy dialogue with Jesus and, by her testimony, she leads others to believe in him as well (4:39). Later the citizens of that city go beyond the testimony of the Samaritan woman. They believe because they have heard and know that Jesus is truly the Savior of the World (4:42). The royal official believes in Jesus' word that his son will live (4:50), and as a result of this sign he and his whole household believe (4:53).[31] After enduring a lengthy interrogation and being expelled from the synagogue, the man born blind confesses and worships Jesus as the Son of Man (9:38). Despite the death of her brother, Martha professes her faith in Jesus as the resurrection and the life (11:25–27). After Jesus' last and greatest sign, the raising of Lazarus, many of the Jewish crowd believe in him (11:45; 12:11). Perhaps the most interesting example of the struggle that faith involves, however, is the case of Nicodemus. Not yet a believer, he comes to Jesus at night (3:1), aware that Jesus is a teacher who comes from God (3:2). At the beginning of the Gospel, Nicodemus is not even able to believe in the earthly mysteries that Jesus discloses (3:2–14).[32] By the middle of the narrative, however, he progresses to the point of defending Jesus from a summary condemnation by the religious leaders (7:51), and by the end of the Gospel he appears to come forth, a secret believer, to anoint the body of Jesus for burial (19:39).[33]

Faith in Jesus involves a profound movement from darkness to light that the Synoptic Gospels call conversion.[34] Those who believe must overcome a variety of obstacles to their faith: a son in danger of dying, the death of a brother, the hard sayings of Jesus' teaching, expulsion from the synagogue. But the greatest difficulty is the offense of the incarnation: the Gospel's claim that the Word became flesh (1:14).[35] To accept that Jesus is the incarnate Word challenges all that the world knows and understands about itself and requires a painful journey from darkness to light. Aware of Jesus' earthly origin (6:42; 7:52), the world cannot conceive of him as the one sent by God or as the light of the world. Such a claim contradicts the very way in which the world understands itself. Faith is an ethical action, then, because it requires those who believe to alter the fundamental way in which they know and understand themselves.

It is not surprising, then, that unbelief is a major concern in John's Gospel. The world does not believe that Jesus comes from above, that he has been sent by the Father, and that God's Word became flesh. The Johannine Gospel presents "the Jews," especially the Jewish leadership, as the outstanding example of a world that refuses to believe. When the authorities try to arrest Jesus during the feast of Tabernacles, the Pharisees insist that none of their company or any of the authorities have believed in him (7:48). Even when Jesus opens the eyes of a man born blind, the Pharisees do not believe that he comes from God (9:29). Afraid that the whole world will believe in him (11:48), the chief priests and Pharisees convene a meeting of the Sanhedrin to condemn him to death, even though, ironically, he has just raised Lazarus from the dead.

At the end of the Book of Signs, the Evangelist explains the world's unbelief as something that was tragically inevitable and foreseen by the prophet Isaiah (John 12:37–41, quoting Isa. 6:1). Nevertheless, says the Evangelist, many of the rulers believed but refused to confess their faith openly lest the Pharisees expel them from the synagogue. They preferred human praise (*doxa*) to God's praise (*doxa;* 12:43–43). Unbelief, then, is a complicated phenomenon. Although scripture foresaw that the world would not believe, the world remains responsible for its unbelief because, like the religious leaders, it prefers human praise to God's glory.

The words of the Johannine narrator (3:16–21) summarize the essential elements of John's theology and what has been said thus far. God's love for the world leads him to give his Son so that those who believe in the Son might have eternal life. Those who believe are not condemned, while those who do not believe are already condemned. The judgment upon the world is that, despite the sending of God's Son, it preferred darkness to light because its works were evil.

LOVE AND DISCIPLESHIP

In the Book of Signs (John 1:19–12:50), the Johannine Jesus comes into the world performing signs that reveal his glory and teaching the world what he has heard from the Father. By the end of the Book of Signs, however, it is clear that the world prefers to dwell in darkness rather than in the light. Nonetheless there are some who dwell in the light, forming a new community characterized by love for one another. As Jesus prepares to return to the One who sent him into the world, therefore, he turns his attention to the disciples whom the Father has given him in order to prepare them for his departure and for the time when they must live in the world without him. Aware that the hour has come for him to pass from this world to the Father (13:1), Jesus gathers his disciples for a final supper at which he delivers an extended farewell discourse (13:31–17:27) that climaxes with a prayer for the disciples, who will remain in the world after his departure (17:1–27).[36]

As in most farewell discourses, Jesus reminds his disciples of what he has taught them and encourages them to remain faithful to his commandments.[37] Warning them of the hostility they will face from the world after his departure, he promises to send them a Paraclete, the Spirit of Truth, who will act as his successor and remind them of everything he has said. As a final legacy, he leaves his disciples a new commandment: that they should love one another. In his farewell discourse, then, Jesus provides the disciples and those who will believe because of their word with moral or ethical instruction for living in the world in the time after his departure.

Ethical Teaching in
Jesus' Farewell Discourse

The farewell discourse occurs immediately after Jesus washes the feet of his disciples (John 13:1–20) and indicates his betrayer (13:21–30), who then leaves the supper, disappearing into the darkness before Jesus the light of the world begins to speak (13:30). While the present form of the discourse is undoubtedly a composite of several earlier versions, the final edition of the Gospel treats the material as a single unit, as will I.[38]

Jesus' Love for
His Disciples
(John 13:1–30)

Jesus' farewell discourse is set within the context of a meal during which he manifests his love for his disciples by assuming the role of a household slave and washing their feet. Jesus gives two interpretations to his action. The first (13:6–10a) is theological in nature: The foot washing is a parable of his death whereby the disciples will be washed clean (*katharos*). This interpretation is intimated in the dialogue between Jesus and Peter with its subtle shift from talk about washing Peter's feet to washing Peter so that he can share in

Jesus' inheritance. When Peter protests, "you will never wash *my feet*," Jesus replies, "unless I wash *you*, you have no share with me" (13:8). The foot washing, then, is more than an example of self-abasement; it is a parable that points to Jesus' saving death upon the cross.[39] Having disclosed the salvific meaning of his action, Jesus provides a second interpretation (13:12–20) that is paraenetic in nature: his action provides an example for the disciples who must become servants to one another.[40] Thus after washing their feet, he says that he has given them a *hypodeigma*, a "pattern" or "example" of behavior, "that you also should do as I have done to you" (13:15).[41] The washing of the disciples' feet, with its theological and paraenetic dimensions, therefore exemplifies what Jesus means by love and disposes his disciples to hear the following discourse in which his love for them, their love for him and for one another, and the Father's love for the disciples will play a prominent role.[42]

Implications of Jesus' Departure
(John 13:31–14:31)

Jesus' farewell discourse begins with an announcement of his death (13:31). However, since his death is a return to the Father, he speaks of being glorified (13:31). The disciples who have believed that Jesus is the one whom the Father sent into the world must now believe that he is returning to the Father. Jesus' disciples, however, do not understand where he is going and why they cannot follow him (13:36–38). He encourages them not to let their hearts be troubled. Since they believe in God, they are to believe in him as well (14:1). By returning to the Father, he will prepare a place for them so that where he is, they might also be (14:3). When Thomas responds that they do not know where he is going and asks how they can know the way, Jesus announces that he is the Way, the Truth, and the Life (14:6); to know him is to know the Father (14:7); for he is in the Father, and the Father is in him (14:10). After Jesus' departure, the disciples will find themselves in a new situation. But if they continue to believe in him, they will do the works that he does, and whatever they ask in his name, he will do for them (14:12–14). The death/departure of Jesus from the world, then, presents the disciples with a series of ethical challenges: having believed that God sent Jesus into the world, they must now believe that he is returning to the Father and must continue to believe[43] in him despite his absence from the world. Furthermore, they must love one another and manifest their love for Jesus by keeping his commandments.

Jesus' "new commandment" (13:34), that his disciples should love one another as he has loved them, is undoubtedly the focal point of his ethical teaching. The commandment, however, is often seen as narrow and sectarian when compared to the teaching of the Synoptic Jesus, who identifies the most important commandments of the law as the love of God and the love of neighbor and, in his great sermon, calls disciples to love their enemies as well. A comparison between the Johannine and Synoptic teaching on love, however, is like comparing apples and oranges; they have several features in common, but they are different kinds of fruit. To appreciate

Jesus' "new commandment" one must examine it within the context of the Johannine Gospel rather than compare it with the teaching of the Synoptic Gospels.

The first announcement of the love commandment occurs immediately after Jesus announces his departure. Precisely because he is going to the Father, he leaves his disciples with a "new commandment" by which they can live in the world (13:34):

> I give you a new commandment,
> that you love one another.
> Just as I have loved you,
> you also should love one another.
> By this everyone will know that you are my disciples,
> if you have love for one another.

The love commandment is closely associated with the theme of Jesus' departure. Thus while the Book of Signs speaks of God's love for the world (3:16) and the Father's love for the Son (3:35; 10:17), Jesus' teaching on love is reserved for his farewell discourse to his disciples in the Book of Glory.

The love commandment is not an instruction about, or an interpretation of, the law as in the Synoptic Gospels; it is the legacy of the departing Jesus to his disciples. Accordingly, he says that he is "giving" (*didōmi*) his disciples a new commandment; this is the same verb that the Gospel employs when speaking of other gifts given from above: the Spirit (3:34; 14:16), the bread of life (6:11, 27, 31, 32, 33, 34, 37, 39, 51, 52, 65); living water (4:10, 14, 15), peace (14:27), eternal life (10:28; 17:2), glory (17:22, 24), the power to become the children of God (1:12), and the word of God (17:8, 14).[44] Jesus' new commandment is part of the salvific revelation he brings from God.

The distance that John has traveled from the Synoptics can be seen in his use of the word *entolē* (commandment). The Fourth Evangelist does not use *entolē* to refer to an ordinance of the Mosaic law, as do the Synoptics and Paul.[45] Rather *entolē* refers to the commandment of God that directs Jesus' entire mission in the world, which can be summarized as his bringing eternal life (12:50). In the Good Shepherd discourse, for example, Jesus says, "No one takes it [my life] from me, but I lay it down of my own accord. I have power to lay it down, and I have power to take it up again. I have received this *entolēn* from my Father" (10:18; also see 14:31; 15:10). *Entolē* also refers to the commandment or commandments that Jesus gives to his disciples (13:34; 14:15, 21; 15:10, 12).[46] In this case it denotes the teaching that Jesus brings from above rather than a precept of the Mosaic law. Just as Jesus received a commandment from the Father that guides his salvific work in the world, so the disciples receive a new commandment that will guide their mission in the world during the time of Jesus' absence.

Jesus' description of the commandment as "new" raises a further question: in what sense is the commandment to love one another new?[47] Love of one's neighbor, for example, is already found in Lev. 19:18.[48] The newness of Jesus' commandment, however, derives from its christological and eschatological context. The one who gives the commandment is the Son of God who has come from above, and the hour in which it is given is the final hour when the light is about to overcome the darkness of this world. In giving this commandment, Jesus expresses his love for his disciples in the foot washing and thereby provides an example of the kind of love that his disciples must imitate. This love is Jesus' saving death for the disciples, which finds its fullest expression upon the cross. The newness of the love commandment, then, derives from the example of the one who gives it and the time in which it is given.[49] Just as Jesus the Good Shepherd lays down his life for his disciples (15:13), so the disciples should love one another. Although the precise content of the love commandment may not be new—love always entails doing good to the other—the context in which disciples must practice this love is new.

The mark of discipleship in the Johannine community is love for one another. Although the world may not understand this love and may even view it as narrow and sectarian, the disciples' love for each other, patterned after Jesus' love for them, identifies them as his disciples. Conversely, if disciples do not love one another, they will fail as Jesus' disciples. Love for one another is the touchstone of discipleship.

In addition to his speaking of the disciples' love for one another, Jesus on several occasions clarifies what it means to love him. First, if the disciples love him, they will keep his commandments (*entolas;* 14:15). In return, he will ask the Father to give them another Paraclete (14:16). Second, the one who keeps Jesus' commandments is the one who loves him (14:21). In return, such a person will be loved by the Father, and Jesus will love that one and manifest himself to him (14:21). Third, if someone loves Jesus, that person will keep Jesus' word (*logos*). In return the Father will love such a one, and Jesus and the Father will make their abode with him (14:23). Finally, Jesus tells the disciples that if they truly loved him, they would rejoice that he is going to the Father, for the Father is greater than he (14:28). Jesus' commandments, then, do not include any specific directives beyond the commandment to love one another. They consist of the "word" he brings from the Father. By keeping this word the disciples will love Jesus and be loved by the Father.

To summarize, Jesus' departure has ethical implications for his disciples. First, they must continue to believe in him, even during the time of his absence. Second, they must love one another as he has loved them. Third, they must manifest their love for him by keeping his word/commandment and rejoicing that he is returning to the Father.

Abiding in Jesus
(John 15:1–17)

Jesus' parable of the vine and the branches is the most explicit paraenesis of the farewell discourse. As in the Synoptic Gospels, he speaks of the importance of bearing fruit. However, whereas the Synoptics compare the disciples to trees that must bear good fruit, the Fourth Gospel compares them to branches on a vine, which is Jesus, thereby establishing an intimate relationship between him and them. For the Fourth Gospel the moral life is impossible apart from Jesus, and just as a branch cannot bear fruit apart from the vine, so disciples cannot bear fruit without abiding (*menein*) in Jesus. So Jesus says, "apart from me you can do nothing" (15:5). The Father also plays a role in the moral life of the disciples, cleansing (*kathairein*) them so that they can produce even more fruit. Lest one imagine that this intimate association between Jesus and his disciples relieves disciples of moral responsibility, Jesus warns that anyone who does not remain in him will be cast off like a branch and wither and be thrown into the fire to be burned (15:6). By failing to abide in Jesus, the source of the moral life, disciples cease to produce fruit. Therefore, they must remain in his love and keep his commandments (15:8–10). In doing so, they pattern themselves after Jesus, who remains in the Father's love and keeps his commandments. The following pattern appears in Jesus' teaching (15:9–11).

> The Father *loves* Jesus.
> Jesus *loves* the Father.
> Jesus *keeps* the Father's commandments.
> Disciples *keep* Jesus' commandments.
> Jesus *abides* in the Father's love.
> Disciples *abide* in Jesus' love.

In the final portion of this section, Jesus repeats the love commandment twice (15:12, 17) but does not call it a new commandment as he did earlier (13:34). By saying, "No one has greater love than this, *to lay down one's life* for one's friends" (15:13), he grounds the love commandment in his own salvific work as the Good Shepherd who *lays down his life* for the sheep (10:15, 17, 18).[50] Lest disciples imagine that they are the source of the moral life, however, Jesus reminds them that he has chosen (*exelexamēn*) them so that they might go forth and bear fruit (15:16): fruit which finds its culmination in Jesus' commandment to love one another (15:17).

For the Johannine Jesus the moral life is a life of grace because it is rooted in him and patterned after his redeeming love. The world has always known how to love its own, but only those whom Jesus has chosen out of the world, can love one another as Jesus has loved them.

Disciples in the World
(John 15:18–16:4a)

In the parable of the vine and branches the Johannine Jesus focused upon the need for disciples to abide in him in order to bear fruit. While Jesus continues to emphasize the close relationship between himself and the disciples, the central theme of this new section is the relationship of his disciples to the world. What can disciples expect from the world, and how are they to live in it after Jesus has departed? While the Synoptic Gospels speak of the hostility and persecution that the disciples will face during the period between Jesus' death and parousia, the Fourth Gospel develops this discussion even further with its distinctive concept of the world. Before the departing Jesus leaves his disciples, he explains what they can expect from the world, and how they should perceive their relationship to it.

First, the disciples will receive the same reception that the world extended to Jesus. Consequently, if the world hates them, they should recall that it hated Jesus first (15:18). Since the disciples are not greater than Jesus, the world will not accord them any better treatment. If it persecuted him, it will persecute them; if it kept Jesus' word, it will keep their word as well (15:20). In a more specific warning, Jesus tells them that they will be expelled from synagogues (*aposynagōgous;* 16:1), thereby associating them with the fate of the man born blind (9:22), who testified on Jesus' behalf and believed in him. The hour will even come when those who kill the disciples will imagine that they are offering worship to God (16:2), just as the religious leaders viewed their decision to destroy Jesus as necessary to save the nation (11:50). The disciples' intimate relationship with Jesus, therefore, will lead to hostility from the world. Consequently, they must have a clear understanding of themselves and their relationship to it.

As Jesus' disciples they are not of the world (*ek tou kosmou*) any more than Jesus is of the world, for he has chosen them out of the world (*ek tou kosmou*) to be his own (15:19). Discipleship, therefore, leads to a new relationship to the world. Although disciples necessarily remain in the world (*en tō kosmō*), as Jesus will say in his prayer on their behalf (17:11), they are no longer of the world because they have moved from darkness to light. In contrast to the disciples, the world does not know the one who sent Jesus (15:21). If Jesus had not revealed the truth to the world, the world would be unaware of its sin, but now it has no excuse. Jesus has revealed the world's true situation as one of darkness and sin. In return, the world has hated him, and in hating him it has hated the Father (15:22–23).[51]

Because the disciples will find themselves in a situation analogous to that which their master experienced, they must always remember their relationship to the world into which Jesus sends them. The world is a hostile place that will hate them because it hated Jesus. In the ethics of the Johannine Jesus, there can be no accommodation or compromise with the world. People belong to the light or to the darkness, they are from above or from below, they have been taken from the world or belong to the world. There is no middle ground. Disciples are the elected ones whom Jesus has chosen out of the world (15:19). Although the world will hate them for this, they know they belong to the light.

Jesus' Final Reflections on His Departure (John 16:4b-33)

This portion of Jesus' farewell discourse returns to the theme of his death/departure. Although the ethical material of this section is less explicit than what precedes, Jesus' discussion about his departure has ethical ramifications for his disciples. First, he tells them it is to their advantage that he should go, for if he does not go, the Paraclete will not come (16:7). When the Paraclete does come, he will convict the world of sin (*hamartias*), righteousness (*dikaiosynēs*), and judgment (*kriseōs*). How so? The coming of the Paraclete will prove that Jesus truly came from, and returned to, God. Consequently it will be evident to the disciples that the world sinned in refusing to believe in Jesus; that Jesus and not the world stands in the proper relationship to God; and that the world has been judged for refusing to believe in him (16:8–11). Furthermore the Spirit of Truth, the Paraclete, will guide the disciples in all truth, speaking whatever he hears and announcing what will be (16:13). The Paraclete, then, is the disciples' moral guide as was Jesus when he was with them in the world. The ethical and moral life of Jesus' followers will continue to be guided from above. Therefore, even in his absence, the community will hear and know the truth.

When Jesus repeats a new version of the riddle he employed at the beginning of the discourse, "A little while, and you will no longer see me, and again a little while and you will see me" (16:16; see 13:33), the disciples still do not comprehend that he is speaking of his death and return to the Father.[52] At the end of the discourse, however, he tells them that the Father loves (*philei*) them because they have loved him (*pephilēkate*) and believed that he came from God (16:27).[53] Most importantly, he explains the meaning of his departure: "I came from the Father and have come into the world; again, I am leaving the world and am going to the Father" (16:28). At last the disciples think they understand what he is saying (16:29–31). In fact, they do not fully comprehend because they will be scattered and leave him alone (16:32). Despite this, he tells them to take courage for he has conquered the world (16:33).

This final section is instructive for understanding the Johannine notion of discipleship. Jesus' disciples are distinguished by love and faith. On the one hand, they manifest love for Jesus by keeping his commandments, especially the commandment to love one another. On the other, they are the ones who believe that Jesus came from and returned to the Father. Their discipleship in the world has been made possible by Jesus' victory over the world as regards sin, righteousness, and judgment. Because of this victory, they can continue to live in the world as his followers.

Prayer on Behalf
of the Disciples
(John 17:1–26)

Jesus' high priestly prayer provides a fitting climax to his farewell discourse and offers further insight into the nature of discipleship and the relationship of disciples to the world. On the basis of this prayer, disciples gain a deeper understanding of who they are vis-à-vis the world. Moreover, in addition to praying for his disciples (17:6–19), Jesus prays for future generations of disciples who will believe in him through the word of his disciples (17:20–26).[54]

In his prayer, Jesus identifies the disciples in several ways. They are the ones whom the Father *gave* him out of the world and to whom Jesus revealed the name of the Father (17:6). In turn, they have kept the Father's word, which Jesus gave them (17:6). They are the ones who know and believe that the Father sent Jesus (17:8). They are in the world (17:11) but do not belong to the world any more than does Jesus (17:16). Rather than ask the Father to take them out of the world, however, Jesus prays that they be protected from the evil one (17:15). Having consecrated himself for their sake, he asks that they be consecrated in truth (17:17). He will then send them into the world, just as the Father sent him into the world (17:18). The Johannine notion of discipleship places a premium upon the notions of election, consecration, and mission. True disciples know themselves as elected and consecrated for mission to the world. To this extent, their lives parallel the life of Jesus, who was also sent into the world.

In the final part of this prayer (17:20–26), Jesus looks to future generations of disciples who will believe through the word of his first disciples so that all generations of disciples may be one, just as Jesus and the Father are one. In praying for these disciples, Jesus manifests a continuing concern for the world. He prays that the unity of his disciples will lead the world to believe and know that the Father sent him (17:21, 23). Thus, despite the Gospel's negative view of the world, the world is not forsaken, even after it has rejected Jesus. Disciples know that they have been chosen out of the world, but they dare not forsake or abandon the world, for they have been consecrated by the Father and sent into the world by the Son. Despite elements of sectarianism within the Johannine Gospel, then, there are countervailing forces that remind disciples of their mission and responsibility to the world.

JESUS' MORAL TEACHING:
A SUMMARY STATEMENT

The moral teaching of the Johannine Jesus can be summarized in two phrases: (1) "believe in the One the Father has sent into the world," and (2) "love one another as I have loved you." Behind these two phrases, however, stands a major presupposition: the world dwells in a darkness of which it is not aware. Therefore, Jesus insists that he comes into the world as the light of the world to reveal what he has seen and heard in the presence of the Father. Exactly what he has seen and heard, however, is never described. Instead, he presents himself as the Way, the Truth, and the Life, the Good Shepherd, the Bread of Life, the source of life-giving water, the Resurrection and the Life. To see him is to see the Father; to hear him is to hear the Father. In the Fourth Gospel ethics becomes Christology since one passes from death to life by knowing and believing in Jesus.

Believing *in* Jesus as the one sent by the Father into the world, and believing that he is the Son of Man, the Messiah, and the Son of God, rescues one from God's wrath. Such belief is conversion, even though Jesus never employs the term. Instead of calling people to repent, he summons them to

111

believe in himself so that they will move from darkness to life, from slavery to freedom, and from death to life. Those who believe in Jesus are not condemned, but those who refuse to believe pronounce judgment upon themselves. To this extent, the moral life is an eschatological existence in which the future collapses into the present. The life the believer enjoys is eternal life, and yet this eschatological existence does not rule out God's final judgment or life beyond death. People will be judged on the basis of what they have done. The Johannine Jesus, however, does emphasize that faith transforms and changes the believer's present existence.

Jesus does not interpret the Mosaic law or present a new set or rules or regulations, even though he identifies keeping his commandments as proof that one loves him. These commandments consist of Jesus' word of revelation from the Father. Disciples keep Jesus' commandments by believing in him. Despite the lack of specific commandments, the moral and ethical teaching of the Johannine Jesus presents a more systematic view of the moral life than is found in the Synoptic Gospels. Whereas the Synoptic Jesus presupposes the moral teaching of the Mosaic law, and in Matthew's Gospel offers an interpretation of it, the Johannine Jesus appears to replace that law with the word he brings from the Father.

There is, however, one commandment that is specific in Jesus' teaching: his disciples must love one another as he has loved them. The primary beneficiaries of this love are the members of the believing community. Consequently, even though the world is the object of God's love, Jesus never instructs his disciples to love the world. As a realm of darkness and unbelief, the world cannot understand and receive the love shared by Jesus' disciples. This love is not a feeling or emotion but a gift from God. Thus Jesus says that he is "giving" his disciples a new commandment. Since this love presupposes faith in him as the one sent by the Father into the world, the world cannot participate in this love. However, when the world comes to believe that the Father sent the Son into the world, it will participate in Jesus' love. The love that Jesus commands only excludes the world when the world refuses to believe. Faith and love, then, complement each other. Only those who believe in Jesus are capable of loving one another as he loved them. Those who do not believe cannot understand or experience the meaning of such love.

The moral teaching of the Johannine Jesus is intensely communal. Jesus chooses disciples out of the world, whom the Father gave to him so that they might be with him and abide in him. Discipleship is characterized, then, by an intimate relationship between Jesus and the believer. This relationship, however, does not mean that the moral life has been reduced to an individual affair between Jesus and the believer. The love commandment calls disciples to live a life of mutual love so that the world will know and believe that the Father sent Jesus into the world. Disciples are chosen out of the world to form a community of believers who will go into the world and testify that Jesus came from the Father. Since the Paraclete, the Spirit of Truth, will guide them in the truth, the community of believers in the world can be confident even after the departure of Jesus.

Because disciples have been chosen out of the world and given to Jesus by the Father, they are profoundly aware that their moral life is a gift from above. Rooted in Jesus as branches in a vine, believers know that they cannot do anything apart from him. Nonetheless the moral life requires effort, since disciples must "bear fruit." The fruit they bear, however, is not their own but a gift from Jesus.

The moral teaching of the Johannine Jesus manifests a tremendous confidence in the outcome of faith, somewhat akin to Paul's confidence in the power of the Spirit to lead the believer in the moral life. If the world believes in him, all other moral decisions will follow. This may explain why Jesus does not make more specific moral demands upon his followers. The one work that God requires is to believe in the one he sent into the world. From this comes the power to love, and all else besides. Ethics has become Christology.

JOHN AND THE SYNOPTICS

What can we say of the relationship between the Johannine and the Synoptic Jesus? On first appearance, there seems to be little if any relationship between the ethic proposed by each. The Synoptic Jesus preaches the kingdom of God, calls people to repentance and belief in the kingdom and the mighty works that announce it. The Synoptic Jesus summons disciples and teaches them the importance of the cross and the need to become servants to one another. Within the Synoptic Gospels the question of the law, especially in regard to Sabbath observance and the tradition of the elders, remains a central issue. Moreover, the Synoptic Jesus gives specific teaching on the danger of riches, forbids divorce, and teaches people to love their enemies as well as those who do good to them. Finally, the Synoptic Jesus points to the future when he will return as the Son of Man, God's eschatological judge, to repay each one according to his deeds. Is there any relationship between this teaching and what we have encountered in the Fourth Gospel?

There is no legitimate way to harmonize the teaching of the Synoptic Gospels and the Fourth Gospel. The two represent different streams of tradition, both of which, I believe, have their origin in Jesus. Just as rivers cut their own way through the landscape, so the Synoptic and Johannine traditions have made their own way in interpreting the Jesus tradition. Nonetheless, there are indications that both have a common origin in Jesus, as we see if we compare six elements of the Synoptic Gospels with the Fourth Gospel. Those elements are: the kingdom of God, repentance, faith, love, discipleship, and judgment.

The Kingdom of God

The kingdom of God plays a major role in each of the Synoptic Gospels but occurs only twice in the Fourth Gospel, both times in connection with

113

the story of Nicodemus (3:3, 5). Jesus tells Nicodemus that no one can enter the kingdom of God without being born from above (*anōthen*); that is, of water and the Spirit. The notion of the kingdom of God never appears again. The underlying reality of the kingdom of God is replaced by Jesus himself and the life he brings, as indicated by the need for a new birth. The rationale for this, however, is already present in the Synoptic Gospels, where entering the kingdom (Mark 9:47; 10:23, 24) is equated with "entering life" (Mark 9:43, 45) and inheriting "eternal life" (Mark 10:17). While both "eternal life" and "kingdom of God" have a future connotation, the Fourth Evangelist may have favored the former because it allowed him to express more clearly the reality of what the Son of God effects than would the explicitly Jewish and apocalyptic concept of the kingdom of God. While the Synoptics probably remain more faithful to Jesus' terminology of the kingdom of God, the Fourth Gospel expresses the underlying reality of his teaching in language more suitable to the changing circumstances of discipleship in the world.

Repentance

Within the Synoptic Gospels, repentance is the necessary response to Jesus' preaching of the kingdom of God. In the Fourth Gospel, however, the only reference to repentance occurs in a quotation from Isa. 6:10 that the Johannine narrator employs to explain why the world did not believe in Jesus: "He has blinded their eyes and hardened their heart, so that they might not look with their eyes, and understand with their heart and turn (*straphōsin*)—and I would heal them" (12:40). But in the rest of the Gospel neither John the Baptist nor Jesus calls people to repentance. The absence of the Synoptic vocabulary for repentance (*metanoein* and *epistrephein*), however, does not mean that the concept of repentance is not present. Indeed, John's use of the quotation from Isaiah indicates that if the world had understood with its heart and seen with its eyes, it would have repented. Within the Fourth Gospel, the act of believing in Jesus as the one sent by the Father entails a profound change in one's life, a change the Synoptic Gospels call "repentance." For example, when Jesus tells Nicodemus that no one can enter the kingdom of God without being born from above (3:3, 7), Jesus is challenging him to a fundamental reorientation of life. Nicodemus must accept Jesus as the Son of Man who will be exalted upon the cross so that everyone who believes in him might have eternal life (3:14). Jesus' encounter with the Samaritan woman provides yet another example of repentance. In her conversation with Jesus, the woman grows in her understanding of who Jesus is: from a perception that he is a prophet (4:19) to a recognition that he is the Messiah (4:29). By the end of the narrative, she becomes a witness (4:39) to the one she had earlier mocked (4:9). In effect the woman has undergone a profound change in her life; she has moved from darkness to light. The story of the man born blind, as we have already seen, is another example of conversion to the light.

The theme of conversion or repentance is thus not absent from John's

Gospel, but it has been transformed. Whereas in the Synoptic Gospels, John the Baptist and Jesus call for deeds worthy of repentance, the kind of faith that the Johannine Jesus requires *is* repentance, moving from darkness to light. John and the Synoptics, however, point to a similar reality. Because repentance is related to the kingdom of God in the Synoptic Gospels, it entails a profound reorientation of one's life. In light of the in-breaking kingdom of God one must live from the point of view of God. What the Synoptics view as living for the kingdom of God, John views as living in the light.

Faith

In the Synoptic Gospels the object of faith is God, his good news about the kingdom, or Jesus' message of the kingdom. People who come to Jesus for healing must have faith in his power to perform miracles, but the Synoptic Jesus never requires them to believe in himself as does the Jesus of John's Gospel. In the Fourth Gospel, the object of faith is Jesus. One must believe in him, and one must believe certain things about him. The Johannine Jesus has taken the place of the kingdom of God.

There can be little doubt that the Synoptic Gospels stand closer to the original message of Jesus, but this does not mean that the Fourth Gospel has betrayed the substance of that message. When the Synoptic Jesus claims that the kingdom of God has "come to you" (Matt. 12:28; Luke 11:20), or when he tells the Pharisees that the kingdom of God is "among you" (Luke 17:21), he is establishing a relationship between himself and his message of the kingdom that the Fourth Gospel takes a step further. The messenger of the kingdom becomes the message of the kingdom so that the salvation promised by the kingdom is found in the person of Jesus. Thus the Johannine Jesus calls for faith in himself, and the Synoptic Jesus for faith in the kingdom. In both instances faith is the way to salvation.

Love

Love plays a prominent role in the Gospels of Matthew, Luke, and John, and a lesser role in the Gospel of Mark. However, whereas the Synoptics, especially Matthew, tend to relate love to Jesus' interpretation of the Mosaic law, John views it as a "new" commandment given from above that can only be realized in the community of believers. Once more the Fourth Gospel stands at a distance from the Synoptics. Does it also stand at a greater distance from the teaching of Jesus? Here my answer is ambivalent. On the one hand, the Synoptic presentation of Jesus as one who interpreted the law through love is firmly rooted in the tradition. There is little reason to doubt that Jesus proposed love for God (Deut. 6:4–5) and love for neighbor (Lev. 19:18) as the most important commandments of the law. And even though Mark does not report Jesus' teaching on love for one's enemies, this strenuous command seems consistent with a Jesus who made other harsh demands on his disciples. On the other hand, only the Fourth Evangelist reports Jesus' new commandment that his disciples should love one another. That Jesus should have required his disciples to love one another is not surprising. After all, in the Synoptics he calls his disciples to be servants to each other. Thus it is probable that Jesus called the disciples to mutual love, even though the Synoptics lack a specific teaching on this topic.

Once again, however, the Fourth Gospel has taken Jesus' teaching to a new level. Because this Gospel views Jesus as the one who reveals the Father, everything he says comes from the Father. Jesus' words become his commandments, which he brings as "gifts" from the Father. Among these gifts is the new commandment to love one another. While the object of this love is the believing community, the commandment is not meant to exclude others. Rather, within the Johannine logic this commandment can only be practiced by those who believe in Jesus. Thus it is a new commandment precisely because it is a gift from above. What the Synoptic Gospels see as a new teaching, or as a new interpretation of the law, the Fourth Gospel views as a gift from above. To this extent, the Four Gospels agree that Jesus' teaching on love is new and distinctive.

Discipleship

In all the Gospels discipleship is central. One lives the moral life within a community of disciples, not as an isolated individual. Both John and the Synoptics portray Jesus as calling disciples to be with him. There is, however, a greater emphasis upon following Jesus, surrendering one's life and taking up the cross, in the Synoptics. John is not unaware of this dimension of discipleship (12:25–26), but it does not play so prominent a role in his Gospel as in the Synoptics. Within the Fourth Gospel, discipleship is best characterized by "abiding" (*menein*) in Jesus. His first disciples ask him, "Rabbi, . . . where are you staying?" (*meneis*), and he responds, "Come and see" (1:38–39). As the Gospel progresses, they realize that he is the one who abides with God. In the farewell discourse, then, he tells them to abide (*menein*) in him as he abides in them (15:4). Indeed, "abiding" in Jesus is the dominant concept in Jesus' image of himself as the vine and the disciples as the branches.

As one might expect, the Johannine view of discipleship is rooted in its distinctive Christology. In the Fourth Gospel, Jesus' death is the hour of his glorification and return to the Father rather than a moment of humiliation and defeat. Consequently, the Johannine Jesus does not speak of taking up one's cross and following him, as does the Synoptic Jesus. Since Jesus' death is his moment of glorification, his disciples abide in him and share his victory over the world. The Johannine notion of abiding in Jesus, however, is not completely foreign to the Synoptics, for in describing Jesus' choice of the Twelve, the Markan Evangelist writes: "And he appointed twelve, whom he also named apostles, *to be with him*" (3:14). Mark, of course, does not have the Johannine concept of abiding in mind, but it is not difficult to understand how "being with" the earthly Jesus might be transformed into "abiding in" the risen Lord. In effect, the Fourth Gospel

116

has made discipleship accessible to a new generation of disciples for whom following the earthly Jesus is no longer possible.

Judgment

The notion of judgment plays an important role in the Synoptics, especially the Gospel of Matthew. They agree that Jesus will return as the exalted Son of Man at the parousia. Then the elect will be saved and sinners excluded from the kingdom. The Son of Man plays a different role in the Fourth Gospel, however. He is the one who has descended from heaven and will be exalted on the cross, drawing all things to himself. Although the Johannine Jesus knows of the eschatological hour when the dead will be raised and be repaid according to their deeds (5:28–29), he does not speak of the Son of Man as a returning judge. More prominent in John's Gospel, as we have seen, is the present dimension of judgment: those who believe are not judged, whereas those who do not believe are already judged.

Once more John stands at a certain distance from the Synoptics, but it is not as great a distance as one might imagine. When Jesus pronounces woes upon the Galilean cities that have not repented despite his ministry (Luke 10:13–15), and when he tells his disciples, "Whoever listens to you listens to me, and whoever rejects you rejects me, and whoever rejects me rejects the one who sent me" (Luke 10:16), he draws a correlation between a person's response to his ministry and future judgment. The Johannine Jesus has simply placed greater emphasis upon the present than has the Synoptic Jesus, but the essential point is the same: rejection of Jesus results in judgment.

I am not arguing that John has rewritten the Synoptics, nor am I suggesting that all differences between the two can be resolved. In my view, although they represent different streams of the Jesus tradition, both belong to the Jesus tradition. Both testify that the moral demands of Jesus are rooted in God's act of salvation (the kingdom of God—Jesus the Light and Life of the world). Both call for a radical change in the way one views life (repentance—believing in Jesus). Both require faith (in the kingdom of God—in Jesus). Both point to the importance of love in Jesus' teaching (as the proper way of interpreting the law—as Jesus' new commandment). Both emphasize the importance of living in a community of disciples (who take up their cross and follow Jesus—who abide in Jesus). Finally, both warn that judgment is related to one's response to Jesus (whether that judgment is to be in the future or now).

PART TWO
THE LEGACY OF PAUL

For the Synoptic Gospels, the ethical legacy of Jesus is intimately related to Jesus' proclamation of the kingdom of God. The dawning of the kingdom in Jesus' life and ministry and his promise of its final appearance summon people to a moral life characterized by love and faith. In the Fourth Gospel, the moral life is more explicitly related to the person of Jesus: the one who comes from the Father with a salvific revelation. The demands of the moral life in the Fourth Gospel may stand in tension with what is found in the Synoptic Gospels, but they do not contradict it. In the Johannine Gospel people must believe in Jesus as the one sent by the Father and live within a new community whose members love one another as Jesus loved them. While the emphasis is different in the ethical teaching of the Synoptic Jesus when compared to that of the Johannine Jesus, the call for faith and love remains constant.

We now turn to the ethical heritage of the other great figure of the New Testament, Paul of Tarsus, the apostle to the Gentiles. As in the case of Jesus, the moral teaching of Paul has had a tremendous impact upon later generations. It is Paul's ethical stance, alongside that attributed to Jesus, which dominates the New Testament and the Christian moral tradition. However, whereas Jesus' ethical heritage is mediated by the Four Gospels, Paul of Tarsus has left a written record of at least some of his teaching. Thus students of New Testament ethics have more immediate access to the moral teaching of Paul than they do to that of Jesus.

Paul's Letters

Despite the availability of letters from Paul's own hand, the study of his ethical teaching presents certain difficulties and challenges. First and foremost is the question of authorship. Many New Testament scholars agree that Paul did not write all the letters attributed to him in the New Testament. There is no dispute about Pauline authorship of seven letters. To the best of my knowledge, all scholars agree that Paul is the author of Romans, 1 and 2 Corinthians, Galatians, Philippians, 1 Thessalonians, and Philemon. The authorship of the remaining six letters (Ephesians, Colossians, 2 Thessalonians, 1 and 2 Timothy, and Titus) is disputed. When discussing Pauline ethics, therefore, it is advisable to make a distinction between the seven letters about which there is no disagreement, "the undisputed Paulines," and the six letters about which there is considerable discussion, the "disputed Paulines" or "the Deutero-Paulines." The latter represent Paul's ethical heritage in much the same way that the Four Gospels represent Jesus' ethical heritage. Just as the Gospels transmitted and adapted Jesus' moral teaching for the communities they addressed, so the Deutero-Pauline letters transmitted and adapted Paul's moral teaching for the communities they addressed. Paul's ethical heritage, then, comes to us in two ways: in his own writings and in writings attributed to him.

Second, the New Testament collection of Paul's writings has been edited by later compilers. The extent of this editing is disputed. Some scholars maintain that certain letters are composite documents: that is, they consist of two or more Pauline letters joined by later editors to form a single document, for example, 2 Corinthians and Philippians. Others speak of interpolations such as 1 Thess. 2:14–16 and 1 Cor. 14:34–36. Such theories are speculative and disputed, but those intent upon reconstructing the moral teaching of the historical Paul must wrestle with them as well as with the question of authorship.

Third, Paul's letters are "occasional" writings; that is, Paul wrote to answer specific questions raised by the churches and in response to problems they faced. Consequently, his letters must be read with a view to the situations they address. Paul's letters provide the church with an enduring body of teaching, but they were not written in a vacuum. To interpret them one must have some understanding of what occasioned them. Just as one must pay careful attention to the narrative dimension of the Gospels, so one must be attuned to the occasional nature of Paul's writings.

Finally, the relationship between Paul's letters and the Acts of the Apostles remains a point of continuing discussion. While many affirm the essential reliability of Acts as a source for understanding Paul's life and mission, others have all but disregarded it as a source, arguing that the only reliable source of information about Paul is what the apostle himself wrote. How, then, is one to employ information about Paul found in the Acts of the Apostles when discussing his letters? Cautiously, of course! The Lukan portrait of Paul is not pure fiction, but neither is it a scientific historical report. Paul's speeches in Acts, for example, are vehicles for Luke's theology.

Acts can be helpful in providing a framework for Paul's ministry, but what it reports must remain secondary to what the apostle himself writes.

Method and Approach

The course one charts for studying Paul's ethical teaching depends upon one's destination. For example, those attempting a historical reconstruction will place a premium upon questions of authorship, the chronology of Paul's life, the order in which he composed the letters, and the literary integrity and historical setting of each letter. The result will be a historical reconstruction of Paul's ethical teaching that primarily draws upon the undisputed Pauline writings. As for the Deutero-Paulines, they will be viewed as later developments in the Pauline tradition. My work on New Testament ethics, however, proceeds along a different path.

As in the case of the Gospels, my primary concern is the moral teaching of each individual writing rather than a reconstruction of what lies behind the writing. Just as I was chiefly interested in focusing upon the teaching of Jesus as found in the Gospels rather than in reconstructing the moral teaching of the historical Jesus, so I am more concerned with the ethical teaching of the individual letters attributed to Paul than in a historical reconstruction of his teaching.[1] This does not mean that I will abandon all critical sense, making no distinction between Paul's own writings and those attributed to him. Nor will I simply synthesize the moral teaching of the New Testament writings ascribed to Paul. There is no grand synthesis of Paul's ethical teaching in this book. Rather, the second part of this work is guided by the following presuppositions.

First, all the writings attributed to Paul in the New Testament are occasional, some to a greater degree than others. First Corinthians, for example, with its question-and-answer format, is clearly more occasional and situational than Romans, which approaches the form of a carefully composed essay. Consequently, I will describe the moral teaching of each writing in terms of its situation rather than attempt a synthesis of Paul's ethical thought. Readers can find such syntheses in the standard treatments of New Testament ethics. What is more difficult to find, despite the scholarly insistence upon the occasional nature of the Pauline letters, is a presentation of the moral teaching of each writing. There is a twofold danger in synthesizing Paul's thought. (1) When constructing a synthesis, it is difficult to resist viewing Paul' theology through the prism of Romans. As a result, the voices of other writings are often muted. (2) Most syntheses correctly distinguish between the undisputed Paulines and the Deutero-Paulines. But in doing so, they tend to establish a chasm between the undisputed Paulines and the Deutero-Pauline writings. When this happens, some, if not all, of the Deutero-Paulines are seen as a falling away from Paul's pristine theology. But this is not how the New Testament views the letters that are attributed to Paul. For the New Testament each letter makes a contribution. Therefore, I will respect the occasional nature of the letters ascribed to Paul so that each one will have an opportunity to speak.

Second, New Testament ethics need not be so concerned with questions of authorship, dating, compositional integrity, and so on, that it feels unable to proceed. I accept the distinction between the undisputed Paulines and those letters written in Paul's name. I am also aware of the problems regarding the literary integrity of certain letters as well as the difficulties in establishing the chronological order in which the letters were composed. However, since the goal of this study is to uncover the moral teaching of each letter as it is found in the New Testament, I have not organized my work solely in terms of historical considerations. For example, Paul may not be the author of 2 Thessalonians, but it makes more sense to discuss 1 and 2 Thessalonians together than to separate them, since they have similar themes. Again, I doubt that Paul is the author of the Pastorals, but I see little value in restricting a discussion of these letters to the differences between them and the undisputed Paulines. In terms of New Testament ethics, I have found it more helpful to read them as letters of Paul to Timothy and Titus, as does the New Testament itself, viewing each on its own terms rather than in light of Romans or Galatians.

Third, since ethics and theology are one in Paul's writings, one should not separate the two. Pauline ethics is an exercise in Pauline theology but in a different key. Therefore, it is necessary to pay attention to the whole of Paul's argument as well as to its specific moral instructions. Within Paul's letters, however, there are often paraenetic sections that address the moral life more directly. Without neglecting the theological vision of each letter, I will focus upon these sections when possible. This approach, of course, has its own problems since Pauline paraenesis is not always neatly defined. For example, while there is a defined section of paraenesis in Galatians, it is more difficult to find such a section in Corinthians. In the cases of 1 Thessalonians and the Pastorals the letters themselves are paraenetic. Despite these obstacles, I will focus upon Paul's paraenesis in its many forms, always remembering its close relationship to Paul's theology.

In the second part of this work I will examine the Thessalonian correspondence in terms of Paul's election theology and its importance for ethics (chapter 5); the Corinthian correspondence with its concern for the sanctification of the community and the moral example of Paul (chapter 6); Galatians and its teaching on living by the Spirit (chapter 7); Philippians and its call to imitate the examples of Christ and Paul in order to preserve the unity of the community (chapter 8); Romans and the ethical life required of those who have been justified by God's grace (chapter 9); Colossians and Ephesians with their exhortations that believers live according to their baptismal dignity (chapter 10); the Pastorals and the relationship they establish between authentic teaching and ethical behavior (chapter 11). A brief conclusion will summarize a series of observations about the moral life as portrayed in the ethical legacies of Jesus and Paul.

Although I have not dedicated a separate chapter to Paul's letter to Philemon, the major ethical question of that letter (slavery) is discussed in other parts of this work.

5

An Ethic of Election

The Letters to the Thessalonians

I begin my investigation of Paul's ethical legacy with a consideration of his Thessalonian correspondence because there is a general consensus that 1 Thessalonians is among the earliest, if not the earliest, of the Pauline letters.[2] While most Pauline students maintain that the apostle wrote this letter in the late 40s or early 50s, some argue for a date in the early 40s.[3] The authorship and date of 2 Thessalonians is more problematic. The majority of contemporary scholars now view the letter as pseudonymous and assign it a later date. This opinion is not unanimous, however, and although I am inclined to agree with it, I am hesitant to embrace it without reservation.[4] The decision to include a discussion of 2 Thessalonians in this chapter, however, is not based upon my hesitancy regarding the letter's pseudonymity but upon the common ethical themes that it shares with 1 Thessalonians. Even if 2 Thessalonians was not written by Paul, it has much in common with 1 Thessalonians. Therefore, it is advisable, as well as convenient, to study the two letters in a single chapter.

The early date of 1 Thessalonians is not the only reason for beginning our study of Pauline ethics with the Thessalonian correspondence. For 1 Thessalonians—and to some extent 2 Thessalonians—provides an outstanding example of New Testament paraenesis that makes extensive use of "election theology" to encourage and console the Thessalonian community.[5] In both letters Paul[6] reminds the members of his congregation that they are God's elect (1 Thess. 1:4; 2 Thess. 2:13), who have been called (1 Thess. 2:12; 4:7; 5:24; 2 Thess. 1:11; 2:14) and destined (1 Thess. 3:3; 5:9) by God to live in a manner worthy of their election. Because this election theology, with its summons to sanctification, underlies Paul's ethical thought, it provides an excellent entrée to his moral teaching.

Paul's election theology represents a stage in his missionary

123

preaching indebted to that community of believers which first nourished his faith: the church of Antioch in Syria.[7] Accordingly, some contend that the theology and ethics of 1 Thessalonians represent an "early Paul," whereas Philippians, the Corinthian correspondence, Galatians, and Romans witness to the more mature thought of a "later Paul."[8] To be sure, the Thessalonian correspondence does not make any reference to justification by faith, works of the law, the tension between spirit and flesh in the life of the believer, the sacramental dimension of the moral life, and so on. Nevertheless, there is a danger of positing too great a difference between the Thessalonian correspondence and Paul's later letters, as if the apostle made a major midcourse correction in his theology.

The Antioch incident (Gal. 2:11–21) and the controversy that occasioned his letter to the Galatians undoubtedly required Paul to reflect upon the relationship between the Christ event and the Mosaic law in a new way. Moreover, his resulting stance on justification by faith, apart from the works of the Mosaic law, clearly has important consequences for the moral life of believers. Paul's election theology in 1 Thessalonians, however, already implies that believers have been justified by God's grace since those chosen by God in Christ stand in the proper relationship to God.[9] It is more prudent, therefore, to view Paul's teaching on justification by faith as a development of his election theology occasioned by controversies with those who wanted to Judaize his Gentile converts, rather than as a dramatic change in his theology. The situation at Thessalonica did not necessitate a discussion of the law or justification. It did, however, prompt Paul to say a great deal about faith, as well as love and hope. While the ethics of Paul's other letters were often forged in the heat of crisis and controversy, this was not the case with 1 Thessalonians. The moral teaching of this letter affords an example of Pauline paraenesis and recalls the apostle's first moral directives to the church (1 Thess. 4:1–2). To that extent, it is a presentation of the moral life that is not determined by controversy and crisis.

ELECTION AND SANCTIFICATION:
FIRST THESSALONIANS

First Thessalonians provides an excellent example of how Paul tailored his moral teaching to the situations that occasioned his writings. According to this letter, he wanted to visit the Thessalonians, but Satan prevented him from doing so (2:17–18).[10] Consequently, he decided to send Timothy to strengthen and encourage the community's faith, lest the Thessalonians be shaken by the afflictions and persecutions they were experiencing (3:1–5).[11] The letter suggests that Timothy has recently returned with a favorable report of the community's faith and love which has greatly encouraged (*pareklēthēmen*; 3:7) Paul. Reassured by the steadfastness of the Thessalonians, he urges them to continue to stand firm. Paul would like to see them face to face and restore what is lacking in their faith (3:6–10), but since he cannot, he sends this letter.[12] Although there are differences, the situation described here has much in common with what Luke reports in the Acts of the Apostles (17:1–15) about Paul's mission to Thessalonica.[13]

First Thessalonians, then, is a paraenetic letter. It is not a response to a crisis within the community, nor is it concerned with rebuking or advising the community. Moreover, except for Paul's teaching on the parousia (4:13–18), which begins, "But we do not want you to be uninformed . . . ," the letter does not provide the Thessalonians with new teaching or instruction. As Abraham Malherbe notes, the letter presupposes that the Thessalonians already know what Paul encourages them to do.[14] Thus Paul repeatedly writes, "as you know" (1:5; 2:2, 5, 11; 3:4), or "you know" (2:1; 3:3; 4:2; 5:2). He tells the Thessalonians that there is no need for him to write to them (4:9; 5:1). Therefore, he simply reminds them of what he said and did among them (2:9; 3:6). Again and again, Paul writes that the Thessalonians are acting in a manner that conforms with the gospel (4:1, 10; 5:11). He merely wants them to do so all the more (4:1). As is the case with paraenetic letters generally, it is not Paul's purpose to alter the behavior of the Thessalonians so much as it is to encourage and urge them to maintain the course they have undertaken.[15]

Paraenesis is a continuing need in the Christian life. Those who have turned to the living and true God (1:9) must be encouraged to stay the course that they have undertaken. In the case of the Thessalonians the need for paraenesis was especially acute. By turning away from idols to serve the living and true God, they had alienated themselves from their former social situation. Like the Christians addressed in 1 Peter, they were now "aliens and exiles" in their own society. As a result, they needed to be resocialized into a new family, the church.[16] Therefore, Paul makes use of election theology and consistently addresses them as *adelphoi* (brothers and sisters).[17] On the one hand, the use of election theology reminds the Thessalonians that they belong to a new people who are loved by God (1:4). On the other, frequent references to them as *adelphoi* assure them that, as God's beloved people, they belong to a new family whose boundaries are no longer limited by blood and kinship. Alienated from one social group that is now persecuting them, they belong to a new social group in which they will experience love for one another and attain final salvation if they hold to their original faith. Thus there is a perfect "fit" between the situation of the Thessalonians and the type of letter that Paul addresses to them. Because they have turned to the living and true God, they are experiencing tribulation, just as Paul foretold (3:4). To prevent their being overcome by this affliction, Paul sends a letter of exhortation to remind them of their new family and urges them to maintain the course they have undertaken.

Moral Exhortation through Example (1 Thess. 1:2–3:13)

The manner in which Paul achieves his goal of exhorting and comforting the church at Thessalonica constitutes the rhetoric of this letter and has been a point of considerable debate.[18] For example, the beginning of chapter 4 (*loipon oun;* finally) clearly denotes a turning point after which Paul provides the Thessalonians with specific moral exhortation (4:1–5:24). But moral exhortation is not absent from the first part of this letter (1:2–3:13). Thus the question arises: What is the relationship between the first and second parts of the letter? Is the moral exhortation limited to the latter part of the letter? While the second half of 1 Thessalonians (4:1–5:24) contains the most explicit paraenesis of the letter, the first part (1:2–3:13) has an important paraenetic function as well. In addition to preparing for the paraenesis of 4:1–5:24, it develops a moral exhortation based upon the examples of the Lord, Paul, the churches of Judea, and the Thessalonians themselves. For this reason, I approach the entire letter as a sustained work of moral exhortation.

In the first part of the letter Paul (1) makes use of a double thanksgiving to express his gratitude for the continuing faith of the church; (2) reminds the Thessalonians of the manner in which he originally preached the gospel among them; (3) expresses his desire to see the community again; and (4) prays that God will increase their love and strengthen their hearts so that they will be blameless in holiness. The material can be outlined as follows.

First thanksgiving	1:2–10
The example of Paul	2:1–12
Second thanksgiving	2:13–16
Paul's desire to visit the church	2:17–3:10
Paul's prayer for the church	3:11–13

Paul's first thanksgiving. Nearly all of Paul's letters begin with a "thanksgiving" in which he expresses gratitude for the manifestation of God's grace in the community and indicates the major themes he will develop in the letter. First Thessalonians is no exception. Paul thanks God for the community, recalling its "work of faith," its "labor of love," and its "steadfastness of hope in our Lord Jesus Christ" (1:3). He knows that the Thessalonians, whom he now addresses as "brothers and sisters (*adelphoi*) beloved by God," are the beneficiaries of a divine election (*tēn eklogēn hymōn*) because the gospel he preached came to them in power and Spirit (1:4–5). Moreover, because they already know (*kathōs oidate*) what kind of a person Paul is, they have become imitators (*mimētai*) of him and of the Lord (1:6). In turn, they became an example (*typon*) for the churches of Macedonia and Achaia (1:7) by their faith. Having turned from idols to the living and true God, they now await the return of Jesus, who will rescue them from the coming wrath (*orgē;* 1:9–10). Thus this thanksgiving announces a number of ethical themes that Paul will develop in the rest of this letter: faith, love, and hope; divine election; imitation and example; waiting for the Lord's return.

At the outset of the letter, Paul reminds the Thessalonians of their new condition before God. God's election (*eklogē*) gave them a new status formerly reserved to Israel of old. Therefore, Paul addresses them as "beloved by God," language originally applied to Israel but now bestowed on the church.[19] This election resulted in God's call, which came to the Thessalonians through the gospel. Election and call undergird the whole of Paul's moral exhortation, and it was on the basis of their election that Paul originally urged the Thessalonians to lead a life worthy of the God who called them into his kingdom (2:12).

The Thessalonians confirmed their election when they turned (*epestrepsate*) from idols to the living and true God in their response to the gospel. Paul's description of their conversion (1:9–10) establishes a contrast between their former and present status. Then they did not know God, but now they serve the living and true God: the God of Israel, the God and Father of the Lord Jesus Christ (1:1). Because of this change in their status, Paul addresses the Gentile Thessalonians as if they are no longer Gentiles (see 4:5). Their conversion unites them with a new community of brothers and sisters in Christ. But it also has another effect. Because they believe in the living and true God, they now await the return of his Son, Jesus. In doing so they distinguish themselves from their contemporaries by their hope. When Paul gives the Thessalonians further instructions about the parousia, therefore, he does so lest they grieve as do others who have no hope (4:13). The others are those who do not believe.

Divine election, then, results in faith, hope, and love. But Paul is aware that these "virtues" are not simply infused. He speaks of the work of faith (*tou ergou tēs pisteōs*), the labor of love (*tou kopou tēs agapēs*), and the steadfastness of hope (*tēs hypomonēs tēs elpidos*; 1:3). The work of faith suggests an ongoing activity on the part of the Thessalonians,[20] something akin to the "obedience of faith" (Rom. 1:5; 16:26).[21] While Paul clearly praises the Thessalonians for their faith, he suggests that there is something lacking (1 Thess. 3:10): perhaps an adequate understanding of the parousia, the one new issue he addresses in this letter. As for love, Paul views it as a labor that comes with great effort and pain.[22] Thus he exhorts the community to increase and abound in love for one another (4:10). Finally, the steadfastness of hope clearly reflects the situation in which the Thessalonians now find themselves. Despite affliction and persecution, they must maintain their hope in the Lord's parousia.

In remaining steadfast in hope despite persecution, the Thessalonians became imitators of Paul and of the Lord, and because of their faith they became a model for other churches. Thus Paul establishes a chain of imitation that begins with the Lord and includes Paul, the Thessalonians, and other churches. Paul has imitated the Lord, who suffered affliction and persecution. The Thessalonians have imitated Paul, who suffered persecution, and now the Thessalonians have become a model for still other churches by their faith. In the next section, Paul will develop this theme further as he reminds the church of his initial mission among them.

To summarize, this thanksgiving announces several themes that are developed in the rest of the letter. In doing so, it outlines the contours of Paul's moral exhortation. That exhortation is based upon a theology of election that is incarnated in the life and example of Paul and the Thessalonians.

The moral example of Paul's life. Having reminded the Thessalonians how they became imitators of him and of the Lord by receiving the word despite persecution (1 Thess. 1:6), Paul recalls what kind of person he proved to be when he preached the gospel to them (2:1–12). In doing so, he not only presents himself as one whose conduct was beyond reproach, he offers himself as a model to be imitated.[23] Malherbe notes that the self-confidence with which Paul proffers himself as a model for imitation is extraordinary.[24] While ancient moral philosophers made use of imitation for moral exhortation, they rarely pointed to themselves as moral examples,[25] but that is precisely what Paul does because his confidence rests in the gospel. This section is punctuated by the phrases "you know" (2:1, 10) and "as you know" (2:2, 5), because Paul is reminding the Thessalonians of something they should already know. While some argue that Paul is defending himself against false charges and accusations here, it is more likely, as Malherbe has shown, that Paul is presenting himself as a "paradigm for the community," one whose way of life verifies the gospel.[26] In effect, Paul affirms that if the Thessalonians observe his behavior they will learn how to live in accordance with the gospel.

Paul describes his conduct in two ways. He recalls the circumstances in which he first preached the gospel, and he establishes a series of contrasts between what he did and did not do. As the Thessalonians already know (*kathōs oidate*), he declared the gospel to them despite great opposition, even though he had been shamefully treated in Philippi (compare 2:1–2 with Acts 16:20–24). The implication for the persecuted Thessalonians is evident: they too should declare the gospel despite their present circumstances. Next (1 Thess. 2:3–8), Paul draws a series of contrasts that emphasize the integrity of his original appeal (*paraklēsis*).

Not
> from deceit
> impure motives
> trickery
>
> > *But*
> >
> > > as one approved by God

Not
> to please mortals
>
> > *But*
> >
> > > to please God

Not
> with words of flattery
> a pretext for greed
> praise from mortals
>
> > *But*
> >
> > > as a nurse

128

Paul's rhetoric establishes a contrast between two kinds of preachers: those who are approved by and seek to please God, and those who seek to please mortals. The conduct proposed here, however, is not limited to preachers. In the next section, he describes his opponents in Judea as those *who do not please God* (2:15), and at the beginning of chapter 4 he reminds the Thessalonians that he taught them to live and *please God* (4:1). In other words, Paul's conduct is worthy of imitation by those who seek to live in accordance with the gospel.

Finally, Paul again reminds the Thessalonians of the circumstances in which he originally preached to them (2:9–11). While among them he labored and toiled so that he would not be a financial burden to them. His conduct was pure, upright, and blameless (*amemptōs*). He was like a father dealing with his own children, urging them to lead a life worthy of the God who called them. Nearly everything Paul mentions here foreshadows themes he will subsequently develop: the Thessalonians should (1) live quietly, mind their own affairs, and work with their own hands (4:11); (2) be blameless on the day of the parousia (3:13; 5:23); (3) encourage the fainthearted, help the weak, be patient with all (5:14). In his original exhortation to the Thessalonians, he urged them to live in a way worthy of the God who called them (2:12). This way is modeled by Paul's life.

Paul's second thanksgiving. Although it is unusual for Paul's letters to employ a second thanksgiving, the presence of another thanksgiving in 2:13–16 after that of 1:2–10 fits his rhetorical goal of encouraging the Thessalonians to stay on course. As in the first thanksgiving, he praises their behavior because they accepted the gospel as the word of God at work within them. Here again, Paul utilizes the motif of imitation but now in reference to the churches in Judea. By suffering at the hands of their fellow countrymen, the Thessalonians are imitating the churches in Judea who are enduring persecution from their compatriots. As in the first thanksgiving, Paul concludes with the theme of God's wrath. The Thessalonians will be rescued from God's wrath (1:10), but the wrath of God is coming upon those who displease God and hinder Paul from preaching the saving gospel to the Gentiles. The paraenetic goal of Paul's second thanksgiving, then, is to encourage the Thessalonians to maintain their course by comparing their sufferings with those of fellow believers in Judea. In effect, he shows his converts that they belong to a new family whose other members are suffering just as they are. Opposition to the gospel is to be expected, but final vindication awaits those who persevere to the end.

A prayer for the church. Paul concludes the first part of his letter with a prayer-wish for the church (1 Thess. 3:11–13) that foreshadows the moral exhortation he will develop in the last part of the letter. He prays that God who is Father and Jesus who is Lord will direct his way to them. Thus he reinforces a constant theme of this letter: although he cannot now visit the Thessalonians, he longs to see them. In the meantime, he prays (1) that their love for one another and for *all people* will abound just as Paul abounds in love for them, so that (2) their hearts may be blameless in holiness (*amemptous en hagiōsynē;* 3:15) in preparation for the Lord's parousia.

Sanctification, Mutual Love, Waiting in Hope (1 Thess. 4:1–5:24)

Having given thanks for what God has already accomplished in the Thessalonians and presented himself as worthy of imitation, Paul develops a more detailed paraenesis in the second part of his letter, focusing upon (1) the sanctification of the community, (2) mutual love, (3) and the need to wait quietly and vigilantly for the Lord's parousia. The second part of the letter, as I have already noted, is anticipated in the prayer-wish (3:11–13) that serves as a transition to this moral exhortation. Noting the similarity between this prayer-wish and the prayer-wish that concludes this extended moral exhortation (5:23), Raymond Collins suggests a chiastic arrangement of the material.[27]

> A. (3:11–13) a prayer for blamelessness with the parousia as its horizon
> > B. (4:1–8) a paraenesis grounded in the will of God and focusing on the work of the Spirit
> > > C. (4:9–12) a paraenesis introduced by "there is no need to write"
> > > > D. (4:13–18) those who have died and the parousia
> > > C. (4:5:1–11) a paraenesis introduced by "there is no need to write"
> > B. (5:12–22) a paraenesis grounded in the will of God and focusing on the work of the Spirit
> A. (5:23) a prayer for blamelessness with the parousia as its horizon

Collins's structure has several things to recommend it. First, the two prayer-wishes (3:11–13; 5:23) highlight the relationship between the first and second parts of the letter. Second, since Paul's teaching on the parousia (4:13–18) is the centerpiece of this exhortation, the structure points to the relationship between parousia and moral exhortation: the moral life is lived against the horizon of the Lord's imminent return.

Called to holiness. Paul begins his moral exhortation by reminding the Thessalonians of the ethical instructions he has already given to them (1 Thess. 4:1–2). What follows, therefore, is not a new teaching on the moral life but a reminder of an earlier, and undoubtedly more thorough, teaching. Paul writes that they should continue "as you learned (*parelabete*) from us how you ought to live and to please God," and again: "For you know what instructions (*paraggelias*) we gave you through the Lord Jesus." The apostle's initial preaching to the Thessalonians, therefore, was not simply an announcement of the gospel devoid of moral demands. In the beginning, there was moral instruction as well as kerygma.[28] As will become evident from our study of other Pauline letters, although believers are justified by faith, they are not thereby dispensed from the moral life. New life in Christ implies a new way of living.

In that original preaching Paul taught the Thessalonians how they should "walk" (*peripatein*)[29] and please God. In his view, the Thessalonians are continuing to do so, and his purpose in this letter is to encourage such conduct. Therefore, he reminds them of God's will, which is nothing less than their sanctification (*hagiasmos*), the demands of which Paul draws out in the verses that follow (4:3–8).

To most contemporary readers, sanctification or holiness means a surpassing level of moral achievement. People who live ethically blameless lives before God are called holy because they have sanctified their lives. While this active aspect of holiness is not absent from Paul's thought, it is not the main focus. The biblical tradition from which the apostle writes highlights God's activity. God is holy because God is totally other. When the holy God claims or sets aside something or someone for his purpose, that person or object is consecrated to God's service. Such persons and objects are holy because God has made them holy. In the case of the Thessalonians, their sanctification is grounded in God's election and call. So Paul reminds them that God did not call them to impurity (*akatharsia*) but in holiness or sanctification (*en hagiasmō*), which begins with God's electing call.

Those who have been sanctified, consecrated, and made holy must "walk" in a particular manner of life.[30] In the case of the Thessalonians, this means abstaining from *porneia* (a concept that we will encounter several times in Paul's letters) and refraining from exploiting others in this matter. The term *porneia* refers to "sexual immorality of any kind, often with the implication of prostitution."[31] Thus, depending upon the context in which it is found, it can mean "fornication," "sexual immorality," or "prostitution." It is the kind of behavior that especially characterizes the Gentiles, who do not know the God of Israel. Thus Paul exhorts the Thessalonians to control their bodies in holiness (*en hagiasmō*) and honor,[32] "not with lustful passion, like the Gentiles who do not know God" (4:5). Because the Thessalonians have turned from idols to the living and true God (1:9–10), they are to live as a holy and sanctified people so that they will be blameless at the Lord's parousia (3:13; 5:23). Paul establishes this admonition on the strongest possible foundation when he warns that those who reject this teaching reject the God who has given his Holy Spirit (4:8). Although he does not develop a doctrine of the Spirit here, as he will in later letters, he suggests that it is God's Spirit that enables believers to maintain their status as God's holy people.

To abound in mutual love. Having reminded the Thessalonians that their sanctification is God's will, Paul turns to the topic of mutual love (*philadelphia*; 1 Thess. 4:9–12), a theme previously announced (3:6, 12). Once more, he is not writing to rebuke his audience or to provide his readers with new teaching. He begins by noting that they have no need for him to write on this subject because they have been "taught by God" (*theodidaktoi*) to love one another (4:9). Moreover, they already love their brothers and sisters in the churches of Macedonia (northern Greece). But, in the spirit of paraenesis, he urges them to do so all the more.

The literal meaning of *philadelphia* is "brotherly love," and the Greek word normally refers to the love between blood relatives. In Thessalonians, however, this love extends beyond the boundaries of kinship. One's brothers and sisters are those who have been called by God, and they are worthy of the same kind of love that one would extend to a blood brother or sister. The call to mutual love, then, is based upon Paul's election theology and is part of his wider goal: to resocialize the Thessalonians into their new family, the church of God.

The exact meaning of *theodidaktoi* (taught by God) is a matter of considerable discussion. While some interpret it in terms of a philosophical or Hellenistic background,[33] others are inclined to understand it in light of Paul's Jewish heritage.[34] Whatever the precise meaning of the term, it clearly establishes the theological nature of Paul's moral teaching. The love that he urges the Thessalonians to practice is somehow related to divine activity. The Thessalonians have learned this love by the power of God's spirit at work within them (4:8) and from the example of Christ, "who died for us, so that whether we are awake or asleep we may live with him" (5:10). The term further implies that believers have access to a quality of love unavailable to those who do not know the living and true God.

In addition to urging the Thessalonians to practice this love even more, Paul exhorts them to aspire to live quietly, to mind their own affairs, and to work with their hands as he previously directed them so that they will behave properly toward outsiders, not being dependent upon anyone (4:11–12). The advice given here is not unrelated to what Paul has just said about mutual love. Moreover, it prepares for what he will write about the parousia. First, by minding their own affairs and working with their hands, the Thessalonians will assure the good order of their community, a subject that Paul will soon discuss (5:12–24). Such behavior is a concrete example of what Paul means by love. Second, in exhorting the community to aspire to live quietly (*euschēmonōs*), he has more in mind than a quiet philosophical withdrawal from the world. This "quiet life" is an apocalyptic withdrawal, as Calvin Roetzel suggests.[35] Like other apocalyptic groups for whom the form of this world is passing away, the Thessalonians must wait in quiet reliance upon God for Jesus' parousia. As they wait, their life is to be distinguished by mutual love and quiet work.

Waiting in hope. Throughout 1 Thessalonians there have been allusions to Jesus' parousia. It is only in the midst of this extended moral exhortation, however, that the apostle explicitly deals with this topic. Paul's concern is twofold. First, he must explain that those who have already died will not be at a disadvantage when Christ returns, because those who have believed in Christ will be raised with him (4:13–18). Second, although he says that there is no need for him to write on the topic, Paul must exhort the Thessalonians to live soberly as "children of light" and "children of the day" since the day of the Lord's parousia will come suddenly and unexpectedly (5:1–11). Both sections conclude with the same refrain: "therefore encourage one another." Paul not only gives moral exhortation, he expects the community to do the same in his absence.[36]

Paul's description of the Thessalonians as "children of light" and "children of the day," with its attendant exhortation to keep awake and be sober (5:5–6), reminds the Thessalonians that they are engaged in an eschatological battle. While they belong to the day, those outside of the community are in darkness and belong to the night. To survive this battle, the Thessalonians must put on "the breastplate of faith and love, and for a helmet the hope of salvation" (5:8), for God has not destined them for wrath but for salvation (5:8). The reference to faith, hope, and love recalls the Thessalonians' work of faith, their labor of love, and the steadfastness of their hope (1:3). By saying that they have been destined (*etheto*) for salvation, Paul reminds them of their divine election, made possible because Jesus died on their behalf (5:9–10).

The juxtaposition of faith, love, and hope as armor for divine battle on the one hand, and the allusion to election on the other, highlight two aspects of the moral life. First, people are chosen and elected. Second, they must work and struggle so that their election will come to completion. Thus the moral life is both gift and task. This double aspect of the moral life is intimately related to the Lord's parousia. Something has already happened in Christ so that believers are holy and sanctified, but the completion of their sanctification is yet to occur. Until then "the saints" must be vigilant so that they will be blameless at the coming of their Lord (3:13; 5:23).

Community matters. In any discussion of Pauline ethics, it is easy to overlook the most obvious fact: Paul directs his exhortation to a community of believers. The paraenesis of moral philosophers, by contrast, was usually aimed at individuals, for example, the letters of Seneca to Lucillius. For Paul, then, one lives the moral life within the context of a nurturing community. Except for the letter to Philemon, the undisputed Pauline letters are not addressed to individuals but to communities of believers. And even in the case of Philemon, the letter is to be read in the context of the community.

In the final section of his letter (5:12–22) Paul turns his attention to specific community matters. First, the Thessalonians are to respect those who labor among them. Such people are to be esteemed in love because of their work (5:12–13). Second, all members of the community must engage in the work of exhortation. Therefore, Paul urges them to admonish the disorderly (*tous ataktous*),[37] encourage the faint-hearted, help the weak, and be patient toward all (5:14). In an important statement on nonretaliation, he urges the community to pursue what is good for one another *and for all* rather than to render evil for evil (5:15; cf. Rom 12:17). Finally in a series of staccato-like instructions (5:16–22), he exhorts the community to rejoice, pray, give thanks, not extinguish the Spirit or despise prophecy, test everything, hold on to what is good, and abstain from every form of evil (*ponērou*). In a word, the Thessalonian community must live as God's sanctified people. Consequently, Paul concludes with a prayer that God will completely sanctify them in order that they will stand blameless on the day of the Lord's parousia (5:23).

To summarize, a community sanctified by God's election is the setting in which believers are nurtured to live in accordance with the gospel. A life of holiness is impossible apart from, and outside of, this community.

PAUL'S EXAMPLE:
SECOND THESSALONIANS

The relationship of 1 and 2 Thessalonians is problematic since a number of Pauline scholars view 2 Thessalonians as Deutero-Pauline. Although this opinion is the dominant view of contemporary scholarship, " the authorship of 2 Thessalonians is truly an open question."[38] However, even if 2 Thessalonians is not from Paul's hand, it clearly adopts and presupposes important ethical themes from 1 Thessalonians such as the elected status of the Thessalonians (2 Thess. 1:11; 2:13–14) and the value of imitating Paul, who worked night and day among them (3:7–10). In a word, 2 Thessalonians supposes familiarity with 1 Thessalonians. Moreover, while contemporary scholars often highlight tensions between the two letters, such as their different presentations of the parousia, the author of this letter clearly views himself as developing what has already been said in 1 Thessalonians rather than as contradicting it. For these reasons, I treat 2 Thessalonians at this point rather than in a separate discussion of Deutero-Pauline literature, as is done in some works.[39] For the sake of convenience, and in order to highlight the thematic unity of the two letters, I refer to its author as Paul.

Second Thessalonians presupposes a situation of ongoing affliction and persecution at Thessalonica (1:5–6). Whereas 1 Thessalonians gives the impression that the church is relatively free of problems, 2 Thessalonians suggests that Paul must deal with two problems. First, there is a report or letter claiming that "the day of the Lord is already here" (2:1–2). Consequently, Paul must remind the Thessalonians of what he told them while still with them: the Lord's parousia will not take place until the great apostasy has occurred and the lawless one has made his appearance (2:1–12). Therefore they must stand firm and hold fast to the traditions they were taught (2:15). Second, Paul must deal with the disorderly (*ataktoi*) at Thessalonica. Such people were alluded to in 1 Thessalonians (5:14), but in this letter their conduct has become a major problem for the community. Paul commands the community to keep away from such people (3:6, 14–15); he reminds the community of his own example (3:7–10); and he specifically commands the *ataktoi* to work quietly and earn their own living (3:12). Exactly who the disorderly were and why they behaved as they did remain among the most intractable questions posed by this letter.[40]

In response to these difficulties, Paul sends a letter that is both paraenetic and deliberative.[41] Like 1 Thessalonians, it exhorts its readers to maintain the course of action they have undertaken. So Paul tells them that their afflictions are intended to make them worthy of the kingdom of God for which they are suffering (1:5). Unlike 1 Thessalonians, however, this letter does not make frequent use of phrases such as "you know" or "as you know." Nor does it make much use of the verb *parakaleō* (I appeal, I urge, I exhort). Instead, Paul commands (*paraggellō*) the Thessalonians to act or behave in a specific way, giving the letter a more directive character.[42] In addition to encouraging his converts, Paul must persuade the *ataktoi* to alter their behavior.

God's Chosen People

In discussing the ethics of 2 Thessalonians, Willi Marxsen writes that "the author offers no indicative but only imperatives."[43] Marxsen then argues that in this letter salvation can only be expected in the future. In part, he is correct since Paul must dissuade the Thessalonians from embracing a view that proclaims that the parousia is already here (2:1). To argue that the indicative of salvation is no longer present in this letter, however, overlooks the election theology that continues to play an important role in it. As in 1 Thessalonians, Paul's ethical imperatives presuppose a changed status in the life of the Thessalonians. They form a congregation of people who have been called by God. Thus Paul addresses them as "the church of the Thessalonians in God our Father and the Lord Jesus Christ" (1:1). Although they are Gentiles, they have become God's people.

Paul develops this election theology in two thanksgiving statements that enclose his teaching on the day of the Lord. In the first (1:3–12), he thanks God for the love of the Thessalonians that is increasing and for the steadfastness of their faith during all their persecutions and afflictions (1:3–4). He assures them that such trials are meant to make them worthy of the kingdom of God and that God will eventually punish those who are now afflicting them when the Lord Jesus returns at his parousia (1:5–10). Paul then concludes with a prayer-wish: "that our God will make you [the Thessalonians] worthy of his call (*axiōsē tēs klēseōs*) and will fulfill by his power every good resolve and work of faith (*ergon pisteōs*), so that the name of our Lord Jesus may be glorified in you, and you in him, according to the grace of our God and the Lord Jesus Christ" (1:11–12).

In a second thanksgiving (2:13–14), immediately after his discussion about the day of the Lord (2:1–12), Paul says he must continually give thanks because God chose them (*heilato hymas ho theos*) as the first fruits (*aparchēn*) "for salvation through sanctification by the Spirit (*en hagiasmō pneumatos*)." In this thanksgiving Paul calls the Thessalonians "beloved by the Lord" (compare Deut. 33:12, where this epithet is used of Benjamin), saying that God called (*ekalesen*) them through the proclamation of the gospel so that they might obtain the glory of the Lord Jesus Christ.

The election theology of these thanksgivings plays an important role in Paul's moral exhortation. Lest the Thessalonians become overwhelmed by the persecution and affliction they are enduring, he reminds them that they have been called by God, and only God can make them worthy of this call (1:11). Lest the Thessalonians fall prey to a false understanding of the parousia, which claims that the day of the Lord is already here, he writes that God chose them as the first fruits for salvation through sanctification by the Spirit. That salvation is not yet complete, for the day of the Lord has not yet arrived, but God has already called them to it by the gospel. Only when Paul has reminded the Thessalonians of their election does he command them: "So then, brothers and sisters, stand firm and hold fast to the traditions that you were taught by us, either by word of mouth or by our letter" (2:15). As in 1 Thessalonians, there is an intimate relationship between parousia and election theology. Election points to the coming parousia, which in turn requires believers to conduct themselves in a manner that accords with the gospel. In this way, the imperative is grounded in the indicative of Paul's election theology.

Imitating Paul's Example

Second Thessalonians concludes with a rather extended exhortation in which Paul takes up the question of the disorderly (3:1–16). Because the apostle never makes an explicit connection between this disorderly conduct and the mistaken notion that the day of the Lord is already here, Pauline scholars interpret the situation that Paul addresses in one of two ways. While some view the conduct of the *ataktoi* as deriving from this mistaken notion of the parousia (the day of the Lord is here, there is no need to work), others maintain that the problem of the disorderly is a social problem unrelated to the parousia (the poor within the community have become dependent upon the well-to-do). In either case, it is evident that Paul contrasts his behavior to that of the *ataktoi* and presents himself as a model to be imitated.

Although I have called this section an extended exhortation, it is in fact the language of ordering and commanding that dominates (3:4, 6, 10, 12). Paul is confident that the Thessalonians are doing what he *commanded* (3:4), but now he *commands* them to avoid believers who are living disorderly lives that do not correspond to the traditions Paul gave the community (3:6). Paul *commanded* that those who did not work should not eat (3:10); that is, they should not live off the work of others. Consequently, he urges and *commands* such people to work quietly and eat their own bread (compare 1 Thess. 4:11).

To illustrate what he means, Paul reminds the Thessalonians of what they already know: how they ought to imitate him (3:7; compare 1 Thess. 1:6; 2:14). While among them, Paul toiled and labored night and day so that he would not be a burden to the Thessalonians (3:8; compare 1 Thess. 2:9). While some may think that Paul worked for his own living because he did not have the authority to require support from the community, he assures them that he had different motives. By working for a living he provided the Thessalonians with an example (*typon*) to be imitated: as he worked for his own bread, so must they (3:9).

The distinguishing characteristic of the disorderly, in contrast to Paul, is their refusal to work quietly with their own hands for their bread. Instead of busily working (*ergazomenous*) they have become busybodies (*perierga-zomenous*; 3:11). Whereas Paul's behavior is worthy of imitation because it

136

illustrates how one is to live the gospel, the behavior of the *ataktoi* contradicts the gospel. Thus Paul instructs the Thessalonians not to mingle with such people, so that they will be ashamed of their disorderly lives (3:15).

Those who are believers live in the time between their call, which made them God's chosen people, and the day of the Lord when the fullness of salvation will be revealed. In this time between "already" and "not yet," they must not grow weary of doing what is right (3:13). This clearly includes working quietly with one's own hands.

PAUL'S MORAL TEACHING: A SUMMARY STATEMENT

The Thessalonian correspondence provides an outstanding example of moral exhortation to a community of recent converts for whom the parousia is still a vibrant hope. In these letters Paul consistently reminds the community of its elected status. God has called the Thessalonians to a life of sanctification so that they can stand blameless before the Lord on the day of his parousia. To maintain their elected status, they must shun all immorality and uncleanness, and persevere in faith, love, and hope. In their daily lives, they must work quietly as they wait for the Lord's return. Should they need an illustration of what it means to live in accordance with the gospel, they will find it in Paul.

6

Ethics for the
Sanctified Community

The Letters to the Corinthians

y decision to study the moral teaching of Paul's Corinthian correspondence at this point is based upon two considerations, one chronological and the other thematic. First, in terms of chronology, the Corinthian correspondence comes after 1 Thessalonians, and if Paul wrote 2 Thessalonians, after it as well. According to the Acts of the Apostles, he began his ministry in Corinth shortly after leaving Thessalonica. It was probably during this period that he wrote to the Thessalonians. Only later, during his Ephesian ministry, did Paul write to the Corinthians.[1] Second, and more importantly, the Corinthian and Thessalonian letters share several moral or ethical themes, such as the sanctification of the church with the attendant imperative to shun immorality, the importance of love for building up the community, and Paul's presentation of himself as someone whose life is worthy of imitation. In effect the Corinthian correspondence provides a more developed form of the moral exhortation found in the letters to the Thessalonians.

The moral exhortation of the Corinthian correspondence, however, is more than a development of older themes. Whereas the relationship between Paul and the Thessalonians was essentially sound, so that he wrote to encourage and exhort his new converts, Paul finds himself in an entirely new situation when addressing the Corinthians. On the one hand, these letters suggest a deteriorating relationship between the apostle and the Corinthians, who challenge and question his apostolic authority. On the other hand, Paul must do more than exhort and encourage the Corinthians to maintain the course they have undertaken. Because their community suffers from social and moral problems, he must advise, admonish, rebuke, and reproach the congregation as well as exhort and console it. In doing do, he develops familiar ethical themes in new ways, thereby disclosing the process of his moral reasoning.[2]

Given the variety of moral and social issues to which Paul had to respond, it is not surprising that the Corinthian correspondence is both stimulating and challenging. In terms of length, these letters are the largest body of Paul's writings to a single church, and in no other Pauline letter is such a variety of issues addressed: factions and divisions, incest, lawsuits, prostitution, marriage, divorce, celibacy, idolatry, and so on. Small wonder then that biblicists have devoted so much attention to these letters when considering Paul's ethics.[3] Despite the many issues he addresses, however, Paul repeatedly returns to three themes: (1) the moral implications of being God's chosen and sanctified people; (2) the importance of building up the community of the church through love; and (3) the moral example of his own life, which embodies the gospel and allows Paul to say, "be imitators of me" (1 Cor. 4:16; 11:1). I will examine texts that illustrate how Paul employs these themes in developing his ethical stance. First, however, it is necessary to discuss certain literary and historical questions important for the interpretation of these letters.

PAUL AND THE CHURCH AT CORINTH

The Corinthian correspondence raises two related questions: How many letters did Paul write to the Corinthians? What historical circumstances occasioned this correspondence? The answers to these questions are most important, of course, for those interested in a historical reconstruction of Paul's Corinthian ministry, but they also have implications for New Testament ethics since they provide a concrete historical context for interpreting Paul's moral instruction.

Generally speaking, there is more agreement about the literary unity of 1 Corinthians than of 2 Corinthians.[4] In the view of many scholars Paul wrote 1 Corinthians in light of (1) an oral report delivered to him by "Chloe's people" about discord within the community (1 Cor. 1:11), and (2) a letter from the Corinthians that was delivered, perhaps by Stephanas, Fortunatus, and Achaicus (16:17). *For the most part,* Paul responds to the content of the oral report in the first part of his letter (1:10–6:20) and to the letter from the Corinthians in the second part of this correspondence (7:1–16:24).[5] Despite its title, however, 1 Corinthians is not the first letter that Paul sent to the Corinthians, as is clear from a statement he makes when discussing immoral people: "I wrote to you *in my letter* not to associate with sexually immoral persons" (5:9). In a letter that we no longer possess, therefore, Paul had already warned the Corinthians about *porneia.* The background to 1 Corinthians can be summarized as follows.

1. Paul writes a letter to the Corinthians that we no longer possess (1 Cor. 5:9).
2. The Corinthians write a letter to Paul in which they express their opinion about, or ask questions about, the following: sexual abstinence, marriage, divorce, attendance at temple

banquets, spiritual gifts, the resurrection of the dead, the collection for Jerusalem, and Apollos.

3. Paul learns of factions within the community and of a case of gross immorality, from Chloe's people (1:11).
4. In response to this oral report and the letter from the Corinthians, Paul writes 1 Corinthians.
5. Paul sends Timothy to Corinth (4:17; 16:10).

While there is rather general agreement about the above scenario for 1 Corinthians, there is no unanimity when it comes to 2 Corinthians. A goodly number of scholars believe that, in its present form, the letter is a composite of several Pauline letters to Corinth. There is, however, no consensus about the letter's composition. For example, many argue that 2 Corinthians 10—13 was once a separate letter in which Paul responded to criticism of his ministry made by "false apostles" (11:13).

As for chapters 1—9, the disagreement is even more pronounced. While many defend the integrity of these chapters, others maintain that they consist of fragments from several letters addressed to the Corinthians during different stages of the conflict between Paul and the community. Some, for example, propose that 2 Cor. 2:14–7:4 represents a letter from an early stage of the conflict in which Paul discussed the nature of his ministry. When this letter failed to resolve the matter, he sent a harsh apologetic letter (10:1–13:13). After Titus reported that this letter led to repentance (7:5–16), Paul then wrote a letter of reconciliation (1:1–2:13; 7:5–16; 8:1–9:15). Later, according to those who support this partition theory, a scribe joined these fragments together and formed what is now called 2 Corinthians.[6] I subscribe to a simpler scenario that can be summarized as follows.[7]

1. Foreign missionaries come to Corinth with letters of recommendation and criticize Paul's ministry (see 3:1).
2. Learning of the problem, Paul visits the community but his visit ends in humiliation (2:1).
3. Paul sends the community a harsh letter written in tears, a letter that we no longer have (2:3–4; 7:8, 12). He also sends Titus to the community (2:12–13; 7:5–16).
4. Titus informs Paul that the letter has resulted in the community's repentance (7:5–16), leading Paul to write another letter in which he discusses the nature of his ministry, calls for reconciliation, and takes up the question of the Jerusalem collection (chapters 1—9).
5. Controversy breaks out anew, causing Paul to write yet another letter (chapters 10—13).

Even this superficial survey indicates that 1 and 2 Corinthians are very different kinds of letters. Whereas 1 Corinthians appears to be a literary unity that deals with a number of social questions with important ethical implications, 2 Corinthians is probably a composite letter and focuses upon the nature of Paul's apostleship. In 1 Corinthians the apostle rebukes and admonishes the Corinthians for their behavior. In 2 Corinthians he must defend *his* behavior and explain the nature of his apostleship. From one point of view, 1 Corinthians presents a richer field from which to mine Pauline ethics, but there is an unexpected dividend found in 2 Corinthians, where the apostle proposes himself as the model apostle.

SAFEGUARDING THE SANCTIFIED COMMUNITY: FIRST CORINTHIANS

The material of 1 Corinthians cannot be neatly divided into doctrinal and ethical sections.[8] More than in any other letter, nearly everything that Paul discusses here has immediate moral implications. Thus 1 Corinthians contains an embarrassment of riches as regards moral instruction. As in all of Paul's letters, however, morality is rooted in his exposition of the gospel, and his exposition of the gospel has moral implications. In what follows, I will consider a number of texts that exemplify this process, in order to illuminate the process of Paul's moral reasoning.

A Community Called and Sanctified (1 Cor. 1:1–2, 4–9)

As we have already seen in the Thessalonian correspondence, Paul constantly reminds his readers of their Christian identity since their new status before God has ethical implications for their behavior. In 1 Corinthians, as in the letters to the Thessalonians, he also recalls the elected and sanctified status of his converts.[9] Although Gentiles by birth, they now form the church of God in Corinth and are in a state of permanent consecration,[10] sanctified in and by Christ (*hēgiasmenois en Christō Iēsou*). As such they are called to be "saints" (*klētois hagiois*) by living out this state of consecration. In doing so, they are united with all those, in every place, who call upon the name of the Lord (1:2). In sum, Paul affirms that his Gentile converts belong to a cultic and holy people that is God's possession and upon whom God alone has exclusive rights. As the letter unfolds, Paul will draw out the moral implications of these statements.

In thanking God for this community of believers (1:4–9), Paul further defines their identity. They have been enriched with every kind of speech and knowledge and are not lacking in any spiritual gift as they await the revelation of their Lord. So Paul is confident that God will strengthen the community in order that it will be blameless (*anegklētous*) on the day of the Lord's parousia. Such blamelessness entails living in the state of holiness or consecration that has been bestowed upon the community because of its elected status. Paul concludes by assuring the Corinthians of the reliability of the God (*pistos ho theos*) who called them into communion (*eis koinōnian*) with his Son.[11]

141

Those familiar with the rest of this letter will notice the relationship between Paul's description of the Corinthians and the problems that he will address in it. Paul identifies the Corinthians as a consecrated people endowed with spiritual gifts, awaiting the Lord's parousia. But in what follows, it is evident that some are endangering their consecrated status and *koinōnia* with God's Son, that spiritual gifts have become a cause of division and strife, and that those who question the bodily resurrection of the dead have an insufficient understanding of the parousia. At the outset of this letter, then, Paul points to many of the issues he will later address. He also indicates how he will deal with these problems: he will draw out the doctrinal and ethical implications of what it means to be God's chosen people, consecrated and set aside for God.

Elected in Light of the Cross
(1 Cor. 1:10–4:21)

Paul states the goal of his instruction in the opening verse of this section.

> Now I appeal (*parakalō*) to you, brothers and sisters, by the name of our Lord Jesus Christ, that all of you be in agreement and that there be no divisions among you, but that you be united in the same mind and the same purpose (1:10).

At the end of this section, he concludes with yet another appeal that, if heeded, will result in this desired unity.

> I appeal (*parakalō*) to you, then, be imitators of me (4:16).

The reason for Paul's appeal is not difficult to discern. According to a report from Chloe's people, there are rivalries and quarrels (*erides*) among the Corinthians.[12] Some members of the community have laid claim to the wisdom (*sophia*) of the apostles who baptized and preached to them. In making such claims, they have caused rivalries, each faction supposing that the gospel it received from a particular apostle represents a wisdom superior to that preached by other apostles. Because of their superior wisdom, the Corinthians also understand themselves as *pneumatikoi* (spiritual people). In Paul's view, however, they are still *sarkikoi* (carnal people), mere infants in Christ (3:1), because there is jealousy and quarreling among them (3:3). Their alleged wisdom cannot be authentic since it threatens to destroy the church's unity. What then is Christian wisdom? To answer this question Paul turns to his election theology, but now as seen in light of the cross.

According to Paul, the "word of the cross," the proclamation of the crucified Messiah, is God's wisdom. However, to the Jewish world this message is a stumbling block and to the Gentile world utter folly, even though it is the power and wisdom of God for all who are being saved. In Christ,

God has contradicted human power and wisdom by identifying wisdom and power with what the world considers foolish and weak: the cross of Christ.

To establish his point, Paul reminds the Corinthians of their election (1:26–28), which exemplifies God's paradoxical wisdom because God chose the foolish to shame the wise, the weak to shame the strong, the low and the despised in the world "to reduce to nothing things that are" (1:28).[13] Thus Christ has become their righteousness (*dikaiosynē*), their holiness (*hagiasmos*), and their redemption (*apolytrōsis;* 1:31).

Paul's own preaching among the Corinthians also exemplifies God's wisdom, since he announced the gospel to them "in weakness and in fear and in much trembling" (2:3). Thus their faith rests upon the power of God rather than upon an eloquent proclamation of human wisdom (2:5). The first task of the Corinthians, then, is to learn that God's wisdom is found in the weakness and folly of the cross.

To teach this lesson, Paul points to the pattern of life that he and Apollos exemplify. They are mere servants (*diakonoi*) through whom the Corinthians have believed (3:5). Paul planted, Apollos watered the plant, but God gave it the growth. Paul and Apollos are God's coworkers, and the Corinthian community is God's field and building (3:9). The Spirit of God dwells in them so that they are the holy temple of God (*ho gar naos tou theou hagios estin;* 3:17). By calling the Corinthians the temple of God, Paul again invokes his election theology, reminding them that they are a holy people consecrated and devoted to God.[14] And by warning them that God will destroy the person who destroys God's temple (which the Corinthians are), he admonishes those who are endangering the unity of the community by their claims to a superior wisdom. In contrast to such worldly wisdom, wisdom rooted in the "word of the cross" builds up rather than tears down the holy building of God.

The Corinthians must think of apostles as servants and stewards of God's ministry (4:1) rather than as spiritual guides (4:15) who initiated them into wisdom. In the case of Paul and Apollos, for example, the word of the cross is exemplified in their lives. While the Corinthians view themselves as wise, strong, and held in honor, Paul and Apollos are fools for the sake of Christ, weak, and held in disrepute (4:10). In the first of many "hardship lists" found in the Corinthian correspondence (4:9–13), Paul points to the sorry spectacle that distinguishes those who are ministers of Christ from those who are not.[15] Ministers of Christ go hungry and thirsty, are poorly clad, beaten, and homeless. They grow weak from laboring with their own hands. But it is their ministry, despised and rejected by the world, that cleanses and purifies the world![16]

Put another way, the Corinthians are standing on the wrong side of the equation. Instead of exemplifying the weakness and foolishness of the cross, they are aligning themselves with a wisdom that manifests a merely worldly point of view. As a result, their understanding of wisdom threatens to lead them into immoral and unethical conduct. As will become even more apparent in the pastoral epistles, good conduct is related to sound teaching. If the Corinthians are to live as a sanctified people and as the temple of God, they must appreciate their elected status in light of the cross. Should they have any question of what this status means for their behavior, they should look to Paul and Apollos. Such is the implication of Paul's words, "I appeal to you, then, be imitators of me" (4:16).

Moral Implications of Election and Sanctification (1 Cor. 5:1–7:40)

The material in chapters 5—7 represents the final part of Paul's response to the oral report that he received from Chloe's people (5:1–6:20) and the beginning of his response to a letter that the Corinthians had sent to him (7:1–40). The two units, however, have much in common. In both, Paul draws out the implications of what it means to be God's holy and elected people, warning the community to avoid sexual immorality (*porneia*) lest it endanger the community's sanctified status. Here, as in few other places, the apostle discloses his understanding of the sanctified community's relationship to the world. Though the world is filled with immoral people and is passing away, the community need not flee from the world. In regard to its own members, however, the community is held to a different standard. Those who are holy must not associate with those who identify themselves as believers but live immorally.

The material in this section consists of a variety of problems and questions: a serious case of sexual immorality (5:1–13); lawsuits among members of the community (6:1–11); prostitution (6:12–20); sexual abstinence, marriage, and divorce (7:1–40). From Paul's point of view, these problems and questions have arisen because the Corinthians have not understood the wisdom of the cross and the implications of their elected status, which has made them a sanctified community. In dealing with these issues, therefore, he returns to his election theology introduced in the first part of this letter. Moreover, he implies that the Corinthians are not truly wise, otherwise they would not act as they do.[17]

The consequences of arrogance (5:1–6:20). In defining the nature of Christian wisdom (1:10–4:21), one of Paul's purposes was to protect the Corinthians from arrogance (4:6). Thus he asks those who have become arrogant if they want him to come "with a stick, or with love in a spirit of gentleness?" (4:21). From Paul's point of view, the arrogance of the Corinthians is rooted in their failure to grasp the wisdom of the cross. Three examples illustrate their moral and ethical failure. First, they have allowed a gross case of *porneia* in their midst: a man living with his father's wife (5:1–13). In Paul's view, the case is so serious that such immorality is not even found among the Gentiles (5:1). By this rebuke, Paul implicitly reminds the Corinthians of their elected status, for although they are ethnically Gentiles they have become God's sanctified people. The most serious aspect of the case, however, is the failure of the community to condemn the perpetrator. Instead of expelling him from its midst, the community is arrogant (*pephysiōmenoi;* 5:2). The Corinthians no longer view themselves as constrained by the ordinary rules of morality.

The second example is closely related to the first. Some members of the community are consorting with prostitutes (6:12–20). Again, the Corinthians have found a justification for their behavior. Viewing themselves as spirit-endowed people already living in the eschaton, they employ slogans such as "all things are lawful for me" (6:12) to justify their behavior. Considering such sexual relationships to be as casual as the relationship between the body and the ingesting of food, they do not understand the importance of the body in sexual matters.

The third example actually is cited between these two cases of *porneia*. Some members of the community are taking each other to court, where they allow unbelievers to judge between them (6:1–11). On first reading, it may appear that there is no relationship between this and the two cases of *porneia* noted above, but the material is related in a rather interesting manner. The fact that the Corinthians are going to unbelievers to settle their disputes is a further indication of their lack of wisdom. Having failed *to judge* a gross case of immorality in their midst, they are unable *to judge* ordinary disputes among themselves. In effect they have forgotten their status as God's consecrated community. Those who belong to the sanctified community are destined *to judge* the world, *not to be judged* by it. In sum, all three cases point to a lack of wisdom and a failure on the part of the community to live as the sanctified people of God.

Paul's response to these problems provides an interesting insight into his moral discernment. In each instance, he offers a series of reasons why the Corinthians must alter their behavior. Moreover, he focuses upon the community rather than upon the individuals who have committed the wrong. In effect, the failure of the individual becomes the failure of the community. This is why Paul must remind the Corinthians that they are a people who have been consecrated by God. They no longer belong to themselves but to God, and their new status requires appropriate moral conduct. Throughout this section, therefore, he repeatedly employs the formula "do you not know that" (*ouk oidate hoti*).[18] The Corinthians have forgotten or do not fully appreciate their sanctified status.

In responding to the case of incest (5:1–13), Paul concludes with a phrase drawn from Deuteronomy: "Drive out the wicked person from among you" (5:13).[19] Just as Moses instructed the Israelites to expel certain offenders from the community lest it become polluted by their evil, so Paul commands the Corinthians to expel the incestuous man from their midst.[20] Because Paul's wisdom is rooted in the cross, it does not fail him as does the worldly wisdom of the Corinthians who are unable to recognize even a serious case of immorality. Therefore, he orders the community to expel the immoral man from its midst (5:3–5).

Paul uses yet another image to remind the community of its sanctified status. It is like a batch of unleavened dough, which a little yeast (a frequent symbol of evil) will infect. Therefore they must cast out the immoral man

145

who is the old yeast so that they can become a new batch (5:6–8). In making this exhortation Paul notes that the community is already a new batch of unleavened dough, seemingly contradicting himself. How can the community cast out the old yeast if it is already a new batch? The answer is Christ, the Paschal lamb, who has been sacrificed for the Corinthians and has purified them of all wickedness. They are like unleavened bread, but their sanctified status is in danger of being reversed by the immoral man.[21]

In reminding the Corinthians that they are a sanctified community, Paul does not require them to withdraw from the world, as some of the Corinthians mistakenly think (5:9–13). His primary concern is to maintain the holiness of the community. Therefore, the Corinthians can carry on their daily business with "the immoral of this world." They are not to associate, however, with a believer who is "sexually immoral or greedy, or is an idolater, reviler, drunkard, or robber" (5:11). To do so would compromise the community's holiness. Paul's concern, then, is with insiders rather than outsiders. He will not judge those who are outside the community, but he does judge those who are within it (5:12–13). The Corinthians should do the same by expelling the incestuous man from their midst.

By telling the Corinthians that the church should be concerned with judging its own affairs rather than those of the world (5:13), Paul anticipates the discussion of the second problem that he will address: lawsuits among believers (6:1–13).[22] In doing so, he immediately distinguishes between the Corinthians and the world. While the Corinthians have been numbered among the saints (*hagioi*), the unbelievers to whom they bring their lawsuits are the unrighteous (*adikoi*). Drawing upon apocalyptic traditions, Paul reminds the Corinthians that, as God's holy ones, they are destined to judge the world (6:2).[23] The behavior of the Corinthians, then, belies their elected status and the wisdom of which they so arrogantly boast, causing Paul to ask if any of them is not wise enough to judge between one believer and another (6:5).

Despite their elected status, the Corinthians are still wronging and defrauding one another; they are acting like the unrighteous (6:8). Their behavior leads Paul to remind them that the *adikoi* (the unrighteous) will not inherit the kingdom of God.[24] To insure that the community knows what he means by this term, he provides a brief list: fornicators, idolaters, adulterers, male prostitutes, sodomites, thieves, the greedy, drunkards, revilers, robbers.[25] The Corinthians had been such sinners, but now they have been washed, sanctified, and justified (6:11). Their new status, of course, does not mean that they are free from sin. After all, Paul has just accused them of wronging and defrauding one another (6:8). Rather, the apostle is eminently practical in a way that his converts are not: their election involves a task to be fulfilled as well as a new status. It is an incentive to live a moral and ethical life rather than a magical protection from immoral and unethical conduct.

That the Corinthians have been washed, sanctified, and justified provides the background for the arguments Paul will employ to dissuade them from sexual commerce with prostitutes (6:12–20). It was God, working in

146

Christ, who washed, sanctified, and justified the Corinthians. Consequently their bodies are no longer their own; they are members of Christ. To give one's body to a prostitute, however, is to become one flesh with the prostitute and to surrender to another what belongs to Christ (6:15). To be joined with Christ, by contrast, is to become one spirit with him. Once more, Paul draws out the ethical implications of his election theology: the Corinthians belong to another. Therefore they must avoid *porneia* lest they sin against their own bodies, which are temples of the Holy Spirit, which has been given to them by God (6:19–20).[26]

Remain as you are (1 Cor. 7:1–40). The beginning of chapter 7 clearly indicates that Paul is responding to a letter he received from the Corinthians: "Now concerning the matters about which you wrote" (7:1). In chapter 7, these matters deal with sexual abstinence, marriage, and divorce. Yet it would be a mistake to view this material as a systematic presentation of what Paul has to say about these topics. As in the rest of this letter, the apostle is responding as a pastor to problems and questions raised by the church. What he writes about these issues, therefore, is a response to a specific situation rather than a systematic or philosophical reflection on them. Paul undoubtedly had more to say about these topics and might have stated his position differently if he were simply writing as a theologian. But such was not the case.

While we do not have access to the letter the Corinthians sent Paul, many believe that it was a statement of their views on these topics rather than a series of polite questions addressed to the apostle. To be more specific, it appears that some members of the community adopted an ascetical posture in regard to sexuality. Already enjoying the eschatological life of the Spirit, they undertook a regime of sexual abstinence. Moreover, they may have forced the same asceticism upon others. If so, some members of the community may have sought to divorce their spouses in order to practice sexual abstinence, while widows and engaged couples may have had second thoughts about marriage.

The problem that Paul faced was complicated since he was celibate and preferred that others be celibate like himself (7:7). The Corinthian ascetics, however, took his position a step too far. While Paul preferred celibacy, he recognized that each person has particular gifts (7:7). If one cannot practice sexual self-control, therefore, it is better to marry than to burn with passion (7:9). Paul must assure the Corinthians that it is not sinful for widows to remarry (7:9, 39) or for engaged couples to complete their marriage plans (7:36). In effect, he must walk a narrow path between his own preference for the celibate life and the ascetical stance of some who would impose sexual abstinence upon all.

The issues discussed in chapter 7 are noticeably different from those in chapters 5 and 6. Paul now finds himself trying to curb excessive zeal rather than immorality. In doing so, he applies the same moral reasoning that he employed in chapters 5 and 6. First, *porneia* is a threat to the purity of the community, even in the case of those who espouse sexual abstinence on the basis of their slogan, "It is well for a man not to touch a woman" (7:1).[27]

147

Paul is aware that the eschaton has not yet arrived, and so he responds, "But because of cases of sexual immorality (*porneias*), each man should have his own wife and each woman her own husband" (7:2).[28] He realizes that the Corinthian ascetics are endangering the purity of the sanctified community by imposing a regime of sexual abstinence upon all that many will be unable to observe.

Second, Paul returns to his election theology. Nowhere is this more apparent than in the central section of this chapter (7:17–24), where he articulates the ethical principle that undergirds this discussion: "In whatever condition you were *called*, brothers and sisters, there remain with God" (7:24; see vv. 17 and 20 as well). Given the imminence of the parousia and the transitory nature of this world (7:29–31), Paul argues that people should continue living in the state in which God called them. Circumcision or the lack of it no longer matters. What counts is keeping the commandments of God (*alla tērēsis entolōn theou*), which the elect can and must do. Even the degrading condition of slavery does not alter one's status before God, since the slave has become the Lord's freed person, and the free person has become Christ's slave (7:21–22).[29] Real slavery results from sin; therefore, believers, who have been "purchased" by God, must avoid carnal enslavement to others.

This principle underlines nearly all that Paul says in this chapter. For example, the married may practice sexual abstinence "by way of concession," but they must not deny each other the conjugal rights due their spouses since they are married. If the unmarried and widows can practice self-control, they should remain unmarried (7:8), but if they cannot, let them marry. Divorce among believers is not permitted, but if it occurs the spouses should remain unmarried in hope of reconciliation (7:10–11).[30] Believers who are married to unbelievers should remain in their marriages if the unbelieving spouse consents, since even unbelievers are made holy through their spouses.[31]

The principle of remaining in the state in which one was called is closely aligned with Paul's understanding of the world. Since the present form of the world (*to schēma tou kosmou toutou*) is passing away (7:31), believers must live in the world with an eschatological reservation: a recognition that this world is not the final reality that determines their lives. Believers live in a dialectical relationship to the world, between what has happened and what is yet to take place. Aware of this dialectical relationship, Paul treats the world with realism as well as respect, whereas the spirit-filled Corinthians have tipped the scale in favor of what has not yet taken place. Such an attitude, be it libertine or ascetic, cannot deal with *porneia*.

Building Up a Community
Through Love
(1 Cor. 8:1–11:1)

The Corinthians' question about food sacrificed to idols provides Paul with an opportunity to develop his election theology even further. Because the Corinthians are God's holy people they must, like Israel of old, avoid idolatry as well as immorality. Consequently, just as Paul issued a strong admonition against *porneia* in the earlier chapters of this letter (6:18), he now warns the Corinthians to avoid idolatry (10:14). The Corinthians must not participate at the table of demons since they belong to God alone.

While chapter 9, with its emphasis upon Paul's apostolic rights, appears as a digression to some, most scholars recognize the essential role it plays in Paul's argument. In chapter 8, he introduces the question of food sacrificed to idols (*eidōlothytos*): May believers participate at cultic meals where the food they eat has been sacrificed to idols? After advising the "stronger" members of the community to refrain from such meals lest they harm the weaker members of the community,[32] Paul points to the example of his own life in chapter 9. Although he possesses many rights as an apostle, he has set them aside to build up the community of the church. In chapter 10, Paul points to the history of God's first sanctified people, the community of Israel, which, despite its status, fell into idolatry (10:1–13). On the basis of this lesson, he warns the Corinthians to flee from the worship of idols since they cannot participate at the table of demons and remain God's sanctified community (10:14–22). Paul concludes with two practical cases: buying meat sold in the marketplace and eating in the homes of unbelievers (10:23–30). At the end of his discussion he boldly says, "Be imitators of me, as I am of Christ" (11:1; see 4:16). The behavior that the Corinthians are to imitate is described in chapter 9. Chapter 9, then, provides the Corinthians with a concrete example, taken from Paul's life, that illustrates what it means to build up a community through love. I begin with a discussion of chapters 8 and 10, food sacrificed to idols and idolatry, and conclude with a consideration of chapter 9, Paul as a model to be imitated.[33]

Love rather than knowledge (1 Cor. 8:1–13). As was the case in chapter 7, it is probable that the Corinthian letter stated the position of a certain group within the community; for the sake of convenience, I will call this group "people with knowledge." On the basis of their knowledge, they came to the firm conviction that idols do not exist since there is only one God (8:4). Therefore, participation in cultic meals, where the food had been sacrificed to idols, was a matter of indifference. For Paul, however, knowledge is not a sufficient norm for making ethical decisions. He reminds the Corinthians that whereas knowledge can make one arrogant (*physioi*), only love can build up (*oikodomei*) the community (8:1). Drawing upon his election theology, he says that the one who loves God is known by God (8:2–3), implying that being known by God is more important than knowing. Love precedes knowledge and builds up the community. It, not knowledge, is the basis for making moral choices.

To illustrate that knowledge is not a sufficient moral guide, Paul points to the case of a person of knowledge eating food sacrificed to idols in a cultic setting (8:7–10). Faced with such a situation, weaker believers may be tempted to eat such food, contrary to their conscience.[34] In contrast to knowledge, love refuses to scandalize the believer for whom Christ died (8:12). So Paul declares: "If food is a cause to their falling, I will never eat meat, so that I may not cause them to fall" (8:11). As Wendell Lee Willis perceptively notes, Paul is not merely limiting or tempering knowledge by love; he is contrasting two ways of relating to God, only one of which is sufficient.[35]

Flee from the worship of idols (1 Cor. 10:1–33). In chapter 10 Paul returns to the issue of food sacrificed to idols, settling two practical questions: what to do about food sold in the marketplace, much of which had been sacrificed to idols (10:23–26), and what to do when invited to the home of an unbeliever (10:27–30). In both instances, Paul's response manifests remarkable freedom. Believers need not raise questions about the food, on the basis of conscience, in either case. The only exception is if another, perhaps a believer of weaker moral sensibility, should point out that the food has in fact been sacrificed to idols. Before issuing these practical directives, however, Paul introduces a lengthy warning against idolatry (10:1–22).

Although it is possible that the Corinthians' letter raised the question of idolatry, I am inclined to think it did not. Rather, in Paul's view, those with knowledge are in danger of entering a forbidden zone by their attendance at cultic meals. To forestall what has not yet occurred, he reminds the Corinthians of their cultic status as God's people in two ways. First, he compares them with Israel of old, which was also a sanctified community but fell into idolatry, even though it had been baptized into Moses and drank from the spiritual rock that was Christ (10:1–13). Second, Paul points to the exclusive claims that God has upon the Corinthian community (10:14–22). Just as the people of Israel became "partners in the altar" (*koinōnoi tou thysiastēriou*) because they ate the sacrificial food offered to idols (10:18), so the Corinthians become partners with those at whose altar they eat.[36] As a sanctified community elected by God, the Corinthians have become God's exclusive possession. To participate in idol worship, even if one "knows" that there is no such thing as an idol (8:4), is to become partners with those who eat at the altar of idols. Those who do so betray their elected status.

Imitate me (1 Cor. 9:1–27). At the beginning of chapter 11, Paul calls upon the Corinthians to imitate him as he imitates Christ (11:1). In making this appeal, he echoes an earlier appeal (4:16) and reminds the Corinthians of his behavior described in chapter 9. Although free, and although an apostle, he has surrendered certain rights for the sake of the community: most notably the right of being supported by the community. Paul notes that just as those employed in the temple are entitled to a living from the temple (9:13), so those who proclaim the gospel should get their living from the gospel (9:14). Since the Corinthian community is the temple of God and Paul its priest, he has every right to be supported by them, but for the sake of the gospel he has not made full use of his rights (9:15). Although free, he has enslaved himself to all, becoming all things to all people so that he might save some (9:19–23). Furthermore, Paul takes nothing for granted. Like an athlete who exercises self-control in all things to win the race, he punishes and enslaves his body lest he be disqualified (9:24–27).

The implications of Paul's behavior for the Corinthians are apparent.

Those who are strong in conscience must enslave themselves through love for the benefit of the community. Lest their "knowledge" puff them up with pride, they must exercise self-control. So Paul warns them in chapter 10, "If you think you are standing, watch out that you do not fall" (10:12), and, "Do not seek your own advantage, but that of the other" (10:24). The fundamental moral imperative is the edification of the community, and the norm for such behavior is love.

A More Excellent Way
(1 Cor. 13:1–13)

Paul has already referred to love at two strategic points in this letter. At the conclusion of his discussion about wisdom, he asked the Corinthians what they preferred: should he come to them with a stick, or "with love in a spirit of gentleness?" (4:21). Then at the beginning of the discussion about food sacrificed to idols, he reminded those who boasted of their knowledge that knowledge puffs up but "love builds up" (8:1), and that anyone who "loves God is known by him" (8:3). It is not surprising then that Paul should provide the Corinthians with an explanation of what he means by *agapē*.

Although chapter 13 is sometimes referred to as a "hymn to love," the passage is prose.[37] It is not, however, a philosophical or theological treatise on the topic of love. As in Paul's discussions about sexual abstinence, marriage, and divorce, this passage is part of a broader treatment of spiritual gifts and their importance for building up the community (12:1–14:39). More specifically, it appears that some members of the community have exaggerated their status within the church because they speak in tongues.[38] While it is not Paul's intent to forbid speaking in tongues (14:40), he must demonstrate that this gift is not as important for building up the community as are other gifts such as prophecy. Love, as exemplified in Paul's own life, is the more excellent way, and it is this way above all else that the community should seek.

Chapter 13 functions in much the same way as does chapter 9. On first reading it appears to interrupt the discussion about spiritual gifts found in chapters 12 and 14. But on closer examination it becomes apparent that the intervening discussion on love provides the community with the moral guidance necessary to overcome its divisions. As Carl Holladay argues, chapter 13 presents the community with an "apostolic paradigm."[39] Paul himself is the great example of love that the community must imitate. If the Corinthians imitate the love exemplified in his ministry they will build up rather than divide the church.

Drawing upon his election theology, Paul reminds the Corinthians that they were enticed and led astray to idols when they were Gentiles (12:2). Now, they have been baptized into one body (12:13) and have received a diversity of spiritual gifts (12:4–11). Their many gifts are for the good of all (*sympheron;* 12:7) so that the church may be built up, a theme to which Paul has already alluded (6:12; 7:35; 10:23, 33) and which he will develop further

151

(14:3, 4, 5, 12, 17, 26). Indeed, the diversity of gifts within the church is meant to forestall dissention and ensure that the Corinthians will care for each other (12:24–25). Listing the gifts that God has bestowed upon the church in the order of their importance for building up the community, Paul places the gift of tongues last (12:28).

In chapter 14, he encourages the Corinthians to be zealous for spiritual gifts, but especially for the gift of prophecy (14:1). In an extended comparison between prophecy and tongues, he shows the superiority of the former to the latter. Whereas prophecy builds up the church, the gift of tongues builds up those who utter them (14:4). As for Paul, he would rather instruct others with a few words than utter ten thousand words in tongues, even though he speaks in tongues.

In summarizing Paul's argument I have passed over chapter 13. What then is the purpose of this chapter if his argument can be made without reference to it? The question is well put. Chapter 13 does not alter the essential argument that spiritual gifts are intended for building up of the church. Its inclusion, however, provides a personal dimension to Paul's exhortation, demonstrating by example what he requires of his converts.

Paul's own example (1 Cor. 13:1–3). At the end of chapter 12 (12:31) and at the beginning of chapter 13 (13:1–3), Paul shifts to the first-person singular. In doing so, he asks a series of questions that follow a similar pattern. "If I do a particular action, or have a particular gift, but do not have love, I am [or: I gain] nothing." Paul's point is not difficult to discern: love must undergird all spiritual gifts as well as all ethical activity. Without love, moral action and spiritual gifts lose their value.

Although Paul's questions are normally taken in a hypothetical sense as referring to anyone, Carl Holladay suggests that they are self-referential. That is, what Paul describes in these questions is "anchored in his own apostolic behavior."[40] For example, Paul speaks in tongues (14:6, 18). Called by God, he has prophetic status (Gal. 1:15); he reveals heavenly mysteries (1 Cor. 2:9–13; 4:1; 15:51); he has knowledge (2:6–16; 2 Cor. 11:6); he has faith powerful enough to perform miracles (2 Cor. 12:12; Rom. 15:19); he has voluntarily made himself poor for the sake of the gospel (1 Cor. 4:11; 2 Cor. 6:10; 11:7–11); and having given himself up to death for Jesus' sake (2 Cor. 4:11), he can boast.[41] In effect, Paul presents himself to the Corinthians as an example to be imitated. Endowed with spiritual gifts, he is the spiritual person par excellence. Nevertheless, he understands that all gifts and activity are subordinate to love. The Corinthians should do the same.

What love is (1 Cor. 13:4–7). Next, Paul describes the nature of *agapē* in a series of positive and negative statements. Whereas his positive characterization of love corresponds to his own behavior, his negative characterization of love is reminiscent of behavior in the Corinthian community. For example, Paul says that love is patient and kind and he later refers to his own behavior in the same way (2 Cor. 6:6). Likewise, he writes that love bears all things and endures all things, a frequent description of his own way of life (9:12b; 2 Cor. 6:6; 12:12). Negatively stated, "Love . . . is not envious or boastful or arrogant (*physioutai*) or rude. It does not insist on its own way; it is not irritable or resentful; it does not rejoice in wronging" (13:4–5). Such an attitude, however, describes the Corinthians' conduct. There is jealousy and quarreling among them (3:3); they have become puffed up and arrogant in their wisdom and knowledge (4:6, 18, 19; 5:2; 8:1); and by taking others to court they appear to rejoice in what is wrong (6:7–8).[42] While Paul has made himself a slave to all (9:19), the Corinthians insist on their own way. They have yet to heed Paul's advice, "Do not seek your own advantage, but that of the other" (10:24).

Love endures (1 Cor. 13:8–13). The ultimate value of love, however, derives from its enduring quality. Whereas the gifts that the Corinthians most prize (prophecy, tongues, and knowledge) will come to an end, love will endure. Establishing a series of contrasts between love on the one hand, and knowledge and prophecy on the other, Paul implies that the Corinthians have not yet come to maturity, a point already made in an earlier discussion (3:1–4). Love alone is perfect and complete, and it is the hallmark of those who are adult in their faith. In comparison to love, gifts such as tongues, knowledge, and prophecy are incomplete and belong to a stage of spiritual infancy. They provide an imperfect reflection of God but do not allow one to see him face to face. Only love allows one to be known fully by God. To boast in gifts other than love, therefore, is folly.

The example of Paul's life provides a sure moral guide for the Corinthians. This example, however, is also present in the many hardships he bears for the sake of the gospel.

A LIFE TO BE IMITATED:
SECOND CORINTHIANS

On first reading, it might well appear that 2 Corinthians contains little, if any, moral instruction. To be sure, Paul exhorts the Corinthians not to be yoked with unbelievers (6:14–7:1) and to mend their ways (12:19–21; 13:5, 11), but readers of this letter will not encounter the extended discussions about community conduct that characterize 1 Corinthians. Instead they find Paul explaining and defending his own behavior! Thus it is tempting to pass over this letter and move to the more explicitly ethical discussions of Galatians, Romans, and so on. To succumb to this temptation, however, would be a mistake, for in defending and explaining himself to the Corinthians, Paul ultimately recommends his behavior as a model for them to imitate. The moral and ethical content of this letter, as we shall see, is embedded in the example of the apostle's life and ministry, especially his apostolic sufferings on behalf of the gospel. As John T. Fitzgerald notes, "Hellenistic moralists made constant use of the figure of the suffering sage as a pedagogical and paraenetic device for depicting the ideal and exhorting and admonishing their hearers in regard to it."[43] Paul does something similar in 2 Corinthians.

Consoled and Consoling
(2 Cor. 1:3–11)

The theme of Paul's hardships is already announced in the opening benediction of this letter (1:3–11) through repeated references to affliction (*thlipsis*), consolation (*paraklēsis*), and suffering (*pathēma*). The God and Father of Jesus Christ is the God of all consolation who has already consoled Paul in all the afflictions by which Paul participates in the sufferings of Christ. Having been consoled by God, Paul is able to offer consolation to those who will share in similar afflictions. In effect, he says that people are consoled to the degree that they are participants (*koinōnoi*) in Christ's sufferings. In doing so, he implicitly establishes a chain of imitation similar to that found in 1 Thessalonians: namely, Paul's affliction on account of his participation in Christ's sufferings leads to God's consolation. God's consolation allows Paul to console the Corinthians and all others who find themselves in similar circumstances. The Corinthians, in turn, will be able to console still others provided that they share in Christ's sufferings. However, since many of the Corinthians do not comprehend the importance of participating in these sufferings, Paul must explain what he means by the example of his life.

A Man of Integrity
(2 Cor. 1:12–2:13)

Before developing his theme further, Paul clears up a misunderstanding between himself and the Corinthians that has led the community to question his integrity.[44] He had promised to visit the Corinthians on his way to Macedonia, and then again on his return so that they could send him on to Judea (1:16). Paul, however, altered his plans,[45] leading some to accuse him of not keeping his word. At the outset of this letter, therefore, he must defend his integrity. He affirms that he behaves with "frankness and godly sincerity, not by earthly wisdom but by the grace of God" (1:12). Earthly wisdom (*sophia sarkikē*), of course, has already caused jealousy and strife among the Corinthians, but it plays no part in Paul's behavior. He protests that he was not deceitful when he promised to visit the community but was unable to do so. Rooting his faithfulness in the faithfulness of the Son of God, Paul affirms the reliability of his word and the integrity of his character (1:18). The problem was not with Paul but with the community that was not yet reconciled to him (1:23–2:4). Now that the time of reconciliation has come, Paul is ready to forgive the one who offended him on his previous visit to Corinth. Indeed, Paul is solicitous that the community forgive and even console the offender lest the man become overwhelmed with grief. Paul, who has an abundance of love for the community (2:4), encourages the Corinthians to reaffirm their love for the offender (2:8).

In sum, Paul presents himself as a man of integrity who does not seek to exercise excessive authority over the Corinthians (1:24). If he treated the community harshly and postponed a promised visit, he only acted out of love for his converts. Like the Son of God, he is faithful and reliable.

Worthy of Recommendation
(2 Cor. 2:14–6:10)

The difficulties Paul experienced at Corinth were due, in no small part, to the intrusion of rival missionaries.[46] Although our knowledge of them is limited, it appears that they arrived with letters from other Christian communities that recommended them to the Corinthians. In the course of their stay, the rival apostles, and perhaps the Corinthians themselves, questioned the nature of Paul's ministry. Faced with this situation, Paul found it necessary to explain the character of his apostolic service. In doing so, he implicitly compares himself to the rival missionaries. He is not a peddler of God's word like so many of them but a person of sincerity sent by God (2:17; see 1:12, where Paul also describes himself in terms of sincerity). Unlike other missionaries, he does not need letters of recommendation to the Corinthians, since the community itself is his letter of recommendation (3:1–3). Paul's competence is not from himself but from God, who has made him the minister of a new covenant (3:5–6), the glory of which surpasses the fading glory of the Mosaic covenant. Sustained by the hope that derives from this covenant, Paul acts with boldness (*parrēsia;* 2:12). Making a daring comparison between himself and Moses, who veiled his face "to keep the people of Israel from gazing at the end of the glory that was being set aside" (3:13), Paul insists that his gospel is not veiled. He has put aside shameful things, and he refuses to practice cunning or to falsify God's word (4:2). Paul does not proclaim himself but Jesus Christ, for whose sake he has become the community's slave (4:5).

The heart of Paul's argument, however, is not the glorious aspect of his ministry but two lists of apostolic hardships (4:8–9; 6:4–10). Aware that his opponents could also point to the glorious aspects of their ministry, he turns to the very hardships that led the Corinthians to question the authenticity of his ministry. In doing so, he provides them with an important moral lesson: apostolic ministry must not be divorced from participation in Christ's sufferings.

Treasures in clay jars. Having described the glorious aspect of his ministry, Paul now compares himself to a clay jar that contains a glorious treasure. The treasure is the ministry of the new covenant and the clay jar represents Paul's earthly existence. In the first of two hardship lists (2 Cor. 4:7–8), he openly admits his weakness and fragility.[47] He is *afflicted,* but he is not crushed; he is *perplexed,* but he has not yet been driven to despair; he is *persecuted,* but he has not been forsaken; he has been *struck down,* but he is not destroyed.[48] By the hardships that he suffers, Paul carries within his body the death or the dying (*nekrōsis*) of Jesus (4:10).[49] That is, the apostle is in constant danger of death, to the point that he is already participating in the sufferings of Jesus: the afflictions to which he referred in the opening benediction. While others may view Paul's hardships as signs of weakness and as reasons for calling his apostolic credentials into question, he understands them in terms of Jesus' death. Paul is constantly being given up, or is giving himself up, to death[50] for Jesus' sake, so that Jesus' life might be manifested in his mortal flesh (4:11). The net effect of Paul's hardship catalogue is twofold. First, it demonstrates his composure in trying circumstances. Second, it shows God's power at work in his ministry.[51] Paul's hardships recommend him as a model to be imitated.

But how is it possible for anyone to endure hardships without losing faith? Paul provides a series of answers to this question. In doing so he further describes the motivation for his moral and ethical conduct, especially vis-à-vis the Corinthian community. First, he lives by the same faith that sustained the psalmist: "I believed, and so I spoke" (4:13). Second, he knows that the God who raised the dead "will raise us also with Jesus" (4:14). Third, because of his faith in the resurrection, Paul does not lose heart. Although the mortal aspect of his life is wasting away, the enduring aspect is being renewed daily. What he now endures is only a momentary affliction soon to be replaced by an eternal glory. In a paradoxical statement, Paul affirms that he does not look to what he can see but to what he cannot see (4:16–18). He confidently endures his afflictions because he walks by faith and not by sight (5:7). Emphasizing the importance of the body, as he does throughout his Corinthian correspondence, Paul notes that he tries to please God.

> For all of us must appear before the judgment seat of Christ, so that each may receive recompense for what has been done *in the body*, whether good or evil (5:10).

Paul does not fear this judgment, since he knows that he is already-known by God (*theō de pephanerōmetha*), even if he is not yet fully known by the Corinthians (5:11). His faith makes him a man of utter confidence, but not arrogant. He carries out his apostolic ministry compelled by Christ's love for him, as well as his love for Christ (*agapē tou Christou;* 5:14). He comes to the Corinthians as Christ's ambassador, entreating them to be reconciled to God (5:20).

As servants of God. Having described his apostolic ministry in terms of glory and suffering, and having presented himself as Christ's ambassador, Paul urges the Corinthians "not to accept the grace of God in vain" (2 Cor. 6:1). In an urgent appeal to the community with which he is seeking personal reconciliation, he commends himself as one of God's servants. His self-recommendation takes the form of a second and more extended hardship list (6:4–10). The list begins with the all-important virtue of endurance and continues with three triads of nine hardships. Eight virtues follow the hardships so that a list of nine virtues encloses the nine hardships. Next there are three phrases, each introduced by the preposition *dia* (through), which explain how Paul endures his hardships. The list concludes with seven statements pointing to the paradoxical nature of his ministry, indicating that appearances are deceiving. The material can be structured as follows.[52]

through great endurance,
   in afflictions, hardships, calamities,
   in beatings, imprisonments, riots,
   in labors, sleepless nights, hunger;
by purity, knowledge, patience, kindness, holiness of spirit,
    genuine love, truthful speech, and the power of God;
   through the weapons of righteousness . . . ,
   through honor and dishonor,
   through ill repute and good repute. . . .
as impostors, and yet true;
as unknown, yet well known;
as dying, and see—we are alive;
as punished, and yet not killed;
as sorrowful, yet always rejoicing;
as poor, yet making many rich;
as having nothing, and yet possessing everything.

Paul has already spoken of his afflictions several times (1:4, 8; 2:4; 4:17; 7:4), and many of the afflictions he lists here will be repeated later: hardships (12:10), calamities (12:10), beatings (11:23), imprisonments (11:23), labors (11:23, 27), sleepless nights (11:27), and hunger (11:27). Moreover, Paul's description of himself as acting through great endurance with patience, kindness, and genuine love clearly echoes 1 Corinthians 13. In effect, his second hardship list presents him as the embodiment of one who claims to be an ambassador for Christ. Through his apostolic hardships, he is participating in Christ's work of reconciliation. As Christ was made sin so that humanity might become the righteousness of God (5:21), Paul endures his apostolic sufferings so that his appeal for reconciliation (5:20) will bear fruit. By enduring affliction, he provides the Corinthians with a vivid example of what it means to live according to the gospel and implicitly calls the community to imitate him.

Power in Weakness
(2 Cor. 12:1–13:10)

As noted earlier, the last three chapters of this letter probably represent part of another letter written by Paul.[53] Since I am primarily interested in the canonical shape of the material, however, that hypothesis will have little bearing on what follows. Whatever the circumstances at Corinth, it is apparent that Paul faced a severe challenge to his apostolate from those whom he calls "false apostles, deceitful workers, disguising themselves as apostles of Christ" (11:13).[54] Once more he will call upon his apostolic hardships to authenticate his ministry, but in doing so he will introduce yet another motif: boasting in weakness.

The charges against Paul can be summarized as follows. First, there is no correspondence between Paul and his letters (10:1–18). Quoting his critics, he writes, "His [Paul's] letters are weighty and strong, but his bodily presence is weak, and his speech contemptible" (10:10). Second, he is not an authentic apostle because he refuses to be supported by the Corinthian church (11:1–15). Paul's immediate response to these accusations is straightforward and sarcastic. As regards the first, he insists that, although he lives as a human being (*en sarki*), he does not behave in a merely human fashion (*kata sarka*; 10:2–3). He is like a powerful soldier armed with divine power: he destroys the fortresses of those who rely on merely human wisdom, he takes captives, and he punishes (10:3–5).[55] In effect, there is a perfect correspondence between the man and his letters. What he writes, he will do (10:11), for he is a man of perfect integrity.

As regards the second, Paul voluntarily humbled himself by not accepting support from the Corinthians so that he could preach the gospel to them free of charge. Because others supplied his needs, he did not burden them. His refusal to accept support was another manifestation of his apostolic love for the community. What others have interpreted as demeaning behavior, he calls "this boast of mine" (11:10); namely, to preach the gospel free of charge (11:7–11).

Foolish boasting (2 Cor. 11:16–12:10). The centerpiece of Paul's defense, however, is his foolish speech (11:16–12:10) in which he engages in the boasting game of his detractors. However, whereas they boast in their power, he will boast in his weakness and acknowledge that he is, and has acted as, a fool (11:16, 21; 12:11). Paul begins by boasting of his Jewish ancestry (11:22). When he comes to his credentials as Christ's minister, however, he employs yet another hardship list (11:23–29). Following this list, he boasts of a humiliating escape from Damascus (11:30–33). Next he turns to visions and revelations (12:1–9) that culminated in a "thorn in the flesh," given to him lest he become too elated. The entire section ends with a brief hardship list in which Paul paradoxically but triumphantly proclaims, "for whenever I am weak, then I am strong" (12:10).

Paul begins his first hardship list (11:23–29) by explicitly comparing himself with the false apostles on four points. Next comes a series of five ways in which he faced death. Then, he lists eight kinds of danger he has faced, followed by five further examples of hardship. The list closes with a reference to his daily anxiety for the churches and two rhetorical questions. The whole can be outlined as follows.

> greater labors
> far more imprisonments
> countless floggings
> often near death
> > forty lashes minus one (five times)
> > beaten by rods (three times)
> > stoning (once)
> > shipwrecked (three times)

adrift (a night and a day)
in danger from rivers
in danger from bandits
in danger from my own people
in danger from Gentiles
in danger in the city
in danger in the wilderness
in danger at sea
in danger from false brothers and sisters
   in toil and hardships
   in many a sleepless night
   in hunger and thirst
   in famine
   in cold and nakedness
still other things: the daily pressure of anxiety
   Who is weak, and I am not weak?
   Who is made to stumble, and I am not indignant?

Unlike the other hardship lists that make reference to Paul's endurance and virtues, this list catalogues only his hardships. The reason for this change of strategy is plain. Paul's intent is to confound his opponents by boasting of precisely those things which they say manifest his weakness and call his apostolic credentials into question. The point Paul wishes to make serves to conclude the brief hardship list of 12:10: "I am content with weakness, insults, hardships, persecutions, and calamities for the sake of Christ; *for whenever I am weak, then I am strong.*"

In the opening benediction of this letter Paul writes, "For just as the sufferings of Christ are abundant for us, so also our consolation is abundant through Christ" (1:5). In light of these hardship lists, it is clear that the afflictions Paul suffered in his ministry are his participation in the sufferings of Christ. While those who judge by appearance question his apostolic credentials, those who walk by faith understand the integrity of the apostle who founded their community. Paul's life is worthy of imitation, and his behavior provides a sure moral guide for living in accordance with the gospel of the crucified Messiah.

PAUL'S MORAL TEACHING:
A SUMMARY STATEMENT

At the beginning of this chapter I suggested that the ethical teaching of the Corinthian correspondence can be organized around three themes: (1) Paul's election theology, (2) the importance of building up the community through love, and (3) the moral example of Paul's life that allows him to say, "imitate me," much as Jesus said, "follow me." In light of his election theology, Paul has reminded the community that it is the temple of God and the sanctified people of God in whom God's spirit dwells. Therefore it is imperative to flee from immorality. The community must live in the world without compromising its elected identity. Since it belongs exclusively to God, it cannot give itself to another. Building up the community through love requires that the strong bear with the weak and that none seek their own good at the expense of others. In the life and example of Paul, the demands of love and election theology meet. His self-sacrificial love for the community exemplifies the paradoxical wisdom of the cross, while his total devotion to God shows what it means to belong to God. To imitate Paul is to practice the love demanded of those who have been sanctified by the crucified Christ.

7

Walking
by the Spirit

The Letter to the Galatians

Thus far, there has been no occasion to discuss what many view as the centerpiece of Pauline ethics: justification by faith apart from works of the Mosaic law. To be sure, we have already encountered the language of righteousness and justification. In 1 Corinthians, for example, Paul writes that Christ Jesus became "for us wisdom from God, and *righteousness* and sanctification and redemption" (1:30), and in 2 Corinthians he states that God made Christ to be sin for our sake, "so that in him we might become the *righteousness of God*" (5:21). Moreover, in warning the Corinthians to flee immorality, he reminds them that they were washed, sanctified, and "*justified* in the name of the Lord Jesus Christ and in the Spirit of our God" (1 Cor. 6:11). Apart from these texts, however, the concepts of righteousness and justification do not play an important role in the letters that we have examined thus far.[1] Rather, the ethical teaching of the Thessalonian and Corinthian correspondence is conveyed by the language of election and sanctification rather than by the doctrine of justification by faith.[2] In Paul's letter to the Galatians, however, the theme of justification comes to center stage, and he offers a profound theological reflection on the moral and ethical life of those who have been justified.[3]

Although the doctrine of justification by faith dominates Paul's letter to the Galatians, the significance of his teaching on this point is disputed. What has become a complex scholarly debate can be stated in a simple question: What is Paul opposing in Galatians by his teaching on justification by faith? The traditional answer, developed in the crucible of the Reformation debates, is righteousness by works: any attempt on the part of human beings to secure their own salvation by doing good works.[4] In more recent years, however, a "new perspective on Paul" has argued that the problem at Galatia was more cultural and social than personal and individualistic: one group of Christians (Jewish Christians) attempted to impose its cultural and national identity upon another (Gentile Christians).[5] The interpretation that one chooses in regard to justification, as we shall see, has important ramifications for Pauline ethics.

On the one hand, those who proceed along the venerable Reformation path emphasize the importance of God's grace in the moral life, and they oppose any attempt on the part of human beings to boast in their moral achievements before God. Put another way, this approach resists all forms of Pelagianism and synergism, arguing that one is not saved by good works but by the saving grace of God alone. On the other hand, those who proceed along the path cut by the new perspective on Paul define the issues in terms of inclusion and exclusion, entitlement and disadvantage. People are not justified before God on the basis of national or ethnic heritage but by the saving grace of God. In the words of James Dunn,

> Justification by faith is a banner raised by Paul against any and all such presumption of privileged status before God by virtue of race, culture or nationality, against any and all attempts to preserve such spurious distinctions by practices that exclude and divide.[6]

To be sure, these two positions continue to have much in common. Both, for example, emphasize the primacy of God's grace as manifested in the cross of Christ, the need for faith, and the impossibility of being justified by God on the basis of "the works of the law" (Gal. 2:16). However, whereas the more traditional Reformation approach tends to view justification in terms of the sinful individual, the new perspective on Paul emphasizes the communal and social dimensions of justification: how one group of people is to relate to another. Moreover, since this approach no longer frames the issue in terms of faith versus "works righteousness," the new perspective finds a more positive role for Paul's moral exhortation in this and other letters.[7] For reasons that I will explain below, I have aligned myself with this new perspective on Paul.[8]

THE BACKGROUND TO A DEBATE

Paul's letter to the Galatians presupposes a crisis situation.[9] Shortly after he preached the gospel to the churches of Galatia, other missionaries arrived and proclaimed a "different gospel" that, in Paul's view, perverted the gospel of Christ (Gal. 1:7). This different gospel would have required the Gentile Galatians to become circumcised. Although Paul attributes motives of deception and cowardice to those who were "disturbing" his converts (4:17; 6:12), the agitators or Judaizers undoubtedly viewed themselves and their work differently. Like Paul, they were Jewish Christians but of a more conservative stripe and with strong ties to the Jerusalem church headed by James. Although there is no record of the gospel that they preached at Galatia, I suggest the following.

First, and most importantly, they taught that faith in Christ does not exempt people from circumcision, the sign of the eternal covenant that God made with Abraham (Genesis 17). To be sure, it was now possible for those Gentiles who believed in Christ to share in the blessings of Abraham. To participate fully in these blessings, however, they must attach themselves to God's covenant people by embracing circumcision, the sign of the covenant (Gen. 17:11).

Second, in addition to advocating circumcision, the agitators would have required Gentile believers to live "under the law." In speaking of the law, they focused primarily upon dietary prescriptions (2:11–14) and the observance of particular days and feasts (4:10). In effect, they attempted to "Judaize" Gentiles by requiring them to adopt those aspects of the Mosaic law that identified Jews as Jews in the ancient world: circumcision, dietary prescriptions, and the observance of particular days and feasts. Furthermore, the agitators undoubtedly pointed to the value of the Mosaic law as a guide to moral and ethical behavior.[10] Thus they emphasized the importance of the law as a marker of identity and as a pattern for behavior.[11]

While the theological stance of the agitators is no longer convincing to most contemporary Christians, it contains a compelling logic. God sent his Son, Jesus the Messiah, to save the covenant people of Israel. Therefore, Gentiles who believe in the Jewish Messiah must attach themselves to the covenant people of Israel by accepting the sign of circumcision and placing themselves under the law if they wish to share in the blessings of the covenant people. By circumcision, the Gentiles will become descendants of Abraham, and by placing themselves under the law, they will find a sure moral guide.

In making their argument, the agitators undoubtedly raised questions about Paul's missionary activity. For example, they may have questioned his relationship to Jerusalem, his apostolic credentials, his motives, and the integrity of the circumcision-free gospel that he preached at Galatia. Consequently, Paul is faced with a series of challenges. First, he must explain and defend the "truth of the gospel" that he preached at Galatia. Second, he must show the Galatians that they are already Abraham's descendants in virtue of faith, apart from circumcision and other works of the law. Third, and most important for New Testament ethics, he must explain how the Galatians can live a moral and ethical life if they are not under the law.

WORKS OF THE LAW AND
THE TRUTH OF THE GOSPEL

Galatians can be divided into three parts: (1) an autobiographical statement in which Paul draws upon events from his own life to explain the "truth of the gospel" that he preached to the Galatians (1:11–2:21); (2) an extended argument in which he shows the Galatians that they are already Abraham's descendants because they have been incorporated into Abraham's singular descendant, who is Christ (3:1–5:12); and (3) a moral exhortation in which Paul explains that the Galatians will fulfill the law by the love commandment if they walk by the Spirit (5:13–6:10). Although some view the letter's paraenesis as an appendage to the letter's main argument,[12] there is in fact an integral connection between the moral imperative and the indicative of salvation developed in this letter: having told the Galatians that they are not under the law because they are in Christ, Paul explains in his paraenesis that being in Christ enables one to fulfill the law. Before making his moral exhortation, however, he must explain the truth of the gospel that he preaches.

In the first part of Galatians (1:11–2:21), Paul employs the expression "the truth of the gospel" twice: first in reference to himself (2:5), and then in reference to those who withdrew from table fellowship with Gentile believers at Antioch (2:14). In the first instance, he informs the Galatians of his conduct at Jerusalem when a number of false brethren would have compelled Titus to be circumcised (2:1–5). Paul affirms that he refused to submit to their demands so that the truth of the gospel might remain intact for the Galatians. If he had circumcised Titus, he would have robbed the Galatians and all Gentile converts of their freedom to remain uncircumcised.

Shortly after this episode, in which Paul successfully defended the truth of the gospel, others betrayed its truth at Antioch (2:11–14). Prior to the arrival of Jewish Christians aligned with James, Peter and other Jewish believers shared table fellowship with the Gentile believers of Antioch. At the arrival of the delegation from James, however, all, including Peter and Barnabas, withdrew from such table fellowship. Thus Paul writes:

> But when I saw that they were not acting consistently with *the truth of the gospel,* I said to Cephas before them all, "If you, though a Jew, live like a Gentile and not like a Jew, how can you compel the Gentiles to live like Jews?" (2:14).

In effect, Paul compares two kinds of behavior. On the one hand, he defended the truth of the gospel at Jerusalem, despite intense opposition from false brethren, so that he could preserve the freedom of his Gentile converts as regards circumcision. On the other hand, Peter, Barnabas, and other Jewish Christians acted hypocritically at Antioch and compromised the freedom of the Gentile converts as regards table fellowship and dietary restrictions. In making this comparison, Paul demonstrates that his moral behavior corresponds to the truth of the gospel that he preaches and suggests that the Galatians will find a pattern worthy of imitation in him.

Paul's account of his conduct at Jerusalem and Antioch clearly indicates that freedom from circumcision and dietary prescriptions are integral to the truth of the gospel that he preaches. It is only at the close of chapter 2 in a major statement about justification by faith, however, that Paul formulates what he means by the truth of the gospel (2:15–21).

Not by works of law (Gal. 2:15–17). Paul begins with a distinction between those who are Jews by birth and those who are sinners from among the Gentiles. The first group belongs to the covenant people by birth and knows God's will because its members possess the gift of the Mosaic law. In contrast to this group, Gentiles are not part of the covenant people and live without the knowledge of God's will that the law affords. In effect, they are sinners from birth to death because they stand outside of the covenant and are ignorant of God's law.

Having made this traditional statement, Paul explains the new situation that God has effected through the death of his Son. Because of Christ, even those who are Jews and not Gentile sinners know that

> a person is justified (*dikaioutai*) not by the works of the law (*ex ergōn nomou*) but through faith in [or: through the faith of] Jesus Christ (*dia pisteōs Iēsou Christou*). And we have come to believe in Christ Jesus (*eis Christon Iēsoun*), so that we might be justified (*dikaiōthōmen*) by faith in [or: by the faith of] Christ (*ek pisteōs Christou*), and not by doing the works of the law (*ex ergōn nomou*), because no one will be justified (*dikaiōthēsetai*) by the works of the law (*ex ergōn nomou*).

Stated simply, the truth of the gospel concerns the basis upon which people are justified or acquitted before God so that they stand in the right relationship to God. In this statement Paul sets forth two possibilities, only one of which is correct: one is justified on the basis of works of the law, or on the basis of faith in, or the faith of, Jesus Christ.[13] Paul implies that previous to Christ, he and other Jews relied upon works of the law, but now even they realize that no one is justified on the basis of works of the law; one is justified only through faith in, or through the faith of, Jesus Christ. Therefore, even they have believed in Christ.

While the point Paul wishes to make is clear, the precise meaning of his language is not. What does he mean by "works of the law," and why is it impossible for anyone to be justified by them?[14] Here two points must be made. First, when Paul speaks of the works of the law, he is *not* referring to moral or ethical activity in general. Rather, he has in mind the Mosaic law with its many commandments and prescriptions. Second, the context of this letter suggests that circumcision and dietary prescriptions are the principal works of the law that Paul has in view since these works of the law identified Jews as Jews and separated them from Gentiles. Thus Paul is arguing against a "Judaizing gospel" of the agitators that implicitly equates justification before God with Jewish identity. In my view, there is no indication in the immediate context that Paul was combatting a legalistic attitude that sought salvation by doing good works, either among the agitators or the Galatians.[15]

An objection (Gal. 2:17). Paul's statement on justification leads to an objection. If Jewish Christians like him seek to be justified in Christ rather than on the basis of the works of the law, their conduct will be no different from that of sinful Gentiles. Like Gentiles, they will eat unclean foods and be deprived of God's law to guide their conduct. In effect Christ, the instrument of God's salvation, will be made an agent of sin. Therefore it is necessary to do the works of the law that identify and separate God's chosen people from the nations and to live under the law since it provides a pattern for correct ethical behavior. The objection is serious, and Paul will provide a full answer only in the paraenesis of this letter.[16] In the verses that follow, however, he anticipates what he will say there.

Crucified with Christ (Gal. 2:18–21). Ethics, for Paul, are eschatological ethics; that is, they are rooted in the cross of Christ where God's eschatological future already breaks into the present through the power of the Spirit.[17] To be in Christ is to be a new creation (6:15; 2 Cor. 5:17). So he writes,

> For through the law I died to the law, so that I might live to God. I have been crucified with Christ; and it is no longer I who live, but it is Christ who lives in me. And the life I now live in the flesh I live by faith in [or: by the faith of] the Son of God, who loved me and gave himself for me (2:19–20).

As Paul will explain in chapter 3, the law's role in salvation history was temporary. Inaugurated 430 years after God's promise to Abraham (3:17), it functioned as humanity's disciplinarian (*paidagōgos*) until Christ came (3:24). Because Paul understands the law as pointing to Christ rather than to itself, he says, "I died to the law, so that I might live to God." In effect, he has been transferred from the realm of the law to the realm of Christ. No longer living under the law, he is crucified with Christ, a striking metaphor of the eschatological existence that he now lives. Christ lives in Paul through the power of the Spirit, and Paul lives on the basis of faith in (or the faithfulness of) the Son of God who loved him and gave his life for him. Although Paul does not employ the technical language of justification here, its reality underlies everything he writes. To be justified is to participate in the eschatological future by sharing in Christ's death.

The works of the law, by which people are identified on the basis of national or cultural heritage, cannot justify because they belong to the old age that merely points to Christ. God never intended that righteousness should come through the law; if so, Christ's death would have been in vain (2:21; see 3:21). That God sent his Son into the world, however, indicates the inability of the law and its works to justify. Christ, then, is not the agent of sin but of righteousness. If Paul reestablishes the "works of the law" that once separated Jew from Gentile, he will show himself to be a transgressor.

To summarize, the truth of the gospel concerns the basis upon which people are justified or acquitted before God: namely, faith in Jesus Christ, or the faithfulness of Jesus Christ in whom one must believe. As a result, the ethical life of the believer is based upon life with and in Christ rather than upon doing the "works of the law."

CHILDREN OF ABRAHAM
CALLED TO FREEDOM

Having stated the truth of the gospel that he preaches, Paul must explain how the Galatians can be included among Abraham's descendants without being circumcised (Gal. 3:1–5:12). At the conclusion of this section (5:1–12), he will warn the Galatians that anyone who lets himself be circumcised is "obliged to obey the entire law" (5:3). Moreover, those who want to be justified by the law will cut themselves off from Christ and fall from grace (5:4). What matters in the realm of Christ is not circumcision or the lack of it but faith expressing itself through love (5:6; see 1 Cor. 7:19). For Paul there is no middle ground or room for compromise; the Galatians must choose between being justified by Christ and being justified by the law.

Children of Abraham. If Paul is to dissuade the Galatians from accepting circumcision, he must demonstrate that they are already descendants of Abraham on the basis of faith. To accomplish this, he draws a sharp distinction between the promise God made to Abraham and the law given to Moses through the mediation of angels. In doing so, he argues that God proclaimed the essence of the gospel to Abraham when he promised the patriarch, "All the Gentiles shall be blessed in you" (Gal. 3:8; compare Gen. 12:3). Because Abraham believed this promise, "it was reckoned to him as righteousness" (Gal. 3:6; compare Gen. 3:6). Consequently, Abraham's real descendants are the people of faith (*hoi ek pisteōs*), and they will be blessed along with faithful Abraham (Gal. 3:7, 9).

In contrast to the people of faith, those who rely on the works of the law (*hosoi ex ergōn nomou*) are under a curse (3:10). Paul makes this bold statement on the basis of a text from Deuteronomy: "Cursed is everyone who does not observe and obey all the things written in the book of the law" (Gal. 3:10; compare Deut. 27:26). Employing yet another text from Deuteronomy ("Cursed is everyone who hangs on a tree," Gal. 3:13; compare Deut. 21:23), he argues that the purpose of Christ's death upon the cross was to redeem "us"[18] from the law's curse so that the blessings of Abraham might come upon the Gentiles, and the Spirit might be given through faith. In effect, then, the Gentiles are Abraham's descendants if they live on the basis of faith.

Paul's argument, however, has not yet taken into account the appearance of the law. Perhaps the Mosaic covenant changed the original stipulations of the promise that God made with Abraham. If so, it is imperative for the Galatians to do the works of the law as well as to believe in Christ. Anticipating the objection, Paul compares the promise God made to Abraham to a will that is incapable of being altered by later codicils. That will, argues Paul, had a single beneficiary in view, "who is Christ" (Gal. 3:16). Since the law came 430 years later, it could not and did not alter the original stipulation of the will; namely, that the inheritance would be granted to Abraham's singular descendant through promise rather than the law (3:18). Having made this point, Paul states that if the Galatians belong to

167

Christ they are Abraham's descendants and heirs according to the promise God made to him (3:29).

The ethical implications of Paul's exegesis are far-reaching. For those baptized into Christ, Abraham's singular descendant, any distinction based upon ethnic, social, or sexual differences has become a matter of indifference (Gal. 3:28; compare 1 Cor. 12:13; Col. 3:11). Here, more than anywhere else, it is clear that justification by faith has a profound social dimension. Whereas circumcision divided Jew from Gentile, faith in Christ establishes a new creation (Gal. 6:15) in which there is neither Jew nor Gentile, slave nor free, male nor female. To be sure, believers continue to live in a world where these distinctions are the basis for privilege and oppression. In the realm of Christ, however, they have come to an end.

The role of the law. Having shown the priority of the promise to the law of Moses, Paul must explain the purpose of the law.[19] If God intended that the Gentiles would be blessed through Abraham, and if this inheritance comes through promise rather than through the law, why did God give the law? Paul answers, "It was added because of transgressions (*tōn parabaseōn charin prosetethē*), until the offspring would come to whom the promise had been made" (Gal. 3:19). The meaning of Paul's language here is not clear, since the Greek preposition *charin* can be interpreted in two ways: (1) God added the law *because* it was necessary to curb and control transgressions; (2) God added the law *in order to* provoke and manifest transgressions so that people would rely upon grace. In either case, Paul asserts that the law had a temporary role in salvation history that ended with the arrival of Christ, Abraham's singular offspring whom the promise had in view. If God had given a law capable of giving life, Paul says, then righteousness would be from the law (3:21). But this is not the case. Previous to Christ, the law functioned as humanity's disciplinarian (*paidagōgos;* 3:24). Like a household slave who watched over and disciplined the young boy destined to become the master of the estate, the law corrected, reprimanded, and instructed those under its power.[20] The law belonged to the period of Israel's legal minority, and those under it were under the power of a servile force. With the appearance of the faith made possible through Christ (3:25), the role and power of the law have come to an end.

Unless one believes that the sole purpose of the law was to provoke transgressions, Paul's image of the *paidagōgos* suggests that the law established a pattern for the moral and ethical conduct of those under its power. The law, however, was and remains incapable of making people righteous before God.

The example of Paul. As in the first part of this letter, Paul now points to the example of his life, which embodies the gospel he preaches. In a personal appeal to the Galatians (4:12–20), he begs them, "become as I am, for I also have become as you are" (4:12). By leaving behind the works of the law, especially those that distinguished him as a Jew, he became like a Gentile (see 1 Cor. 9:21). In the view of those who insist upon doing the works of the law, Paul is now no different from a Gentile sinner. In exhorting the Gentile Galatians to become as he is, he asks them to maintain their Gentile status in the face of Judaizing opposition. Paul embodies the gospel he preaches.

The correspondence between Paul and his gospel includes persecution for the sake of the gospel. He asks, "Why am I still being persecuted if I am still preaching circumcision?" (Gal. 5:11). Paul's circumcision-free gospel has resulted in personal suffering. In contrast to him, the agitators urge circumcision lest they be persecuted for the cross of Christ (6:12). Although it is not clear who is persecuting Paul,[21] it is apparent that the circumcision-free gospel he preached resulted in severe personal suffering (6:17). The conduct of his life, then, verifies the gospel he proclaims and provides the Galatians with a model to imitate. Because they are in Christ, there is no need for them to put themselves under the law to become Abraham's descendants. But if they are not under law, how can they live a moral life?

FULFILLING THE LAW OF CHRIST

In light of Paul's teaching on justification by faith, the moral exhortation of his letters is somewhat problematic. If God justifies people on the basis of faith, is it necessary to live a moral life? Paul's answer is an unequivocal "yes." Others, however, faulted his teaching on faith and justification as disregarding the moral life. In Romans, for example, Paul reports that some slandered him by accusing him of saying, "Let us do evil so that good may come" (Rom. 3:8). And in the same letter, he states an objection against his own position when he writes, "What then? Should we sin because we are not under law but under grace?" (Rom. 6:15). It is not surprising, then, that the epistle of James insists that "a person is justified by works and not by faith alone" (James 2:24), especially if its author misunderstood or received a distorted report of Paul's teaching. Because of such objections, the final section of Galatians (5:13–6:10) is crucial to Paul's argument. Unless he can convince his Gentile converts that they can live a moral and ethical life without placing themselves under the law, they will accept circumcision and do the works of the law. What Paul says can be summarized as follows: those who walk by the Spirit, those who are led by the Spirit, and those who follow the Spirit's lead will fulfill the (Mosaic) law through the love commandment.

Love fulfills the law (Gal. 5:13–15). Throughout Galatians, Paul employs the concepts of freedom and slavery. When the Galatians did not know God, for example, they were "enslaved to beings that by nature are not gods" (4:8). The period before Christ was the period of their minority when they were enslaved to "the weak and beggarly elemental spirits" (4:9). But now that the Spirit of God's Son dwells in their hearts, the Galatians are no longer slaves but sons and daughters, heirs of the promise made to Abraham (4:7). They belong to the lineage of the free woman and are children of the promise according to Isaac (4:21–31). Therefore, Paul exhorts them, "For freedom Christ has set us free. Stand firm, therefore, and do not submit again to a yoke of slavery" (5:1). As members of the "Israel of God" (6:16) they have been called to freedom (5:13).

The freedom to which Paul refers is freedom from living under the law. It is not necessary for the Gentile Galatians to do those works of the law that would identify them with the Jewish people. Lest they misunderstand their freedom in terms of a license to do whatever they wish, Paul warns them that their freedom must not become a staging ground for "the flesh" (*eis aphormēn tē sarki*) to exercise its power. Having been set free from the law and the powers that once enslaved them, they must *enslave* themselves to each other through love! Freedom is not absolute so that people may do whatever they wish. It is exercised in and through love for others.

Paul spoke of this love when he affirmed that the Son of God loved and gave himself for him (2:20), and when he reminded the Galatians that in Christ the only thing that counts is faith working through love (5:6). Such love is hardly an empty concept, and it is much more than feeling, sentiment, or emotion. Rooted in the pattern of Christ's life, it is sacrificial in nature. Those who love as the Son of God loved, then, will hand themselves over for the sake of one another. Because Paul understands love in light of Jesus' life and death, he writes that the whole law is fulfilled (*peplērōtai*) in a single commandment, "You shall love your neighbor as yourself" (5:14; Lev. 19:18). What Paul says here recalls his earlier warning that those who let themselves get circumcised are obliged to do (*poiēsai*) the entire law (5:3). In effect, he establishes a contrast between those under the law of Moses and those who have been set free from it. While the former must do the entire law, the latter fulfill its deepest requirements through the love commandment.

In writing that the whole law is fulfilled by observing the commandment to love one's neighbor, Paul is still referring to the Mosaic law. Those who are no longer under the law because they have been freed from it still fulfill the law. In much the same way that God's promise found its fulfillment in Christ, the law finds its fulfillment in the love commandment.[22] Because the essence of what the law requires is found in the commandment to love one's neighbor, justification by faith does not result in moral laxity. To be sure, the justified no longer need to do the "works of the law" such as circumcision, dietary prescriptions, and the observance of certain days and feasts, all of which function as signs of Jewish identity.[23] But by enslaving themselves to each other through love, the Galatians will fulfill all that the law requires of them.

Walking by the Spirit (Gal. 5:16–26). The difference between doing and fulfilling the law, however, is not merely a matter of knowledge, as if Jesus taught an aspect of the law that others had neglected. For Paul, "doing" and "fulfilling" the law are two different approaches to the moral life which correspond to living according to the flesh and living according to the Spirit. Viewed from this vantage point, the ethical life is lived either in the realm of the flesh (*sarx*) or in the realm of the Spirit (*pneuma*). Each realm, in turn, corresponds to living under the law or in Christ.

Having told the Galatians that they fulfill the law through the love commandment, Paul exhorts them to walk by the Spirit, promising that if they do so, they will not fulfill the desires of the flesh (5:16), since the realm of the Spirit and the realm of the flesh are diametrically opposed (5:17). Those who give themselves to the one will not render allegiance to the other (5:17). To use a military image, just as one cannot simultaneously fight for two opposing armies, so one cannot live both in the realm of the Spirit and the realm of the flesh. One belongs to one or the other, and then acts accordingly. If the Galatians are led by the Spirit, they are not under the law, but if they put themselves under the law, they cannot be led by the Spirit. Thus Paul relates the law to the realm of the flesh (*sarx*; 5:18).

In the first part of this letter *sarx* is used in a variety of ways, all of which are ethically neutral. For example, Paul says that he did not confer with flesh and blood after his call (1:16), by which he means that he did not ask the advice of other human beings. Again, he says that although he lives in the flesh, he lives by faith in the Son of God (2:20). Here Paul simply means that although he is confined by the ordinary circumstances of human life, he now lives by a new principle.[24] In chapters 5 and 6, however, he employs *sarx* as a moral or ethical category (5:13, 16, 17, 19, 24; 6:8). Used in this way, *sarx* functions as a metaphor for what is opposed to God's Spirit. Deeply rooted in unredeemed humanity, *sarx* still remains a threat to those who have been justified. *Sarx* can use the freedom of the believer as an opportunity for self-indulgence (5:13), has desires that are opposed to those of the Spirit (5:16–17), and produces works (5:19) that result in corruption (6:8). The justified, therefore, must crucify *sarx* with its passions and desires (5:24). When used as a moral or ethical category, then, *sarx* does not refer to that which covers the human skeleton.[25] To crucify the flesh, for example, means to die to all that is opposed to God.

Rather than define *sarx*, Paul lists the "works of the flesh" (5:19–21), which he contrasts with the "fruit of the Spirit" (5:22–23). Neither list is exhaustive, but both demonstrate the results of doing the works of the flesh or allowing the Spirit to produce its fruit in the believer. The works of the flesh begin with *porneia* ("sexual immorality"), the evil that Paul continually warns his Gentile converts of. The central and longest portion of the list, however, refers to the kind of conduct that destroys the fabric of community life: enmities, strife, jealousy, anger, quarrels, dissensions, factions, envy. The "works of the flesh" include, but are hardly limited to, sexual immorality. Those who do them will not inherit the kingdom of God.

In contrast to the works of the flesh stands the singular fruit of the Spirit. The list consists of three triads of three, reflecting the perfect harmony the Spirit produces in a community:

love, joy, peace,
patience, kindness, generosity,
faithfulness, gentleness, self-control

Paul insists that there is no law against these things (5:23), by which he means that the fruit of the Spirit is in perfect accord with what the law intends.[26] Because the fruit of the Spirit is the perfect expression of *agapē*, it fulfills the deepest intention of the law.

The expression "the works of the flesh" is undoubtedly meant to remind readers of Paul's expression "the works of the law," suggesting that the law is related to the realm of the flesh. Therefore, if the Galatians want to be under the law (4:21) and justified by it (5:4) after having known Christ, they are still in the realm of the flesh. In light of the Christ event, the ethical life has been redefined for them. If they walk by the Spirit and are guided by the Spirit, the Spirit will produce its fruit within them, allowing them to fulfill the law. But lest they think that such a moral life is automatically produced in the believer, Paul reminds them that those who belong to Christ have crucified the flesh with its passions and desires (5:26), a vivid image recalling his self-description as crucified with Christ (2:19). Because it is a cruciform existence, the moral life of believers is both a gift and a task.

The law of Christ (Gal. 6:2). Paul's understanding of the moral life is summarized in yet another exhortation: "Bear one another's burdens, and in this way you will fulfill the law of Christ" (6:2).[27] Since this is the only occurrence of the expression in Paul's letters,[28] the precise meaning of the phrase is disputed. Is Paul referring to a body of ethical teaching that comes from Jesus? The love commandment given by Jesus? The Mosaic law as exemplified in the life and death of Jesus? The close relationship between Paul's earlier statement that love fulfills the (Mosaic) law (5:14) and the claim that burden bearing fulfills the law of Christ suggests that the law of Christ is the Mosaic law interpreted and lived by Christ in terms of love. If so, Paul exhorts the Galatians to live the Mosaic law in the way that Christ did. The Son of God loved us and gave himself for our sins to set us free from this evil age (1:3; 2:20). In the words of Romans, he did not please himself (Rom. 15:3).

To summarize, the Mosaic law plays a paradoxical role in Pauline ethics as developed in Galatians. On the one hand, since no one is justified by the works of the law, those who seek to be justified by the law or to place themselves under it will be cut off from Christ. On the other hand, those who believe in Christ fulfill the Mosaic law (now identified as the law of Christ) through the love commandment. The faith of the justified expresses itself in love.

THE MORAL TEACHING OF PAUL:
A SUMMARY STATEMENT

In Galatians, Paul develops moral instruction within the context of a polemical situation. To combat those who would deprive his Gentile converts of their freedom in Christ, he defends the truth of his circumcision-free gospel. In doing so, Paul relates the moral life to justification by faith: those justified by faith are not under the law, yet they fulfill the law by the love commandment through the power of the Spirit. Integral to Paul's argument is the example of his own life, which exemplifies the truth of the gospel he proclaims. Aware of his freedom in Christ, he has become like a Gentile for the sake of the Galatians, suffering persecution for his circumcision-free gospel. Thus he presents himself as a model and asks the Galatians to become as he is. In a word, Galatians manifests the same ethical themes we have already identified in the Thessalonian and Corinthian correspondence but adapted to a new situation. First, Paul reminds the community of its elected and sanctified status, which results from being justified by faith apart from the law. The Galatians are the children of Abraham; they belong to the Israel of God. Therefore, they must act accordingly. Second, love stands at the center of this ethic because it is the perfect expression of faith and the fulfillment of the law. Third, Paul provides an ethical model worthy of imitation because he embodies the gospel that he preaches. Election theology, the demands of love, and the example of Paul continue to hold center stage.

8

An Ethic of
Imitation and Example

The Letter to the Philippians

A t several points in this study, I have pointed to the importance
Paul attributes to the example of his own life. On first hearing, this may appear to contradict what the apostle himself writes:
"For we do not proclaim ourselves; we proclaim Jesus Christ as
Lord and ourselves as your slaves for Jesus' sake" (2 Cor. 4:5).
When Paul calls others to imitate him, however, he does not intend
a slavish mimicking of his actions or a blind obedience to his teaching.[1] Rather, as an apostle of Jesus Christ, he has so conformed
himself to Christ's sufferings that his life now manifests the very
gospel that he preaches. Put another way, because he has conformed himself to the pattern of Christ's death, Paul invites others
to imitate him by conforming themselves to Christ. While the
theme of imitation and example play a prominent role in the moral
teaching of all Paul's writings, it holds a special place in Philippians, and so it is in light of this theme that I will discuss the moral
and ethical teaching of this letter.

THE INTEGRITY OF A LETTER

There is no unanimity among scholars concerning the date,
origin, or literary integrity of Paul's letter to the Philippians.[2]
While the first two questions have little bearing upon the interpretation of the letter for New Testament ethics, the question of the
letter's literary integrity is more important, especially for those interested in a historical reconstruction of Paul's ethical teaching. Although my work is primarily concerned with the canonical form
of the text rather than earlier versions of it, a brief consideration of
the contemporary debate on the letter will be helpful for understanding the letter.

There are two principal reasons for questioning the literary integrity of Philippians.[3] First, beginning with 3:1 there is a dramatic shift in the letter's mood. Whereas previous to this verse Paul writes with a sense of peace and joy, in chapter 3 there is a sudden and unexpected warning about those who would compel the Philippians to adopt a Jewish way of living by relying upon the law. Second, toward the end of this letter Paul thanks the Philippians for the gift of their financial support in a brief thank-you that some view as an independent letter (4:10–20). On the basis of these facts, many suggest that Philippians is a composite work consisting of two or three letters that Paul sent to the Philippi at different times, and perhaps from different places.[4] If this is true, then the canonical form of Philippians presents us with a letter in which earlier letters have received a new liter-ary setting.[5]

Not all commentators, however, have espoused that view. Indeed, re-cent studies based upon Greco-Roman rhetoric, epistolary genre, and liter-ary theory argue on behalf of the letter's literary integrity.[6] For example, those who study Philippians from rhetorical and literary perspectives point to patterns of words and themes such as koinōnia (sharing) that are repeated throughout this letter in light of an overarching goal such as com-munal unity. In an analogous fashion, those who make use of epistolary genre argue that the whole of Philippians manifests the characteristics of a letter that belongs to a particular epistolary genre such as the family letter or the letter of friendship. In my view, proponents for the unity of Philip-pians have the stronger case, and so in what follows I will treat Philippians as a single letter written by Paul, from prison, to the congregation at Philippi.[7] The debate about the letter's literary integrity, however, raises an issue of no little importance for the study of New Testament ethics: Does Philippians have a thematic unity?[8] And if it does, what is the relation be-tween the letter's thematic unity and its moral teaching?

PARTNERSHIP IN THE GOSPEL

It is not difficult to outline Philippians in terms of its contents. After a salutation (1:1–2) and thanksgiving (1:3–11), Paul describes to the Philippi-ans his circumstances, which despite his imprisonment have promoted the gospel (1:12–26). Next, he exhorts the Philippians to stand as one in their present trying circumstances (1:27–2:18). After informing them that he will send Timothy and Epaphroditus to them (2:19–30), he warns the Philippi-ans about those who would Judaize them (3:1–21), makes an appeal for communal unity (4:1–9), thanks them for their financial support (4:10–20), and then concludes the letter (4:21–23). It is more difficult, however, to find a thematic unity in Philippians that explains what Paul hopes to effect among his Gentile converts.[9] Nonetheless, I propose that he gives some in-dication of his purpose in the thanksgiving portion of this letter.

In his thanksgiving (1:3–11) Paul expresses gratitude to God because of the community's koinōnia (sharing, partnership, or participation) in the gospel from the first day until now, confident that God, who has begun a "good work" within the community, will bring it to completion on the day of the Lord Jesus Christ, that is, the parousia (1:3–6). Paul affirms that it is right for him to think of the Philippians in this way since they are his *sygkoinōnous* (fellow participants or partners) in grace, both in his imprisonment and in his defense of the gospel.[10] Therefore, he offers a prayer-wish: that their love (*agapē*) will overflow with knowledge and full insight so that they can approve what is best in order that they will be pure and blameless on the "day of Christ," filled with the fruit of righteousness (*karpon dikaiosynēs*) that comes through Jesus Christ (1:9–11). Although brief, Paul's thanksgiving anticipates the major themes of this letter and already implies a course of ethical action for his audience.

First, by reminding the Philippians of their *koinōnia* in the gospel, he announces the overarching theme of this letter: he and the Philippians share in a common enterprise, the proclamation of the gospel, which requires Paul and the Philippians to behave in a way that accords with the gospel. Paul recalls this theme at the end of this letter when he thanks the Philippians for sharing (*sygkoinōnēsantes*) in his distress (4:14) and acknowledges that in the early days of his preaching no other congregation shared (*ekoinōnēsen*) its resources with him as did the Philippians (4:15). Moreover, in the middle of this letter, Paul makes an appeal for unity among the Philippians on the basis of their common participation in the same Spirit (*koinōnia pneumatos;* 2:1). Finally, in presenting himself as an example for the Philippians, he draws out the consequences of *koinōnia*, "to know Christ and the power of his resurrection and the sharing of his sufferings (*koinōnian tōn pathēmatōn*) by becoming like him in his death" (3:10). In sum, the theme of *koinōnia* occurs throughout this letter and binds it together.

In the present circumstances of the Philippian church, however, this *koinōnia* is in danger, and so Paul prays that their "love may overflow more and more with knowledge and full insight" (1:9), that they may discern what is best. Paul will deal subsequently with the jealousy and strife that endanger the *koinōnia* of the Philippians in two exhortations (1:27–2:18 and 3:1–4:9). In doing so, he will provide the congregation with further knowledge and insight into the demands of love as revealed in Christ (2:5–11). Moreover, he will point to Timothy, Epaphroditus, and himself as examples worthy of imitation. Only if the love of the Philippians grows in knowledge and insight, as Paul prays that it will, will the Philippians maintain *koinōnia* and discern what is truly good (1:10; 4:8–9).

As in Paul's other letters, the goal of the moral life is to stand pure and blameless at the parousia, filled with "the fruit of righteousness" (1:10–11), the righteousness that comes from God based on faith (3:9). To explain what he means by this righteousness, Paul will contrast the example of his life with that of those who have confidence in the flesh, especially in the sign of circumcision. To summarize, then, the organizing theme of Philippians is *koinōnia*, the bond of unity that makes the congregation one because its members share in the proclamation of the gospel, the gift of the Spirit, and the fellowship of Christ's sufferings. To safeguard *koinōnia* Paul will explain that love requires individual members of the community to surrender their selfish ambitions for the good of others.

A LIFE WORTHY OF THE GOSPEL

The main body of Philippians consists of a series of exhortations on behalf of communal unity. Before appealing for unity, however, Paul informs the community of his circumstances (1:12–26) in order to lay the groundwork for the moral exhortations that will follow.

Paul is in prison. Nevertheless, his imprisonment has actually benefited the gospel since many are now proclaiming the Word with even greater boldness and without fear, precisely because of Paul's imprisonment (1:14). In effect, even in prison Paul serves as a model of Christian behavior for others. The implication, of course, is that he should also serve as a model for the Philippians, who are apparently enduring, or about to experience, trying circumstances. Not all is well since some preach the gospel from envy, rivalry, and selfish ambition, hoping to add to Paul's tribulations (1:15–17).[11] Paul, however, is remarkably sanguine since Christ is being preached, albeit for false motives (1:18).[12] Moreover, he appears to be confident that he will be delivered from his present circumstances and not be put to shame (1:19–20). The reason for Paul's confidence, despite his trying circumstances, is plain: the apostle has come to a point in his life when he can say that living *is* Christ and dying *is* gain (1:21). Paul has so oriented his life to Christ that it has no meaning apart from him. Moreover, should he die, he is confident that he will be with the Lord. In effect, Paul finds himself in a situation in which both life and death are advantageous.

By informing the Philippians of his circumstances, Paul accomplishes two things. First, he puts those who are his partners in the preaching of the gospel at ease: there is no need for them to be concerned about his welfare. Second, since the Philippians find, or may soon find, themselves in similar circumstances, he begins the process of presenting himself as a model worthy of imitation. By continuing to rejoice in the midst of affliction (1:18), he embodies the paradox of the gospel that he preaches: God effects life through death.

Having informed the Philippians of his circumstances, Paul turns to their circumstances. Despite their partnership with him in the gospel, all is not well. For reasons he does not explain, there is dissension within the community. Therefore, in what is the central moral exhortation of this letter (1:27–2:18), Paul calls the Philippians to unity. The exhortation begins with a comprehensive admonition that stands as a heading for all that follows.[13] The Philippians, who live in the Roman colony of Philippi, are to live their lives as citizens (*politeuesthe*) "in a manner worthy of the gospel of Christ" (1:27). Whether present or absent, Paul wants to be assured that the Philippians are standing in *one* spirit as they contend (*synathlountes*) with *one* soul on behalf of the faith that underlies and derives from the gospel, in no way intimidated by their opponents (1:27–28). In effect, Paul is calling for a concerted communal effort in the proclamation of the gospel. The Philippians are to act as a single corporate person. In doing so, they will avoid the divisive preaching to which he has just referred (1:15–17). Moreover, as a united community they will be able to manifest the boldness that characterizes Paul in his own imprisonment. Lest the Philippians shrink from their task, Paul reminds them that it has been granted to them by God (*echaristhē*) not only to believe in Christ but to suffer on behalf of him as well (1:29). In effect, the Philippians are experiencing the same struggle (*agōna*)[14] which they saw in Paul when he was imprisoned in Philippi (see 1 Thess. 2:2; Acts 16) and which they now hear that he is enduring at Rome or Ephesus (1:30). The Philippians are to be Paul's partners in suffering, then, as well as in preaching the gospel.[15] To do so, however, they must live and work as a united community.

Having spoken of the external dangers threatening the Philippians, Paul turns his attention to the divisions that endanger the internal life of the community (2:1–4). He begins with a fourfold appeal:

if then there is any encouragement in Christ
if there is any consolation from love
if there is any sharing (*koinōnia*) in the Spirit
if there is any compassion and sympathy

Although each of these phrases begins with "if" (*ei*), Paul is appealing to the encouragement and consolation that he and the community *already* experience in Christ. Thus the conditional clauses could be rendered "since there is" or "if, as indeed is the case."[16] On the basis of what they have already experienced, then, Paul exhorts them to make his joy complete by the following:

being of the *same* mind
having the *same* love
being united in a *common* soul
thinking *one* thing
    doing *nothing* from selfish ambition
    nor from conceit
    but in humility regarding others as better than themselves
each one looking *not* to his own interest
    but to the interests of others

As in the previous section, where he encouraged the community to stand in *one* spirit and contend in *one* soul (1:27) against its external enemies, here Paul exhorts the community to avoid internal division by being of *one* mind (*to auto phronēte . . . to hen phronountes*), each regarding himself or herself in humility (*tē tapeinophrosynē*).

Although biblical writings present humility as the proper attitude of human beings before God, the Greco-Roman world did not prize humility as a virtue but viewed it as the proper demeanor only for those who, like slaves, were base-born. Thus, in exhorting his Gentile converts to regard themselves with humility, Paul challenges them to rethink their moral and ethical values. It is not surprising, then, that he turns to Christ in order to support his exhortation (2:5–11).

Paul has already encouraged the Philippians to "be of the same mind" and to be of "one mind" (2:2). Playing on these phrases, both of which employ the verb *phronein* (to think),[17] he now exhorts them, "Let the same mind (*touto phroneite*) be in you that was in Christ Jesus" (2:5). While the precise meaning of this phrase, as well as its bearing on Paul's argument, is disputed,[18] I suggest that Paul is drawing a comparison between the behavior exemplified by Christ's sacrificial love and the attitude of humility that Paul encourages the Philippians to pursue. Although Christ Jesus was in the "form of God," he did not consider that his equality with God consisted in snatching.[19] Or, to put it another way, Christ saw his divine status in terms of giving rather than of getting. Consequently, emptying himself of all status, he took the "form of a slave," bereft of rights and social status. Thus he humbled himself by becoming obedient to the point of death, even to accepting crucifixion, the punishment especially reserved for slaves. In effect, Christ understood his divinity in terms of giving and surrendering rather than of exercising or receiving power. Therefore God exalted him.

To be sure, there can be no perfect comparison between the situation of Christ and that of the Philippians. Unlike Christ, the Philippians cannot claim a divine status. Moreover, no act of obedience on their part can ever be redemptive as was Christ's obedience. Finally, the Philippians must not expect that their obedience can or will earn a divine recompense. Nonetheless, Paul draws an important analogy between the behavior of Christ and that of the Philippians. Just as Christ did not consider his divine status as consisting in snatching, so the Philippians must not look to their own interests but to the interests of others (2:4). For Paul, Christians are to imitate the self-emptying of Christ. To this extent, the Pauline notion of imitating Christ is rooted in Christ's redemptive act rather than in specific moral or ethical examples taken from Jesus' earthly life.

Having reminded the Philippians of Christ's self-emptying, he draws out the implications of the Christ hymn for the Philippian congregation ("Therefore, my beloved . . . "; 2:12–18). Playing upon the notion of obedience that characterized the redemptive work of Christ, Paul expresses his confidence that the community that obeyed him when he was present will do so all the more now that he is absent and in prison.[20] This obedience requires the Philippians to work out their salvation with fear and trembling (2:12). Since Paul is addressing the entire community, he has more in view than just the personal salvation of the believer, although this is not excluded. From Paul's perspective, the salvation of the individual is intimately related to the destiny of the community. A failure on the part of the community to work out its salvation, therefore, will have profound implications for the individuals who constitute the congregation.

In exhorting the Philippians to work out their salvation, Paul is not contradicting his earlier statement that God will bring to completion the good work he has begun in them (1:6). Rather, having told the Philippians to work out their salvation (*sōtērian katergazesthe*), Paul immediately explains that God is at work within them (*theos gar estin ho energōn en hymin;* 2:13), enabling them to carry out his good pleasure. Whatever work the Philippians carry out, therefore, is accomplished by God, who is already at work among them. Nonetheless, Paul expects his Gentile converts to work in an active manner for the salvation that God is effectively working in them. More specifically, he wants them to do all things "without murmuring and arguing" so that they will be "blameless and innocent, children of God without blemish in the midst of a crooked and perverse generation" in which they will shine like the stars in the world (2:14–15). These two verses are the goal of the moral exhortation Paul has been developing (1:27–2:18). He is writing because there is discord within the church, and if the community is to "work out" its salvation, it must do all things without murmuring and arguing.

In calling upon the community to do all things without murmuring and arguing, and in reminding the Philippians that they are children of God without blemish, meant to shine like the stars, Paul undergirds his moral exhortation with election theology by implicitly comparing and contrasting the Philippians with the elected community of Israel.[21] First, Israel of old murmured against God and Moses in the wilderness (Ex. 16:7; Num. 11:1), thereby endangering its communal unity. The Philippians must not repeat this error. Second, the Septuagint version of the Song of Moses describes the Israelites as "blamable children" (*tekna mōmēta*), who comprise "a crooked and perverted generation" (*genea skolia kai diestrammenē;* Deut. 32:5). In contrast to them, the Philippians are and must remain children of God without blemish (*tekna theou amōma*) in the midst of a crooked and perverse generation. Third, because of its elected status, Israel of old was to be "a light to the nations" (Isa. 42:6) and the wise were to shine "like the brightness of the sky" (Dan. 12:3). Like Israel of old, therefore, the Philippians must shine like stars in the world. Paul is clearly contrasting and comparing the Philippians with Israel in order to remind his Gentile converts of their elected status and the moral implications that this has for their lives. As God's people, they are to maintain their elected status by holding to the word of life until the day of the Lord's parousia (2:16).

To summarize the extensive moral exhortation of 1:27–2:18, the Philippians will live in a manner worthy of the gospel and work out their salvation if, instead of grumbling and arguing, they look to one another's interests in a manner analogous to that of Christ, who humbled himself. By doing so, they will be blameless and innocent children of God on the day of the Lord's parousia.

JOINING OTHERS IN IMITATING PAUL

As we have seen, Paul implicitly points to the example of his own life when he informs the Philippians of his present circumstances (1:12–26). In the latter part of this letter, however, he makes an explicit appeal to the Philippians to join others in imitating him: "Join in imitating me, and observe those who live according to the example you have in us" (3:17). Among those who imitate Paul are Timothy and Epaphroditus. In announcing that he will send both to Philippi (2:19–30), Paul describes the character of each in a manner that recalls the example of Christ he has just proposed (2:5–11). Accordingly, Paul says that he has no one else quite like Timothy. Whereas all others seek their own interests, Timothy is genuinely concerned about the welfare of the Philippian community (2:20–21). His character is self-evident because he serves Paul as a son serves his father. As for Epaphroditus, he came close to death (*mechri thanatou*, 2:30, the same phrase found in the Christ hymn, 2:8) for the work of Christ. Epaphroditus and Timothy, then, have joined in imitating Paul by conforming themselves to the pattern of Christ's self-giving: Timothy no longer seeks his own interests, and Epaphroditus has given of himself to the point of almost losing his life. In sending these coworkers to Philippi, Paul provides the community with concrete examples of his moral exhortation.

It is the example of Paul's own life, however, that controls the latter part of this letter. Having exhorted the Philippians to communal unity (1:27–2:18) and announced the coming visits of Timothy and Epaphroditus (2:19–30), he now undertakes yet another exhortation (3:1–4:9). In him, the Philippians will find someone who has forsaken everything for the righteousness that comes from God (3:1–10) and who continues to pursue the heavenly call of God in Christ (3:11–21). Therefore, they must join others in imitating him and set aside all community dissension (4:2–3).

Chapter 3 is problematic for the study of Philippians, and most commentators read it in terms of a real or impending crisis: Judaizing missionaries have come, or are about to come, to Philippi as they did to Galatia.[22] While I do not dismiss or even dispute this scenario, I suggest that chapter 3 also has a paraenetic function, indicated by its opening phrase, "To write the same things to you is not troublesome to me, and for you it is a safeguard" (3:1).[23] Here, as in 1 Thessalonians, Paul makes use of a traditional paraenetic device; he acknowledges that the Philippians already know what he is about to tell them, yet he repeats what they know. In this case, however, the paraenesis is conveyed by the example of Paul's life.

Paul begins by contrasting two kinds of behavior: his own and that of the Judaizers. Whereas the latter rely upon the sign of circumcision made in their flesh to obtain a righteousness based upon the law, Paul has obtained a righteousness that comes from God and is based upon faith (3:9). This righteousness, however, comes at a price since it has been necessary for Paul to reckon as loss everything he once counted as gain, including the righteousness he enjoyed according to the law. Therefore Paul has suffered the loss of everything in order to gain Christ and be found in him, having the righteousness that comes from God and is based on faith. In a way analogous to Christ, who took on the form of a slave (*morphēn doulou*), Paul seeks to know the power of Christ's resurrection and the sharing of his sufferings by conforming himself to Christ's death (*symmorphizomenos tō thanatō autou*) so that he might attain to the resurrection of the dead (3:10–11). In effect, Paul draws an implicit comparison between himself and Christ: as Christ conformed himself to the condition of a slave, Paul has conformed himself to Christ's death. The process of conforming himself to Christ, however, is not complete. Like an athlete, therefore, Paul strains forward to obtain the prize of the heavenly calling (*brabeion tēs klēseōs*; 3:14).

When Paul exhorts the Philippians to join others in imitating him and to observe those who live in accordance with the example (*typon*) of his life (3:17), there is little doubt what he intends. The Philippians must learn the power of Christ's resurrection and the sharing of his sufferings by a continual process of conforming themselves to Christ's death. Whereas the enemies of Christ's cross set their minds on earthly things, those who are in the process of being conformed to Christ know that their citizenship is in heaven (3:20). From there will come a Savior who will transform (*metaschēmatisei*) their humble bodies so that they will be conformed (*symmorphon*) to Christ's glorious body (3:21). Once more, Paul is alluding to the Christ hymn (2:5–11) here.[24] Christ was found to be in human form (*schēmati*) and humbled himself (*etapeinōsen*), obedient unto death (2:7–8), wherefore God highly exalted him. Those who are conforming themselves to Christ's death currently find themselves in a humble body (*to sōma tēs tapeinōseōs*; 3:21), but on the day of the parousia that body will be conformed to Christ's glorious body. The imitation to which Paul calls his converts, then, is rooted in the salvific pattern of Christ's incarnation, death, and resurrection. Those who imitate Paul in this way are truly circumcised, even if they are not circumcised in the flesh.

Having pointed to the example of his own life, Paul draws out the consequences of what he has been saying: "Therefore (*hōste*), my brothers and sisters, whom I love and long for, my joy and crown, stand firm in the Lord in this way, my beloved" (4:1). The manner in which Paul structures this exhortation (3:1–4:9) parallels the organization of his earlier exhortation (1:27–2:18). Just as he drew out the moral consequences of that exhortation (*hōste*; 2:12) after presenting the example of Christ (2:5–11), so he draws out the consequences of this exhortation (*hōste*; 4:1) after presenting the example of his own life (3:1–21). First, the Philippians are to stand firm (*stēkete*, the same word used in the first exhortation, 1:27) in the Lord in this way. "This way" refers to all that Paul has just said about himself: the Philippians are to rely upon the righteousness that comes from God as they press toward their heavenly goal.

Second, Paul becomes more specific (4:2–3). Euodia and Syntyche are to be of the same mind in the Lord (*to auto phronein en kyriō*). The phrase Paul uses here is the very same one that he employs in his first exhortation, when he urges the Philippians to be of the same mind (2:2), and it is clearly intended to recall the opening of the Christ hymn, "Let the same mind be in you . . . " (*touto phroneite en hymin,* 2:5). While the quarrel among these two women may appear to be of passing importance, it is more likely that it underlies the dissension racking the Philippian community. Euodia and Syntyche have "struggled" with Paul and the rest of his coworkers in the gospel. The word that Paul employs in describing their efforts (*synēthlēsan*) is the same that he used in the first exhortation when he called upon the entire community to "strive" side by side with one mind (1:27). Although there is no certainty in the matter, it appears that Euodia and Syntyche were community leaders who were endangering the life of the community by quarreling. If this is the case, then the rhetoric of the whole letter is in the service of these verses.[25]

Third, Paul calls upon the Philippians to rejoice because the Lord is near (4:4–7), thereby placing their moral and ethical life within the horizon of Christ's parousia. In doing so, he recalls themes that he has already developed: the Philippians are to be pure and blameless on the day of Christ (1:10), and they must press forward to their heavenly call (3:14) because their citizenship is in heaven, whence the Savior will come (3:20).

Finally, Paul provides the Philippians with a list of virtues that would have resonated with those living in the Greco-Roman world (4:8). The manner in which he concludes this list suggests his awareness of, and readiness to embrace, a broader ethical heritage (" . . . if there is any excellence and if there is anything worthy of praise, think about these things").[26] But the final word is about Paul himself! "Keep on doing the things that you have learned and received and heard and seen *in me,* and the God of peace will be with you" (4:9). Not only does Paul teach the moral life, he exemplifies it because he has conformed himself to Christ.

PAUL'S MORAL TEACHING:
A SUMMARY STATEMENT

Philippians, more than any letter studied thus far, focuses upon example and imitation understood as conforming oneself to the pattern of Christ's death. But in addition to this theme, Paul makes use of two other themes found in his letters to the Thessalonians, Corinthians, and Galatians: election and love. As in those letters, he reminds the Philippians that they are God's elected people. They are the children of God in the midst of a perverse generation (2:15). They are the true circumcision (3:3) whose citizenship is in heaven (3:20). Therefore, their love must overflow more and more (1:9) with knowledge and insight that comes from having the mind of Christ Jesus (2:5). In doing so, they will safeguard their *koinōnia.*

9

The Obedience
of Faith

The Letter to the Romans

*I*t is with good reason that Paul's letter to the Romans stands at
the beginning of the Pauline corpus. Not only is it the longest of
the apostle's letters that we possess, but in the judgment of most
scholars it is the most important. Written from Corinth during the
winter of 57–58 before his final journey to Jerusalem,[1] Romans is
Paul's most detailed and systematic discussion of (1) justification
by faith apart from the law, (2) the role and destiny of Israel, and
(3) the moral and ethical demands flowing from the life of faith. It
is not surprising then that many view this letter as a compendium
of the apostle's theology, a kind of theological last will and testament.[2] Romans is, after all, a powerful and compelling document,
and studies in Paul's theology are often filtered through its prism.
While there is some justification for understanding Romans in this
way, there has been a continuing debate concerning its nature and
genre.[3]

Put most simply, what kind of a writing is Romans? Is it a response to a particular situation within the Roman church?[4] Or is
it occasioned by the circumstances of Paul's life? For example,
having completed his work in the Mediterranean basin, and hoping to open a new missionary field in Spain, does the apostle employ this letter as the opportune moment to summarize his teaching on topics such as justification, faith, the law, Israel, and the
moral life?[5] Or is Romans a mixture of the two: a response to a
concrete situation within the Roman church that requires Paul to
present his gospel in a careful and detailed manner? The answer
to these questions is of importance to New Testament ethics since
the paraenesis or moral exhortation of Romans (12:1–15:13), especially the discussion about the weak and the strong (14:1–
15:13), is at the heart of the debate. For example, if Paul employs
Romans as an occasion to lay out his gospel in a somewhat systematic fashion, then his moral exhortation (12:1–15:13) is a gen-

eral paraenesis, something approaching a moral or ethical statement made in light of his gospel. But if Paul writes Romans in response to a concrete situation within the life of the Roman church, then his moral exhortation must be read in light of that situation, for example, a dispute between the strong and the weak regarding dietary prescriptions, festival days, and so on . Paul's moral exhortation would then be the expression of his gospel written for a specific situation.

To be more concrete and specific: One of the most celebrated passages in the whole of the New Testament is Paul's statement concerning obedience to the governing authorities (13:1–7). If Romans is a compendium of his teaching that was not written in response to a specific situation, then one might argue that this text provides the basis for a theology of church and state, though neither word, "church" or "state," is found in the text. But if Paul is responding to a concrete situation at Rome, what he says about the governing authorities is not necessarily the theological basis for a doctrine of church and state so much as an ad hoc response to a specific situation. To be sure, the student of New Testament ethics can and should learn from the manner in which Paul solves this moral and ethical question, but in this case it is no longer advisable to view his response as the unchanging foundation for an apostolic doctrine on church and state.

Scholars have taken and will continue to take different sides in the Romans debate. I favor the third approach listed above: Romans, like Paul's other letters, is an occasional writing that responds to a real situation within the Roman church. That situation, however, requires Paul to compose something akin to an "essay-letter"[6] in which he presents important aspects of his gospel. The moral exhortation (12:1–15:13) of this letter, then, is a response to a concrete situation so that the exhortation explains the moral demands of "the obedience of faith" (1:5) required by the gospel. Understood in this way, Romans sketches the broad contours of a Pauline ethic.[7]

OBJECTIONS TO PAUL'S GOSPEL

Any description of the situation that occasioned Romans will, of necessity, remain at the level of a hypothesis. Such hypotheses are helpful for interpreting Paul's letters because they "fill in" the other side of his conversations, but they remain liable to continuing revision and correction, and in some instances must even be abandoned. With this caution, I propose the following background for the composition of Romans.[8]

I begin with the presupposition that the Roman church represents a type of Christianity which A.J.M. Wedderburn calls "Judaizing," that is,

a form of Christianity which treats Christianity as simply part of Judaism and, more important, requires of all its adherents, whether they are Jews or not, that they observe the Jewish Law as the Jewish Law either in whole or in part.[9]

To speak of a Judaizing Christianity, therefore, implies that "the patterns of thought and behavior of Judaism"[10] were dominant for those who embraced this kind of Christianity, be they Gentiles or Jews. Moreover, for these believers (be they Gentiles or Jews), Paul's gospel was puzzling and threatening inasmuch as it did not require others to accept circumcision and the law.

Second, I presuppose that there were other Christians at Rome who practiced a form of Christianity akin to the gospel Paul preached.[11] Such believers, if they were Gentiles, did not undergo circumcision, and whether Gentiles or Jews, they no longer observed the traditional dietary prescriptions of the law. Thus we can speak of two kinds of believers: the first aligned themselves closely to a Jewish way of life while the second did not. This is not to claim that there were two churches or two congregations at Rome.[12] Indeed, even the expression "the Roman church" is somewhat misleading since it gives the impression that there was a single congregation at Rome.[13] In all likelihood, the Roman church consisted of a number of house churches (see 16:5), some of which were probably associated with various synagogues. The result was a certain tension in the Roman church between believers (be they Jewish or Gentile) who lived a Jewish way of life and those who did not. The former, I submit, are the "weak" and the latter the "strong" of whom Paul speaks in 14:1–15:13.[14]

Third, I presuppose that Paul was aware of these tensions, as well as the misgivings that those Christians who observed Jewish customs had about him and the gospel he preached. Given his desire to visit Rome, and from there to evangelize in the West (perhaps with Roman assistance and monetary support),[15] it was necessary for Paul to respond to the objections and fears that his gospel caused among believers who continued to live a Jewish way of life. Thus the *whole* of Romans, not just Paul's discussion of the weak and the strong (14:1–15:13), is a response to a concrete situation. Paul must explain what he teaches about the law and Israel, and most important for our purposes, he must dispel any notion that his gospel encourages an antinomian way of life. In what follows, I will consider objections Paul raises through a series of rhetorical questions against his own gospel.

Will We Be Judged?
Should We Do Evil?

The first of these rhetorical questions occurs in Rom. 3:1–8 when Paul asks if there is any advantage in being circumcised and being a Jew (3:1), since Jews as well as Gentiles stand under God's wrath. Furthermore, if human wickedness paradoxically leads to God's righteousness, is it not unjust for God to inflict wrath upon humanity (3:5)? And why are we condemned as sinners if human falsehood leads to God's truthfulness and glory (3:7)? Paul's final question is the most important: "And why not say (as some people slander us by saying that we say), 'Let us do evil so that good may come'?" (3:8). To understand why Paul raises these questions, it is necessary to review his discussion on the sinfulness of humanity which precedes these questions (1:18–2:29).

Having announced the theme of his gospel as God's saving righteousness in 1:16–17, Paul embarks upon a description of human sinfulness in 1:18–2:29 in order to show that all, Jew as well as Gentile, are in need of God's saving grace (3:23–24). In the first part of this discussion (1:18–32), Paul focuses upon the sinfulness of the Gentiles. Their root sin is idolatry, for although they knew something of God from the created world, they did not worship God as God (1:21) but "exchanged the glory of the immortal God for images resembling a mortal being or birds or four-footed animals or reptiles" (1:23). The result of Gentile idolatry, according to Paul, is a total breakdown in human society that he describes in three units, each of which begins in a similar way.

First, Paul says that God handed the Gentiles over (*paredōken*) to the impurity of their own hearts and the degradation of their bodies since they worshiped the creature rather than the creator (1:24–25). Second, pointing to the homosexuality of the Gentile world, he states that God handed the Gentiles over (*paredōken*) to degrading passions as they exchanged heterosexual relationships for homosexual relationships (1:26–27).[16] Finally, since the Gentiles did not see fit to acknowledge God, God handed them over (*paredōken*) to their undiscerning mind, this resulting in all kinds of evil behaviors that are detrimental to society (1:28–32).

Any Jewish reader would have applauded Paul's description of the Gentile world, recalling a somewhat similar indictment of Gentile idolatry in Wisdom of Solomon 13—14. Therefore, having gained the goodwill of his Jewish audience, in Romans 2 Paul turns his attention to Jewish sinfulness in order to show that even the Jews stand under God's wrath. From Paul's point of view, the basic problem is as follows. Even though the Jews have the advantage of the law and circumcision, they have failed to fulfill God's will. Indeed, Paul supposes that there are Gentiles who, although they do not have the law, observe by nature what the law commands and so show that at least certain commandments of the law are written in their hearts. In effect, the law and circumcision are advantageous to the Jews so long as they observe the law. Paul writes:

> For he [God] will repay according to each one's deeds: to those who by patiently doing good seek for glory and honor and immortality, he will give eternal life; while for those who are self-seeking and who obey not the truth but wickedness, there will be wrath and fury. . . . For God shows no partiality. All who have sinned apart from the law will also perish apart from the law, and all who have sinned under the law will be judged by the law. For it is not the hearers of the law who are righteous in God's sight, but the doers of the law who will be justified (2:6–13).

This is one of the most disputed texts in the whole of Romans,[17] since it appears to contradict Paul's teaching on justification by faith: "For 'no human being will be justified in his sight' by deeds prescribed by the law, for through the law comes the knowledge of sin" (3:20). To make sense of what Paul is saying in Romans 2, it is important to keep three points in mind. First, Paul's primary audience is composed of believers who have experienced God's justifying grace. Some of these continue to rely on the law and circumcision while others do not. With the former group in view, Paul makes the following point: Although you have been justified by faith, you will be judged by God on the basis of your deeds. God is impartial and does not judge human beings on the basis of externals such as circumcision and the possession of the law. As regards judgment, deeds are important. Justified by faith, all will be judged on the basis of deeds. Their deeds, however, will not justify them.[18]

Second, the opening chapters of Romans are part of a rhetorical argument in which Paul purposely overstates his case since he wants to show that *all*, Jew as well as Gentile, are in need of God's grace. He writes: " . . . since all have sinned and fall short of the glory of God; they are now justified by his grace as a gift, through the redemption that is in Christ Jesus" (3:23–24). Therefore Paul must paint a negative portrait of the Gentile world in chapter 1, and an equally negative portrait of the Jewish world in chapter 2. But in chapter 2, Paul has yet another rhetorical goal: to show the impartiality of God (2:11). Consequently, there is a tension between chapters 1 and 2, for Paul assumes in chapter 2 that there are in fact some Gentiles who do what the law commands. This, in turn, allows Paul to show that God judges Jew and Gentile impartially on the basis of conduct rather than national identity.

Finally, when Paul writes that no one will be justified by the deeds prescribed by the law (3:20), he is working with still another premise: the sinfulness of humankind. Because all are under the power of sin, no one can do the righteous deeds prescribed by the law. Therefore all, Jew as well as Gentile, are freely justified by God's grace. Paul seems to suppose that although human beings can do what is right, at least part of the time, the situation of human sinfulness is so overwhelming that all, without exception, are in need of God's grace.

What Paul says in chapters 2 and 3 can be summarized, somewhat artificially, in two syllogisms. The premise of the first rests on the impartiality of God.

Major:	God is impartial (2:11).
Minor:	One who is impartial does not judge on the basis of appearance.
Conclusion:	God does not judge on the basis of possessing the law and circumcision but on the basis of doing the law (2:6–8).

The premise of the second syllogism is the sinful situation in which humanity finds itself.

Major:	Both Jews and Greeks are under the power of sin (3:9).
Minor:	Those under the power of sin cannot do the just requirements of the law (chapter 7).
Conclusion:	No one is justified by the deeds of the law (3:20) because no one can do them apart from Christ (8:1–4).

Paul is dealing with different premises when he says that the "doers of the law will be justified" (2:13) and that no one will be justified "by deeds prescribed by the law" (3:20). In the first instance, he is concerned with God's impartiality; in the second, he has the sinfulness of Jew and Gentile in view.

Furthermore, although Paul writes that "doers of the law will be justified," he does *not* say that they will be justified by their works. The implication of the passive voice in 2:13 is that the doers of the law will be justified *by God*. Graciously justified by God, they will ultimately be judged on the basis of their deeds. When readers come to the objections that Paul raises against his own gospel in 3:1–8, therefore, two things should be clear. First, his gospel does not do away with God's judgment. Second, Paul does not encourage others to do evil in order to provoke God's mercy.

Do We Overthrow the Law?

At the end of Romans 3 Paul employs yet another rhetorical question in order to clarify his gospel. Having explained that God manifested his righteousness apart from the law, although this righteousness was attested to by the law and the prophets (3:21–26), and having declared that no one can boast before God since all are justified by faith apart from the works prescribed by the law (3:27–30), Paul asks, "Do we then overthrow the law by this faith?" (3:31). Employing a favorite expression, "By no means!" (*mē genoito*), he emphatically answers "no!" To the contrary, his teaching on faith upholds the deepest meaning of the law (*alla nomon histanomen*). To explain what he means, Paul provides a fresh exegesis of Gen. 15:6, "Abraham believed God, and it was reckoned to him as righteousness."[19] In the first half of chapter 4 (vv. 1–12), he explains that God reckoned righteousness to Abraham before he was circumcised on the basis of his faith rather than his works. Then, in the second half of the chapter (vv. 13–25), he describes Abraham's faith as an incipient faith in the resurrection since it did not waver even when he considered his aged body and Sarah's barren womb. Thus Paul is able to conclude that the text of Gen. 15:6 was written for the sake of all who believe in the God who raised Jesus from the dead (4:24). Rather than overthrowing the law by "the law of faith" (3:27), Paul establishes it on the firm foundation of faith (3:31).

Shall We Continue to Sin?

In Romans 6 and 7, Paul raises four more objections to his teaching, all of which have important moral implications.[20] First, having contrasted the incomparable gift of God that leads to justification and eternal life with the trespass that results in judgment and condemnation (Rom. 5:12–21), he asks, "What then are we to say? Should we continue in sin in order that grace may abound?" (6:1). The objection, of course, is similar to that posed earlier: Paul's teaching encourages doing evil in order to provoke God's goodness (3:8). But now Paul responds to the objection in some detail. As in 3:31, he emphatically answers "no!" (*mē genoito*) since believers have died to sin by their sacramental participation in Christ's death. Baptized into his death, they are to walk in newness of life (*en kainotēti zōēs;* 6:4). This is not to say that believers are incapable of sinning. Were that the case, there would be no need for Paul to give any moral exhortation whatsoever. A realist, Paul knows that believers live between two ages, the old and the new. On the one hand, they are justified and already experience the power of God's Spirit, which enables them to fulfill the just requirement of the law (8:1–4). But since the parousia is yet to occur, the justified are not yet saved (5:9–10), and they have not yet attained their goal (see Phil. 3:12–14). Nevertheless, they must consider themselves dead to sin and living for God in Christ Jesus (6:11).

On the basis of this baptismal catechesis, Paul exhorts the Romans not to let sin rule over their bodies but to present themselves to God, for they are no longer "under law but under grace" (6:14). To summarize, sin is incompatible with the new life that believers have embraced. Although Paul teaches that where sin increased, grace abounded all the more (5:20), he does not encourage those justified by faith to continue in sin.

Paul's affirmation that the justified are no longer "under law but under grace" (6:14) allows him to raise a second objection against his own teaching. He asks, "Should we sin because we are not under law but under grace?" (6:15). Once more, he responds *mē genoito*, and then proceeds to answer the objection in detail. In true paraenetic fashion, he begins by reminding his audience of what they should already know (*ouk oidate*, "do you not know?" 6:16). There is no absolute freedom because people are slaves (*douloi*) to whatever or whomever they offer obedience, either to the power of sin, which leads them to death, or to obedience,[21] which leads them to righteousness (6:16). Freed from the power of sin, believers are now enslaved to righteousness (*edoulōthēte tē dikaiosynē;* 6:18). Therefore, they must present the members of their bodies to righteousness[22] for sanctification (*eis hagiasmon*), which leads to eternal life (6:22). Being under grace, therefore, is not a license to sin but a transferal to a new realm of obedience that leads to righteousness and life.

Next, employing an example taken from the law (7:1–6), Paul explains why believers are no longer under the law. Just as a married woman is no longer bound to her husband when he dies, so believers are no longer bound to the Mosaic law, since they died to the law "through the body of

Christ" (7:4), by which Paul means the crucified body of Christ.[23] Before Christ freed them from the law, the law aroused their sinful passions (7:5). But now that they have been freed from the realm of the law by Christ's death, with which they are associated through baptism, believers live in the realm of God's grace. Far from being an encouragement to sin, being "under grace" requires an obedience to righteousness whereby believers give themselves wholly and entirely to God.

By saying that the law aroused the sinful passions of those who were under it (7:5), Paul lays the groundwork for yet another objection to his teaching: "What then should we say? That the law is sin?" (7:7). Once more the question is emphatically denied (*mē genoito*) since the law is holy and the commandment is holy, just, and good (7:12).[24] Sin, however, made use of God's just commandments to arouse all kinds of desire (*pasan epithymian;* 7:8) in those who were not yet redeemed by God's grace. Consequently, when they heard the commandment, those who were not yet under God's grace were tempted by sin to do the very thing that the commandment forbade them to do. Sin, not the law, is the culprit.

Paul's description of the law's commandment as good leads to a final question: "Did what is good, then, bring death to me?" (7:13). The objection is especially serious since it suggests that God's law has failed. Instead of leading those under it to life, it shepherded them to death. Once more, however, it is sin, and not God's law, that is at fault. Therefore, Paul begins by denying the objection (*mē genoito*) and then proceeds with his argument. Sin used what is good, the law, to work death in order that sin might be seen in all of its sinfulness (7:13). The problem, then, is not the law but the human condition apart from Christ. The law is spiritual (*pneumatikos*) because it comes from God, but apart from Christ humanity is carnal (*sarkinos*), sold under and to the power of sin. Those who are *sarkinos* and sold under the power of sin (unredeemed humanity) are incapable of fulfilling the just requirements of the law because they dwell in the wrong realm. Only those who have been transferred to the realm of grace fulfill the just requirements of the law, through the power of God's Spirit.

Has God Been Unfaithful?

In Romans 9—11, Paul raises further objections to his teaching. The questions are most serious because they call into question the very integrity and faithfulness of God.[25] For example, after describing God's elective love (9:1–13), Paul asks: "What then are we to say? Is there injustice on God's part?" (9:14). Next, after describing Israel's failure to attain righteousness, he writes: "I ask, then, has God rejected his people? (11:1). Then after discussing the remnant that has believed he writes, "So I ask, have they [the people of Israel] stumbled so as to fall?" (11:11). In each instance, Paul answers *mē genoito* (by no means) before responding to the objection, indicating that the very objection is objectionable. Nonetheless, he must deal with these questions because others have misunderstood or even purposely distorted the role of Israel in his preaching. Just as his gospel of justification by faith seems to imply that there is little or no room for the moral life, so his teaching that the Gentiles are justified by faith implies, to some at least, that God has rejected and been unfaithful to Israel. Therefore, just as Paul argued in the first eight chapters of this letter that his gospel does not do away with God's judgment, overthrow the law, or make the moral life irrelevant, so in chapters 9—11 he contends that the gospel of grace does not mean the rejection of Israel.

However, Paul has yet to provide the Romans with specific moral instruction. What is the concrete shape of the moral life for those who live "under grace" rather than "under the law"?

LIVING IN THE REALM OF GOD'S GRACE

In addition to being the longest moral exhortation in the Pauline corpus, Rom. 12:1–15:13 provides an excellent example of how Paul grounds his moral imperative in the indicative of salvation by summoning believers to live moral lives because God has acted on their behalf through his saving justice. To be sure, chapters 1—11 are not bereft of ethical teaching. Nevertheless, they deal with matters that are more doctrinal in nature: the righteousness of God, the sinfulness of humanity, the relationship between faith and law, and the destiny of Israel. In the final chapters of Romans, however, Paul focuses more explicitly upon moral and ethical issues such as the need to maintain communal unity, the demands of love, and the obedience that believers owe to those in authority. Moreover, as many commentators point out, this moral exhortation is closely related to his discussion in the first eleven chapters. For example, Paul Achtemeier notes: "How the story of God's relationship to his rebellious creation bears on the way Christians are to conduct their daily lives is the burden of the final chapters of Paul's letter to the Roman Christians."[26] In a similar vein, James Dunn entitles the section of his commentary that deals with this moral exhortation "The Outworking of the Gospel for the Redefined People of God in Everyday Terms,"[27] while Joseph Fitzmyer writes: "This hortatory part of Romans is also an expression of God's uprightness, but now in terms of concrete conduct."[28] In sum, the moral exhortation of this letter is not unrelated to what has preceded and, in fact, can only be understood in light of Paul's teaching on justification by faith apart from the law.

In my view, however, this exhortation is not simply a general paraenesis intended to illustrate the relationship between life and doctrine.[29] To be sure, it does fulfill this function, but as I have already noted, Paul writes in response to a particular situation at Rome. Therefore, while this moral exhortation is the practical working out of the gospel for Christian behavior in the world and the completion of the story about God's dealing with sinful humanity, it has consequences for the conduct of the Roman Christians.[30] In a word, it is intended to unite those who are at odds over dietary prescriptions, the observance of Jewish festivals, and the nature of Paul's gospel, which proclaims justification apart from the prescriptions of the law. The climax of this exhortation, then, comes when Paul appeals to the weak and the strong: "Welcome one another, therefore, just as Christ has welcomed you, for the glory of God" (15:7).

The content of this exhortation can be summarized as follows.[31] In the opening verses (12:1–2) Paul announces the theme of his exhortation: the moral life requires a new way of thinking that derives from a renewed mind. Next he describes this new way of life in four steps. First, those whose minds have been renewed must regard themselves and others with sober judgment (12:3–16). Second, they should not repay evil with evil (12:17–13:7). Third, they should fulfill the Mosaic law through love (13:8–10). Fourth, they should put on Christ, for the day of salvation is near (13:11–14). In the final section of his exhortation, Paul applies what he has said to the situation of the weak and strong at Rome, urging them to accept each other (14:1–15:13).

The Renewal of Your Minds
(Rom. 12:1–2)

> I appeal to you therefore, brothers and sisters, by the mercies of God, to present your bodies as a living sacrifice, holy and accept-able to God, which is your spiritual worship. Do not be conformed to this world, but be transformed by the renewing of your minds, so that you may discern what is the will of God—what is good and acceptable and perfect.

These verses are crucial for understanding Paul's moral exhortation in 12:1–15:13 since, in addition to announcing the themes he will develop, they relate this exhortation to the first part of the letter, thereby rooting the moral imperative in the salvation-historical indicative.[32] For example, in making his appeal "by the mercies of God" (*dia oiktirmōn tou theou*), Paul relates this exhortation to all that has preceded and recalls what he has just said in his discussion of Israel's destiny (11:30–32).

> Just as you were once disobedient to God but have now received mercy (*eleēthēte*) because of their disobedience, so they have now been disobedient in order that, by the mercy (*eleei*) shown to you, they too may now receive mercy (*eleēthōsin*). For God has impris-oned all in disobedience so that he may be merciful (*eleēsē*) to all.

To be sure, Paul employs different Greek words for "mercy" in the above passage, but there is little doubt that he is speaking of the same mercy that God extended to all, Gentile as well as Jew. It is on the basis of this mercy that the apostle makes his exhortation and urges the beneficiaries of God's mercy to act in a new way.[33]

This new way of living stands in sharp contrast to the life of disobedi-ence that Paul described in the opening chapters of Romans (1:18–3:20).[34] There he announced that the wrath of God was being revealed against all ungodliness. Since humanity refused to adore God as God, even though it could know God from the visible world (1:19), "Therefore God gave them up in the lusts of their hearts to impurity, to the degrading of their *bodies among themselves*" (1:24). Sinners *"worshiped* and served the creature rather than the Creator" (1:25). Therefore, "God gave them up to a debased mind and to do things that should not be done" (1:28). The new behavior that Paul urges the Romans to adopt, then, is the mirror image of the disobedient life portrayed at the beginning of the letter. Instead of degrading their bodies (1:24), they are to present them "as a living sacrifice, holy and acceptable to God" (12:1). Instead of worshiping the creature (1:25), they are to offer God spiritual worship (*tēn logikēn latreian hymōn;* 12:1). And instead of living with a debased mind (*adokimon noun;* 1:28), they are to be transformed by the renewal of their minds (*tē anakainōsei tou noos;* 12:2) so that they can discern (*dokimazein*) God's will.[35]

But it is not only the letter's opening chapters that are recalled in these verses. In urging his audience to present (*paristanein*) their bodies as a living sacrifice to God, Paul echoes what he has already said in chapter 6. There he warned his audience not "to present" the members of their bodies to sin as instruments of wickedness but "to present" them to God (6:13), since people are slaves to whomever they "present" themselves as obedient slaves (6:16). As once they "presented" themselves as slaves to impurity and lawlessness, so now they must "present" themselves as slaves to righteousness for sanctification (6:19).

The moral life has taken on a cultic dimension for Paul. Whereas Gentiles and Jews regularly offered agricultural and animal sacrifices in order to please God, Paul envisions a moral life of total obedience to God as the kind of sacrifice that is truly appropriate for human beings. Fittingly, he calls this conscious offering of one's self a living sacrifice (*thysian zōsan;* 12:1) that is holy and pleasing to God since it corresponds to the rational nature of human beings who, unlike other creatures, can consciously offer obedience to God. Such sacrifice is worship in accord with humanity's rational nature (*tēn logikēn latreian hymōn;* 12:1). Therefore, even if some who believe in Christ no longer offer temple sacrifices and should find themselves under suspicion from those who do, they offer a pleasing and acceptable sacrifice to God.

To accomplish this offering believers must not be conformed (*syschēmatizesthe*) to this age but transformed (*metamorphousthe*) by the renewal of their minds (*anakainōsei tou noos*) so that they will be able to discern God's will (12:2). Exactly what this means for the Romans, and how it is to be achieved, Paul describes in the paraenesis that follows. But before turning to that exhortation, it is necessary to make three points. First, as indicated by the passive voice, "be transformed," Paul views the moral life as an ongoing process of transformation effected by the power of God's Spirit. In this regard, the best commentary on this text is 2 Cor. 3:18, which employs the same verb: "And all of us, with unveiled faces, seeing the glory of the Lord as though reflected in a mirror, are being transformed (*metamorphoumetha*) into the same image from one degree of glory to another; for this

194

comes from the Lord, the Spirit."[36] The alternative to this transformation is to be conformed to this age (*tō aiōni toutō*). Once more the passive voice indicates that Paul has more in view than conforming oneself to the mores of this world, although this idea is not excluded. "This age" stands in contrast to the "coming age" inaugurated by Christ's death and resurrection, and it still has power to bend, mold, and control those who are part of the history of sin inaugurated by Adam (Rom. 5:12–21).

Second, in speaking of the renewal of the mind, Paul is not opposing mind (*nous*) and body (*sōma*) as if they were two parts of the human person. Human beings do not merely have a body, they are *sōma* because they are able to make themselves the objects of their own actions and to experience themselves as subjects to whom something happens.[37] Similarly, the *nous* is not so much a faculty of the human person as it is the human person capable of knowing, understanding, and judging.[38] When he employs body and mind in these verses, then, Paul is referring to the entire human person viewed from different perspectives. The human person embodied in the world (*sōma*) must give total obedience to God in a visible and concrete way. To accomplish this, the knowing, judging, and understanding subject (*nous*) must allow God to transform him or her from within.

Third, the goal of the moral life is to discern (*dokimazein*) the will of God. Once more, it is evident that Paul is hardly a libertine. His apostolate stems from God's will (1 Cor. 1:1; 2 Cor. 1:1), and he realizes that his visit to Rome depends upon God's will for him (Rom. 1:10). Moreover, as we have already seen, Paul told the Thessalonians that God's will for them is their sanctification. In order to do God's will, however, one must be able to discern and approve (*dokimazein*) what is the good (*agathon*), the acceptable (*euareston*), and the perfect (*teleion*), precisely what unredeemed humanity cannot do because of its debased mind (*adokimon noun;* 1:28). Now, however, those who allow themselves to be transformed by the power of God's Spirit can discern and do what God requires.

In sum, Paul describes the moral life as a total offering of self made possible by the complete renewal of the self that God has accomplished. Nevertheless, the moral life is not automatic, since the *nous* is corrupt and without understanding so long as human beings refuse to submit to God. In the remainder of his paraenesis, Paul provides the Romans with a series of exhortations that illustrate how they can be transformed in the renewing of their minds in their present circumstances.

A First Principle:
Think with Sober Judgment
(Rom. 12:3–16)

Paul's first admonition appropriately enough is for unity. The Romans are to function as one body in Christ because they belong to each other as do the members of a body. This advice would have been familiar to them, since the proper functioning of the *polis* (city) was often compared to the body in which each member must play a vital, though different, role. The

Greek moralist Epictetus, for example, makes use of this image (*Discourses* 2.10.4–5), as does Paul himself in 1 Corinthians 12 at even greater length than here. The distinctive mark of Paul's usage, however, is the manner in which he relates the life of the community to Christ. Believers are one body *en Christō* inasmuch as faith in Christ undergirds their union.[39] To maintain this communal life they must regard each other in an entirely new way that corresponds to the renewal of their minds. Playing upon the verb "to think" (*phronein*), much as he did in his letter to the Philippians, Paul urges the Romans not to think more highly of themselves (*hyperphronein*) than they ought to think (*phronein*) but to think with sober judgment (*sōphronein*) according to the "measure of faith" that God has assigned to each (12:3). The injunction not to think more highly of oneself than one ought echoes Paul's earlier warning to Gentile believers not to become proud but to stand in awe (11:20), and it foreshadows the final verse of this section: "Live in harmony with one another; do not be haughty, but associate with the lowly; do not claim to be wiser than you are" (12:16).

Rather than thinking too highly of themselves, believers should evaluate themselves according to "the measure of faith" they have received.[40] By this expression Paul suggests that there are different degrees of faith or conviction among the members of the Roman church, a point he will employ again in his discussion of the strong and the weak (14:1–15:13).

To explain what he means by diversity within the church, he lists seven gifts of the Spirit: prophecy, ministry, teaching, exhorting, sharing, leading, and extending mercy. Believers have different functions within the community because they have different gifts in accordance with the grace that God has given to each. Interestingly, Paul highlights prophecy by instructing those who prophesy to do so "in proportion to faith" (12:6). While this injunction could be applied to any of the gifts Paul lists, its application to prophecy here suggests that believers can overstep the limits of the gifts God has assigned to them. If so, then certain prophets among the Roman Christians may have gone beyond the measure of faith allotted to them in prophesying God's will for the believers at Rome.[41]

After listing the diversity of gifts within the community, Paul introduces the topic of love (12:9–13).[42] For most commentators, Paul's opening injunction marks the beginning of a new section (12:9–21): "Let love be genuine; hate what is evil, hold fast to what is good" (12:9). The literary units of Paul's letters, however, are not airtight compartments. For example, even though he turns to the topic of love here, he is still concerned with communal unity and the importance of not thinking more highly of oneself than one ought, mentioned earlier (12:3).[43] Thus, after introducing the topic of love, he returns to the theme of sober judgment (*sōphronein*), urging the Romans to think in the same way toward one another (*to auto eis allēlous phronountes*), not thinking in a haughty way (*mē ta hypsēla phronountes*) but associating with the lowly, not claiming to be wiser (*phronimoi*) than they are (12:16).

By introducing the theme of love here, however, Paul accomplishes two things. First, he lays the groundwork for what he will say about enemy love (12:17–13:7) and fulfilling the law through love (13:8–10). Second, he establishes a relationship between "love" and the mode of thinking required of those whose minds have been renewed. Thus if the Romans are to live in harmony with one another (12:16), their love must be genuine (12:9). To explain what he means by genuine love, he first sets the parameters within which love operates: it hates evil and clings to what is good (12:9). Next, in a series of staccato statements, he describes how love operates (12:10–13).[44]

> love one another with mutual affection
> outdo one another in showing honor
> do not lag in zeal
> be ardent in spirit
> serve the Lord
> rejoice in hope
> be patient in suffering
> persevere in prayer
> contribute to the needs of the saints
> extend hospitality to strangers

These exhortations are primarily directed to the Christian community and exemplify the relationship between the renewed mind and genuine love.

Following these admonitions, Paul makes use of three carefully balanced imperative statements to clarify the demands of love (Rom. 12:14–16).

> 1. Bless those who persecute you;
>   bless and do not curse them.
> 2. Rejoice with those who rejoice,
>   weep with those who weep.
> 3. Live in harmony with one another;
>   do not be haughty,
>   but associate with the lowly,
>   do not claim to be wiser than you are.

The first of these imperatives recalls Jesus' words about enemy-love (Matt. 5:44; Luke 6:28) and anticipates what Paul will say about nonretaliation. Exactly which "enemies" Paul has in view is difficult to say. To be sure, the text could be applied to the enemies of the Christian community at Rome. But if there was hostility between the "weak" and the "strong" at Rome, as many have suggested, Paul may be calling upon the believers at Rome not to retaliate when fellow believers heap abuse upon them. Somewhat paradoxically, then, enemy-love can and must be exhibited to those within as well as to those outside the community. The ethical imperative of Paul's second and third sayings can, of course, be practiced toward those outside the community as well as toward those within it. Given his concern for communal unity in this section, these sayings probably have community members in view.

As we have seen so often, Paul's ethic is intimately bound to community life. Believers live the moral life within the context of the Christian community, where they must "think" about others in a new way that is not conformed to this age. Rather than regarding themselves too highly, they must outdo one another in showing love and honor to others.

A Second Principle:
Do Not Repay Evil with Evil
(Rom. 12:17–13:7)

Having introduced the theme of enemy-love in the previous section, Paul now develops it in two ways.[45] First, he provides a general instruction about enemy-love that he grounds in a series of scriptural texts (12:17–21). Second, he applies his concept of nonretaliation to a specific situation: the responsibility of believers to subject themselves to the governing authorities by paying taxes (13:1–7).[46] I am assuming that here, as throughout this exhortation, Paul is addressing a specific situation in the Roman church.

Although his instruction on enemy-love recalls Jesus' teaching (Matt. 5:44; Luke 6:27), Paul does not quote or refer to Jesus. Instead, he grounds his argument in a series of scriptural texts, the only citations from the Old Testament in the paraenesis of Rom. 12:1–13:7.[47]

12:17b	Take thought for what is noble in the sight of all (Prov. 3:4)
12:18	Live peaceably with all (Ps. 34:14)
12:19a	Never avenge yourselves (Lev. 19:18)
12:19b	Vengeance is mine, I will repay (Deut. 32:35)
12:20	If your enemies are hungry, feed them; if they are thirsty, give them something to drink; for by doing this you will heap burning coals on their heads (Prov. 25:21–22)

Exactly who Paul has in view is not clear. On the one hand, the injunctions not to repay *anyone* evil for evil (12:17) and to live peaceably with all suggest a broader horizon than the Christian community alone. And, in fact, Paul makes just such an application in 1 Thess. 5:15: "See that none of you repays evil for evil, but always seek to do good to one another *and to all*." Thus Paul is clearly aware that the demands of love transcend the parameters of the Christian community. But in this exhortation, it is possible that he primarily has believers at Rome in view. If this is the case, he calls for love toward one's enemies within as well as outside the community.

Whatever the historical situation, the demands for enemy-love are the most difficult that Paul makes upon the church, since they require an end to all selfishness and appear to disregard the balance of justice.[48] Perhaps this is the reason he places his teaching within the eschatological framework of God's judgment, a theme introduced at the beginning of this letter (Rom. 1:18). He will develop this theme further in the remainder of this exhortation (13:11–14; 14:10). Justification by faith does not do away with God's judgment, and believers must wait for the wrath and judgment of God to settle accounts. In the meantime, they are to treat their enemies with mercy, thereby heaping "burning coals" on their heads (12:20). Exactly what these burning coals are is disputed. While some see them as the pangs of shame (enemies will be filled with shame and repent because of the good done to them), others view them as divine punishment (enemies will pile up judgment for themselves by not repenting at the good done to them). Whatever the precise meaning of the image, the wider context suggests that Paul is holding two concepts in tension: the imperative to do good to one's enemy and the assurance that God judges evil. Believers must not and need not retaliate because, if retaliation is necessary, God will avenge the just.[49]

On first reading, it is difficult to see a connection between Paul's teaching on enemy-love and nonretaliation on the one hand, and his exhortation that all should subject themselves to the governing authorities on the other (13:1–7).[50] In light of its opening verses, the latter admonition seems to be a teaching on the divine right of rulers: all authority is from God, therefore whoever resists authority resists God. As we shall see, however, the *purpose* of the exhortation is to provide the Roman Christians with a rationale for paying taxes and to encourage them to continue doing so lest they cause unrest among their fellow believers.

In asserting that "there is no authority except from God," Paul is not developing a doctrine of church and state so much as he is reflecting a common Old Testament view.

By me [divine Wisdom] kings reign,
    and rulers decree what is just;
by me rulers rule,
    and nobles, all who govern rightly (Prov. 8:15–16).

It is I who by my great power and my outstretched arm have made the earth, with the people and animals that are on the earth, and I give it to whomever I please. Now I have given all these lands into the hand of King Nebuchadnezzar of Babylon, my servant, and I have given him even the wild animals of the field to serve him (Jer. 27:5–6).

Listen therefore, O kings, and understand; learn, O judges of the ends of the earth. Give ear, you that rule over multitudes, and boast of many nations. For your dominion was given you from the Lord, and your sovereignty from the Most High; he will search out your works and inquire into your plans (Wisd. Sol. 6:1–3).

God is supreme and no one can resist him. He uses foreign rulers for his purpose (Isa. 45:1) and is powerful in deposing and setting up kings (Dan. 2:21). The premise of Paul's exhortation, then, is as follows: even if those in authority are ignorant of the true God, they are his servants whether they realize it or not. The *purpose* of the exhortation, however, is found in the final two verses:

> For the same reason you also pay taxes, for the authorities are God's servants, busy with this very thing. Pay to all what is due them—taxes to whom taxes are due, revenue to whom revenue is due, respect to whom respect is due, honor to whom honor is due (Rom. 13:6–7).

In other words, Paul has made use of a traditional Jewish teaching on the supreme authority of God in order to provide the Roman Christians with a rationale for paying taxes. Exactly why he encouraged them to pay their taxes is difficult to say.[51] If it derives from a specific situation at Rome, however (for example, the burden of taxation and the behavior of those who abused their responsibility in collecting taxes), Paul's exhortation is part of his teaching on nonretaliation. The Roman Christians should not withhold taxes in order to retaliate against those who maltreat them, since even the authority of the Roman state derives from God, who will avenge all. In effect, Paul calls for a "political quietism"[52] in light of God's supreme authority and the imminent judgment that is to occur. Paul is too consumed by the expectation of the Lord's parousia to consider reforming "this age." Rather than reformation, he seeks transformation by the renewal of one's mind.

A Third Princple:
Fulfill the Law through Love
(Rom. 13:8–10)

Having instructed the Romans to "Pay to all what is due to them (*tas opheilas*)," Paul next exhorts them to "owe (*opheilete*) no one anything, except to love one another; for the one who loves has fulfilled the law" (13:8). In doing so, he returns to the topic of love introduced in 12:9. However, whereas he has recently focused on enemy-love and nonretaliation, now he discusses love in relation to the Mosaic law. By doing so, he clarifies his discussions of the law in the earlier parts of this letter and recalls a similar exhortation in Galatians: " . . . but through love become slaves of one another. For the whole law is summed up in a single commandment, 'You shall love your neighbor as yourself' " (Gal. 5:13–14).

Overall, Romans manifests a more positive estimation of the law than does Galatians. As we have already seen, Paul vigorously denies that the law is sin (Rom. 7:7) or that it brought death (7:13), and he unequivocally affirms that the law is holy and the commandment is holy, just, and good (7:12). Nonetheless, he clearly states that no one is justified by the deeds prescribed by the law, "for through the law comes the knowledge of sin" (3:20). Moreover, in chapter 7 he describes the situation of the human person who is able to agree with the law but is unable to do it because of the power of sin that dwells within the body's members (7:23). Therefore, despite Paul's positive affirmations on behalf of the law, his exposition raises questions about the moral and ethical life of those who live by faith. Are they bound by the commandments? Or is Paul's gospel of justification by faith incapable of dealing with the moral and ethical teaching prescribed by the law? As in Galatians, Paul must address these and similar questions, since many of those to whom he was writing were undoubtedly skeptical of his "new" teaching on the law.

As in Galatians, Paul approaches the question of moral behavior and the prescriptions of the law from the point of view of fulfilling what he calls the "just requirement of the law" (8:4). Rather than view the moral life in terms of the many prescriptions found in the law ("You shall not commit adultery; You shall not murder; You shall not steal; You shall not covet"; 13:9), he begins with the demand of love prescribed in Lev. 19:18, "Love your neighbor as yourself." In doing so, Paul echoes Jesus' teaching, but only in part, since Jesus speaks of two commandments (love for God and love of neighbor) when the scribe asks him, "Which commandment is the first of all?" (Mark 12:28). The differences between Jesus and Paul at this point, however, should not be exaggerated. The "Jesus" portrayed in the Gospels interprets the law in light of God's original will without ever suggesting that its role has ended. In contrast to him, Paul affirms that the law has completed its salvation-historical goal, since "Christ is the end (*telos*) of the law so that there my be righteousness for everyone who believes" (Rom. 10:4). Therefore, Paul does not identify the most important commandments of the law as does Jesus (for whom the law has not yet run its salvation-historical course) but highlights the means by which the just requirement of the law is fulfilled in the new age. In doing so, however, he does not make love the first or the most important of many commandments, since the ability to love derives from the power of the Spirit, who has "poured" God's own love into the heart of the believer (5:5). Thus, those who walk according to the Spirit and not according to the flesh fulfill the just requirement of the law.

In sum, Paul's teaching on the Mosaic law and the ethical life is somewhat paradoxical. On the one hand, believers are no longer under the law, since it has attained its salvation-historical purpose in Christ. On the other hand, it is unthinkable for Paul that Christian behavior should contravene the law, since believers fulfill the law, by the power of the Spirit, through love that "does no wrong to a neighbor" (13:10). Put another way, although the law is no longer in force from a salvation-historical perspective, those who believe in Christ do not violate it.[53]

A Fourth Principle:
Put on Christ
(Rom. 13:11–14)

Paul writes as he does about ethics and the law because he knows that in Christ the end of the old age and the beginning of the new age have overlapped (1 Cor. 10:11). That is to say, although the old age has not yet ended, the new age has already made its appearance so that believers find themselves "walking between the times."[54] They live in the old age and must subject themselves to the governing authorities, even to the point of fulfilling mundane responsibilities such as paying taxes (13:1–7). But believers must not be conformed by this age (12:2), nor should they take upon themselves the eschatological wrath that belongs to God (12:19). Walking between the times, they are engaged in an eschatological battle that requires its own armament ("the armor of light," 13:12). As in 1 Thess. 5:1–11, therefore, Paul employs several images to convey the hour in which believers find themselves. In terms of time, the critical hour is nearer now than when they first believed, the night is far advanced, and the day has drawn near (*hē hēmera ēggiken;* Rom. 13:12). The verb used in the latter expression is the same as that found in Jesus' proclamation of the kingdom (Mark 1:15) and suggests the imminent arrival of the day when Christ will appear and God will render judgment. Just as the imminent arrival of the kingdom requires a profound change in one's moral life, so the impending day summons believers to "lay aside the works of darkness and put on the armor of light" (Rom. 13:12).

Although Paul summons believers to live with the eschatological reservation that the present form of the world is passing away, and although he views the Christian life as life in the Spirit, he remains eminently realistic. He urges believers not to live in reveling, drunkenness, debauchery, licentiousness, quarreling, and jealousy (13:13), suggesting that believers are not immune from immoral behavior. The moral life is a constant process of transformation effected by God (12:2) with which believers must cooperate by putting on Christ and making no provision for the flesh (13:14). Once more, then, Paul presents a somewhat paradoxical view of the moral life inasmuch as believers live between the ages. Though they are justified and freed from sin, it is still possible for them to be enslaved by the powers of this age. Therefore, they must constantly remind themselves that they are living in the final hour of salvation history.

Practical Application:
Welcome Each Other
(Rom. 14:1–15:13)

Although directed to a specific situation, Paul's paraenesis has been somewhat general thus far. In the final part of this exhortation (14:1–15:13), however, he addresses the problem of the weak and the strong, the issue that underlies all he has said hitherto. In doing so, he makes use of principles that he introduced in the first part of his paraenesis, such as not thinking more highly of oneself than is appropriate but evaluating oneself according to the measure of faith (12:3), and practicing genuine love (12:9).

As in 1 Cor. 8:1–11:1, the problem here concerns the weak and the strong, although the identity of the two groups is no longer the same.[55] Whereas "the weak" in 1 Corinthians designates those who refrain from eating meat sacrificed to idols, in Romans "the weak" refers to those who eat only vegetables and observe certain days in honor of the Lord. In both letters, the behavior of the strong scandalizes the weak, and Paul must advise the strong not to offend the weak. There is no indication in Romans, however, that the behavior of the strong might lead to serious misconduct such as idolatry, or that the strong have embraced a libertine perspective that views every kind of behavior as lawful (compare 1 Cor. 10:23). Rather, the situation at Rome has divided believers over issues that, in Paul's view, are matters of indifference and without ultimate consequence for salvation. The moral issue, therefore, is: How should a community regulate itself when its members quarrel about questions that are important to the disputing parties but not essential for faith and salvation? Paul proceeds in three steps. First, he outlines the problem and urges the strong and the weak not to despise or judge each other (14:1–12). Second, he urges the strong not to become a stumbling block to the weak (14:13–23) or to please themselves (15:1–6). Third, he exhorts the weak and the strong to welcome each other as Christ welcomed them (15:7–13).

Do not despise or judge (Rom. 14:1–12). Although Paul identifies the weak as those who eat only vegetables and observe certain days, and the strong as those who eat anything and view all days as the same, there is no further indication of their identity, except Paul's statement that he belongs to the strong (15:1).[56] The fundamental problem, however, is not difficult to discern. While the faith of the strong has led them to the conviction that all food is clean and all days are the same, the faith of the weak convinces them to abstain from certain foods and to observe particular days in honor of the Lord. It should be noted that in this section Paul's understanding of "faith" is related to his earlier statement about the measure of faith that God has assigned to each person (12:3): the personal conviction of each believer based upon his or her understanding of what God has done in Christ. While both the weak and the strong believe *in* Christ, their faith leads them to draw different conclusions about the manner in which they must live out their faith. Paul understands this, for in his view both weak and strong seek to honor the Lord and give thanks to God when they act from conviction (14:6).

Nonetheless, Paul is disturbed that the strong despise the weak, and the weak judge the strong (14:3, 10). Consequently, he returns to the theme of judgment that he introduced in chapter 2. All believers are mere servants of the Lord and must stand before the judgment seat of God to give an account of themselves (14:10–12). Therefore, it is not their place to judge other believers who, they must presume, are acting from conviction and in accord with the measure of faith that God has granted to them.

Walking in love (Rom. 14:13–23). Paul's moral sensibility allows him to distinguish between what is and what is not important in the moral life.

For example, he is fully convinced that there is nothing unclean in itself (14:14) and that all things are clean (14:20). Therefore, it does not matter whether or not one observes dietary prescriptions. The kingdom of God is not a matter of what one eats or drinks but of righteousness, peace, and joy in the Holy Spirit (14:17). These are the matters of supreme importance about which one can never compromise. Nevertheless, Paul realizes that people are at different stages in the life of faith, and that the weak commit sin if they eat food that they think is unclean. Thus "those who have doubts are condemned if they eat, because they do not act from faith; for whatever does not proceed from faith is sin" (14:23). Once more, Paul is speaking of faith in a specific sense that is akin to conscience or conviction.[57] He means that people commit sin, even in matters of indifference, if they act contrary to what they believe is right or wrong. Conversely, Paul does *not* mean that everything that does not proceed from faith *in* Christ is sinful.

As in 1 Corinthians, Paul realizes that building up the community often requires believers to make personal sacrifices. Therefore, if the strong are injuring the weak (on behalf of whom Christ died) by what they eat, the strong are no longer behaving in a manner that accords with love (*ouketi kata agapēn peripateis*; 14:14). There are moments, then, when it is best to keep one's faith before God (14:22). Once more, Paul is speaking of faith as personal conviction rather than as faith in Christ. Understood in this way, there are moments when the demands of love are best expressed by keeping personal convictions a matter between oneself and God rather than insisting upon these convictions and injuring those whose measure of faith is weak.

The example of Christ (Rom. 15:1–7). Continuing to address the strong, Paul urges them to bear (*bastazein*) the failings of the weak rather than please themselves (15:1), much as he instructed the Galatians, "Bear (*bastazete*) one another's burdens, and in this way you will fulfill the law of Christ" (Gal. 6:2). Since the law is summed up in the words "Love your neighbor as yourself" (Rom. 13:9), the strong should please their neighbor "for the good purpose of building up the neighbor" (15:2). As in Philippians, Paul draws upon the example of Christ in order to motivate the behavior that he urges. Since Christ did not seek to please himself but bore the insults of those who insulted God (Ps. 69:9), the strong must bear with the failings of the weak, even to the point of enduring insults from the weak, who now judge them for not abstaining from certain foods or observing certain days (14:3, 10).

In a brief prayer-wish (15:5–6), Paul prays that God will grant the Romans the gift of living in harmony (*to auto phronein en allēlois*) so that they may glorify the God and Father of Jesus Christ with one voice. In making this prayer, he recalls the first part of his paraenesis, where he urged the Romans to "live in harmony with one another" (*to auto eis allēlous phronountes*; 12:16). Most importantly, he identifies the ultimate purpose of the moral life as giving praise to God, thereby recalling the very beginning of his paraenesis, "present your bodies as a living sacrifice, holy and acceptable to God, which is your spiritual worship" (12:1). The moral and ethical life is a cultic act of the entire community, which, having set aside all differences for the sake of the neighbor, praises God with a single voice.

Welcome one another (Rom. 15:7–13). As I have already mentioned, the appeal that Paul makes in 15:7 is the goal of his paraenesis: "Welcome one another, therefore (*dio proslambanesthe allēlous*), just as Christ has welcomed you, for the glory of God" (15:7). In making this appeal, Paul reminds the Romans of Christ, who became "a servant of the circumcised" in order to confirm the promises made to the patriarchs and in order that the Gentiles might glorify God for his mercy toward them. Thus Christ once more functions as an exemplar for Christian behavior inasmuch as his entire life was at the service of others. In referring to him as the "servant of the circumcised," Paul clearly reminds the weak and the strong of the central role that Israel plays in salvation history, thereby dispelling any notion that his gospel implies the rejection of Israel (9:1–11:36). In referring to God's mercy (*eleous*) on behalf of the Gentiles so that they might glorify God (15:9), Paul echoes the language of mercy found in his discussion of Israel's destiny (11:28–32), as well as in the opening appeal of this paraenesis, "I appeal to you therefore, brothers and sisters, by the mercies of God . . . " (12:1). Finally, the exhortation to receive one another recalls the opening appeal of this section on the weak and the strong, an appeal that is addressed to all: "*Welcome* those who are weak in faith; . . . those who abstain [the weak] must not pass judgment on those who eat [the strong]; for God has *welcomed* them" (14:1, 3). Making use of Old Testament quotations from the Septuagint that have in common the word "Gentiles" (*ethnē;* Ps. 17:50; Deut. 32:43; Ps. 117:1; Isa. 11:10), Paul shows that God had already announced his purpose in scripture: that the Gentiles should join Israel in praising God. Paul makes his moral exhortation, therefore, against the horizon of salvation history. Weak and strong must welcome each other, as Christ welcomed them, so that both Gentiles and Jews might glorify the God and Father of Jesus Christ.

PAUL'S MORAL TEACHING:
A SUMMARY STATEMENT

Romans echoes many of the ethical themes we have uncovered in Paul's other letters, for example, the centrality of love, the importance of unity within the Christian community, the example of Christ, and the moral life that should characterize the elect, who have been freely justified by God's grace. Romans, however, also presents the most mature statement of Paul's reflection on the moral life, and it responds to objections that his teaching on justification by faith cannot provide believers with reliable moral guidance since it affirms that "Christ is the end of the law" (Rom. 10:4).

For Paul the moral life has become a cultic act whereby believers make a complete offering of themselves to God within the context of the Christian community in order that all, Gentile and Jew, might glorify God. As for the law, it no longer forms the basis of the ethical life since its salvation-historical role has ended. Nevertheless, believers fulfill its just requirement by willingly repaying the debt of love that they owe each other in light of what God has done for them in Christ.

Romans does not represent a systematic development of ethical theory or a compendium of Paul's moral teaching. Rather, as with his other letters, its rhetoric and argumentation have the concerns of a particular community in view. It would be a mistake, therefore, to employ it as the summation of Paul's thought. Romans does, however, present the logical starting point for those who would develop a systematic ethic in a Pauline trajectory. More than any other Pauline letter, it challenges believers to frame ethics within the horizon of worship and thanksgiving, so that the moral life will become the total giving of oneself within the context of a believing community for the praise and glory of God.

10

Ethics for a
New Creation

The Letters to the Colossians and the Ephesians

Colossians and Ephesians provide an especially rich source for those interested in New Testament ethics since both writings function as moral exhortations with clearly defined units of paraenesis (Col. 3:1–4:6; Eph. 4:1–6:20). Moreover, since there is a striking similarity in the language, style, and theology of these letters, it is convenient to study them in a single chapter.

Nonetheless, both letters are problematic since there is considerable debate, on literary and theological grounds, regarding their authorship.[1] In terms of literary style, for example, they make use of elaborate and extended sentences that are characterized by participles and seemingly endless genitive constructions.[2] In contrast, Paul's undisputed writings tend to employ shorter and crisper sentences. As regards theology, there are a number of new emphases.[3] In Colossians the work of Christ, the firstborn from the dead, is cosmic in scope so that God reconciles all things, "whether on earth or in heaven" in him (1:20). In both letters, the church is viewed as the "body" of Christ, but not in the functional sense described in Rom. 12:4–8 and 1 Cor. 12:12–31. Rather, there is a unique relationship between Christ and the church inasmuch as Christ is the head, and the church is the body (Col. 1:18; Eph. 1:22–23). The church, in turn, has become universal and even cosmic in scope through its union with him. Given their emphasis upon the redemptive work of Christ, it is not surprising that these letters stress the present dimension of salvation. To be sure, there is an awareness that the fullness of salvation is yet to come (Col. 3:4), but one no longer finds the lively hope for an imminent parousia that characterizes the undisputed Pauline letters. It is not surprising, then, that while several scholars maintain the Pauline authorship of one or both of these letters, a growing majority views them as pseudonymous. Thus the question arises: If Paul did not write Colossians and Ephesians, what is the relationship

207

between their moral teaching and the moral teaching of Paul's undisputed correspondence? Does the moral teaching of Colossians and Ephesians represent an authentic expression of the apostle's ethical teaching, or is it a retreat, perhaps even a fall, from Paul's pristine doctrine?

THE LEGACY OF PAUL

As I have already noted, the question of authorship is crucial for anyone who seeks to reconstruct the moral and ethical teaching of Paul. If Paul did not write 2 Thessalonians, Colossians, Ephesians, and the pastoral epistles, these letters should not be employed in any synthesis of his ethics or theology, no matter how much they reflect the spirit of his writings. To be sure, such letters may be viewed as Paul's legacy, since his writings and ministry undoubtedly provided the inspiration for those who wrote in his name, but properly speaking they are Deutero-Pauline writings. In this work, however, I am more interested in the literary integrity of each writing—understood in light of the situation that occasioned it—than in synthesizing or reconstructing Paul's ethical teaching. Consequently, while the question of authorship remains important, it is not crucial to the argument of this book. One can investigate the ethical teaching of Colossians and Ephesians even if Paul is not their author. The more important questions are: What is the ethical teaching of each letter, and how does Paul (or whoever writes in his name) persuade his audience to embrace the moral and ethical behavior that he proposes?

In what follows, I shall refer to Paul as the author of Colossians and Ephesians even though they may have been written by someone else. There are two reasons for this. First, Colossians and Ephesians identify Paul as their author, and in doing so, they clearly invoke his authority. Second, the argument of these letters is, in no small measure, dependent upon the assumption that it is Paul who writes. In both letters, Paul is presented as the apostle par excellence who reveals "the mystery" (Col. 1:27; 4:3; Eph. 3:2–6)[4] and is now suffering on behalf of the church (Col. 1:24; Eph. 3:13). It is his authority as well as the persuasive argument of these letters, then, that strengthens the moral resolve of those who hear or read them. Put most simply, much of the argumentation in these letters rests upon Paul's authority, even if he did not write them.

The importance of Paul's authority in persuading the audience to adopt a particular way of life raises yet another question. Is the moral instruction of these letters a faithful development of what is found in the undisputed Pauline correspondence? Such a question can only be answered after one has investigated and compared all the material, and even then it will undoubtedly receive different answers.[5] In my own view, Colossians and Ephesians represent an organic development of the Pauline tradition. To be sure, they introduce new material such as the household codes (Col. 3:18–4:1; Eph. 5:21–6:9), emphasize themes such as good works (Eph. 2:10), and no longer stress other themes, such as the imminent parousia and justification. In the main, however, they repeat important Pauline themes that we have already uncovered, such as the moral implications of being God's people, the communal aspect of morality, the centrality of love, and the example provided by Paul's own life. One suspects that if Paul were faced with the new situation that those who followed him encountered, he would have approved of their "Pauline" solutions.

RESCUED FROM THE POWER OF DARKNESS: COLOSSIANS

Colossians gives every indication of being an authentic letter written in response to a situation in the Colossian community. In addition to Paul, Timothy is named in the salutation (1:1–2), as he is in 2 Corinthians, Philippians, 1 and 2 Thessalonians, and Philemon, suggesting that he had some role in the letter's composition.[6] In the closing of the letter (4:7–18), Paul commends Tychicus and Onesimus to the community, saying that they will tell the Colossians "about everything here" (4:7–9). As for Paul, he is in prison (4:3); nonetheless he sends greetings from numerous people (4:10–17), among whom are his fellow prisoner, Aristarchus, and Epaphras, the founder of the church at Colossae (1:7). The place of Paul's imprisonment is not mentioned, since the Colossians supposedly know where he is incarcerated.[7]

Overall, Paul is pleased with the progress that the community is making. Epaphras has told him of the community's "love in the spirit" (1:8), and Paul rejoices at their morale and the firmness of their faith in Christ (2:5). Nonetheless, he finds it necessary to warn the Colossians lest they be deceived by the arguments of others (2:4) and led astray "through philosophy and empty deceit, according to human tradition, according to the elemental spirits of the universe, and not according to Christ" (2:8). It is difficult, if not impossible, to determine precisely what Paul means by this rather enigmatic verse.[8] For our purposes, it is sufficient to say that there are people at Colossae who are promising mystical or angelic experiences (2:16–19) to those who adopt certain religious and ascetical practices (2:20–23).[9] In Paul's view, however, there is a radical opposition between this teaching and Christ, whose death has made such teaching and practice superfluous (2:9–15). Although some of the Colossians appear to have already adopted ascetical practices (2:20–21), there is no indication that the situation at Colossae has become a crisis comparable to that at Galatia.[10] Indeed, the first part of this letter is primarily a celebration of the Colossians' faith.

In my view, Colossians is primarily a letter of moral exhortation and only secondarily a warning about "the philosophy"[11] mentioned in chapter 2. It exhorts the Colossians to live as the new creation they have become in Christ. The ethic it proposes is grounded in Christology, eschatology, and the sacrament of Baptism. Through their baptism, the Colossians have been raised up with Christ. Thus they belong to Christ who is the head of the body—that is, the church—and now live on the basis of what is prepared for them in heaven. Despite the theological underpinnings of this ethic, its content is rather commonplace. The paraenesis contains lists of virtues and vices and a household code with which most Gentiles and Jews would readily agree.[12] In effect Colossians provides its audience with a new and more profound motivation to do what is good and explains what it means to live in and with Christ.[13] The hymnic passage that stands at the beginning of this letter (1:15–20), therefore, has important implications for ethics. Paul identifies Christ as the "firstborn of all creation," "the head of the body, the church," "the first born from the dead." Later he calls upon the Colossians to put on the new person that they have become (3:10) in Christ. Thus the moral life is the life of Christ, who is the beginning of the new humanity that is now manifested in the church.

To convince the Colossians to live as the new humanity that they have become in Christ, Paul reminds them of what they were and who they are (1:1–2:5). Next, in warning them of "the philosophy," he recalls what Christ has done for them (2:6–23). Finally, he draws out the ethical consequences of their having died and risen with Christ (3:1–4:6).

Then and Now
(Col. 1:1–2:5)

The first part of Colossians is an example of epideictic rhetoric inasmuch as Paul celebrates what God has already done for the Colossians. In recalling God's activity on their behalf, however, Paul is already laying the foundation for the explicit paraenesis he will employ at the end of this letter (3:1–4:6). Thus Colossians exhibits a pattern found in Paul's undisputed correspondence of rooting the moral imperative in the indicative of salvation.

Colossians recalls and celebrates the identity of its recipients in several ways. For example, from the opening salutation it is evident that they form a holy and faithful community in Christ (1:2), and Paul reports that he has already heard of their faith in Christ as well as their love for all the saints (*tous hagious;* 1:4). While he prays that they will be filled with the knowledge of God's will so that they will live (*peripatēsai*) in a manner worthy of the Lord (1:9–10), he knows that the gospel is already bearing fruit and growing among them. Therefore, he rejoices to see their morale and firmness of faith (2:5). In effect, Paul celebrates the community's faith in order to remind the Colossians that they are a chosen and elect people.

When compared with his other letters, however, Colossians extends the horizon against which Paul views this holy people. The redemption that God has effected for them is cosmic in scope. They share in the inheritance of God's holy ones because God has rescued them from the power of darkness and transferred them into the kingdom of his beloved Son in whom they have redemption, which is the forgiveness of their sins (1:12–14). The Son is the firstborn of creation, and his work is cosmic in scope; he is the head of the church, which is his body (1:18, 24). Through him, God reconciled everything in heaven and on earth (1:19–20). Thus the redemption that the Colossians experience is not an isolated phenomenon; it belongs to the cosmic reconciliation accomplished in Christ.

Paul explains the nature of this redemption by contrasting the former existence of the Colossians with their present circumstances. Once (*tote*) they were alienated and hostile in mind toward God on account of their evil deeds (1:21). But now (*nyni*) they have been reconciled to God through Christ's death (1:22), and the mystery hidden for ages has been revealed to them inasmuch as they are numbered among God's holy ones (1:26). This mystery is Christ, who is present among them (1:27; 2:2).

As a servant of the gospel (1:23) and of the church (1:24–25), it is Paul who makes this mystery known. His ultimate goal is to present "everyone mature (*teleion*) in Christ" (1:28). What he means by this is best interpreted in light of Christ's redemptive work. Christ redeemed the Colossians in order to present them to God: holy, blameless, and irreproachable (1:22). The goal of the moral life, then, is part of the divine economy of salvation that is cosmic in scope. The Colossians were alienated from God without any knowledge of God's plan on their behalf. But by his death on the cross, Christ, the firstborn from the dead, has initiated a new creation and reconciled all things to God. Seen against the horizon of the divine economy, the goal of the moral life is to be mature in Christ; that is, holy, blameless, and irreproachable before God. The practical steps for achieving this, however, are yet to be discussed.

While the opening of Colossians celebrates what God has already accomplished and congratulates the Colossians for their steadfastness, Paul is clearly aware of the moral struggle they face. Thus he does not cease to pray that they will be filled with the knowledge of God's will, prepared to endure everything with patience (1:11). Most importantly, when Paul contrasts the former and present existence of the Colossians, he adds an important proviso (1:21–23). Once (*tote*) they were estranged from God, but now (*nyni*) they are reconciled and will be presented to God as holy, blameless, and irreproachable, provided that (*ei ge*) they continue "securely established and steadfast in the faith, without shifting from the hope promised by the gospel" they have heard (1:23). In effect, there is an intimate relationship between the gospel, redemption, and the moral life. Those who misrepresent the gospel, and those who are led astray by such people, will ultimately fall from the moral life—a theme that will be fully developed in the pastoral epistles.

The Sufficiency of Christ
(Col. 2:6–23)

The middle section of Colossians has attracted an inordinate amount of attention since it deals with what is sometimes called "the Colossian heresy," or "the false teaching." My concern, however, is the ethical implications of this section.

The very manner in which Paul begins the section suggests that he is concerned about the moral and ethical life of the Colossians. Drawing a conclusion from all that he has said thus far, he writes:

> As you therefore have received Christ Jesus the Lord, continue to live your lives (*peripateite*) in him, rooted and built up in him and established in the faith, just as you were taught, abounding in thanksgiving (2:6–7).

Although the precise nature of the problem at Colossae is no longer known to us, there is little doubt about Paul's solution: the Colossians must live their lives in Christ in accordance with the gospel they were taught.

At one point in their history they were dead to God because of their trespasses. Drawing upon the imagery of circumcision, Paul refers to the uncircumcision of their flesh (2:13), by which he means an existence apart from God. Like all of humanity that did not know God, the Colossians had lived their lives on a purely carnal level. By the death of Christ upon the cross, however, God did away with the bill of indictment (*cheirographon*) that stood against them and forgave their trespasses. As a result, God made them alive to himself (2:13–14). When the Colossians were baptized, they appropriated this salvation for themselves. Again, drawing upon the imagery of circumcision, Paul refers to their baptism as a circumcision made without hands by which they stripped away the old self, the body of the flesh (*tou sōmatos tēs sarkos*; 2:11). Thus Baptism has become the Christian's circumcision, "the circumcision of Christ." But whereas the old circumcision merely removed the male foreskin, the circumcision of Christ strips away the carnal self that is humanity's unredeemed nature. It now becomes possible for believers to clothe themselves with a new self (3:10) since, buried with Christ in baptism, they are also raised with him from the dead (2:12).[14] In effect, the lives of believers are now patterned after Christ, the firstborn of the dead.

This baptismal catechesis has profound ethical implications for the moral life of believers. Thus Paul asks the Colossians why they are living as if they still belong to the world, since they died with Christ to the elemental spirits of the universe (*tōn stoicheiōn tou kosmou*; 2:20) in their baptism. The precise meaning of this phrase, like much of the language in Colossians, is no longer available to us.[15] But it is clear that Paul sees a sharp contrast between Christ and the *stoicheia*. Here it may be helpful to draw a comparison with Galatians. Just as those who seek to be justified by the law cut themselves off from Christ (Gal. 5:4), so those who live for the *stoicheia* do the same. There are two kinds of existence for Paul, each of which has profound ethical implications: the life of unredeemed humanity characterized by living under the elemental spirits of the universe, and the life of redeemed humanity determined by Christ, the head of the body, the firstborn of the dead. In what follows, Paul describes how believers live this life in the world.

Consequences for Life in Christ
(Col. 3:1–4:6)

The paraenesis of Colossians rests upon two theological assumptions that Paul has developed in the first two parts of this letter. First, Christ is the forerunner and exemplar of a renewed humanity. The firstborn from the dead, he is the beginning of a new creation that is already present in the church. Second, having been buried with him through baptism and raised with him through faith, the Colossians are part of this new creation. As the community of the church, which is the body of Christ, they form a new humanity in whom there is no distinction between "Greek and Jew, circumcised and uncircumcised, barbarian, Scythian, slave and free" (3:11). Therefore, although the material of this paraenesis contains a great deal of commonplace ethical teaching, it is firmly rooted in the gospel and cannot be fully understood apart from it.

The paraenesis falls into a number of clearly defined units. It begins with a statement (3:1–4) that grounds its moral teaching in the baptismal catechesis that Paul developed in the previous section. Since the Colossians have been raised with Christ, they must set their minds on things that are above, for they have died to their old life. Next, he develops this baptismal theology in two ways (3:5–17). First, since the Colossians have died with Christ, they must put to death (*nekrōsate*) those aspects of their lives that are merely earthly (3:5–11). To show what he means, Paul provides the Colossians with two lists, each of which contains five items.

Put to Death

fornication	anger
impurity	wrath
passion	malice
evil desire	slander
greed	abusive language

Second, continuing his baptismal imagery, Paul exhorts the community to clothe (*endysasthe*) itself in a manner appropriate to God's holy and elect people (3:12–17). In doing so, he makes use of yet another list of five items: compassion, kindness, humility, meekness, patience (3:12), and then encourages the Colossians to cover this "garment" with the garment of love, "which binds everything together in perfect harmony" (3:14).

Next, Paul turns to the Christian household, addressing wives and husbands, children and parents, slaves and masters (3:18–4:1). At the end of this chapter, I will return to this material in conjunction with the Ephesian household code. Finally, he encourages the community to persevere in prayer, requests their prayers, and exhorts them to conduct (*peripateite*) themselves wisely toward outsiders (4:2–6).

Although this paraenesis contains a variety of material, it never loses its central focus that the moral life is the consequence of a new creation effected by Christ's death and resurrection. Because believers have died with Christ, Paul calls upon them to put to death those aspects of their lives which are earthly. And because they have been raised with Christ, he calls upon them to clothe themselves as God's holy and elect people. Despite the exalted character of this baptismal ethic, it never removes believers from this world. When Paul exhorts the Colossians to die to the old self and embrace the new, his lists of virtues and vices are ordinary and mundane. And while he calls upon the Colossians to seek the things that are above, he also requires them to respect the social structures of family and society in which they live, and to conduct themselves wisely toward outsiders. In a word, the new creation is not an escape from creation. Nor does it disregard those aspects of the moral life which Jew and Gentile recognize as good. Unlike the proponents of "the philosophy" who embrace ascetical practices in order to escape this world, Paul's ethic is fully engaged with the created world. To be sure, this is an ecclesial ethic intended for the community of the church rather than for outsiders. Moreover, one suspects that, in Paul's view, it can only be fully lived within the community of the church, under the headship of Christ. But the church to which it is directed lives in the world as the first fruits of a new creation.

A LIFE WORTHY OF GOD'S CALLING:
EPHESIANS

Although Ephesians precedes Colossians in the New Testament canon, I have elected to treat it second for two reasons: First, there is greater doubt about the Pauline authorship of Ephesians than about Colossians. Second, in all probability the author of this letter knew and employed Colossians.[16] The author of Ephesians, however, is not slavishly dependent upon Colossians. For example, he employs the basic structure of the household code found in Colossians but thoroughly revises it in light of his ecclesiology, thereby presenting the most exalted picture of marriage in the New Testament. Again, the author of Ephesians readily takes up ideas present in Colossians and the undisputed Pauline letters, but recasts them in new ways appropriate to the author's situation.[17] Thoroughly acquainted with Paul's thought, this author could well be styled the first Pauline theologian. Thus, while I suspect that Ephesians is Deutero-Pauline, I refer to its author as "Paul." Moreover, as I will explain below, Paul's authority is an integral part of the letter's rhetorical strategy for persuading its audience to adopt and maintain the patterns of behavior it presents.

Ephesians purports to be a letter from Paul who is in prison (3:1; 4:1; 6:20). The place and circumstances of his imprisonment, as well as the addressees of the letter, are not clear.[18] While several manuscripts read, "To the saints who are *in Ephesus* and are faithful in Christ Jesus," other important witnesses have rather, "To the saints who are faithful in Christ Jesus," suggesting that this is a general or circular letter intended for several communities, perhaps in and around Ephesus.[19] Unlike Colossians and the majority of Paul's undisputed correspondence, there is no mention of a coauthor such as Timothy or Silvanus. The sole authorship of Paul is almost required by this letter, given its portrayal of Paul in chapter 3: he is *the* apostle to the Gentiles who has been granted special insight into the mystery of Christ (3:1–13).

The letter's closing is brief and impersonal when compared to other Pauline letters. There are no greetings from, or to, other believers. In a phrase dependent upon Colossians, only Tychicus is named.

> Tychicus will tell you everything. He is a dear brother and a faithful minister in the Lord. I am sending him to you for this very purpose, to let you know how we are, and to encourage your hearts (Eph. 6:21–22; see Col. 4:7–8).

Furthermore, there is little indication that a specific problem or crisis has occasioned Ephesians, as is the case in Paul's undisputed letters, or even Colossians. If, as most commentators suppose, the author knew and employed Colossians, this is all the more striking since that letter deals at length with some sort of false teaching (see Col. 2:8–23). To be sure, Ephesians does contain occasional warnings not to be deceived by people whose words are empty (4:14; 5:6–7), but there is no specific warning about a present or impending danger such as is found in Colossians.

Having said this, I do not wish to imply that Ephesians is simply a theological tract with the trappings of a letter. In my view, it is a real, albeit circular, letter addressed to several churches for the purpose of exhorting its recipients to live a moral life worthy of their exalted calling as members of the universal church.[20] Moreover, it appears that this exhortation is sorely needed, since those who were chosen are now tempted by the deceptive allure of their former way of life. Indeed, all too much of the world that Paul criticizes has penetrated the church that he depicts in such a grand manner.[21] His rhetorical task in Ephesians, then, is to remind his audience of their status so that they will lead a life worthy of the vocation to which they have been called (4:1).

Aside from its initial greeting (1:1–2) and brief closing (6:21–24), Ephesians is easily divided into two parts. The first (1:3–3:21) is an outstanding example of epideictic rhetoric that recalls and celebrates the divine election of the addressees. Although it contains important doctrinal matter, it is marked by benediction, thanksgiving, anamnesis, and prayer, which suggests to some that these texts derive from, or are closely related to, the liturgical life of the church.[22] The second part (4:1–6:20) is an example of deliberative rhetoric intended to persuade the addressees to conduct themselves in accordance with their elected status. Except for Rom. 12:1–15:12, this section comprises the longest paraenesis of any letter attributed to Paul in the New Testament. Overall, the letter's rhetorical strategy is clear, and that strategy will guide my exposition of this writing: Paul celebrates and reminds the Ephesians of their chosen status in order to reinforce their identity and strengthen their resolve to live in accordance with the gospel they have received. He establishes a series of contrasts between the former and present life of the addressees in order to remind them of their identity vis-à-vis the world.[23] Finally, he will remind them that they are engaged in a cosmic struggle that requires them to put on the full armor of God if they are to prevail. Such a strategy does not excuse the Ephesians from living in the day-to-day world, as the letter's household code makes clear. Thus Ephesians draws a sharp line between church and world, but it does not require the church to disengage itself entirely from the world.

Saved by Grace

If moral conduct is related in any way to a person's self-identity, then Ephesians provides one of the most persuasive arguments in the whole of the New Testament for living an ethical life. In the first three chapters of Ephesians, Paul employs a variety of images to remind the recipients that they have become God's chosen and elect people. Thus, after an initial greeting, he begins with an extended benediction (Eph. 1:3–14), rather than the traditional thanksgiving, in which he praises God for his redemptive work accomplished on behalf of the Ephesians. The major points can be summarized in the following statements. First, God chose them[24] in Christ, from the foundation of the world, to be holy and blameless (*hagious kai amōmous;* 1:4; see 5:27, where the same expression occurs). From the outset of the letter, therefore, Paul establishes an intimate relationship between divine election and the moral life. Second, their moral life is grounded in Christ, since God destined them for adoption through Jesus Christ for the praise of his glorious grace that was bestowed upon them in Christ (see 2:5, 8, where the theme of grace is developed further). Third, in Christ and through his blood, believers already have redemption, understood as the forgiveness of their sins, thanks to the richness of God's grace. Thus the moral life is a present reality inasmuch as their sins have been forgiven. Fourth, it is possible and incumbent upon the elect to live a moral life because God has made known the mystery of his will to them: that all things are to be gathered up in Christ. Fifth, they are to live for the praise of God's glory because they were allotted an inheritance in Christ. Sixth, in Christ they have heard the word of truth that is the gospel and were marked with the seal of the Holy Spirit, the pledge of the full inheritance yet to come. Thus, despite the strong emphasis upon what has already been attained, Paul indicates that the completion of their salvation is yet to occur. In a word, he celebrates their election, adoption, redemption, the revelation of the mystery, and the inheritance they are to receive. In doing so, he lays the foundation for the moral demands he will soon make.[25]

In a more traditional thanksgiving section (1:15–23) that follows the benediction, Paul praises the community for its faith in the Lord Jesus and its love for all the members of the church (*tous hagious*). But then, lest there be any notion that the community has already attained to the fullness of its salvation, he prays that God will give them a spirit of wisdom and revelation as they come to know God so that their hearts will be enlightened to know the hope to which he has called them and the glorious inheritance that awaits them among the holy ones, as well as the surpassing greatness of his power. The thanksgiving, then, intimates that the Ephesians must continue to grow in the knowledge of what God has already done for them. They have been elected and called, they are already living a life of faith and love, but there is need for a more profound understanding of the hope and inheritance that is theirs. Although Paul does not explicitly employ moral or ethical language in this section, his prayer-wish for the Ephesians has moral and ethical implications.

These moral implications become more explicit in chapter 2, where Paul draws a series of contrasts between the life of the Ephesians then (*pote*) and now (*nyn*). The first of these contrasts (2:1–10) is explicitly moral and ethical in nature and makes use of Paul's teaching on justification, but in such a way that the teaching is updated for a new generation of Gentile believers.[26] Before they were "saved by grace," they were dead to God on account of their trespasses and sins. *Then* they lived (*periepatēsate*)[27] in accordance with the spirit of this age and were destined for God's wrath. But when they were dead, God made them alive. To emphasize the gracious aspect of what God did for them, Paul writes "by grace you have been saved" (2:5), and then repeats the thought in a slightly expanded form, "for by grace you have been saved *through faith*" (2:8). Without using the explicit vocabulary of justification, he reminds them that their salvation is a gift of God, not their own doing or the result of their works. In effect, Ephesians rethinks the doctrine of justification for the church and makes it more intelligible to Gentiles with no Jewish background. Whereas Romans and Galatians speak of justification by faith apart from the works *of the Mosaic law*, Ephesians uses the language of being saved by faith apart from one's good works.[28] The old battle between Paul and the Judaizers has been settled, and "works" now refers to good deeds in which believers might be tempted to boast.[29] As in the undisputed Pauline letters, however, believers must persevere in the moral life even though they have been "justified," to use the language of Galatians and Romans, or "saved," to use the language of Ephesians. These "good works," however, are the work of God, since believers have been "created in Christ Jesus for good works, which God prepared beforehand" (2:10).

In the second part of this chapter (2:11–22), Paul again points to the "then" and "now" of the Ephesians. In doing so, he draws out the social implications of justification by faith, much as do Galatians and Romans, but without using the vocabulary of justification. *Then* they were without Christ, alienated from the commonwealth of Israel, strangers to the covenants and their promises, without hope, and without God. But again, they received salvation from God through Christ, who reconciled Jew and Gentile into a single person (*kainon anthrōpon;* 2:15). Through his death, Christ abolished the law[30] (the only reference to the law in this letter) with its commandments since it acted as a wall separating Jew from Gentile. *Now* the Ephesians and all Gentile believers are fellow citizens and saints, members of the household of God. In Christ they have been built into a holy temple, a dwelling place for God.

When Paul writes that Christ abolished the law with its commandments and ordinances (2:15), one might legitimately ask if the apostle has not done away with an important element of moral instruction. As this section intimates, and as the rest of this letter will show, however, Paul establishes the moral life of believers on a new basis. The church is the new humanity (*kainos anthrōpos*) that is growing and maturing into Christ its head (4:13, 15). In effect, then, Paul establishes the moral life on Christ. Those who belong to the body, which is the church, form this new humanity that finds its moral maturity in Christ. What Torah was to the moral life of Israel, Christ has become to the community of the church: the revelation of God's will.

At this point, it might appear that Paul is ready to begin his paraenesis proper. But before doing so, he points to himself as one uniquely entrusted with the mystery of Christ (3:1–13). Whereas Colossians defined this mystery as "Christ in you, the hope of glory" (Col. 1:27), Ephesians explains it thus: "The Gentiles have become fellow heirs, members of the same body, and sharers in the promise in Christ Jesus through the gospel" (Eph. 3:6). This mystery, as I have already intimated, is the basis of the moral life, since God's purpose in sending Christ was to establish a new humanity devoid of enmity and hostility. Inasmuch as Paul is the apostle to the Gentiles who has a unique insight into this mystery (3:4), his apostolic instruction is essential for the moral life of Gentile believers such as the intended recipients of this letter. The letter, then, is not one exhortation among others; it is an *apostolic* exhortation from one specially gifted by God to understand the mystery of Christ. Thus, whether or not Paul is the author of Ephesians, its moral persuasion is intimately related to his person. It is Paul who writes to the Ephesians, disclosing the mystery of Christ. In doing so, he shows them a way of life worthy of their calling.

In the final verses of part one (3:14–21), Paul returns to the genre of prayer that characterized the opening benediction and thanksgiving. The great apostle of the Gentiles prays that the Ephesians will be strengthened in their inner being (*ton esō anthrōpon*; 3:16) through the power of God's Spirit, that Christ will dwell in their hearts, and that they will comprehend and know the love of Christ. Such a prayer-wish indicates Paul's understanding of the moral life and is more than a mere formality. One must understand the mystery if one is to live the moral life that Paul urges the Ephesians to embrace. Moreover, as he will explain at the conclusion of his paraenesis, the moral life requires divine assistance, since believers are struggling against more than flesh and blood.

Imitators of God

The paraenesis of Ephesians expands upon that of Colossians.[31] In the central section of this paraenesis (4:17–6:9), for example, Paul urges the Ephesians to cultivate certain virtues and avoid specific vices, and he employs an expanded household code that is modeled upon the one found in Colossians. The paraenesis of Ephesians, however, is prefaced by an exhortation to maintain the unity of the church (4:1–16), and it concludes with an exhortation to put on the armor of God, since believers are engaged in a cosmic struggle (6:10–20). Consequently, whereas the paraenesis of Colossians exhorts its readers to live out the baptismal implications of dying and rising with Christ (Col. 3:1–4), Ephesians views the moral life against the horizon of the church universal, which is engaged in a cosmic struggle. The material may be outlined as follows.[32]

4:1–16	An initial exhortation to maintain the unity of the Spirit so that the church will grow, in love, into its head, who is Christ
4:17–5:14	Three exhortations not to live morally dissolute lives as the Gentiles do: 4:17–24; 4:25–5:2; 5:3–14
5:15–6:9	An exhortation concerned with the internal life of the church, especially the Christian household
6:10–20	An exhortation to take up the armor of God in order to be strengthened in the moral life

As can be seen from this outline, the paraenesis begins with a consideration of the church (4:1–16), moves to the life of believers in the world (4:17–5:14), returns to a consideration of life within the church (5:15–6:9), and concludes with a cosmic view of the moral life (6:10–20).

Maintaining the unity of the Spirit (Eph. 4:1–16). The beginning of this paraenesis recalls what Paul has just said and foreshadows what he will say.[33]

> I therefore, the prisoner in the Lord, beg you to lead a life (*peripatēsai*) worthy of the calling to which you have been called, with all humility and gentleness, with patience, bearing with one another in love, making every effort to maintain the unity of the Spirit in the bond of peace (4:1–3).

By making his appeal as a prisoner in the Lord, and by exhorting his addressees to lead a life (literally, "to walk") worthy of their calling, Paul binds his paraenesis to what he has written about election, adoption, and heritage in the opening benediction (1:3–14), and to his unique role as Christ's prisoner on behalf of the Gentiles (3:1). A life "worthy of their calling," therefore, cannot be understood apart from what he has just said.

In appealing to them to "walk" in a manner worthy of that calling, he employs a familiar Old Testament metaphor for the moral life that he will use several times in this paraenesis.

4:17	You must no longer *walk* as the Gentiles *walk*
5:2	*Walk* in love, as Christ loved us
5:8	*Walk* as children of light
5:15	Be careful then how you *walk*

The metaphor suggests the following about the moral life: (1) it is dynamic inasmuch as it involves progress; (2) it has an ultimate goal; (3) the way is prescribed by God; (4) the way that one walks is either pleasing or displeasing to God.[34] In the present circumstances of the Ephesians, three virtues are needed (humility, gentleness, patience), all of which are modes of bearing with one another in love. Love will occur again at the end of this section (4:15–16) and is the appropriate way for believers to become imitators of God (5:1–2).

The most distinctive aspect of this section, however, is the ecclesiological and corporate dimension it brings to the moral life, an aspect already announced in the first part of the letter. The Ephesians are to maintain the unity of the Spirit in the bond of peace because, as the church, they are one body.[35] The language Paul employs recalls what he said earlier about the salvation God effected for the Gentiles. Christ has become their peace, making Jew and Gentile a new humanity (*kainos anthrōpos*) by reconciling both in one body, the church (2:14–16). Therefore, the moral requirement of bearing with one another in love is nothing less than maintaining the peace that God has effected for the church. Those who destroy the unity of the Spirit deny God's work of salvation, while those who promote the unity of the Spirit affirm that salvation. In effect, just as the gift of salvation implies moral responsibility, the moral life is the proper response to the gift of salvation.[36]

The ultimate goal of the moral life is related to the new humanity that God has inaugurated in Christ (2:15). As the one body of Christ, the church has been given a variety of ministerial gifts so that its members, "the saints," might be equipped for the work of service (*diakonia*), that is, for building up the body of Christ. Thus, by the unity of faith and knowledge, the church is meant to attain to mature manhood (*eis andra teleion*; 4:13), growing into the head, who is Christ (4:15). The moral vision here is both corporate and individual. Individual believers must live out the moral life. But the moral life is worked out in community with others, making it a corporate as well as an individual project.

Living not as the Gentiles live (Eph. 4:17–5:14). Having set the moral life within its ecclesial setting, Paul turns his attention from the internal life of the church to Christian existence in a hostile environment.[37] The section begins with another reference to "walking" that announces the main theme: "you must no longer walk as the Gentiles walk" (4:17). Then, in three units (4:17–24; 4:25–5:2; 5:3–14), he describes two different and opposing kinds of existence. Each unit begins by depicting the godless existence the Ephesians have left behind and then turns to the kind of behavior that should characterize their new life.[38] While Paul draws a sharp

220

contrast between these two kinds of existence, suggesting that there is no good in the world and no wrong in the church, one suspects that he so writes precisely because too much of the world has penetrated the church.[39]

In the first of three units (4:17–24), Paul appeals to the Ephesians not to "walk" as the Gentiles do, reminding his addressees of what they learned in Christ: to put off the old self (*ton palaion anthrōpon*) and to cloth themselves with the new self (*ton kainon anthrōpon*). Borrowed from the paraenesis of Colossians (3:9–10), this metaphor stands for the two kinds of existence that Paul juxtaposes. The first is the utterly futile existence of those who are incapable of grasping what is good because they are alienated from God's life. Their attempts at the moral life are utterly frustrated since they are guided by a mind that is useless (*en mataiotēti*) so that they have no understanding of God's will. Such people surrender themselves to licentiousness (*aselgeia*) and practice every kind of impure deed. Such was the former existence of the Ephesians. The second is the existence of those whose minds are renewed because they have put on the new self created in the likeness of God, in righteousness and holiness, enabling themselves to become "imitators of God" (5:1). Such is the new existence of the Ephesians. The fact that Paul urges them to adopt this new existence, however, indicates that it has not yet become a complete reality for them.

The most interesting aspect of this exhortation, however, is the distinction Paul makes between his addressees and their Gentile compatriots. Even though the recipients of the letter are Gentiles, Paul no longer views them as such. A new person in Christ, they form a new race that is neither Jewish nor Gentile. Therefore, they must live in an entirely new way.

This new existence is more fully described in the next unit (4:25–5:2). Once more, Paul begins with a negative type of behavior and concludes with the kind of conduct appropriate to those who have put on the new self. They are to put away falsehood; they are not to sin when they are angry; they are not to steal; they are not to talk in an offensive way; they are not to grieve the Holy Spirit by their evil conduct. Although the behavior listed here is rather commonplace, Paul provides his addressees with a series of reasons for reforming their conduct which appears to have the community in view. Thus, they are to put away falsehood because they are members of one another. They must work rather than steal so that they can contribute to the needs of the less fortunate. They must watch over their speech so that they will speak what is useful for building up the church.[40]

Having told his audience what they must avoid, Paul urges the Ephesians to imitate God.[41] They must be kind, tenderhearted, and forgiving toward one another because, in Christ, God has forgiven them (4:32). Therefore, they must become imitators of God as his beloved children (5:1). While Paul often calls upon his converts to imitate himself or Christ (1 Cor. 4:6; 11:1; Gal. 4:12; Phil. 3:17; 4:9; 1 Thess. 1:6; 2 Thess. 3:7, 9), this is the only place in the Pauline corpus that believers are urged to imitate God. The notion, however, is thoroughly Jewish and can be found in the Gospels (Matt. 5:48; Luke 6:36) as well as in the Old Testament (Lev. 19:2: "You shall be

221

holy, for I the LORD your God am holy"). The manner in which the addressees are to imitate God, however, is christologically grounded. They are to "walk in love" as Christ loved them and handed himself over for them (Eph. 5:2).

The third and final unit of this section (5:3–14) continues the process of distinguishing the recipients of this letter from their unbelieving environment. There is no room for fornication, impurity, and greed (*porneia, akatharsia, pleonexia*) in their lives since such behavior is not worthy of those who are holy (*hagioi*). Nor will those who practice such deeds inherit the kingdom of Christ and God. The Ephesians are not even to associate with such people (5:7), since once (*pote*) they were darkness, but now (*nyn*) they are light. Therefore they are to walk as children of light (5:8).

The Paul who writes Ephesians has clearly gone beyond the Paul who wrote the Corinthian correspondence. While Paul told the Corinthians to shun fornication (1 Cor. 6:18) and not to associate with sexually immoral people (1 Cor. 5:9), he insisted that he did not mean the immoral of this world, since otherwise it would be necessary for the Corinthians to flee from the world. Paul's primary concern in Corinthians is with immoral believers (1 Cor. 5:9–11).[42] But the Paul who writes Ephesians envisions a stronger separation between church and world. The world is a place where the disobedient dwell in darkness while the church is—or should be—populated by children of light. The moral life, according to Ephesians, requires a strong sense of moral identity and clear lines of demarcation between the children of light and the children of darkness.

Redeeming the time (Eph. 5:15–6:9). Having appealed to the Ephesians to distinguish themselves clearly from the world by not behaving as the Gentiles do, Paul once more turns his attention to the internal life of the church. This new section begins with an exhortation: the Ephesians should be careful how they "walk" (*pōs peripateite*) lest they behave as senseless or foolish people (*asophoi*). But instead of contrasting two kinds of existence as he did in the previous section, Paul now focuses his attention on how believers should relate to one another within the community of the church. As people who are wise (*sophoi*), they should understand the will of the Lord and be inebriated with God's Spirit rather than with wine. Employing four participial phrases (5:19–21), he describes the conduct of those intoxicated with the Spirit in terms of addressing (*lalountes*) one another in psalms, hymns, and spiritual songs; singing and making melody (*adontes kai psallontes*) to the Lord; giving thanks (*eucharistountes*); and being subordinate (*hypotassomenoi*) to one another. The last phrase serves as the introduction to an extended household code that will be considered below. Once more, the Paul who writes Ephesians is keenly aware of the danger that the world poses for the church. Characterizing the present time as evil, he encourages his audience to redeem or make the most of the time, suggesting perhaps that the moment of God's judgment is near (see 5:6, where there is an explicit threat of God's wrath).

The armor of God (Eph. 6:10–20). When he reminded the Ephesians that once they were darkness but now they are light (5:8), Paul intimated that there is a cosmic dimension to the moral life. In the final section of this paraenesis, he explicitly describes the moral life as a struggle with more than human opponents. The Ephesians are contending "against the cosmic rulers (*tous kosmokratoras*) of this present darkness" (6:12). In order to compete with them, they must put on the full armor of God:[43]

the belt of truth
the breastplate of righteousness
shoes: a readiness to proclaim the gospel of peace
the shield of faith
the helmet of salvation
the sword of the Spirit, that is, the word of God

The most striking aspect of this passage, however, is its implicit claim that one cannot live the moral life apart from God. In this regard, this passage states in yet another way one of the central themes of the letter: in accordance with the riches of God's grace (1:7), the elect have been saved by grace (2:5, 8). While the elect must take personal responsibility for their conduct, the moral life is more than their own doing, for God has created them for good works (2:10) and strengthens them with his armor in their daily struggle against appeasing spiritual powers. For the Paul of Ephesians, the church is God's fighting force in the world, equipped with the whole armor of God.[44]

The paraenesis of Ephesians concludes with an exhortation to prayer, and a request for prayers that Paul will be able to make known the mystery of the gospel with all boldness (6:19–20). Thus it recalls his special role in making known the mystery to the Gentiles (3:1–13). For the Paul of Ephesians the moral life is rooted and grounded in this mystery, and apart from this mystery it is impossible to please God.

CONDUCT FOR CHRISTIAN HOUSEHOLDS

Household codes are among the most significant aspects of the paraenesis in Colossians and Ephesians. In both letters, Paul outlines how members of a believing household are to relate to one another (Col. 3:18–4:1; Eph. 5:21–6:9). It is not surprising then that the origin, and significance, of these codes has been a topic of ongoing discussion and debate.[45] Especially in recent years, there has been a movement toward tracing them back to Hellenistic discussions of household management, as found in Aristotle's discussion of the household in the *Politics*, Book 1.[46] Whatever the origin of these codes, there is little doubt that they were Christianized in order to respond to the new situation in which believers found themselves.

Although household codes are found in Colossians and Ephesians, they do not occur in any of the undisputed Pauline letters. Moreover, while there are similar codes in 1 Tim. 2:8–15; 6:1–2, in Titus 2:1–10, and in 1 Peter 2:18–3:7, these codes do not exhibit the clear pattern or structure of the

Colossian and Ephesian codes. In both of these letters, Paul turns his attention to three household relationships: husband and wife; parent and child; master and slave. In doing so, he always begins with those who are more socially dependent (the wife, the child, the slave), directly addressing all of the parties involved.[47]

In the view of most commentators the Ephesian code is dependent upon that of Colossians, allowing readers to compare the manner in which Ephesians makes use of earlier material for its own theological purposes. In this regard, the most dramatic editorial activity occurs in the first and most important relationship, husband and wife. Whereas Colossians simply reads, "Wives, be subject to your husbands, as is fitting in the Lord" (3:18), and, "Husbands, love your wives and never treat them harshly" (3:19), the Ephesian code begins with the statement, "Be subject to one another out of reverence for Christ" (5:21). Next, it substantiates what it says about the relationship between husband and wife in light of the church's subordination to Christ. Wives are to be subject to their husbands because the husband is the head (*kephalē*) of the wife in a manner analogous to Christ, the head of the church. The subordination of wife to husband, therefore, is not a servile obedience[48] but the loving submission that the church renders to Christ. As regards husbands, the Ephesian code is at pains to describe the love that they owe to their wives. Calling attention to the relationship of Christ and the church, the code commands them to love their wives as Christ loved the church; he manifested his love by handing himself over for the sake of the church (*paredōken hyper autēs*), an unmistakable reference to Christ's death. Thus Christian husbands are called to a self-sacrificial love that imitates the very love of Christ, who did not come to be served but to serve and give his life a ransom for many (Mark 10:45).

To be sure, the Paul of Ephesians does not go beyond the social structures of his day, which ordinarily required wives to be subordinate to their husbands,[49] but by prefacing this code with the injunction, "Be subject to one another out of reverence for Christ" (Eph. 5:21), and by drawing an analogy between the husband and Christ on the one hand, and the wife and the church on the other, he creates an entirely new context of mutual and loving service for understanding the marital relationship.

There is less editorial activity in the rest of the code, suggesting that the Paul of Ephesians was especially interested in the relationship of husband and wife. The redactional work that does occur, however, is of interest. Whereas Colossians exhorts children to obey their parents in everything, for it is their acceptable duty in the Lord (3:20), Ephesians adds a scriptural justification: the commandment to honor one's parents contains a promise, "so that it may be well with you and you may live long on the earth" (6:1–3, quoting Ex. 20:12; Deut. 5:16).[50] In a similar vein, whereas Colossians exhorts fathers not to provoke their children lest they lose heart (3:21), Ephesians adds, "but bring them up in the discipline and instruction of the Lord" (6:4).

Except for that given to husbands in the Ephesian code, the appeal to slaves is the longest exhortation of both codes (Col. 3:22–25; Eph. 6:5–8).

Both codes begin, "Slaves, obey your earthly masters . . . ," and then make a number of similar points: The obedience of slaves should not be limited to times when they are being watched, or in order to please their earthly masters. Rather it should be wholehearted as if they were serving the Lord, knowing that they will receive a recompense from the Lord, who is impartial. In the Ephesian code, however, slaves are enjoined to obey "as *slaves of Christ*, doing the will of God from the heart" (6:6). As for masters, both codes remind them that they also have a "Master in heaven" (Col. 4:1; Eph. 6:9), but Ephesians adds "and with him there is no partiality." The tendency of the editorial activity in Ephesians vis-à-vis Colossians is clear. Whereas Colossians Christianizes standard household injunctions by a series of simple phrases—for example, "as is fitting in the Lord" (3:18), "for this is your acceptable duty in the Lord" (3:20), "fearing the Lord" (3:22), "as done for the Lord" (3:23)—Ephesians has thoroughly reworked the material in light of its ecclesiology. To be sure, the desired conduct remains the same, but the Ephesian code provides reasons for such behavior that are more theologically grounded.

Since I have identified this work of New Testament ethics as primarily descriptive, I have generally refrained from discussing the normative value of the texts under study. In most instances, I suspect that this has not caused great difficulty for the reader, especially when the moral teaching of the New Testament calls believers to a rather heroic kind of virtue. In such instances, the question is more often about the practicality of such an exalted ethic. But in the present instance, if the question concerning the normative value of the text is not addressed, the ethic of the New Testament will seem totally irrelevant since, as theologically sophisticated as these texts may be, they command wives to be submissive to their husbands and slaves to be obedient to their masters. While there are undoubtedly cultures in which the first of these injunctions is still socially plausible, that is hardly the case in most Western democratic societies, in which the social equality of women is acknowledged in principle, if not always in fact.

This issue, of course, demands more than the brief discussion that follows, for it raises fundamental questions about the normative value of scripture within the church.[51] All too aware of this, I offer the following points.

First, it is the gospel above all else that is normative for the life and teaching of the church: the proclamation of God's saving work in and through Jesus Christ. And yet, since the gospel is proclaimed in human words, it is impossible to extract from the writings of the New Testament a series of propositions about the gospel that transcend time and culture. Even those propositions which all would acknowledge as central to the gospel, such as Paul's statement on justification by faith apart from the works of the law (Gal. 2:16), are expressed in the language of a particular time and culture. Were they not, there would be no need to exegete their meaning! The content of the gospel—understood as God's saving act in Jesus Christ—transcends time and culture, but its human expression is necessarily incarnated in human words and culture. Moreover, while it often criticizes and challenges society's values, the gospel is always lived within a specific culture.

Second, the household codes, like all New Testament texts, derive from, and reflect, a specific time and culture. Since human beings always live within a particular social structure whose plausibility they accept, the human writers of the New Testament were no more able to transcend their time and culture than we are. The authors of Colossians and Ephesians, for example, assumed the social legitimacy of the world in which they lived because it was part of the plausibility structure that gave meaning to their lives. Consequently, while the modern reader is offended by the notion of slavery or the idea that women are inherently subordinated to men, the New Testament was born in a very different world. For that world, the institution of slavery was plausible, since society was economically dependent upon it. Likewise, since the domain of the man was in the public forum and that of the woman in the household, the subordination of a wife to her husband was taken for granted.

Third, the normative value of texts such as the household codes does *not* extend to the cultural and social customs that they necessarily reflect. Those living in the twentieth century are no more bound to the social institutions of the first century than those living in the twenty-fifth century will be to the social institutions of the twentieth century. This would be true even if the household codes reflected cultural values that were more amenable to twentieth-century democracy. Rather, the normative value of these texts resides in the manner in which they relate gospel and culture to each other. In doing so, they show believers how to live the gospel in their daily lives, given the limitations of time and culture.

To be more concrete, whether or not the authors of Colossians and Ephesians agreed with the institution of slavery, they clearly presupposed that it constituted an important dimension of their social world. Likewise, they assumed that the wife was to take the subordinate role in the marital relationship. The Christ event, however, also made an impact upon them and those to whom they wrote. If Jesus is *Kyrios* (Lord), and believers are his *douloi* (slaves), what has become of the master and slave relationship? And if in Christ there is no "male and female," how is one to interpret the traditional relationship of husband and wife?[52]

In some quarters of the early church, there may have been an attempt by Christian slaves to attain social equality vis-à-vis their Christian masters. Likewise, Christian wives may have questioned their subordination to their believing husbands. Thus, many suggest that the codes of Colossians and Ephesians represent a regression from the doctrine of a more egalitarian-minded Paul as seen in Gal. 3:28. But given Paul's insistence that each one should remain in the state in which he was called (1 Corinthians 7), his admonitions to women (1 Cor. 11:2–16; 14:34–36), and his acceptance of the master-and-slave relationship in his letter to Philemon, I am not so sure that he was as egalitarian in practice as the famous couplet in Gal. 3:28 suggests.[53] Nonetheless, the early church did find itself in a dilemma, since the social structures in which it lived did not always correspond to the deeper meaning of the Christ event it proclaimed.

The authors of Colossians and Ephesians resolved their dilemma by trying to give new meaning to their social structures in light of the Christ event. Thus, the work of slaves gains a certain dignity because the slave ultimately belongs to the Lord. Masters are faced with new responsibilities toward their slaves because they have a Master in heaven, and God is impartial. Christian wives and husbands, at least in the case of Ephesians, are now related to each other as are Christ and the church, even though the wife remains subordinate to her husband.

Contemporary believers can no longer accept these culturally bound solutions unless they are ready to embrace slavery and the innate subordination of woman to man. But they can learn an important lesson from these New Testament writings: namely, that the gospel must be lived within the context of a specific social structure, as ambiguous as that structure may be. While the gospel may call upon believers to question and challenge the values of this age, it does not relieve them of the responsibility of living in this world, in the social and cultural structures of their time and place. These texts call each generation of believers to live the gospel within its particular culture and social setting, criticizing and challenging when necessary, but always living in a real world.

PAUL'S MORAL TEACHING:
A SUMMARY STATEMENT

At the beginning of this chapter I raised the question of the relationship between the moral teaching of these letters and that of the undisputed Pauline correspondence. I will now provide a brief response to that question.

On several points, there is a remarkable similarity between the ethical instruction of these letters and the undisputed Pauline correspondence. First, both letters emphasize the elected dignity of their addressees before specifically exhorting them to a particular course of action, thereby reaffirming the Pauline relationship between the indicative of salvation and the moral imperative. Second, the content of the virtues to be embraced, and the vices to be avoided, does not essentially differ from what is found in Paul's other letters. Believers are to avoid everything that is immoral and unclean, and they are to be gentle, compassionate, and forgiving. Third, in both letters, as in Paul's other writings, there is an emphasis upon the centrality of love, which is the bond of perfection. Fourth, both letters ground their ethics in Christology and ecclesiology and make specific references to Baptism. Fifth, as in all of Paul's correspondence, there is a deep concern for the unity of the church, the community within which believers live the moral life. In sum, there is little doubt that Paul would have approved of the moral life of believers who lived in the manner recommended by these letters.

The most noticeable difference between these letters and the undisputed correspondence is in the area of eschatology and ecclesiology. The lively hope for the parousia that characterizes the undisputed Pauline correspondence is no longer present in these letters, especially Ephesians. To be sure, both letters speak of the believer's hope that sustains and underlies faith, but there is a sense that believers will continue to live in a rather hostile world for a longer period than Paul expected. Given this situation, Colossians and Ephesians provide a slightly different perspective on the moral life when viewed from the angle of ecclesiology. Stressing the cosmic dimensions of Christ's work, they view the church as his body so that the church becomes universal in scope. This church is the first fruits of a new creation forming a new humanity, the basis of a new moral life. At the present time, the church lives in a hostile world and must contend with spiritual powers and forces, but the final victory is assured. To be sure, there is a danger of viewing this church as merely the church triumphant, but both letters are keenly aware that Christians can fail and have failed. Given the new times and circumstances in which Colossians and Ephesians were written, it is difficult to imagine Paul finding fault with them.

11

Reliable
Moral Guides

The Pastoral Epistles

The pastoral epistles (1 and 2 Timothy, Titus) are among the most fascinating yet problematic writings of the New Testament. They are fascinating because their emphasis upon the role of bishops, presbyters, and deacons foreshadows the ecclesial structure espoused by early church writers such as Ignatius of Antioch. It is not surprising, then, that these writings have been especially attractive to Anglican, Roman Catholic, and Orthodox Christians in whose churches the threefold order of bishop, presbyter, and deacon plays a central role. Yet these writings are problematic inasmuch as scholars question their Pauline authorship, arguing that Paul did not write them and that Timothy and Titus were not their original recipients.[1] Thus the question arises: Are these writings faithful to the Pauline tradition? This question, of course, requires more than a simple yes-or-no response.

ASSESSING THE "PAUL"
OF THE PASTORALS

Each of the Pauline letters inevitably leaves its readers with an impression or portrait of Paul. For example, 1 Thessalonians portrays him as a founding father and nursing mother deeply concerned for the needs of his community, whereas Galatians presents him as the valiant apostle who refuses to compromise the truth of the gospel. The pastoral epistles are no exception to this rule. In them Paul is the herald, preacher, and teacher of the gospel whose life and teaching assures the truth of what he has entrusted (the *parathēkē*) to Timothy and Titus. The Pastoral Paul is *the apostle*[2] who transmits sound teaching so that the church can lead "a quiet and peaceable life in all godliness and dignity" (1 Tim. 2:2). What are we to make of this portrait of Paul?

A Decline in the Pauline Tradition?

For some, the pastoral epistles mark a decline in the vibrant Pauline tradition of justification by faith, charismatic ministry, and hope in an imminent parousia. In place of Paul's doctrine of justification by faith, they find a renewed interest in good works and civic virtue. In place of charismatic ministry, they perceive an attempt to restrict ministry to certain groups within the church. And in place of Paul's lively hope for the Lord's imminent return, they see the church reconciling itself to living in the world and accommodating itself to it. In their view, the charismatic community of the end time has become a well-ordered household in which subordinates, especially women and slaves, must learn their place. The ethical life is no longer guided by the Spirit so much as it is by the virtues and ideals of Hellenistic philosophy. In their view, then, the Pastoral Paul has retreated from the bold stance taken by the real Paul vis-à-vis the world.

An important commentary by Martin Dibelius and Hans Conzelmann on the pastoral epistles[3] has been especially influential in solidifying this position, portraying the ethics of these letters as *bürgerlich* (middle class, bourgeois, pertaining to good citizenship). For example, in an excursus titled "The Ideal of Good Christian Citizenship,"[4] Dibelius and Conzelmann write:

> Here, as in Luke-Acts, the ethics of good citizenship serve to regulate the time until the parousia, which is no longer felt to be imminent. The components of the regulation are: a good conscience, the idea that the Christian life aims at good works, faith and love, piety and dignity.[5]

Dibelius and Conzelmann maintain that the Pastorals are the only writings in the New Testament that structure life under the ideal of good Christian citizenship.[6]

Reggie M. Kidd, however, has noted that Dibelius and Conzelmann never give a full explanation of what they mean by *bürgerlich*.[7] On the basis of other writings by Dibelius, however, Kidd suggests that Dibelius meant that the Christians of the pastoral epistles were socially ascendant, culturally accommodative, and unheroically conservative. In contrast to the Christians of the Pastorals, Paul's original converts supposedly belonged to the lower classes of society, did not accommodate themselves to the prevailing culture, and therefore were ethically heroic. Although Kidd does not agree with this assessment of the pastoral epistles, he has identified what many mean when they label the Pastorals *bürgerlich*. These labels imply that the Pastorals represent a fall from a pristine Pauline theology that demanded a more heroic ethic.

A Development of the
Pauline Inheritance

In recent years there has been a renewed appreciation of the Pastorals even among scholars who work with the hypothesis that Paul was not their author. This "rehabilitation" has resulted from at least two lines of research: (1) an analysis of the social situation in and for which the Pastorals were written; (2) a further investigation into the ethical argumentation of these letters.

An investigation of the social situation of the Pastorals has led some to argue that the use of terms such as *"bürgerlich,"* "bourgeois," and "middle class" to describe the ethics of the Pastoral Paul is not only anachronistic but inaccurate.[8] The terms are anachronistic because the ancient world did not have a middle class comparable to that of modern Western industrialized society. Consequently, the application of these terms to the Pastorals has the potential of misrepresenting them as advocating a quiet middle-class existence that was foreign to their original intent. More importantly, it now appears that there is greater continuity between the social status of the Christians of Paul's churches and the social status of the believers represented in the Pastorals than previously thought. The pastoral epistles address a new phase in the church's life but not necessarily a different class of Christians. Their audience is not a group of socially ascendant—in comparison to Paul's converts—Christians who must now accommodate themselves to the world.[9]

Other studies have examined the relationship between theology and ethics in the pastoral epistles and shown that they maintain the connection between the indicative of salvation and the imperative of ethical conduct found in Paul's moral teaching.[10] As Philip Towner discovered, within the Pastorals it is God's salvation that makes the ethical life possible as well as imperative. There is no need to dispute the long-standing claim that the Pastorals make use of ethical teaching similar to that found in the moral philosophy of the Greco-Roman world. What must be contested, however, is the assumption that there is little or no connection between the salvation these letters proclaim and the ethical life they propose. In a word, there is more continuity between the undisputed Pauline correspondence and the pastoral epistles than is often thought. How then are we to approach these letters?

Letters of Moral Exhortation

The pastoral epistles are, apart from the letter to James, the most explicitly ethical writings of the New Testament. The Pastoral Paul employs these letters to instruct his delegates, Timothy and Titus, in what it means to shepherd the church and live in accordance with the gospel. In turn, Timothy and Titus are to instruct others who will instruct still others. Thus the letters initiate an ethical tradition that purportedly has its roots in Paul's own teaching.

As firmly rooted as the pastoral epistles are in that Pauline tradition, they present a problem of no little importance for New Testament ethics. How are they to be employed in this study? We have already encountered a similar problem in dealing with 2 Thessalonians, Colossians, and Ephesians. The problem, however, is more acute for the pastoral epistles. First, there is greater agreement among scholars that the Pastorals are pseudepigraphal.[11] Second, the ethical argument of the pastoral epistles rests upon the authority of Paul and the tradition he entrusts to Timothy and Titus (the *parathēkē*). Lewis Donelson goes so far as to conclude: "If the fiction of the letters is not believed by its readers, then the theology of the letters loses its reliable status."[12]

For those who argue that the Pastorals come from Paul's hand, the question I have raised is not pertinent since the Pastorals represent authentic Pauline instruction. To be sure, these letters manifest a different tone when compared with Paul's other writings, but this could be explained in light of the Pastorals' distinctive character: they are private correspondence to Paul's "apostolic delegates" written at a later stage in the apostle's career rather than letters addressed to communities of believers. For those convinced that the letters are pseudonymous, however, the question is more difficult to resolve. Some maintain that, although written by another in Paul's name, the Pastorals are an authentic development of the Pauline tradition; others contend that they betray that tradition.

As was the case in my study of 2 Thessalonians, Colossians, and Ephesians, I maintain that those engaged in the study of New Testament ethics need not be overly concerned with the question of authorship unless their primary concern is a historical reconstruction of Paul's moral teaching. In that case, one must clearly distinguish between what Paul wrote and what was attributed to him, as well as the chronological order and literary integrity of the authentic Pauline letters. This work of New Testament ethics, however, has charted a different course, since its primary task has been to describe the ethical teaching in the letters attributed to Paul by the canon of the New Testament. Therefore, although I am generally convinced by those who argue that Paul is not the author of the Pastorals, I will study them as part of Paul's ethical legacy, just as I treated the four Gospels as the ethical legacy of Jesus.

In the case of 2 Thessalonians, Colossians, and Ephesians this approach meant reading the letters "as if" they were Paul's in order to determine the ethical impact that Paul (or someone writing in his name) intended to effect upon his audience. In the case of the Pastorals, I propose a similar strategy. Rather than synthesizing their teaching and comparing and contrasting them to the undisputed Pauline correspondence,[13] I will read each letter as paraenesis or moral exhortation addressed to Timothy or Titus by Paul.[14] In doing so, I will pay attention to the manner in which "Paul" persuades "Timothy" or "Titus" to live an ethical life in accord with the gospel, as well as to the instruction he provides for the churches in their care. In my view, this approach preserves the integrity of each writing as well as the canonical claim of the New Testament that the letter is Pauline. It also avoids reducing the moral teaching of the Pastorals to household codes and lists of virtues and vices. Just as the ethical impact of the Gospels comes from the stories they communicate, so the ethical impact of the pastoral epistles derives from the exhortation each letter makes in light of the purported circumstances that caused "Paul" to write to "Timothy" and "Titus." This approach does not require one to set aside all critical judgments about authorship. The differences between these letters and the undisputed Pauline correspondence should be evident to those who have read earlier chapters of this work, and later I will make some comparisons between the Pastorals and the undisputed Pauline correspondence. These comparisons, however, are not the primary goal of this work, which endeavors to appreciate the ethical teaching of each writing.

LIVING IN THE HOUSEHOLD OF GOD: FIRST TIMOTHY

The pastoral epistles differ from the other canonical correspondence attributed to Paul inasmuch as each letter is addressed to an individual rather than to a community of believers.[15] In all likelihood, however, these letters were intended for communities of believers and read in a communal setting.

The scenario of 1 Timothy presupposes that, before departing for Macedonia (see Acts 20:1), Paul left Timothy in Ephesus to counter certain false teachers (1:3). Timothy is portrayed as a young man (4:12) prone to frequent ailments (5:23). He has, however, been ordained by a council of elders in accordance with prophetic spirit (1:18; 4:14). Most importantly, Paul identifies him as his legitimate son (*gnēsiō teknō*, 1:2) in the salutation of this letter. Because of this, the letter's salutation foreshadows the difference between Timothy, who is Paul's legitimate son and heir, and false teachers, who are not legitimate heirs of his authority.[16]

First Timothy is a paraenetic letter[17] intended to exhort the young Timothy to carry out Paul's original charge despite the difficult circumstances in which he finds himself. In exhorting Timothy, Paul charges him to live as an example of moral integrity (4:12) and to instruct others how to live in the household of God, which is the church (3:15).[18] It would be a mistake, however, to view this letter as merely an extended household code or as a handbook for church order. Despite the role these elements play, they are only part of a broader strategy. As we shall see, in 1 Timothy Paul alternates between charging Timothy to live a life in accordance with the gospel and providing him with specific instructions for the household of God.

Paul's Former Charge to Timothy (1 Tim. 1:3–20)

Paul begins by reminding Timothy of the original charge Paul gave him: Timothy must instruct certain people not to teach other doctrines that Paul characterizes as "myths and endless genealogies" (1:4). In contrast to such teaching, he asserts that the goal of Timothy's instruction should be love based upon a pure heart, a good conscience, and sincere faith. Thus Paul establishes an initial contrast between his teaching, which he characterizes as "sound" (1:10), and that of those who teach "other things." However, because he sees an intimate connection between what one teaches and how one acts, Paul is more interested in contrasting his behavior with that of the false teachers than in rehearsing the precise details of their teaching.[19] Consequently, in a prayer of thanksgiving (1:12–17) he presents himself as an example (*hypotypōsin;* 1:16) of what God's grace can accomplish in sinners. Paul was the foremost of sinners: a blasphemer, a persecutor, and an arrogant man. Jesus Christ, however, was merciful toward him because Paul acted "ignorantly in unbelief" (1:13). The purpose of such mercy was to make him an "example" for all those who will come to faith.

Paul's image of himself as the converted sinner who has experienced God's grace stands in sharp contrast to that of the false teachers evoked by his list of lawless and disobedient people (1:9–10).[20] Whereas the false teachers are akin to the lawless and disobedient for whom the law is intended, Paul stands on the side of the just who have no need of the law because they already do what it requires. Consequently, when he tells Timothy that he is giving him "these instructions" (*tēn paraggelian;* 1:18), Timothy and other readers of the letter can be confident in what Paul commands because the moral quality of Paul's life is in harmony with his teaching. Jesus Christ has made him an example for all who will come to believe. In contrast to Paul, false teachers like Hymenaeus and Alexander have rejected the moral sensibility provided by a good conscience and their faith has run aground (1:19–20). It is precisely such moral sensibility that Timothy must maintain by following Paul's example. In a word, Paul offers himself as an example of good ethical conduct and establishes a relationship between sound teaching and ethical conduct.

Instructions for the Household of God (1 Tim. 2:1–3:16)

Having reminded Timothy of the charge given to him, Paul instructs his delegate how to teach others to live in the household of God that is the church. To summarize briefly, Paul requests prayers for those in authority (2:1–8) so that the church can live "a quiet and peaceable life in all godliness and dignity" (2:2). He desires women to dress/live modestly and decently and does not permit them to teach or have authority over men within the church (2:9–15). Next, he lists the character traits necessary for bishops (3:1–7) and deacons (3:8–13). It is especially important that such men be above reproach (*anepilēmēton;* 3:2) and blameless (*anegklētoi;* 3:11), capable of managing their own households. Finally, Paul reminds Timothy of the "mystery of our religion" (3:14–16), thereby indicating that the conduct he is advocating is rooted in the mystery of salvation.

Because of the material in this section, many view the pastoral letters as bourgeois and oppressive. There is no doubt that this section reflects the household values of patriarchal culture. It would be a mistake, however, to view the material as simply an accommodation to that culture. Paul requests prayers for everyone, especially those in authority, because God "desires everyone to be saved and to come to the knowledge of the truth" (2:4). The "quiet and peaceable life" (2:2), therefore, is the means to an end, providing the proper setting in which the gospel can be preached.[21] In a similar way, Paul's desire that women learn in silence "with full submission" (*en pasē hypotagē*; 2:11) has the church's mission in view. As Margaret MacDonald notes: "A woman's religious practices were generally seen as indicative of the stability of the household, and indeed, of society as a whole."[22] For women to teach and have authority over men would, in the mind of the Pastoral Paul, discredit the church's mission by destabilizing the household and society. When the Pastoral Paul forbids women to teach or have authority over men, then, it is for the sake of the church's mission. For similar reasons, he requires bishops to be above reproach and well thought of by outsiders, and deacons to be blameless (3:10). Paul intends the church and its householders to reflect what is best in society for the sake of a greater good, "the mystery of our religion" (3:16).

Paul's Charge to
Timothy Renewed
(1 Tim. 4:1–16)

Having instructed Timothy about living in the household of God, Paul renews his charge that Timothy should command and teach these things (4:6, 11). As was the case in the first charge, Paul begins with a warning about false teachers (4:1–3; compare 1:3–4). Now, however, the warning is given an apocalyptic tone and the teaching of the false teachers is more explicitly defined. Timothy is living in the last times, when people are turning away from the faith (4:1). False teachers have arisen, forbidding marriage and requiring abstinence from foods. In light of this situation, it is imperative that Timothy instruct the church as Paul directed him in the previous section. Timothy is to train himself for godliness (*eusebeia*; 4:7) and, like Paul, to set an example (*typos ginou*) "in speech and conduct, in love, in faith, in purity" (4:12). In a word, he must become like Paul, who is "an example to those who would come to believe" (1:16).

Further Instructions
for the Household of God
(1 Tim. 5:1–6:2a)

Having charged Timothy to command and insist upon these things (4:11), Paul once more instructs his delegate how to teach and behave in the household of God when dealing with older and younger men and women (5:1–2), with widows (5:3–16), with presbyters (5:17–22), and with slaves (6:1–2a). First, Timothy is to treat others with proper regard for their age. Second, he is to distinguish between those who are really widows and those who can and should be provided for by their families (5:3–8, 16). As regards the "enrolled widows," only those who meet stringent qualifications and whose lives are characterized by "good works" are to be enrolled (5:9–15).[23] Third, elders who rule well are worthy of financial compensation, while those who persist in sin are to be publicly rebuked (5:17–22). Fourth, slaves must honor their masters so that the name of God and "the teaching" may not be blasphemed. Slaves whose masters are believers must not take advantage of this fact but serve them because their masters, who devote themselves to good works (*tēs euergesias*; 6:2), are faithful and beloved.[24]

Once more, the controlling thought of this section is proper order within the church for the sake of the church's mission. Those who are not real widows but insist upon support, presbyters who persist in sin, and slaves who are disrespectful toward their masters threaten the stability of the household that is the church and undermine its mission of preaching salvation to the world. In effect, Paul subordinates the individual to the mission of the church.

Paul's Final Charge to Timothy
1 Tim. (6:2b–21)

In the final section of this letter, Paul extends a solemn charge to Timothy. Timothy is to teach and urge all that Paul has said thus far (6:2b). He is to avoid love of money, which is the root of all evil, pursuing "righteousness, godliness, faith, love, endurance, gentleness" (6:11). He is charged to keep the commandment (*tēn entolēn*)[25] "without spot or blame until the manifestation of our Lord Jesus Christ" (6:14). In a word, Timothy is to guard all that Paul has entrusted to him (*tēn parathēkēn*; 6:20). Throughout this section Paul continually warns Timothy of the dangers of riches. Whereas the false teachers imagine that there is gain in godliness (*eusebeia*; 6:5), Paul instructs Timothy that there is great gain in godliness only when it is combined with contentment (*autarkeia*; 6:6). Timothy, in turn, must instruct the rich "to be rich in good works, generous, and ready to share" (6:18).

Summary

First Timothy employs a rhetorical strategy in which Paul alternates between charging Timothy to act in a particular manner and instructing him what to teach in the household of God.

1:3–20	Charge to Timothy
2:1–3:16	Instruction for the household of God
4:1–4:16	Charge to Timothy
5:1–6:2a	Instruction for the household of God
6:2b–21	Charge to Timothy

Consequently, Timothy's authority to instruct the household of God is rooted in the charge that he has received from Paul and the tradition entrusted to him (the *parathēkē*). Paul's own life witnesses to sound teaching and morally good behavior; now Timothy must provide a similar example for the household of God. In contrast to Paul and Timothy, the behavior of false teachers has led them to teach other things, and their teaching of other things has resulted in morally irresponsible behavior. So the Pastoral Paul establishes a connection between sound teaching rooted in the mystery of salvation and a morally upright life.

SHARING IN THE HARDSHIP
OF THE GOSPEL:
SECOND TIMOTHY

Paul's second letter to Timothy finds the apostle in prison, presumably in Rome (1:17). Early in the letter, Paul reminds Timothy that all in Asia have turned away from him (1:15), and in the letter's conclusion he informs him that everyone deserted him at his first defense (4:16). Despite being chained like a common criminal (2:9) Paul is not ashamed (1:12), and a major aim of this letter is to encourage Timothy not to be ashamed "of the testimony about our Lord or of me his prisoner, but join with me in suffering for the gospel" (1:8). The letter reaches its climax in Paul's solemn charge that Timothy "proclaim the message; be persistent whether the time is favorable or unfavorable; convince, rebuke, and encourage, with the utmost patience in teaching" (4:2). It concludes with a moving statement in which the apostle intimates that his death is at hand, leading many commentators to view this letter as Paul's farewell testament.[26]

Paul does not provide Timothy with instructions for the household of God in this letter as he does in 1 Timothy, nor is there the sustained appeal to the civic virtues found in that letter. Indeed, it is difficult to understand how anyone could label the ethic of this letter bourgeois since Paul unrelentingly urges Timothy to join with him in suffering for the gospel (1:8; 2:3; 4:5). As in 1 Timothy, personal example plays a major role as Paul contrasts the conduct of his life with that of those who have strayed from sound teaching.

An Exhortation to Join
in Paul's Suffering
(2 Tim. 1:6–2:13)

After a thanksgiving (1:3–5) in which he speaks of his "clear conscience" and Timothy's "sincere faith," Paul begins a sustained exhortation, urging Timothy to suffer with him (*sygkakopathein*) for the gospel (1:8) like "a good soldier of Jesus Christ" (2:3). In order to convince Timothy to adopt this pattern of behavior, Paul presents himself as a model of the conduct that he urges Timothy to adopt. Paul is already suffering, but he is not ashamed because he knows the one in whom he has put his trust: the God "who saved us and called us with a holy calling, not according to our works but according to his own purpose and grace" (1:9). Consequently, Timothy is not to be ashamed of the testimony about the Lord, or of Paul the Lord's prisoner.

In addition to his own example, Paul points to the contrasting behavior of Phygelus and Hermogenes on the one hand, and Onesiphorus on the other. While the former were among those who turned away from Paul, the latter was not ashamed of him and diligently searched for Paul in Rome (1:15–18). Thus Onesiphorus, as well as Paul, provides a model for Timothy. As a soldier of Christ Jesus, Timothy can also learn from the behavior of soldiers who seek to please those who have enlisted them, of athletes who compete according to the rules, and of farmers who work for the crop (2:3–7). Finally, Paul returns to the example of his own suffering (2:8–13). He endures everything for the sake of the elect because he is confident that "If we have died with him, we will also live with him; if we endure, we will also reign with him" (2:11–12). The one for whom Paul suffers, Jesus Christ, will be faithful because he cannot deny himself. Paul's behavior in adverse circumstances, then, provides Timothy with a model for moral and ethical behavior in similar circumstances.

An Exhortation in the Face of False Teachers (2 Tim. 2:14–3:9)

If Timothy is ashamed of Paul's chains and hesitant to suffer with him as a soldier of Christ Jesus,[27] it is due in no small measure to the difficult situation that Paul now faces. Not only is Paul in prison, but distressing times have arrived (3:1). Hymenaeus and Philetus are claiming that believers have already experienced the fullness of the resurrection (2:18), and others are disrupting whole households, captivating certain women by their novel ideas that are opposed to the truth (3:6–7).[28] Consequently, Paul encourages Timothy to stand fast. In doing so, he juxtaposes the behavior of those who have strayed from sound teaching and the behavior that should characterize Timothy.

Timothy is to avoid the behavior that characterizes false teachers: arguing over words (2:14), profane chatter (2:16), and senseless controversies that breed quarrels (2:23). In the "last days," which presumably have begun, people will hold to the outward form of godliness (*morphōsin eusebeias;* 3:5) but deny its power. Consequently, it is important for Timothy to set aside youthful passions and pursue "righteousness, faith, love, and peace" (2:22). As the Lord's servant he must be "kindly to everyone, an apt teacher, patient, correcting opponents with gentleness" (2:24–25) so that God may grant them repentance to know the truth.

By acting in this way, Timothy will present himself as one approved by God, a worker who does not need to be ashamed (*anepaischynton*) since he is correctly explaining the word of truth (2:15). Therefore, if Timothy embraces the behavior Paul urges, he will not be ashamed to suffer with Paul for the gospel. Conversely, if he does not, he will surely be ashamed of Paul and his witness to Jesus Christ. In effect, Paul establishes a connection between moral behavior and suffering for the gospel. Those who are not ashamed of the gospel and suffer for it live moral lives. In turn, their behavior results in suffering and not being ashamed of the gospel. Conversely, those who do not suffer for the gospel are an easy prey to false teachers and immoral conduct.

A Solemn Charge to Timothy
(2 Tim. 3:10–4:8)

Having exhorted Timothy to share with him in suffering for the gospel and to stand fast in the face of false teachers, Paul solemnly charges his young delegate "in the presence of God and of Christ Jesus, who is to judge the living and the dead" (4:1). This solemn charge (4:1–5) is skillfully sandwiched between two examples of Paul's behavior. In the first (3:10–17), Paul reminds Timothy that he has observed his (Paul's) teaching, his conduct, the purpose of his life, and his faith, patience, love, and steadfastness as well as the sufferings and persecutions he endured. Most importantly, Timothy knows that the Lord rescued Paul from all these persecutions. Therefore, it is time for Timothy to imitate his mentor, since those who want to live a godly life (*eusebōs zēn*) will be persecuted (3:12). In contrast to false teachers who deceive and are being deceived, Timothy can be confident of what he has learned and believed because he has received it from Paul, whose exemplary moral life authenticates his teaching. Furthermore, Timothy has been nourished on the sacred writings, which have equipped him "for every good work" (3:17).

The second example of Paul's conduct occurs immediately after the solemn charge to Timothy (4:6–17). Aware that his death is imminent, Paul tells Timothy that he has fought the good fight like a loyal soldier; like an athlete he has finished the race; and as the herald, apostle, and teacher of the gospel (see 1:11) he has kept the faith. Consequently, Paul awaits the crown of righteousness that the Lord will give him on the day of his appearance (*epiphaneian;* 4:7–8). Earlier, Paul encouraged Timothy to suffer as a good soldier of Jesus Christ and to compete as an athlete for the crown of victory (2:3–4). Since Paul has already done what he encourages Timothy to do, there is a perfect correspondence between how he lives and what he teaches, assuring Timothy and subsequent generations that Paul is a reliable moral guide.

The Paul of 2 Timothy stands alone and abandoned by all except Luke (4:9–18). Demas has deserted him, Alexander the coppersmith has done him great harm, and no one supported him at his first defense. Only the Lord stood by Paul and gave him strength. Therefore, Paul is confident that the same Lord will rescue and save him for his heavenly kingdom.[29] The implications for Timothy are evident. Despite the young delegate's difficult situation, he can and should draw confidence from Paul's example. Even if

Timothy must stand alone, the Lord will not abandon him. Consequently, it is time for Timothy to join Paul in suffering for the gospel.

Second Timothy, more than any of the Pastorals, makes sustained use of personal example to communicate moral teaching. The ethical instruction of this letter is embodied in the life and ministry of Paul. The manner of his life authenticates his teaching, and his teaching requires a corresponding manner of life from those who accept it.

TRAINED BY GOD'S GRACE:
TITUS

According to this letter, Titus is on the island of Crete, where Paul has left him to "put in order what remained to be done" and "appoint elders in every town" (1:5). As for Paul, he has decided to spend the winter in Nicopolis (3:13), on the western coast of Greece.

In many ways, the content of the letter to Titus resembles that of 1 Timothy. Paul lists the qualifications necessary for the presbyter-bishop (Titus 1:5–9; compare 1 Tim. 3:1–7)[30] and provides Titus with teaching that he must impart to various groups within the church (Titus 2:1–15; compare 1 Tim. 2:1–15; 5:1–6:2). However, whereas the church at Ephesus already has bishops, presbyters, deacons, and perhaps an order of widows, the development of church offices is still in progress on the island of Crete.[31] One of the purposes of this letter, then, is to guide Titus in choosing appropriate leaders and to provide him with sound moral teaching for the presbyter-bishops he will appoint.

As in the other pastoral epistles, the church is threatened by false teachers who live immoral lives. Paul does not provide a detailed description of their teaching.[32] Rather, as in his letters to Timothy, he focuses upon the morally corrupt character of the teachers, which makes them "unfit for any good work" (1:16). As in 1 and 2 Timothy, therefore, Paul establishes a strong connection between "sound" teaching and the moral life.

The Need for Sound Teachers
(Titus 1:5–16)

Since a morally good life is dependent upon sound teaching, Paul insists that the presbyter-bishop be "blameless" (*anegklētos*; 1:6, 7) and "have a firm grasp of the word . . . so that he may be able both to preach with sound doctrine (*en tē didaskalia tē hygiainousē*) and to refute those who contradict it" (1:9). In a list of vices to be avoided and virtues to be cultivated, Paul explains what he means by *anegklētos* (blameless). First, as God's steward, the presbyter-bishop must have control over his own household; thus he must be "married only once" and his children must not be rebellious (*anypotakta*; 1:6). As for himself, he must avoid the following vices: being arrogant, quick-tempered, addicted to wine, violent, or greedy for gain (*aischrokerdē*; 1:7). Rather, in his conduct he must be hospitable, a lover of goodness, prudent (*sōphrona*), upright (*dikaion*), devout, and self-controlled (*egkratē*; 1:8). In effect, one who is blameless has "a firm grasp of the word" and exhibits self-control as well as control over his household.

The character of the false teachers is diametrically opposed to that of the presbyter-bishop. First, they are rebellious (*anypotaktoi*), idle talkers, and deceivers (1:10). Rebelliousness, of course, is one of the character traits that must not be found in the children of the presbyter-bishop, while those who are idle talkers and deceivers cannot be prudent, upright, and devout. Second, the false teachers are "upsetting whole families by teaching for sordid gain (*aischrou kerdous*) what it is not right to teach" (1:11). In contrast to them, the presbyter-bishop assures stability within households and is not greedy for gain. Third, the false teachers are pictured as totally lacking in the self-control that characterizes the presbyter-bishops; they verify in their lives the saying: "Cretans are always liars, vicious brutes, lazy gluttons" (1:12). Most importantly, they are not sound in the faith, and their minds and consciences are corrupt (1:13, 15). Paul's final judgment upon them is that they are "unfit for any good work" (*pros pan ergon agathon adokimoi*; 1:16). This judgment foreshadows a motif developed in the rest of the letter: the importance of doing good works for which God has trained the believer. In summary, the false teachers are incapable of living moral lives or teaching others to do so. It is all the more important, then, that Titus appoint blameless leaders from whom others can learn to live a virtuous life.

Sound Teaching and God's Grace (Titus 2:1–3:7)

Having established the need for sound teachers, Paul provides Titus with several examples of the sound teaching that he and those appointed by him must insist upon. As in 1 Timothy, this teaching is directed to various groups within the church. While the teaching may appear highly moralistic to some, it is deeply rooted in the Pastoral Paul's understanding of God's grace. Thus after providing Titus with instructions for older and younger men and women, and for slaves (2:1–10), Paul relates the behavior he requires to God's grace (2:11–14). Next, after calling for submission and obedience to those in authority (3:1–2), he explains why believers must act in a morally acceptable manner (3:3–7). Thus in addition to providing Titus with sound teaching, Paul explains the soteriological reasons for the conduct that he urges.

Sound teaching	2:1–10
God's grace	2:11–14
Declare these things	2:15
Sound teaching	3:1–2
God's grace	3:3–7

Older men are to be temperate, serious, and prudent (*sōphronas*), as well as sound (*hygiainontas*) in faith, love, and endurance. Older women are to be reverent in their behavior, teaching what is good (*kalodidaskalous*): that is, they are to teach younger women to love their husbands and children and manage their homes well. Like the older men, young men must be prudent (*sōphronein*). As for Titus, he must be a "model of good works" (*typon kalōn ergōn*), a person whose "sound speech" cannot be censured (2:8). Finally, slaves are to be submissive to their masters, manifesting complete and perfect fidelity.

The virtues Paul presents in his instruction to Titus undergird a moral outlook that values an orderly household, thereby complementing the character traits necessary for the presbyter-bishop. Such behavior will assure the church's reputation vis-à-vis the world. Thus the word of God will not be discredited if younger women exercise their role within the home (2:5), and opponents will have nothing evil to say if Titus's speech is sound (2:8). In 2:11–14, these instructions to Titus are undergirded by an understanding of God's grace that has made its appearance in Jesus Christ.

> For the grace of God has appeared, bringing salvation to all, training us (*paideuousa hēmas*) to renounce impiety (*asebeian*) and worldly passions, and in the present age to live lives that are self-controlled (*sōphronōs*), upright (*dikaiōs*), and godly (*eusebōs*), while we wait for the blessed hope and the manifestation (*epiphaneian*) of the glory of our great God and Savior, Jesus Christ. He it is who gave himself for us that he might redeem us from all iniquity and purify for himself a people of his own who are zealous for good deeds (*kalōn ergōn*).

These words highlight three aspects of the Pastoral Paul's ethical stance that have strong connections with the moral teaching of the undisputed Pauline letters. First, the believer stands between two decisive periods: the appearance of God's grace in Jesus Christ and Jesus' future appearance, which the undisputed Paulines call the *parousia* and the pastoral epistles the *epiphaneia*. The moral life for the Pastoral Paul, then, is not a matter of "settling down" in the world any more than it is for the Paul of the undisputed letters. Having been the beneficiaries of God's salvific work in Christ, believers live the moral life in hope of a final salvation that is yet to occur. They are never completely at home in the present age.

Second, although the performance of "good works" plays a more prominent role in these letters than in other letters attributed to Paul, the Pastoral Paul nonetheless makes such works subordinate to God's grace. God's grace "trains" believers to live in a way that shuns impiety and worldly passions and embraces self-control, uprightness, and godliness. Whatever good works believers perform, these ultimately derive from a divine pedagogy. Self-control, uprightness, and godliness are not merely the result of character training. In the view of the Pastoral Paul, they are only fully attained in a life of grace. Piety (*eusebeia*), for example, is moral behavior that derives from the true knowledge of God.[33]

Third, the Pastoral Paul has not forgotten the election theology found in earlier letters such as the Thessalonian and Corinthian correspondence. He insists that Jesus Christ has purified a people for his own (*laon periousion*) who are zealous for good works (2:14). Once more, the implication is that good works are performed by those who have been washed from all iniquity by the death of Christ. The moral life is hardly separable from the salvific effects of the Christ event. Although the vocabulary may be different from that found in other Pauline letters, the major motifs enunciated here are not.

Having provided Titus with instruction for different members of the church, Paul reminds him to teach everyone to be subject and obedient to rulers and authorities (3:1–2). In doing so, he provides a motivation that is reminiscent of a familiar Pauline pattern: "once we were . . . but now we are." So Paul reminds Titus that once we were foolish and disobedient (3:3), but now we have become heirs to eternal life (3:4–7) through God's grace and mercy. Consequently, the moral life is predicated upon change in the situation of the believer. What the Pastoral Paul says here is the clearest statement of justification by faith found in these letters.

> But when the goodness and loving kindness of God our Savior appeared, he saved us, not because of any works of righteousness that we had done, but according to his mercy, through the water of rebirth and renewal by the Holy Spirit. This Spirit he poured out on us richly through Jesus Christ our Savior, so that, having been justified by his grace (*dikaiōthentes tē ekeinou chariti*), we might become heirs according to the hope of eternal life (Titus 3:4–7).

Any idea that the Pastoral Paul has displaced grace by good works should thus be set aside. It is God's grace that has saved and justified the believer. It is precisely the gift of redemption that enables believers to live differently than they did in the past. This is why they must subject themselves, and be obedient, to rulers and authorities.

In the closing of this letter (3:8–15) Paul returns to the theme of good works. Whereas false teachers pursue genealogies and discussions over the law, Paul wants those who believe in God to devote themselves to "good works" since they are profitable to everyone (3:8). Those who belong to the church should learn to devote themselves to "good works" in order to meet urgent needs (3:14). The contrast between false teachers and what Paul expects from those who follow sound doctrine could not be greater. Whereas false teachers are simply unfit for any good work (1:16), those who follow the teaching of Paul, Titus, and those appointed by Titus will devote themselves to good works because God's grace has trained them.

MORAL TEACHING IN THE
PASTORAL EPISTLES

This chapter has proceeded on the assumption that the moral teaching of the pastoral epistles can best be discerned by paying careful attention to the rhetorical argument of each letter. Such an approach allowed us to appreciate the distinctive contribution of each letter by associating ourselves with the purported recipient of the letter, be it Timothy at Ephesus or Titus on Crete. The advantage of this approach is verified by the dramatic difference we uncovered between 2 Timothy on the one hand, and 1 Timothy and Titus on the other. Whereas the former makes extensive use of personal example to call Timothy to share in suffering for the gospel, the latter letters make use of material akin to household codes to assure good order in the household of God. And whereas one might be tempted to call the ethic of 1 Timothy and Titus bourgeois, it is clearly inappropriate to view the ethics of 2 Timothy as such. Having studied the moral argument of each letter, I now offer a modest synthesis of moral teaching in the pastoral epistles.

Salvation and the
Ethical Life

The pastoral epistles do not present an autonomous moral or ethical system. As in the case of other New Testament writings, their ethical stance is theological, given the close relationship between theology and ethics in these writings.[34] God is the Savior God (1 Tim. 1:1; 2:3; Titus 1:3; 2:10) of all people, "especially of those who believe" (1 Tim. 4:10). This God desires "everyone to be saved and to come to the knowledge of the truth" (1 Tim. 2:4). God does not save people because of their righteous works but according to his mercy (Titus 3:5). But when the grace of the Savior God appeared, it trained those who received it to live lives of self-control, uprightness, and godliness (Titus 2:11–13).

The one mediator between the Savior God and humankind is Christ Jesus (1 Tim. 2:5), who is also called Savior (2 Tim. 1:10; Titus 1:4; 3:6) and, at one point, "our great God and Savior" (Titus 2:13).[35] He is the Savior who came into the world to save sinners (1 Tim. 1:15). At his first epiphany, he "abolished death and brought life and immortality to light through the gospel" (2 Tim. 1:10). Through this Savior, God's Spirit has been richly poured out on those who believe (Titus 3:6). While believers already enjoy something of salvation, they eagerly await the final epiphany of this Savior who will complete God's salvific work (Titus 2:13) Therefore although the Pastorals can say God saved us (Titus 3:5), they do not neglect the future dimension of salvation (1 Tim. 2:15; 4:16; 2 Tim. 4:18). So Christ Jesus is called "our hope" (1 Tim. 1:1).

To come to the knowledge of the truth (1 Tim. 2:4) is to participate in the economy of salvation. To conduct one's life in a manner that accords with this knowledge of the truth is to live a life of godliness (*eusebeia*). Thus the godly behavior that the pastoral epistles urge is inseparably linked to

God's plan of salvation manifested in Jesus Christ. Salvation enables one to live a moral and ethical life; and, inasmuch as the church is a household of salvation, it affords the proper setting for living a virtuous life.

Sound Teaching and the
Ethical Life

One of the most noteworthy features of the pastoral epistles is their insistence upon "sound" teaching. For example, at the beginning of 1 Timothy, Paul provides an extensive list of behavior that is contrary to sound teaching (1:9–11) and, at the end of the same letter, he says that "whoever teaches otherwise and does not agree with the sound words of our Lord Jesus Christ and the teaching that is in accordance with godliness" (6:3) is conceited and understands nothing. In 2 Timothy, Paul urges Timothy to hold on to the example of sound teaching that he heard from him (1:13), warning him that a time is coming when people will not endure sound doctrine. In the letter to Titus, Paul says that the presbyter-bishop must have a grasp of the word so that he can preach with sound doctrine and refute opponents (1:9) in hope that they will become "sound" in the faith (1:13). Titus must teach what is consistent with sound doctrine (2:1), and his speech is to be sound so that it cannot be censured (2:8).

This insistence upon sound teaching and sound speech is closely related to the concept of the *parathēkē*, the tradition Paul has entrusted to Timothy and Titus (1 Tim. 6:20; 2 Tim. 1:14). This entrusted tradition is never explicitly defined, but one surmises that it includes the moral instructions given in these letters, which are integral to the gospel for which Paul has been appointed herald, preacher, and teacher (1 Tim. 2:7; 2 Tim. 1:11). Sound teaching, therefore, includes moral and ethical instruction: more specifically, the moral and ethical instructions of these letters.

Within the pastoral epistles there is a dialectical relationship between "sound teaching" and the moral life. Sound teaching enables people to conduct their lives in a moral and ethical way that accords with the gospel: to live in a godly manner (*eusebōs*). Those, like the false teachers, who do not follow sound teaching will behave in an immoral and godless way. It is imperative, therefore, to have reliable teachers such as Paul, Timothy, Titus, and their successors whose lives exemplify the teaching they propose, and so assure its authenticity. Thus reliable teachers provide sound teaching, and sound teaching points to reliable teachers. This is why the pastoral epistles insist that those who exercise the role of bishop, presbyter, deacon, and widow must live exemplary lives.

God's Grace and
Good Works

Those who live their lives in accordance with sound teaching necessarily perform good works. Therefore, Paul instructs women to adorn themselves with good works (1 Tim. 2:10). The good works performed by the enrolled widows are the rearing of children, hospitality, washing the feet of the saints, helping the afflicted, doing good in every way (1 Tim. 5:10). As in society at large, so also in the church, office and wealth provide an opportunity to perform good works. Therefore, Paul says that those who aspire to become bishops aspire to a good work (1 Tim. 3:1), and he urges the wealthy to become wealthy in good works (1 Tim. 6:18) by employing their wealth for the good of others. People must cleanse themselves from every evil so that they will be prepared for every good work (2 Tim. 2:21). Trained in righteousness by scripture, people will be equipped for every good work (2 Tim. 3:17). While false teachers are unfit for any good work (Titus 1:16), it is Paul's desire that believers devote themselves to good works (Titus 3:8, 14).

There is no tension between God's grace and good works within the pastoral epistles. God "saved us and called us with a holy calling, not according to our works but according to his own purpose and grace" (2 Tim. 1:9). God "saved us, not because of any works of righteousness that we had done, but according to his mercy" so that we have been justified by his grace (Titus 3:5–7). This doctrine of justification by faith, however, differs from that in the undisputed Pauline letters. In Galatians and Romans Paul has the works of the Mosaic law in view. He argues that Gentiles need not adopt a Jewish way of life by doing the works of the law in order to stand in a right relationship with God, since faith in, or the faithfulness of, Jesus Christ has justified them. In the Pastorals, however, the Gentile question is no longer an issue. Here "good works" refers to charitable deeds toward others. They do not justify a person, but they are required in order to live a godly life.

Creation and the Social Order

The pastoral epistles view both creation and the social order in a positive manner. Marriage and the bearing of children are positive goods. Ascetical practices are of little value since "[t]o the pure all things are pure" (Titus 1:15). Therefore, the Pastoral Paul vigorously opposes those who forbid marriage and demand abstinence from foods (1 Tim. 4:1–5). In his view, everything that God created is good.

This positive vision of creation is complemented by an essentially affirmative view of the social order. The Pastoral Paul encourages prayers for, and obedience to, those in authority (1 Tim. 2:1–8; Titus 3:1), even though he will eventually find himself imprisoned by those same authorities (2 Timothy). He values the social structures of his day, whose essential unit is the household. Therefore, wives must learn in silence from their husbands with full submission (1 Tim. 2:11; Titus 2:5), and slaves must honor their masters (1 Tim. 6:1–2) and be submissive to them (Titus 2:9–10). Although there are precedents for these instructions in the undisputed Pauline letters, there is no doubt that the approach of the Pastoral Paul is decidedly more conservative. Masters of slaves are no longer urged to treat their slaves kindly as in Philemon, Colossians, and Ephesians, and there is no indication of the radical equality that all enjoy in Christ despite race, social class, or sex (Gal. 3:28). The Pastoral Paul wants each to find his or her place in the social order of the day so that the church can carry out its mission of salvation. In my view, the *enduring* moral teaching of the pastoral epistles consists in their attitude toward the broader culture rather than their specific teaching about women, slaves, and so on. Christians must come to terms with the social structures of their day without compromising the faith. For the Pastoral Paul, this meant coming to terms with the patriarchal household in light of the gospel; for contemporary Western Christians it may mean coming to terms with a democratic society in light of the same gospel.

The Virtuous Life

Virtues play an important role in the pastoral epistles. For example, Paul specifies the qualities necessary for church officials (1 Tim. 3:1–7, 8–13; Titus 1:6–9). On two occasions he explicitly lists virtues that Timothy is to pursue:

> righteousness, godliness, faith, love, endurance, gentleness
> (1 Tim. 6:11)
> righteousness, faith, love, and peace (2 Tim. 2:22)

On another occasion, Paul describes his own behavior in terms of his faith, his patience, his love, and his steadfastness (2 Tim. 3:10). He says that women will be saved through childbearing provided that they persevere in faith, love, holiness, and modesty (1 Tim. 2:15). Older men are to be "temperate, serious, prudent, and sound in faith, in love, and in endurance" (Titus 2:2). Younger women are to be "self-controlled, chaste, good managers of the household, kind" (Titus 2:5). Finally, God's grace has trained people to be self-controlled, upright, and godly (Titus 2:12). While these lists contain virtues such as self-control (*sōphrosynē*), godliness (*eusebeia*), seriousness (*semnotēs*), and uprightness (*dikaiosynē*) that were highly valued by Greek moral philosophers, it is the combination of faith and love that appears most frequently (1 Tim. 1:5, 14; 2:15; 4:12; 6:11; 2 Tim. 1:13; 2:22; 3:10; Titus 2:1). The reason for this is not difficult to discern. The ethics of the pastoral epistles are thoroughly theological, and the goal of this instruction is "love that comes from a pure heart, a good conscience, and sincere faith" (1 Tim. 1:5). Although written for a new time and situation, the pastoral epistles are an authentic expression of Paul's ethical legacy.

CONCLUSION

The Ethical Legacy
of Jesus and Paul

*T*hroughout this work I have spoken of the ethical legacies of Jesus and Paul as they are found in the four Gospels and the Pauline epistles. But now, having investigated both sets of writings, I offer some overtures toward a more synthetic view of the ethical legacy that Jesus and Paul bequeathed to the church. To be sure, the work of synthesizing this legacy requires more than the few pages that follow. Indeed, it merits another volume. In what follows, however, I merely propose a number of theses that, in my view, summarize the enduring legacy of the moral teaching attributed to Jesus and Paul. The reader might view these theses as a first tentative sounding toward a systematic presentation of New Testament ethics.

1. The moral life of believers is a response to God's work of salvation. One of the constant themes of this book has been the relationship between the moral imperative (what humanity ought to do) and the indicative of salvation (what God has done for humanity). The moral demands of Jesus as portrayed in the four Gospels, and the ethical teaching of Paul as found in the letters attributed to him, presuppose God's work of salvation. Thus the Synoptic Jesus calls people to repentance on the basis of the gospel he preaches: God's kingly rule is making its appearance. Because this salvific act was unfolding in his own life and ministry, Jesus called and gathered a community of disciples to live in a way that already witnessed to the hidden presence of the kingdom. While each of the Synoptic Evangelists describes this new life in a slightly different way, all of them focus in varying degrees upon the need for faith in the gospel that Jesus preaches, love for God and neighbor, and a willingness to surrender everything that would prevent one from following Jesus, be it one's livelihood, family, or possessions.

Although the Johannine Jesus does not proclaim the kingdom

of God, his moral imperative is rooted in the indicative of salvation: God so loved the world that he sent his only begotten Son, not to condemn the world, but to save it. People must believe in the one whom the Father has sent into the world for the purpose of saving the world. Put another way, one could say that in the Fourth Gospel Jesus embodies the salvation that the kingdom of God proclaims. He has seen and heard the Father, and the Father has sent him into the world to proclaim and witness to the truth. The essential ethical act, then, is to believe in the one whom God has sent into the world.

But in addition to believing in the Son of God, the community of disciples that Jesus has chosen from the world must love one another as he has loved them. As in the Synoptic Gospels, then, Jesus' moral imperative rests upon a prior act of salvation: the redemptive revelation of God's Son. In the Fourth Gospel, the one who proclaimed the gospel becomes the content of the gospel.

In the Pauline letters Jesus, the herald of the gospel, becomes the subject of the gospel in an even more explicit manner. The gospel has as its content God's act of salvation accomplished in the death and resurrection of his Son, Jesus Christ. Through the death and resurrection of his Son, God has justified the ungodly and reconciled the world to himself. While the Deutero-Pauline letters emphasize the present aspect of salvation more than the undisputed Paulines do, they recognize that the fullness of salvation will only occur in the future. In the present time, believers are summoned and empowered to live the moral life in light of what God has already accomplished for them in Christ and in hope of what is yet to come.

The moral legacy of Jesus and Paul is so intimately united with God's act of salvation that one could speak of a soteriological ethic. Indeed, were there no act of salvation, the ethical teaching of Jesus and Paul would be emptied of all meaning since it is God's salvific work that grounds their moral instruction. The way of living that they propose is a response to the in-breaking rule of God (Synoptic Jesus), the salvific revelation of the Son whom God has sent into the world (Johannine Jesus), the redeeming death and resurrection of the Christ (Paul).

2. Believers live the moral life in light of God's coming salvation and judgment. This thesis is closely related to the first. But whereas the first focuses upon the salvation that God has already effected in and through Jesus, this thesis looks to the future, when God's in-breaking rule will have become a reality that none can deny. At that moment the risen Lord will return as the triumphant Son of Man to gather the elect and then, as God's eschatological regent, judge all the nations.

Among the Synoptics, we noted the central role that judgment plays in the Gospel according to Matthew. But the threat of judgment and the promise of future salvation are found in Mark and Luke as well. All of the Synoptics agree that the hidden kingdom will be revealed with the glorious Son of Man's parousia. Therefore, it is imperative that disciples live their lives as faithful and vigilant servants. Because moral actions have eschatological consequences that no one can escape, the promise of sharing in the banquet of the kingdom and the threat of being excluded from that divine fellowship function as powerful motivational factors in the moral life of believers.

Although the Johannine Jesus proclaims that there will be a future judgment when the dead will be raised, he emphasizes the present dimension of salvation and judgment more so than does the Synoptic Jesus. Thus, in the Fourth Gospel Jesus says that those who believe in him have passed from death to life so that they already enjoy eternal life and hence do not come to judgment at a future date. Conversely, those who refuse to believe in him are already judged and dwell in darkness. As in the Synoptic Gospels, then, Jesus stresses the eschatological consequences of one's moral decisions.

In the Pauline letters the threat of judgment and the hope of future salvation continue to play a vital role. Although Paul does not speak of the Son of Man, he is keenly aware that there will be a moment when Jesus will return to gather the elect. While the hope for that parousia is more vivid in the undisputed Paulines than in the Deutero-Paulines (the terminology "parousia" does not occur in these letters), hope is present in these letters as well. God's act of salvation, inaugurated in the death and resurrection of Christ, has not yet been completed. Moreover, there will be a judgment that will be salvific for some and disastrous for others. Consequently, Paul and those who write in his name remind believers that certain kinds of behavior will exclude them from the kingdom of God.

To be sure, believers have already been justified, and God has reconciled the world, indeed the entire cosmos, to himself. Nonetheless, believers are not yet saved, and it is still possible to fall from God's grace. Therefore, they must persevere in doing what is good, for, though justified by grace, they will be judged according to what they do.

The moral legacy of Jesus and Paul is deeply rooted in God's grace. God's act of salvation empowers them, as well as summons them, to lead a life worthy of their calling and pleasing to him. God's grace and the power of his Spirit working within them, however, do not result in an effortless moral life that relieves believers of moral responsibility. The moral life is a struggle comparable to an athletic contest. It is part of a cosmic battle, and all conduct will have to be accounted for at a future judgment. What believers do now, therefore, is vitally important, since their actions have eschatological consequences.

3. The moral life is lived in and with a community of disciples who form the church. One of the most overlooked aspects of the New Testament's ethical teaching is its communal dimension. Jesus addresses his moral instruction to a community of disciples, and Paul instructs communities of believers, the churches. All of the Gospels agree that Jesus gathered a community of disciples to be with him, to follow him, and to share in his distinctive way of life. Likewise, except for Philemon and the pastoral epistles, the Pauline letters are addressed to communities of believers rather than to individuals. But even in the cases of Philemon and the Pastorals, the instruction they contain has important implications for the moral life of the church.

The moral teaching of Jesus and Paul, then, has an intensely communal dimension. Jesus does not give private instruction in the moral life to individuals, and Paul does not write essays for those embarking upon the moral life as did Cicero and Seneca. Proclaiming that the kingdom of God is at hand, Jesus calls for national repentance so that Israel will be prepared for the in-breaking kingdom of God. The disciples he calls are the first fruits of this national renewal for the purpose of providing Israel with a concrete example of what it means to repent and believe in the gospel. Therefore, Jesus insists that they become servants of one another; that they practice a greater righteousness; that they do the will of their heavenly Father; and that they love one another as he loved them. Although he delivers his great sermon (the Sermon on the Mount, the Sermon on the Plain) in the hearing of the crowd, the ethic he proposes is meant for disciples. Indeed, Jesus' "strenuous ethic" makes little sense apart from the call to discipleship, and it cannot be fulfilled outside of a community of disciples. The farewell discourse of the Johannine Jesus, which is spoken only to the disciples, is especially insistent upon the communal life that disciples must live in the world during the period of Jesus' absence. The command to love one another becomes a "new commandment" that can only be lived in a community of disciples who have experienced Jesus' love and the comfort that the Paraclete brings. In a word, then, in calling others to live moral or ethical lives, Jesus summons them to live their lives in a community of like-minded disciples.

It is not surprising, then, that Paul addresses the majority of his letters to a community of believers. The church is the post-resurrection community of disciples; it is the place in which the moral life is learned and lived. For Paul and those who wrote in his name, this church is the sanctified community, a community of saints, God's chosen and elect people, the body of Christ, nothing less than God's own temple. Because of its new status, the church is necessarily different from the world, although Paul and those who wrote in his name generally expect that believers will continue to interact with the world. Nonetheless, since believers live in a new and distinctive manner that the world does not understand, there should be clear boundaries between the sanctified community and the world. Indeed the church has been empowered to live in a way that the unbelieving world cannot.

Because he sees the church as a sanctified community, Paul views the failure of individual believers as a failure of the entire community. Moreover, if the community fails to maintain its status as a holy and elect people, it will be difficult if not impossible for individuals to live their lives in accordance with the gospel. To be sure, believers do not lose their individuality when they enter the sanctified community, nor are they relieved of personal responsibility, since each must stand before the judgment seat of God. But there is an undeniable and important relationship between individual and community in the Pauline letters so that the fate of one is deeply affected by the fate of the other.

The ethical legacy of Jesus and Paul, then, stresses the importance of living the moral life within a community of like-minded believers. There can be no solitary believer who lives the moral and ethical life isolated from or independent of the community of faith. The moral life is lived by, and in, the church.

4. The personal example of Jesus and Paul instructs and sustains believers in the moral life. Personal example plays a major role in the ethical instruction of both Jesus and Paul. Jesus calls disciples to follow him, and Paul urges his converts to imitate him. Both are able to make these demands because their moral lives incarnate the instruction that they propose.

In calling disciples to follow him, Jesus summons them to a new way of life that is energized by the in-breaking kingdom of God. Deeply aware that God's kingly rule is breaking into this world, the Synoptic Jesus lives his own life in such a way that he views and judges everything from the point of view of God. The Johannine Jesus, who has been sent into the world by the Father, speaks and teaches what he has seen and heard while dwelling in God's presence. The moral life of Jesus, then, is determined by God's kingdom (the Synoptic Gospels) and the consciousness of having been sent into the world by the Father to do the work of God (the Fourth Gospel). In calling disciples to follow him, Jesus asks them to orient their lives to God in a similar way.

Thus it is not surprising that the "story" of Jesus provides a rich source of moral instruction. Because the life of Jesus incarnates the moral and religious message he proclaims, those who hear the story are already instructed in the moral life. How Jesus acts *is* moral instruction. What he says and how he responds provide disciples with patterns of behavior to follow and imitate. Jesus' most important moral instruction, however, comes at the moment of his death. Although he is the Son of God, he refuses to save his life by miraculously descending from the cross. Instead he trusts in God because he knows that only God can save him.

Paul does not say "follow me," but he does not hesitate to say "imitate me." On first hearing, this imperative appears to deflect attention from Jesus to Paul. But as we have already seen, Paul makes this statement because he has been conformed to Christ's sufferings. It is no longer Paul who lives but Christ Jesus who lives in him. Because Paul has been crucified with Christ and continues to participate in Christ's sufferings through his apostolic hardships, he manifests the dying of Jesus in his life. In exhorting others to imitate him, then, he is inviting them to follow Christ by entering into the mystery of his death and resurrection. Furthermore, one must remember that Paul was addressing people who did not know Jesus of Nazareth personally, and many of them had little acquaintance with Jewish morality. In calling others to imitate him, therefore, Paul was providing them with a concrete example of the Christian moral life.

In the pastoral epistles, the function of personal example comes to center stage as Paul presents himself as a model for Timothy and Titus, who, in turn, are to become models of ethical conduct to others. Moreover, the Pastoral Paul establishes a strong relationship between moral conduct and correct teaching. Immoral behavior leads to false teaching, and false teaching results in immoral behavior. The church, then, is ever in need of reliable moral guides who teach what they have received from Paul, Timothy, Titus, and those duly appointed by them.

Thus one of the subtle but often overlooked ways in which the New Testament communicates moral teaching is personal example, especially the personal example of Jesus and Paul. Indeed, one might say that the most enduring ethical legacy of these great figures is the example of their lives. The stories of Jesus and Paul inevitably affect the lives of believers, leading them to inquire further about their teaching. Would anyone follow Jesus if he had been unfaithful to God at the moment of his death? Or would anyone imitate Paul if the apostle did not embody the gospel of Christ's death and resurrection that is so central to his message?

5. The moral life consists in doing God's will. The ultimate goal of the moral life is to please God by doing his will. Thus the four Gospels present Jesus as the obedient Son of God who comes to do God's will and teaches others to do the same. In obedience to God's will, Paul is an apostle of Jesus Christ. As Christ's apostle, he seeks to do God's will in all that he does and to communicate the mystery of this will to his converts. Thus he tells them that their sanctification is God's will so that they must flee from all immorality and uncleanness that defile the sanctified community.

Because the moral life is ultimately rooted in God's will, the ethical legacy of Jesus and Paul is profoundly theological in nature: the norm for what is good and evil is God's will rather than an anthropological norm such as human nature or reason. This is not to say that God's will contradicts either nature or reason or that there is no place for rational discourse in the ethical legacy of Jesus and Paul. Jesus, for example, makes use of moral reasoning in his great sermon and his controversies with the religious leaders, and Paul does the same when he seeks to persuade his Gentile converts to adopt a particular way of behaving. But neither Jesus nor Paul proposes an ethic that is autonomous or independent from God. The prerequisite for doing what is good is to know God's will. For the Synoptic Jesus, God's will is being revealed through the in-breaking rule of God. In the Fourth Gospel, Jesus himself reveals God's will since he has been sent into the world by the Father. And in the Pauline epistles the Christ event, as seen in the death and resurrection of Christ, provides the starting point for understanding what pleases God.

The Law (Torah) provided Israel of old with a gracious expression of God's will that was unavailable to the Gentiles. While Jesus criticized the manner in which certain religious groups practiced and interpreted this law, the Gospels do not portray him as explicitly abolishing it. Instead of abolishing it, he interprets and intensifies the law by emphasizing and focusing upon the commandment to love God and neighbor. In his controversies with the religious leaders, Jesus places the commandment of God before their human traditions, no matter how hallowed these may be.

In the Pauline correspondence, the problem is more complicated since Paul views the Christ event as the end of the law's role in salvation history. Nevertheless, he does not abolish or contradict what our contemporary mind views as the moral or ethical aspects of the law. Indeed, on more than one occasion, he even calls upon the law to sustain his argument. Aspects of the law that are identity markers, such as circumcision, the observance of particular festivals, food laws, and so on, are, however, matters of indifference according to Paul. They may be observed by Jewish Christians, but they need not be, and indeed they should not be observed by Gentiles lest the sufficiency of the Christ event be called into question. What contemporary believers call the moral or ethical dimension of the law, for example, the Decalogue, remains an authentic expression of God's will. But for Paul, and perhaps those who write in his name, it is the commandment to love one's neighbor that fulfills the law.

The moral legacy of Jesus and Paul, then, is a theological ethic rather than a philosophically autonomous ethic. According to Jesus, the purpose of the moral life is to do God's will. Paul gives a similar answer but would undoubtedly add, "as revealed in Jesus Christ." For Jesus and Paul, there is no moral life apart from God.

6. *The moral life expresses itself in love for God, love for neighbor, and love for one's enemy.* In the discussion of God's will, I have already touched upon the centrality of love in the moral teaching of Jesus and Paul. Both agree that the law finds its perfect expression in love. However, although love is the central component in the moral teaching of Jesus and Paul, they express this commandment in a variety of ways. For example, the Matthean and Markan Jesus speaks of the love of God and the love of neighbor as the two most important commandments of the law. The Matthean Jesus adds that the law and the prophets are dependent upon these commandments. In Luke's Gospel, a lawyer recites the two commandments as though they were a single commandment, and then Jesus illustrates this commandment through the parable of the good Samaritan. Furthermore, in the Sermon on the Mount and the Sermon on the Plain, Jesus teaches his disciples to love even their enemies. In the Johannine Gospel, love for one another becomes a "new commandment" that characterizes the community of Jesus' disciples: they must love one another as he loved them so the world will know that they are his disciples. As for Paul, all of the commandments are fulfilled in the love of neighbor so that love is the fulfillment of the law. Although the law plays a less important role in the Deutero-Pauline letters, love continues to have a central role. It is the bond of perfection—the "virtue" that embraces all others.

But what do Jesus and Paul mean by love? For Jesus, it clearly entails compassion and mercy, the very mercy and compassion manifested by God. Thus the demands of love lead Jesus to heal on the Sabbath and to associate with those who are ritually unclean. As for Paul, love finds its deepest meaning in the example of Jesus' self-surrender upon the cross. Paul is keenly aware that the Son of God loved him and gave his life for him. The love of Jesus is a self-sacrificing love that Paul seeks to imitate in his own ministry by giving and spending himself for the sake of his churches. Thus it is not surprising that he calls those who believe to do the same. Nothing is more important than the communal life of the church. Therefore, believers must exercise their freedom by loving one another, even if this means surrendering legitimate rights for the sake of the community's weaker members. Believers must love the church by giving themselves to one another in mutual service just as the Son of God loved the church by handing himself over for it.

Love is not a sentiment or emotion, although it does not necessarily exclude these. And although it is the key to interpreting all the commandments, it does not make them obsolete. It is, however, the distinctive mark of the moral life that Jesus and Paul urge. Its demands cannot be codified one time for all but must be discerned again and again as believers live their life in a community of disciples.

7. The moral life is an expression of faith. Throughout this summary, I have repeatedly and purposely employed the term "believers" when speaking of the moral life. In doing so, I have tried to communicate the essential role that faith plays in the moral legacy of Jesus and Paul. The Synoptic Jesus summons people to faith in the God whose rule is claiming their lives; the Johannine Jesus calls people to believe in himself as the one sent by the Father; and all of the Pauline letters are addressed to believers. Put most simply, the moral demands and teaching of Jesus and Paul make little sense apart from faith. To be sure, nonbelievers may be edified by Jesus' Sermon on the Mount as recorded by Matthew and his Sermon on the Plain as presented by Luke. Moreover, there are moving passages of moral exhortation such as 1 Corinthians 13 that even unbelievers will find persuasive. Overall, however, the moral instruction of the New Testament makes little sense apart from a community of faith.

Jesus and Paul proclaim a message of salvation that has ethical implications. Apart from their proclamation of salvation, their ethical teaching, while inspiring, is not necessarily compelling or persuasive. Nor is it meant to be! Neither develops, or seeks to develop, a new ethical system. Both presuppose the moral teaching of Israel, even though that instruction has been rethought in light of the gospel. Put most simply, the moral legacy of Jesus and Paul is primarily for believers, for the community of faith. To be sure, it invites others to heed its demand, but in doing so it calls them first of all to faith.

What I have called New Testament ethics, then, is an integral part of the gospel; indeed, it is the gospel viewed from the point of view of humanity's response to God's work in Christ. Believers will find guidance in the moral teaching of Jesus and Paul, and they will undoubtedly supplement that guidance with still further ethical reflection. Nonbelievers may be inspired, but the ethic of the New Testament makes no immediate claim upon them except the most basic of all claims, to repent and believe in the gospel.

Abbreviations

AB	Anchor Bible
ABD	*Anchor Bible Dictionary*
AnBib	Analecta biblica
BARev	*Biblical Archaeology Review*
BETL	Bibliotheca ephemeridum theologicarum lovaniensium
Bib	*Biblica*
BNTC	Black's New Testament Commentary
BZNW	Beihefte zur *ZNW*
CBQ	*Catholic Biblical Quarterly*
CBQMS	Catholic Biblical Quarterly Monograph Series
ConBNT	Coniectanea biblica, New Testament
EBib	Études bibliques
EQ	*Evangelical Quarterly*
ETR	*Études théologiques et religieuses*
FilNeot	*Filología neotestamentaria*
FRLANT	Forschungen zur Religion und Literatur des Alten und Neuen Testaments
GNS	Good News Studies
HTKNT	Herders theologischer Kommentar zum Neuen Testament
HUT	Hermeneutische Untersuchungen zur Theologie
ICC	International Critical Commentary
Int	*Interpretation*
ITQ	*Irish Theological Quarterly*
JAAR	*Journal of the American Academy of Religion*
JBL	*Journal of Biblical Literature*
JSNT	*Journal for the Study of the New Testament*
JSNTSS	Supplements to *JSNT*
JTS	*Journal of Theological Studies*
LD	Lectio divina

LS	*Louvain Studies*
MarTS	Marburger theologische Studien
MDB	Le Monde de la Bible
NAC	New American Commentary
NCB	New Century Bible
NICNT	New International Commentary on the New Testament
NIGTC	New International Greek Testament Commentary
NovT	*Novum Testamentum*
NRSV	New Revised Standard Version
NTM	New Testament Message
NTS	*New Testament Studies*
NTT	New Testament Theology
OBT	Overtures to Biblical Theology
RelStRev	*Religious Studies Review*
RevExp	*Review and Expositor*
RTL	*Revue théologique de Louvain*
SB	Sources Bibliques
SBLDS	Society of Biblical Literature Dissertation Series
SBLSBS	SBL Sources for Biblical Study
SNTSMS	Society for New Testament Studies Monograph Series
SR	*Studies in Religion/Sciences religieuses*
SwJT	*Southwestern Journal of Theology*
TRu	*Theologische Rundschau*
WBC	Word Bible Commentary
ZNW	*Zeitschrift für die neutestamentliche Wissenschaft*
ZSNT	Zacchaeus Studies: New Testament
ZTK	*Zeitschrift für Theologie und Kirche*

Notes

Introduction

1. Throughout this work I use the adjectives "moral" and "ethical" interchangeably.

2. The fundamental meaning of *diachronic* is "through time," suggesting a method that goes back through time to see how a particular writing grew and developed. The basic sense of *synchronic* is "with time" or contemporaneous, suggesting a method that deals with a work in its present form rather than the stages of its growth.

3. For a recent review of the literature, see F. W. Horn, "Ethik des Neuen Testaments 1982–1992," *TRu* 60 (1995) 32–86.

4. In speaking of "submerged voices," I have in mind material such as the sayings source (Q).

5. Allen Verhey, *The Great Reversal: Ethics and the New Testament* (Grand Rapids: Eerdmans, 1984).

6. Ibid., 61.

7. Wolfgang Schrage, *The Ethics of the New Testament* (Philadelphia: Fortress, 1988; originally published in 1982 by Vandenhoeck & Ruprecht, Göttingen, as *Ethik des Neuen Testaments*).

8. Siegfried Schulz, *Neutestamentliche Ethik*, Zürcher Grundrisse zur Bibel (Zurich: Theologischer Verlag, 1987).

9. Rudolf Schnackenburg, *Die sittliche Botschaft des Neuen Testaments*, vol. 1, *Von Jesus zur Urkirche*; vol. 2, *Die urchristlichen Verkündiger* (Freiburg: Herder, 1986, 1988). This is a thorough revision of a work that first appeared in 1954, in a single volume, and was subsequently revised in 1962. The second revised edition of 1962 was translated by J. Holland-Smith and W. J. O'Hara as *The Moral Teaching of the New Testament* (London: Burns & Oates, 1964). I employ the two-volume German edition, which has not been translated into English.

10. Schnackenburg is not unique in this regard. Schrage devotes 105 pages to Jesus and 29 to the Synoptic Evangelists; Schulz devotes 63 pages to the historical Jesus and 53 to the Synoptic Evangelists.

11. Ceslas Spicq, *Théologie morale du Nouveau Testament*, 2 vols., EBib (Paris: Gabalda, 1965).

12. After each chapter Spicq studies a number of subthemes that he titles "Themes annexes."

13. On p. 15 of vol. 1, Spicq writes: "[N]otre 'théologie morale' sera une collection de *themes majeurs*, communs à presque tous les auteurs du Nouveau Testament."

14. See Karl H. Schelkle, *Theology of the New Testament*, vol. 3, *Morality*, translated by W. A. Jurgens (Collegeville, Minn.: Liturgical Press, 1973). (Originally, *Theologie des Neuen Testaments*, Düsseldorf: Patmos Verlag, 1970.)

15. Basic Concepts: Morality as Obedience Dictated by Faith, Sin and Grace, Reward and Punishment. Basic Attitudes: Conversion and Repentance, Faith, Hope, Love of God, Love of Neighbor. Objectives: Freedom, Peace and Joy, Renunciation and Abnegation, Holiness, Righteousness, Purity, Perfection. Various Areas for Consideration: Virtue and Virtues, Divine Worship and Prayer, Life, Marriage and Celibacy, Unchastity, Truth and Falsehood, Oaths, Work, Property, Poverty and Wealth, Honor and Glory, Family, Civil Government.

16. Here, of course, I am referring to the revised work of Schnackenburg.

17. Jean-François Collange, *De Jésus à Paul: L'Éthique du Nouveau Testament*, Le Champ Éthique 3 (Geneva: Labor et Fides, 1980).

18. *Ibid.*, 31.

19. *Ibid.*, 32.

20. Eduard Lohse, *Theological Ethics of the New Testament*, translated by M. G. Boring (Minneapolis: Fortress, 1991). (Originally, *Theologische Ethik des Neuen Testaments*, Stuttgart: W. Kohlhammer, 1988.)

21. Ibid., 5.

22. This point is made by J. L. Houlden, *Ethics and the New Testament* (New York: Oxford Univ. Press, 1977), chap. 1. His own work proceeds in this manner. It should noted, however, that this is not a perfect analogy, since literary and historical questions are closely related in the New Testament. Those seeking the historical Jesus must also attend to literary matters, while those seeking the theology of the Evangelists must attend to historical as well as literary matters.

23. E.g., I subscribe to the "Two Source" theory as the best way of explaining the literary relationships between the Synoptic Gospels, and I make use of redaction-critical insights. Moreover, in my study of the Pauline literature, I have tried to ascertain the historical circumstances that occasioned each letter.

24. At the beginning of part 1 (The Legacy of Jesus), and at the beginning of part 2 (The Legacy of Paul), I describe my method and approach to the Gospels and Pauline literature in more detail.

25. There are seven letters whose Pauline authorship is not disputed: Romans, 1 and 2 Corinthians, Galatians, Philippians, 1 Thessalonians, and Philemon. The authorship of Ephesians, Colossians, 2 Thessalonians, 1 and 2 Timothy, and Titus is disputed; hence these letters are often called "Deutero-Pauline." While there is consensus that Ephesians and the Pastorals were not written by Paul, there is considerable discussion about the authorship of Colossians and 2 Thessalonians.

Chapter 1: Ethics for the Kingdom of God

1. To the best of my knowledge, the only full-length book devoted to the ethics of Mark's Gospel is that of D. O. Via, *The Ethics of Mark's Gospel—in the Middle of Time* (Philadelphia: Fortress, 1985). Other authors have dedicated chapters to Mark's ethics: A. M. Ambrozic, *The Hidden Kingdom: A Redaction-Critical Study of the References to the Kingdom of God in Mark's Gospel*, CBQMS 2 (Washington, D.C: The Catholic Biblical Association of America, 1972), 136–82; H. C. Kee, *Community of the New Age: Studies in Mark's Gospel* (Philadelphia: Westminster, 1977), 145–75. I have also consulted the following general works on New Testament ethics, all of which dedicate chapters to the ethics in Mark's Gospel: Schnackenburg, *Die sittliche Botschaft*, 1: 110–21; Schrage, *Ethics*, 138–43; Schulz, *Ethik*, 434–46; Verhey, *Great Reversal*, 74–82.

2. For interesting discussions of the ethical dimensions of narrative, see W. C. Booth, *The Company We Keep: An Ethics of Fiction* (Berkeley: Univ. of California Press, 1988), and S. Hauerwas, *A Community of Character: Toward a Constructive Christian Ethic* (Notre Dame, Ind.: Univ. of Notre Dame Press, 1981).

3. The story of Jesus that functions as a narrative norm for most believers is, in fact, a composite story taken from all four Gospels. In this work I am focusing upon the distinctive story of Jesus presented by each Evangelist in order to show how each narrative functions as a norm for moral behavior.

4. Literary critics speak of "suspending one's disbelief." For example, readers of science fiction must suspend their disbelief that space travel is possible, even if such travel is not possible at the present time. To be sure, the Gospels are not pure fiction, but readers of the biblical narrative must accept a narrative world in which angels and demons are active characters, even if readers have no experience of such beings.

5. Literary critics speak of the "discourse" of a story, by which they mean *how* the story is told. Each of the four Gospels tells the same basic story, but the "discourse," the way in which the story is told, is different. The discourse of a story provides readers with narrative enjoyment, encouraging them to read old stories anew.

6. This may even happen to a reader who is not sympathetic to the viewpoint of the Evangelist. Caught up and persuaded by the narrative logic of an Evangelist, such a reader may even experience a moral conversion.

7. Whether or not the historical Jesus explicitly abolished the food laws is open to debate since, as far as we know, the early church did not appeal to this saying of Jesus in its disputes about the observance of these laws. Perhaps, then, the Markan community is drawing out what it sees as the implications of Jesus' teaching.

8. On the prologue of Mark's Gospel, see R. A. Guelich, *Mark 1–8:26*, WBC 34A (Dallas: Word, 1989), 3–46, and my article, "The Prologue as the Interpretative Key to Mark's Gospel," *JSNT* 34 (1988) 3–20.

9. The NRSV usually translates *euaggelion* as "good news," but I will translate it as "gospel."

10. The expression "the gospel *of* God" can be understood in two ways: (1) the good news about God, or (2) God's own good news. The context seems to require the second interpretation.

11. On the kingdom of God, see R. Schnackenburg, *God's Rule and Kingdom* (New York: Herder & Herder, 1968); the dictionary articles of D. C. Duling, "Kingdom of God,"and "Kingdom of Heaven," in *The Anchor Bible Dictionary*, ed. D. N. Freedman, 6 vols. (New York: Doubleday, 1992), 4: 49–69; and that of C. C. Caragounis, "Kingdom of God/Heaven," in *The Dictionary of Jesus and the Gospels*, ed. J. B. Green, S. McNight, and I. H. Marshall (Downers Grove, Ill.: InterVarsity, 1992), 417–30. Also helpful is the April 1993 issue of *Interpretation*, vol. 47, which is dedicated to the theme "The Reign of God."

12. See J. L. Mays (to whom I am indebted in this section), "The Language of the Reign of God," *Int* 47 (1993) 117–26.

13. See J. Marcus, *The Way of the Lord: Christological Exegesis of the Old Testament in the Gospel of Mark* (Louisville, Ky.: Westminster John Knox, 1992), esp. chap. 2, "The Gospel according to Isaiah."

14. The identity of the "holy ones of the Most High" is disputed. While some scholars view them as angelic figures, others regard them as representatives of the Maccabean martyrs.

15. I will employ "the kingdom of God" since it is a traditional expression. The reader should understand, however, that I am using it in its dynamic sense, the kingship of God.

16. See Mark 1:15; 4:11, 26, 30; 9:1, 47; 10:14, 15, 23, 24, 25; 12:34; 14:25; 15:43.

17. I am indebted to C. D. Marshall (*Faith as a Theme in Mark's Narrative*, SNTSMS 64 [Cambridge: Cambridge Univ. Press, 1989], 34–36) for this insight.

18. The majority of Jesus' miracles occur in the first part of Mark's Gospel: the cure of a demoniac (1:21–28), the healing of Peter's mother-in-law (1:29–31), the healing of a leper (1:40–45), the healing of a paralytic (2:1–12), the cure of a man on the Sabbath (3:1–6), the rescue of the disciples at sea (4:35–41), the healing of the Gerasene demoniac (5:1–20), the healing of a woman with a hemorrhage and the raising of Jairus's daughter (5:21–43), the feeding of the five thousand (6:34–44), the second rescue of the disciples at sea (6:45–52), the cure of the Syrophoenician woman's daughter (7:24–30), the cure of a deaf man (7:31–37), the feeding of the four thousand (8:1–9), the cure of a blind man (8:22–26). In the second part of the Gospel, Mark reports only three miracles: the healing of a boy possessed by a demon (9:14–29), the cure of a second blind man (10:46–52), and the cursing and withering of the fig tree (11:12–14, 20–21). For Mark, Jesus' miracles are a concrete proclamation of the kingdom of God.

19. On the hidden presence of God's kingdom, see Ambrozic, *Hidden Kingdom*.

20. Note the allusion here to Ezek. 17:23; 31:6; Dan. 4:12, 21.

21. The discussion with Jesus' disciples about being saved (Mark 10:26–27) and Jesus' references to the age to come (10:30), however, suggest that Jesus is speaking of a future reality.

22. Exactly what this saying refers to is disputed: the transfiguration, the resurrection, the parousia. Within the context of Mark's narrative, it could refer to either Jesus' resurrection or parousia, since at least some of the disciples will be alive—according to Mark's narrative—for both events. I find the reference to the transfiguration unconvincing since the kingdom of God does not come in power at this time.

23. Marshall, *Faith as a Theme*, 236.

24. Ibid., 236.

25. Thus Mark draws a sharp distinction between the preaching of John and that of Jesus; Jesus not only calls people to repentance but to faith in the kingdom.

26. The meaning of this quotation from Isaiah within Mark's Gospel is disputed. Some would argue that Jesus speaks in parables so that the crowd will not be converted. But I have taken the phrase to mean that the crowd does not want to see or hear lest they find it necessary to repent.

27. I am aware that the Markan disciples fail at many other points in this narrative and that Mark also uses them as examples of failure. But in this incident, at least, he presents them as making a generous response to the gospel.

28. On this point, see D. Rhodes (to whom I am indebted here), "Mark's Standards of Judgment," *Int* 47 (1993) 358–69.

29. Except for the preaching of John the Baptist, Mark does not relate repentance and the forgiveness of sins when speaking of Jesus' ministry. This does not mean that Jesus' ministry has nothing to do with the forgiveness of sins, however. In 2:1–12, Jesus forgives the sins of a paralytic, and in 2:17 he describes his ministry as calling sinners. Mark, however, does not add "to repentance," as does the parallel text in Luke 5:32. He seems to presuppose that repentance entails turning from sin.

30. Marshall, *Faith as a Theme*, 62.

31. On the miracles in Mark's Gospel, see my article, " 'He Saved Others, He Cannot Save Himself': A Literary-Critical Perspective on the Markan Miracles," *Int* 47 (1993) 15–26.

32. See Marshall, *Faith as a Theme*, 63–64.

33. The literature on the disciples in Mark's Gospel is immense, and the precise role that they play within the Gospel is disputed. Some believe that Mark views the disciples as representatives of a viewpoint that is completely false, e.g., a false Christology and a false notion of church leadership. Others see the disciples as flawed characters who, nonetheless, are generous, and whose story Mark uses to instruct the church of his day. I agree with this latter view. On the Markan disciples, see E. Best, *Following Jesus: Discipleship in the Gospel of Mark,* JSNTSS 4 (Sheffield: JSOT Press, 1981), and idem, *Mark: The Gospel as Story,* Studies of the New Testament and Its World (Edinburgh: T. & T. Clark, 1983). The study of M. A. Tolbert, *Sowing the Gospel: Mark's World in Literary-Historical Perspective* (Minneapolis: Fortress, 1989), while helpful, tends to take a more negative view of the disciples than I do.

34. On this important section of the Gospel, see my article "The Incomprehension of the Disciples and Peter's Confession (Mark 6,14–8,30)," *Bib* 70 (1989) 153–72.

35. Tolbert (*Sowing the Gospel*) sees the parable of the sower as the key to understanding Mark's Gospel. She argues that Jesus' interpretation of the parable of the sower details the different responses to his preaching of the kingdom. Thus the parable functions as the proverbial story within the story.

36. It is important to remember that the religious leaders of the Gospels are literary characters. They do not always accurately reflect the historical religious leaders of Jesus' day but play a literary role within the Gospels. On their literary role, see J. D. Kingsbury, *Conflict in Mark: Jesus, Authorities, Disciples* (Minneapolis: Fortress, 1989), 63–88.

37. The principle law codes of the Old Testament are the Decalogue (Ex. 20:1–17; Deut 5:6–21); the Book of the Covenant (Ex. 20:22–23:33); the Priestly Law (Leviticus 1—16); the Holiness Code (Leviticus 17—26); and the Deuteronomic Law (Deuteronomy 12—26). For an interesting discussion of how the law functions in a narrative context, see W. Janzen, *Old Testament Ethics: A Paradigmatic Approach* (Louisville, Ky.: Westminster John Knox, 1994), 55–105.

38. E. P. Sanders (*Paul and Palestinian Judaism: A Comparison of Patterns of Religion* [Philadelphia: Fortress, 1977]) has coined the expression "covenental nomism," which means that one maintains status in God's gracious covenant by observing Torah.

39. This is the solution proposed by Matthew's Gospel and a number of Jewish Christians, often called "Judaizers," who opposed Paul's law-free gospel.

40. This point is made by Schulz, *Ethik*, 434–46.

41. On the theme of conflict in Mark's Gospel, see Kingsbury, *Conflict in Mark*.

42. This is how the Form Critics interpreted these controversies.

43. The accusation of the religious leaders that Jesus has blasphemed foreshadows Jesus' trial, when he is condemned to death for blasphemy (Mark 14:64).

44. The text, however, is not clear about the identity of those who pose the question to Jesus.

45. For a helpful discussion of what the purity laws entailed, see E. P. Sanders, *Judaism: Practice and Belief, 63 BCE–66 CE* (Philadelphia: Trinity Press International, 1992), 190–240. A more technical discussion is found in his *Jewish Law from Jesus to the Mishnah* (Philadelphia: Trinity Press International, 1990).

46. On this point, see W. H. Kelber, *Mark's Story of Jesus* (Philadelphia: Fortress, 1977), 30–42.

47. The story of the Syrophoenecian woman also plays a role here (Mark 7:24–30), for she is clearly a Gentile. At first Jesus refuses to "feed" her with the bread of the children (7:27); because of her persistent faith, however, he "feeds" her by healing her daughter. Thus Jesus breaks down the barrier between Jew and Gentile, clean and unclean.

48. Notice that this is the same phrase used in the Galilean controversies.

49. See R. F. Collins, *Divorce in the New Testament*, GNS 38 (Collegeville, Minn.: Liturgical Press, 1992), 65–103.

50. Note that the verbs "commanded" and "allowed" suppose that whereas Moses allowed divorce, divorce was never commanded by the law. The law commanded that a husband should write a bill of divorce and give it to his wife. See Deut. 24:1–4.

51. The "house" appears frequently in Mark's Gospel and serves as a place of private instruction for Jesus' disciples. Perhaps Mark's original readers were intended to relate it to the house churches in which they assembled and were instructed by the risen Lord. See Best, *Following Jesus*, 226–29.

52. I have not included the question about David's son because the scribes do not pose this question to Jesus. Rather, Jesus asks the crowd why the scribes say that the Messiah is David's son.

53. I understand "Son of Man" as a technical term employed by the

Markan Jesus to describe his destiny of rejection, suffering, death, and vindication.

54. On Jesus' prayer in the garden of Gethsemane, see R. E. Brown, *The Death of the Messiah: From Gethsemane to the Grave, A Commentary on the Passion Narratives in the Four Gospels*, 2 vols., Anchor Bible Reference Library (New York: Doubleday, 1994), 1:147–215.

Chapter 2: Doing the Greater Righteousness

1. In recent years there has been a revival of the Griesbach hypothesis (Matthean priority), but it has not won the assent of the majority of scholars. Two recent examples are B. Orchard and H. Riley, *The Order of the Synoptics: Why Three Synoptic Gospels* (Macon, Ga.: Mercer Univ. Press, 1987), and H. Riley, *The Making of Mark: An Exploration* (Macon, Ga.: Mercer Univ. Press, 1989). On the manner in which Matthew revised Mark, see J. D. Kingsbury, *Matthew*, Proclamation Commentaries, 2d rev. ed. (Philadelphia: Fortress, 1986), 20–26.

2. While the material designated Q may have come from a written source, it is less likely that the material designated M represents a single written source. M is best taken as a designation of material and traditions peculiar to Matthew. For a reliable guide to what material is designated as Q, see F. Neirynck, *Q-Synopsis: The Double Tradition Passages in Greek*, Studiorum Novi Testamenti Auxilia XIII (Louvain: Peeters, 1988). Also helpful is J. S. Kloppenborg, *Q Parallels: Synopsis, Critical Notes and Concordance*, Foundations and Facets: New Testament (Sonoma, Calif.: Polebridge, 1988).

3. For studies on the ethics of Matthew's Gospel, see these works on New Testament ethics: Houlden, *Ethics*, 47–54; W. Marxsen, *New Testament Foundations for Christian Ethics* (Minneapolis; Fortress, 1993), 231–48; Schnackenburg, *Die sittliche Botschaft*, 2: 122–33; Schrage, *Ethics*, 143–51; Schulz, *Ethik*, 447–65; and Verhey, *Great Reversal*, 82–91. In addition to these works, the following monographs are important: J. P. Meier, *The Vision of Matthew: Christ, Church, and Morality in the First Gospel* (New York: Crossroad, 1991 [originally published in 1979 by Paulist Press]); R. Mohrlang, *Matthew and Paul: A Comparison of Ethical Perspectives*, SNTSMS 48 (Cambridge: Cambridge Univ. Press, 1984); and G. Strecker, *Der Weg der Gerechtigkeit: Untersuchung zur Theologie des Matthäus*, FRLANT 92 (Göttingen: Vandenhoeck & Ruprecht, 1971).

4. On the social background of Matthew's Gospel, see R. E Brown and J. P. Meier, *Antioch and Rome: New Testament Cradles of Catholic Christianity* (New York: Paulist, 1982); and D. L. Balch, ed., *Social History of the Matthean Community: Cross-Disciplinary Approaches* (Minneapolis: Fortress, 1991).

5. Those peculiar to Matthew are 3:2; 4:23; 5:10, 19 (twice), 20; 7:21; 8:12; 9:35; 13:19, 24, 38, 41, 43, 44, 45, 47, 52; 16:19; 18:1, 4, 23; 19:12; 20:1, 21; 21:31, 43; 22:2; 23:13; 24:14; 25:1, 34.

6. They are Matt. 5:3; 6:10, 33; 8:11; 10:7; 11:11, 12; 12:28; 13:33.

7. The expression "the kingdom of heaven" is probably "a stylistic variation" of "the kingdom of God," the word "heaven" serving as a periphrasis for "God." See W. D. Davies and D. C. Allison, *A Critical and Exegetical Commentary on the Gospel according to Matthew*, 2 vols., ICC (Edinburgh: T.& T. Clark, 1988, 1991), 1:389–92.

8. One element that is new, however, is Matthew's reference to the kingdom of the Son of Man. Matthew seems to suppose that in the period after the resurrection, Jesus the Son of Man has a kingdom over which he rules. That rule is not yet acknowledged by all but, at the parousia, it will be. See J. D. Kingsbury, *Matthew: Structure, Christology, Kingdom* (Philadelphia: Fortress, 1975), 143–44.

9. What follows is not intended to be a full presentation of the kingdom-of-heaven theme as found in Matthew's Gospel. For such a study, see Kingsbury, *Matthew: Structure,* 128–60, and idem, *The Parables of Jesus in Matthew 13: A Study in Redaction Criticism* (St. Louis: Clayton, 1969).

10. I am making use of the structure of Matthew's Gospel as proposed by Kingsbury in *Matthew: Structure:* Matt. 1:1–4:16, the genesis and significance of the person of Jesus; 4:17–16:20, the nature and effect of his proclamation; and 16:21–28:20, the reason and finality of his suffering, death, and resurrection.

11. It will, however, break in when Jesus inaugurates his ministry.

12. Matthew's omission of "believe in the gospel" does not mean that he disregards the importance of faith. Faith and the need to believe continue to play a significant role in this Gospel, even though I do not devote a specific section to the topic. The verb occurs 11 times (8:13; 9:28; 18:6; 21:22, 25, 32 [3 times]; 24:23, 26; 27:42), and the noun 8 times (8:10; 9:2, 22, 29; 15:28; 17:20; 21:21; 23:23). The verb (14 times in Mark and 11 in Matthew) and the noun (5 times in Mark and 8 times in Matthew), however, occur proportionally more frequently in Mark's Gospel, which is about 40 percent shorter than Matthew's. Without neglecting the importance of believing, Matthew places more emphasis on doing than on believing.

13. C. C. Caragounis ("Kingdom of God/Heaven"), however, claims that the verb should be interpreted according to "a well-attested but little-known and generally misunderstood Greek idiom" that "implies an advance but not quite the presence of the kingdom of God" (423).

14. The literature on the parables is vast, and the study of the parables is complicated since authors employ such diverse methodologies to interpret them. My primary interest is how the parables function within the context of Matthew's Gospel. Two helpful works for interpreting the parables from this vantage point are Kingsbury, *Parables,* and J. Drury, *The Parables in the Gospels: History and Allegory* (New York: Crossroad, 1985), 70–107.

15. This parable, of course, does not make any reference to righteousness, nor does it identify the oil in the lamp as works of righteousness. I suggest this interpretation because of the highly allegorical nature of Matthew's parables. The bridegroom is clearly Jesus, the virgins represent disciples, the marriage feast is the kingdom of heaven. Given the allegorical nature of the parable, and its setting within a Gospel that emphasizes the need for righteousness, it does not seem unreasonable to interpret the oil as the deeds of righteousness with which the elect must meet their Lord.

16. The present form of the Sermon on the Mount, as found in Matthew's Gospel, is a Matthean literary construction. This does not mean that the moral content of the sermon is Matthew's creation; the moral teaching of the sermon finds its origin in Jesus. However, it is Matthew who has given the sermon its distinctive shape and orientation. The literature on the sermon is immense. I have depended upon the following works: R. A. Guelich, *The Sermon on the*

Mount: A Foundation for Understanding (Waco, Tex.: Word Books, 1982); and J. Lambrecht, *The Sermon on the Mount: Proclamation and Exhortation,* GNS 14 (Wilmington, Del.: Glazier, 1985). In addition to these, one should consult the standard commentaries, especially those of Davies and Allison, *Matthew;* U. Luz, *Matthew 1—7: A Commentary* (Minneapolis: Augsburg, 1989); and J. P. Meier, *Matthew,* NTM (Wilmington, Del.: Glazier, 1980).

17. For example, Schrage (*Ethics,* 152) writes: "In any case, righteousness is a gift of grace, not just a requirement to be fulfilled."

18. The major study proposing that righteousness refers to conduct is that of B. Przybylski, *Righteousness in Matthew and His World of Thought,* SNTSMS 41 (Cambridge: Cambridge Univ. Press, 1980). Others who view righteousness in Matthew as conduct are Luz (*Matthew,* 237–38), Mohrlang (*Matthew and Paul,* 45), and Schnackenburg (*Die sittliche Botschaft,* 2:124).

19. The verb "to fulfill" has been interpreted in different ways. For a discussion of the possibilities, see Luz (*Matthew,* 26–61) and Davies and Allison (*Matthew,* 1:484–87). In my view, Jesus is the eschatological fulfillment of the law, and he carries out the demands of the law in his life and ministry.

20. It is noteworthy that the Matthean Jesus does not exclude those who violate the least of the commandments from the kingdom, although they will be called least in the kingdom. Perhaps Matthew employs this saying as a response to those members of his audience who mistakenly think that they can do away with such commandments.

21. Mohrlang, *Matthew and Paul,* 19.

22. The precise meaning of *porneia* is debated. While some argue that it refers to serious immorality, such as adultery, others interpret it as referring to unlawful marriages between people too closely related by blood. In the former case, Jesus would allow divorce for a specific case of immorality on the part of the woman. In the latter, he says that certain marriages should be divorced because they were illegal from the start. On this "exception clause," see Collins, *Divorce,* 184–213; Luz, *Matthew,* 301–10; and Meier, *Matthew,* 52–53.

23. There is no commandment in the Old Testament to hate one's enemy. By adding the phrase "and hate your enemy," Matthew may be providing his audience with a current interpretation of the commandment to love one's neighbor, understood as fellow countrymen, i.e., you shall hate those who are not your compatriots because they are the enemies of your people.

24. My colleague John Meier has pointed out that there is a distinction between completely abrogating the Mosaic law and abrogating individual commandments in the law, which is still affirmed. Thus some argue that Jesus abrogated certain individual commandments while still affirming the general validity of the law.

25. Przybylski, *Righteousness,* 83.

26. A. E. Harvey (*Strenuous Commands: The Ethics of Jesus* [Philadelphia: Trinity Press International 1990], 92) makes the point that the strenuous part of Jesus' moral teaching about nonresistance, love of enemies, giving to all who ask, and so on does not follow the form of legal constraints. Legal constraints prefer a more casuistic form or a straight prohibition, "thou shall not."

27. Przybylski, *Righteousness,* 88.

28. This portrayal of the hypocrites blowing trumpets before themselves as they give alms may be a comical portrait rather than a historical fact.

29. The point is made by Luz (*Matthew*, 211–13), who places the Lord's Prayer at the very center of the sermon.

30. Luke places the Lord's Prayer during the course of Jesus' journey to Jerusalem (Luke 11:2–4).

31. An ethical interpretation of the petitions "thy kingdom come" and "thy will be done" is suggested by Luz, *Matthew*, 378–80.

32. This is not to imply, however, that God's kingdom comes by or because of human ethical action.

33. Not all manuscripts have "of God."

34. Matthew seems to suppose an extramission theory of sight (light flows from the eye) rather than an intromission theory (light enters through the eye). See Davies and Allison, *Matthew*, 1:635. This means it is the eye that illuminates the body. Since Matthew is using "eye" metaphorically, it must refer to something that enlightens the whole person, such as total dedication to God, seeking the kingdom of heaven.

35. The admonition not to throw one's pearls before swine presents another crux. To what do "pearls" and "swine" refer? One possibility is that "pearls" refer to the knowledge of the mysteries of the kingdom that has been given to the disciples (Matt. 13:11), the kingdom being the pearl of great price (13:45–46). The pejorative "swine" would refer to those who are unclean because they have refused the message of the kingdom (10:14–15). Since such people are hard-hearted, the disciples should not squander the message of the kingdom on them once they have refused it. See Davies and Allison, *Matthew*, 1:674–77.

36. I will return to the Golden Rule in my discussion of Luke's version of Jesus' great sermon, the Sermon on the Plain.

37. Przybylski (*Righteousness*, 105–15) points to the relative significance of the concept of righteousness in Matthew's Gospel. He argues that "the will of God" is a more inclusive term than righteousness, and that "[p]roperly religious followers of Jesus are disciples whose conduct is governed by the will of God" (114).

38. In this part of the Gospel, Matthew presents Jesus as son of Abraham, son of David, Messiah, Emmanuel, Israel's Shepherd-King, and the Son of God.

39. On this point, see Luz (*Matthew*, 177–78), who interprets Jesus' righteousness as conduct; Meier (*Matthew*, 27), who interprets it as God's saving activity; and Davies and Allison (*Matthew*, 1:325–27), who try to combine these two positions. Righteousness refers to moral conduct, Davies and Allison say, but "Jesus, knowing the messianic prophecies of the OT, obediently fulfills them and thereby fulfils all righteousness. Because prophecy declares God's will, to fulfil prophecy is to fulfil righteousness" (327).

40. On this episode, see B. Gerhardsson's chapter on Matthew in *The Ethos of the Bible* (Philadelphia: Fortress, 1981), esp. pp. 54–60, where he discusses Jesus as a model of righteous behavior.

41. Gerhardsson (ibid.) draws a comparison between Jesus' testing in the wilderness and his testing on the cross. He notes that in both episodes Jesus is deprived of all food and drink, the last vestiges of power and property, and is also deprived of protection and deliverance from death (59).

42. Meier (*Matthew*, 169), however, points to Matt. 15:11 to support his view that Jesus does annul the food laws. If this is so, I do not understand why

Matthew omitted Mark's side comment (Mark 7:19) that Jesus declared all food clean.

43. So, D. J. Harrington, *The Gospel of Matthew*, Sacra Pagina 1 (Collegeville, Minn.: Liturgical Press, 1991), 337. For an opposing view, see Meier, *Matthew*, 284.

44. In the parallel passage of Mark 10:19, the Markan Jesus lists commandments from the Decalogue, but not Lev. 19:18 as does the Matthean Jesus here. Again, it appears that Matthew wants to emphasize the centrality of love more explicitly than his Markan source.

45. In Mark 10:28 the scribe asks which commandment is first of all, but in Matt. 22:36 he asks which commandment *in the law* is the greatest. Matthew's editorial activity shows his interest in the law. Mark has Jesus uphold God's commandments, but he never explicitly discusses the law.

46. As noted above, in his answer to the rich man, the Matthean Jesus includes the commandment from Leviticus to love one's neighbor as oneself (Matt. 19:19).

47. For a discussion of the literary portrait of the religious leaders in Matthew's Gospel, see J. D. Kingsbury, *Matthew as Story*, 2d ed. rev. and enlarged (Philadelphia: Fortress, 1988), 115–28.

48. Unfortunately, the Gospel of Matthew can lead to immoral behavior by supporting the anti-Semitic convictions of some who take the Gospel's literary portrait of the religious leaders as historical fact.

49. On the tradition of the elders, see Davies and Allison, *Matthew*, 2:520. They write, "The tradition of the Pharisees had a controversial status before A.D. 70. . . . Jesus and the gospel writers were not alone in rejecting the Pharisaic *paradosis* as a later innovation."

50. Hypocrites are mentioned in Matthew 6, but they are not explicitly identified as the religious leaders.

51. Jesus' woes against the Pharisees are spoken in the presence of the crowd and the disciples (Matt. 23:1). The Pharisees do not appear to be present. Thus the woes are meant to instruct the crowd and disciples, as much as condemn the Pharisees.

52. On the theme of judgment and reward in Matthew's Gospel, see K. Weber, "The Events of the End of the Age in Matthew" (Ph.D. diss., Catholic University of America, Washington, D.C., 1994). In this section, I am indebted to many of her insights.

53. Mohrlang, *Matthew and Paul*, 48.

54. There has been considerable debate about the least of Jesus' brethren. Some argue that the least of his brethren are the disciples, since a similar expression, which refers to the disciples, occurs in Matt. 10:42 (*hena mikron touton*). But others maintain that Jesus has a more universal vision in this scene of the final judgment: all who suffer. See Schnackenburg, *Die sittliche Botschaft*, 2:130.

55. In this particular passage, "the heirs of the kingdom" seems to refer to the people of Israel.

56. For a comparative study of law and righteousness in Matthew and Paul, see Mohrlang, *Matthew and Paul*, 7–47.

57. Mohrlang, *Matthew and Paul*.

58. On the soteriology of Matthew's Gospel, see A. Hultgren, *Christ and*

His Benefits: Christology and Redemption in the New Testament (Philadelphia: Fortress, 1987), pp. 69–90. He describes Matthew's soteriology as "redemption confirmed through Christ." This has a parallel with Matthew's ethical vision in which salvation is confirmed by living a life of righteousness.

59. In reading Matthew's Gospel, one must remember that the disciples within the narrative can be viewed in two ways. First, they represent the disciples chosen by Jesus during the time of his ministry. Second, for the post-resurrection church they represent all believers. Therefore, as members of the church read about Jesus' original disciples, they are invited to associate themselves with the disciples of the narrative.

60. J. D. Kingsbury, "The 'Eager' Scribe and the 'Reluctant' Disciples (Matt 8. 18–22)," *NTS* 34 (1988) 45–59.

61. Notice that in the parallel passage of Mark 4:38 Jesus is called "Teacher" but not "Lord". Matthew retrojects the exalted Lord into the time of the earthly Jesus more explicitly than does Mark.

62. Mohrlang, *Matthew and Paul*, 80.

Chapter 3: Ethics in an Age of Salvation

1. Luke places most of his Q material in two major blocks called the small insertion (6:20–8:3) and the large insertion (9:51–18:14). Scholars believe that he was more faithful to the original order of Q than is Matthew, since Luke tends to respect Mark's order more than Matthew does. It is, however, impossible to prove that Luke preserves the order of Q more faithfully than Matthew since we do not have the Q document.

2. "L" should be viewed as a sign which designates Luke's special traditions rather than as a single source or document. For a list of the L material, see C. F. Evans, *Saint Luke*, TPI New Testament Commentaries (Philadelphia: Trinity Press International, 1990), 26–27; and J. A. Fitzmyer, *The Gospel according to Luke*, 2 vols., AB 28, 28A (Garden City, N.Y.: Doubleday, 1981, 1985), 1:83–84.

3. For a discussion of the situation that Luke addressed, see R. Maddox, *The Purpose of Luke-Acts* (Edinburgh: T. & T. Clark, 1982), as well as the standard commentaries.

4. Here I am paraphrasing Luke's prologue (1:1–4). This elegant Greek sentence provides readers with Luke's own statement of why he wrote, but it is notoriously difficult to interpret. On the preface, see Evans, *Saint Luke*, 115–36, and the monograph of L. Alexander, *The Preface to Luke's Gospel*, SNTSMS 78 (Cambridge: Cambridge Univ. Press, 1993).

5. On Luke's understanding of the law, see Schulz, *Ethik*, 466–84 and S. G. Wilson, *Luke and the Law*, SNTSMS 50 (Cambridge: Cambridge Univ. Press, 1983).

6. Luke omits Mark's discussion of the tradition of the elders with its declaration that Jesus declared all foods clean (Mark 7:1–23) because this issue will be resolved at the Jerusalem conference (Acts 15).

7. For a summary of the ethics in Luke's Gospel, see Houlden, *Ethics*, 55–60; Schnackenburg, *Die sittliche Botschaft*, 2:134–47; Schrage, *Ethics*, 152–62; Schulz, *Ethik*, 466–85; and Verhey, *Great Reversal*, 92–101.

8. On the theme of salvation, see I. H. Marshall, *Luke: Historian and Theologian* (Grand Rapids: Zondervan, 1970), esp. 77–102.

9. Caragounis, "Kingdom of God/Heaven," 428.

10. Those references peculiar to Luke are 1:33; 4:43; 8:1; 9:11, 60, 62; 10:11; 12:32; 13:28; 14:15; 17:20–21; 18:29; 19:11; 21:31; 22:16, 29–30; 23:42.

11. These are Luke 6:20; 7:28; 9:2; 11:2, 20; 12:31; 13:20, 29; 16:16.

12. These are Acts 1:3, 6; 8:12; 14:22; 19:8; 20:25; 28:23, 31.

13. These are Luke 8:10; 9:27; 13:18; 18:16, 17, 24, 25; 22:18; 23:51.

14. In Luke this saying is spoken to the crowds, whereas it is directed at the religious leaders in Matthew's Gospel.

15. Here I am following the interpretation of Luke 16:16 presented by Fitzmyer, *Luke,* 2:1114–18. Matthew employs this saying in a different way: the kingdom of God is suffering violence from violent men (Matt. 11:12).

16. This saying could also be taken as a comparison of John and Jesus: Jesus who is lesser (younger) than John is greater than John. The context of Luke's Gospel, however, suggests that Jesus is making a comparison between John and the least in God's kingdom. See Fitzmyer, *Luke,* 1:675.

17. The additional phrase found in Matt. 6:33, "and his righteousness," is absent from Luke's version of the saying. Given Matthew's interest in the concept of righteousness, it is likely that he added this phrase to the original Q saying.

18. On the difficulty of translating this phrase, see Fitzmyer, *Luke,* 2:1160–62. Among the possible translations are: "within you," "among you," "in the midst of you," "within your reach, grasp, or possession."

19. The man in the parable who goes off to a distant country to receive a kingdom is clearly Jesus, who at his return is the triumphant Son of Man.

20. On this point, see R. C. Tannehill, *The Narrative Unity of Luke-Acts: A Literary Interpretation,* vol. 1, *The Gospel according to Luke,* Foundations and Facets (Philadelphia: Fortress, 1986), 13–44.

21. After the infancy narrative, John the Baptist preaches a baptism for the forgiveness of sins (Luke 3:3), fulfilling the prophecy of Isa. 40:3–5. While Matthew and Mark view John's ministry as the fulfillment of Isaiah's prophecy, only Luke extends the Isaiah quotation to include "and all flesh shall see the *salvation* of God" (Luke 3:6). The ministry of John the Baptist prepares for God's salvation by turning the children of Israel to the Lord their God so that they will be a people prepared for the Lord (1:16–17). But this coming salvation will bring a reversal of fortunes, for when the Baptist sees the crowds coming for his baptism, he warns them that God can raise up new children to Abraham (3:7–8). Therefore they must repent. This reversal of fortune occurs in Acts, when the majority of Israel does not repent and God's offer of salvation is extended to the Gentiles.

22. See Tannehill, *Narrative Unity,* 26–32.

23. In Luke 1:33 the angel tells Mary that the kingdom of her son will endure forever. While this brings to mind the kingdom of David as described in the prophecy of Nathan (2 Sam. 7:8–16), the reference here is to God's kingdom.

24. For a discussion of Jesus' inaugural sermon, see D. L. Tiede, *Prophecy and History in Luke-Acts* (Philadelphia: Fortress, 1980), 19–64.

25. The emphasis upon the "today" of salvation is characteristic of Luke's Gospel. See 2:11; 4:21; 5:26; 19:9; 23:43.

26. A review of Jesus' ministry shows that he cures a leper (Luke 5:12–16) and heals a paralytic (5:17–26), "releasing" the man from his sins. He heals a

man with a withered hand (6:6–11), cures the ills of a great multitude (6:17–19), announces good news to the poor (6:20–21), heals a centurion's servant (7:1–10), and raises a widow's son (7:11–17).

27. The year of favor refers to the year of Jubilee (Lev. 25:8–55), when all debts were to be forgiven. S. H. Ringe (*Jesus, Liberation, and the Biblical Jubilee: Images for Ethics and Christology*, Overtures to Biblical Theology [Philadelphia: Fortress, 1985]) provides a helpful background to this concept and shows how it applies to Jesus' ministry, especially as portrayed in the Gospel of Luke.

28. On this theme, see J. O. York, *The Last Shall Be First: The Rhetoric of Reversal in Luke*, JSNTSS 46 (Sheffield: JSOT Press, 1991).

29. On the theme of repentance in Luke, see "La Conversion," in A. George, *Études sur l'oeuvre de Luc*, SB (Paris: Gabalda, 1978), 351–68, to which I am indebted in this section; and R. D. Witherup, *Conversion in the New Testament* (Collegeville, Minn.: Liturgical Press, 1994), 44–73.

30. Unless otherwise noted, the underlying Greek words in my references to "repentance" and "to repent" are *metanoia* and *metanoein*, respectively.

31. On the role of John the Baptist in Luke's narrative, see the study of J. A. Darr, *On Character Building: The Reader and the Rhetoric of Characterization in Luke-Acts*, Literary Currents in Biblical Interpretation (Louisville, Ky.: Westminster John Knox, 1992), 60–84.

32. For a provocative discussion of who were the sinners and who were the righteous, see J.D.G. Dunn, *Jesus' Call to Discipleship*, Understanding Jesus Today (Cambridge: Cambridge Univ. Press, 1992), 62–91. For a different view, see E. P. Sanders, *Jesus and Judaism* (Philadelphia: Fortress, 1985), 174–211.

33. On this theme, see the essay by J. Jervell, "The Divided People of God: The Restoration of Israel and Salvation for the Gentiles," in *Luke and the People of God* (Minneapolis: Augsburg, 1972), 41–74.

34. On the responsibility for the death of Jesus as presented in the Acts of the Apostles, see F. J. Matera, "Responsibility for the Death of Jesus according to the Acts of the Apostles," *JSNT* 39 (1990) 77–93.

35. In contrast to his first two speeches, Peter does not call the religious leaders to repentance; this suggests that Luke does not see as much hope for them as he does for the people of Israel.

36. For other instances where repentance is associated with Peter's ministry, see Acts 8:22; 9:35.

37. It is interesting to note that as important as repentance is in Judaism and in the writings of the Synoptic Gospels, it plays a minor role in Paul's letters; this makes the references in Acts to Paul as a preacher of repentance all the more noteworthy.

38. Some would designate the Lukan sermon as Jesus' sermon *at* the Mountain because he delivers the Sermon after descending from the mountain.

39. Most studies focus upon the Sermon on the Mount, the Sermon on the Plain receiving little or no attention. The following works are helpful, however, for understanding the Sermon on the Plain. J. Dupont, *Les Béatitudes*, vol. 1, *Le problème littéraire*, EBib (Paris: Gabalda, 1969); and J. Lambrecht, *The Sermon on the Mount: Proclamation and Exhortation*, GNS 14 (Wilmington, Del.: Glazier, 1985), 206–32.

40. Dupont (*Les Béatitudes*, 1:127–28, 203–4) thinks that Matthew and Luke had slightly different versions of the Q sermon.

41. Luke 11:1–4, 9–13, 34–36; 12:22–32, 33–34, 57–59; 13:23–24, 25–27; 14:34–35; 16:13, 16–17.

42. Luke is the only Evangelist to make a clear distinction between Jesus' many disciples and his twelve apostles. In Acts, the Twelve function as the eschatological regents of a restored Israel. See J. Jervell, "The Twelve on Israel's Thrones: Luke's Understanding of the Apostolate," in *Luke and the People of God*, 75–132.

43. This is essentially the outline proposed by Dupont, *Les Béatitudes*, 1:196–200. Others outline the sermon in a slightly different way. For example, Fitzmyer and Lambrecht see the conclusion consisting of 6:46–49 rather than 6:43–49. Evans makes the main body of the sermon consist of 6:27–38 and 6:39–45 rather than 6:27–36 and 6:37–42.

44. The actual poor are in view here: those who have few possessions and those who are wholly without possessions and must therefore acquire the necessities of life through begging. In the Old Testament, the poor stand under God's protection. According to Deut. 15:4 there should be no poor (LXX, *endeēs*) in Israel since God has given the land to the whole people of Israel.

45. On this theme, see York, *The Last Shall Be First*.

46. On the love of enemies, see V. P. Furnish, *The Love Command in the New Testament* (Nashville: Abingdon, 1972), 45–58; S. Légasse, *"Et qui est mon prochain?" Étude sur l'objet de l'agapè dans le Nouveau Testament*, LD 136 (Paris: Cerf, 1989), 71–116; W. M. Swartley, ed., *The Love of Enemy and Nonretaliation in the New Testament* (Louisville, Ky.: Westminster John Knox, 1992); and P. Perkins, *Love Commands in the New Testament* (New York: Paulist, 1982), 27–41, 89–96.

47. The *chitōn* is the garment worn next to the body, whereas the *himation* is the cloak worn over the tunic.

48. A. E. Harvey (*Strenuous Commands*, 106) says that the Golden Rule, at least in its negative form, was known in antiquity from as early as the fourth century B.C. (see Herodotus 3:142; 7:136, where it is given as advice to rulers). The rule is also attributed to Hillel (B. Shab. 31a; "What is hateful to you, do not do to your neighbor"), and it is found in the book of Tobit, "And what you hate do not do to anyone" (4:15). What is unusual about Jesus' version, however, is that it is formulated positively. Harvey believes that while the negative formulation "is fundamentally a common-sense rule of thumb" (107), i.e., don't do evil to others because you will probably have to pay for it in the end, Jesus' positive formulation does not involve this inner logic. You cannot reasonably expect that if you do good to another it will be repaid in kind (107–8).

49. Harvey (*Strenuous Commands*, 104) notes that the pagan world commended acts of generosity and mercy, but usually toward social equals or superiors who would be obligated to repay in kind. This principle of reciprocity has no place in Jesus' teaching.

50. Note that in the infancy narrative the angel tells Mary her child will be called the "Son of the Most High" (1:32). Thus the Lukan Jesus establishes a relationship between himself and his disciples who are merciful as God is merciful.

51. See Sir. 18:8–14, where God is described as compassionate, especially v. 13 ("The compassion of human beings is not for their neighbors, but the compassion of the Lord is for every living thing"). In Sirach, however, the Greek word for compassion is *eleos*.

52. The passive voice makes it clear that God will effect this.

53. For a full-length study of the journey, see D. Moessner, *Lord of the Banquet: The Literary and Theological Significance of the Lukan Travel Narrative* (Minneapolis: Fortress, 1989).

54. Luke's account is longer than those of Matthew and Mark because, in addition to material from Mark, Luke makes extensive use of material from Q and his L sources.

55. In contrast to this, the announcement of Jesus' journey in Mark 10:1 and Matt. 19:1 does not mark a turning point in the narrative. For Mark and Matthew, the turning point in Jesus' ministry is Peter's confession at Caesarea Philippi.

56. Thus Luke's Gospel may be outlined in this fashion: The Prologue (1:1–4); The Infancy Narrative (1:5–2:52); Preparation for Jesus' Public Ministry (3:1–4:13); Jesus' Ministry in Galilee (4:14–9:50); Jesus' Journey to Jerusalem (9:51–19:46); Jesus' Ministry in Jerusalem (19:47–21:38); Passion, Death, Resurrection, Ascension (22:1–24:53).

57. For a review of theories about the journey section, see H. L. Egelkraut, *Jesus' Mission to Jerusalem: A Redaction Critical Study of the Travel Narrative in the Gospel of Luke, Lk. 9:51–19:48,* Europäische Hochschulschriften, 80 (Frankfurt: Lang, 1976), 30–41; and J. L. Resseguie, "Interpretation of Luke's Central Section (Luke 9:51–19:44) since 1856," *Studia Biblica et Theologica* 5 (1975), 3–36.

58. Texts that indicate that Jesus is on a journey are Luke 9:51, 53, 56, 57; 10:1, 38; 13:22, 33; 14:25; 17:11; 18:31, 35–36; 19:1, 11, 28, 29, 37, 41, 45. Texts that actually mention Jerusalem as Jesus' destination are 9:51, 53; 13:22; 17:11; 18:31; 19:11, 28.

59. These speeches are Luke 10:2–16 (the seventy-two); 11:2–13 (the disciples); 11:17–36 (the crowd); 11:39–52 (the Pharisees and lawyers); 12:1–13:9 (the disciples and the crowd); 13:23–30 (the crowd); 14:8–24 (the Pharisees); 14:26–35 (the crowd); 15:3–17:10 (the Pharisees, scribes, and disciples); 17:22–18:14 (the disciples); 19:12–27 (the audience is not specified).

60. The fact that both sayings speak of "taking up one's cross" suggests a time after the resurrection when the church has begun to theologize about the meaning of discipleship.

61. On this point, see P. Liu, "Did the Lucan Jesus Desire Voluntary Poverty of His Followers?" *EQ* 64 (1992) 291–317.

62. The manager is also a slave, but a slave in charge of other slaves. See Luke 12:43, where he is referred to as a slave.

63. On the theme of possessions in Luke-Acts, see H. J. Degenhardt, *Lukas Evangelist der Armen: Besitz und Besitzverzicht in den lukanischen Schriften, Eine traditions- und redaktionsgeschichtliche Untersuchung* (Stuttgart: Katholisches Bibelwerk, 1965); J. Gillman, *Possessions and the Life of Faith: A Reading of Luke-Acts* (Collegeville, Minn.: Liturgical Press, 1991); and L. Schottroff and W. Stegemann, *Jesus and the Hope of the Poor* (Maryknoll, N.Y.: Orbis, 1986).

64. Once more it is important to remind readers that I am speaking about the religious leaders as portrayed in the Gospel and not the historical religious leaders of Jesus' day.

65. The meaning of this phrase is a notorious *crux* for commentators. The Revised English Bible offers the following interpretive translation: "But let what is inside be given in charity, and all is clean." The real problem is the

meaning of the phrase "what is inside." I take it to mean the wickedness and greed of the Pharisees. If they give alms, they will be cleansed of this.

66. Note the relationship between the situation of poor Lazarus who wished *to be satisfied* with the scraps that fell from the rich man's table (Luke 16:21) and the hungry who *will be satisfied* (6:21), as well as the situation of poor Lazarus who *is comforted* in the afterlife (16:25) and the rich who have received their *comfort* in this life (6:24).

67. On this point see Fitzmyer, *Luke*, 2:1225.

68. This "exodus" refers to his death, which leads to his resurrection and ascension to the Father.

69. Wilson, *Luke and the Law*, 56.

70. Notice, however, that Luke 6:11 softens the language of Mark 3:6. The religious leaders become enraged and discuss what they should do, but they do not plan to destroy Jesus as in Mark's Gospel.

71. Wilson, *Luke and the Law*, 56–58.

72. On the role of women in Luke's Gospel, see J. van Cangh, "La femme dans L'Évangile de Luc: Comparison des passages narratifs propres à Luc avec la situation de la femme dans le judaïsme," *RTL* 24 (1993) 297–324.

73. Brown (*Death of the Messiah*, 2:971–81) argues that the text is authentic.

74. The mentions of *pistis* in Luke's Gospel are 5:20; 7:9, 50; 8:25, 48; 17:5, 6, 19; 18:8, 42; 22:32. All but 7:9, 50; 17:19; 18:8 come from Mark. The uses of *pisteuein* in the Gospel are 1:20, 45; 8:12, 13, 50; 16:11; 20:5; 22:67; 24:25. Except for 8:50, these do not have a parallel in Mark. However, only 8:12, 13; 24:25 are relevant to discipleship.

75. To the extent that repentance in the Gospel of Luke requires accepting Jesus' message about the kingdom of God, Luke upholds what Mark understands by believing in the gospel.

76. Love for one's enemy is also a concern in Matthew's Sermon on the Mount, but it plays a more central role in Luke's Sermon on the Plain.

Chapter 4: Ethics Becomes Christology

1. While I will refer to the author of the Gospel as an individual, e.g., "John" or "the Fourth Evangelist," the final edition of the Gospel is probably the result of a long and complicated literary history involving the work of more than one author. On the question of authorship, see R. E. Brown, *The Gospel according to John*, 2 vols., AB 29, 29A (New York: Doubleday, 1966, 1970), 1:xxiv-xl; R. Schnackenburg, *The Gospel according to John*, 3 vols. (New York: Crossroad, 1968, 1980, 1982), 1:59–104.

2. The only references to the kingdom of God in the Fourth Gospel occur in Jesus' conversation with Nicodemus (3:3, 5), and the only reference to conversion appears in a quotation from Isaiah (12:40).

3. The majority opinion among scholars is that the Fourth Gospel is not dependent upon one or more of the Synoptics. This view, however, has been challenged by Franz Neirynck. For a reliable guide to the debate, see D. Moody Smith, *John among the Gospels: The Relationship in Twentieth-Century Research* (Minneapolis: Fortress, 1992).

4. This is the approach of two works dedicated to the moral teaching of the Johannine writings: N. Lazure, *Les valeurs morales de la Théologie Johannique*

(*Évangile et Épîtres*), EBib (Paris: Gabalda, 1965), and O. Prunet, *La Morale Chrétienne d'après les Écrits Johanniques (Évangile et Épîtres)* (Paris: Presses Universitaires de France, 1957).

5. For a brief exposition of the theology of the letters, see Judith Lieu, *The Theology of the Johannine Epistles*, NTT (Cambridge: Cambridge Univ. Press, 1991). The works of Lazure and Prunet mentioned in n. 4 provide helpful summaries of the moral teaching of the letters. R. E. Brown (*The Community of the Beloved Disciple: The Life, Loves, and Hates of an Individual Church in New Testament Times* [New York: Paulist, 1979]) investigates the life situation that occasioned the letters. He suggests that many of the ethical questions addressed by the letters may have been caused by a misunderstanding of the Gospel's ethical teaching (123–35).

6. Here I am following the outline proposed by Brown, *John*, 1:ix–xii.

7. The transformation of water into wine (John 2:1–11), the cure of the royal official's son (4:46–54), the cure of the paralytic (5:1–9), the feeding of the crowd in the wilderness (6:1–15), walking on the sea of Galilee (6:16–21), the cure of the man born blind (9:1–41), and the raising of Lazarus (11:1–44).

8. For a survey of the ethical teaching of the Johannine writings, see the volumes of Lazure and Prunet mentioned in n. 4 and the following works on New Testament ethics: Marxsen, *New Testament Foundations*, 286–309; Schnackenburg, *Die sittliche Botschaft*, 2:148–92; Schrage, *Ethics*, 295–320; Schulz, *Ethik*, 253–63, 486–526; and Verhey, *Great Reversal*, 142–52. Also important, especially for the Johannine understanding of the human plight, is R. Bultmann's section on Johannine theology in *Theology of the New Testament*, 2 vols. (London: SCM Press, 1952, 1955), 2:3–94.

9. J. Ashton (*Understanding the Fourth Gospel* [Oxford: Clarendon, 1991], 206–7) says that there are two distinct opposites implied by *kosmos*. One is vertical, the earth as opposed to heaven; the other is horizontal and implies a moral or ethical dualism.

10. For an insightful study of the different levels of meaning found in the Fourth Gospel, see J. Louis Martyn, *History and Theology in the Fourth Gospel*, 2d ed. (Nashville: Abingdon, 1979). Martyn uses the cure of the man born blind as a case study.

11. Note the inclusion formed by John's announcement that Jesus is the Lamb of God who takes away the sins of the world and Jesus' commission to the disciples to forgive sins. In the Fourth Gospel, there is a parallelism between Jesus being sent into the world by the Father, and the disciples being sent into the world by Jesus in order to continue his mission.

12. It should be noted that Jesus addresses this critique at those Jews who had believed in him (John 8:31). Read in the context of what was occurring in the Johannine community, these Jews probably represent crypto-Christians who, to the dismay of the Evangelist, remained in the synagogue, or Christians with too low a Christology in the estimation of the Johannine author. See Brown, *Community of the Beloved Disciple*, 71–81.

13. One must remember that the Fourth Gospel contains different levels of interpretation. On the surface level the Gospel appears to be a story of Jesus, but below the surface lies the story of the Johannine community and its struggle with "the world," which is often identified with the Jewish world that does not believe in Jesus. This polemic is especially vitriolic in chaps. 7—8; therefore

it is important that readers do not identify all that the Johannine Jesus says as the words and teaching of the historical Jesus. Two helpful studies of the social world of John's Gospel are J. H. Neyrey, *An Ideology of Revolt: John's Christology in Social-Science Perspective* (Philadelphia: Fortress, 1988), and D. Rensberger, *Johannine Faith and Liberating Community* (Philadelphia: Westminster, 1988).

14. I call John 20:31 the conclusion of the Gospel because most scholars believe that chap. 21 is a later addition to the Gospel. Thus chap. 21 can be viewed as an epilogue.

15. Bultmann *(Theology of the New Testament,* 2:76) writes: "It would not violate Johannine meaning to add: faith is 'conversion' or 'repentance.'"

16. This statement does not mean that Jesus' death has no redemptive value in John's Gospel. Jesus' action of washing his disciples' feet points to the "cleansing" effect that his death will have for his disciples. For John, however, the revelation that Jesus, the eternal word of God, brings from the Father has redemptive value.

17. In John's Gospel Jesus and the Evangelist also speak of Jesus as the one who "came into the world" (3:19; 9:39; 11:27; 12:46; 16:28; 18:37), "came from the Father" or "from God" (8:42; 13:3; 16:27–28, 30; 17:8), or "has come" (5:43; 7:28; 8:14; 10:10; 12:47; 15:22). In this section I am limiting myself to those texts which speak of Jesus having been "sent" *(apostellō* or *pempō)* into the world.

18. Brown *(John,* 1:343–44), says that there was a ritual of lighting four golden candlesticks in the Court of the Women on the first night on the feast of Tabernacles, and that it was from this court that Jesus proclaimed that he is the light, not only of Jerusalem, but of the world.

19. This is the only occurrence in the Gospel of Jesus calling people to "believe in the light." It makes perfect sense, however, since Jesus is the light.

20. On the notion of truth in the Fourth Gospel, see Schnackenburg, *John,* excursus 10, "The Johannine Concept of Truth," 2:225–37, and the brief but informative article by I. De La Potterie, "The Truth in Saint John," in *The Interpretation of John,* ed. J. Ashton (Philadelphia: Fortress, 1986), 53–66.

21. On the notion of life in the Fourth Gospel, see Schnackenburg, *John,* excursus 12, "The Idea of Life in the Fourth Gospel," 2:352–61; and Ashton, *Understanding the Fourth Gospel,* 214–20.

22. Ashton *(Understanding the Fourth Gospel,* 216) writes: "In these passages eternity undoubtedly includes the notion of endlessness, but also (particularly at Qumran) a special quality of life peculiar to the new age. It is this special quality—not endlessness—that is suggested by John's term *zōē aiōnios,* which might therefore be translated 'the life of the new age.'"

23. John 1:12; 2:11, 33; 3:16, 18, 36; 4:39; 6:29, 35, 40; 7:5, 31, 38, 39, 48; 8:30; 9:35, 36; 10:42; 11:25, 26, 45, 48; 12:11, 36, 37, 42, 44, 46; 14:6, 12; 16:9; 17:20. Taken from Schnackenburg, *John,* 1:559–60.

24. In John 1:7, 50; 3:15, 18; 4:41, 42; 5:44; 6:36, 47; 9:38; 10:25, 26; 12:39; 14:11; 16:31; 20:8, 25, 29, 31 the content can be determined from the context. In 4:28, 53; 6:64; 11:15, 40; 14:29 the context is not so helpful. Taken from Schnackenburg, *John,* 1:561.

25. Jesus is the object in John 4:21; 5:38, 46; 6:30; 8:31, 45, 46; 10:37, 38; the words of Jesus in 2:22; 4:15; 5:47; the Father in 5:24; the scriptures in 2:22; Moses or his writings in 5:46, 47; and the works of Jesus in 10:38. Ibid., 562.

26. Jesus is in the Father and the Father is in him (John 14:10, 11), he comes from God (16:27), and the Father has sent him (11:42; 17:8, 21); Jesus is "I am" (8:24; 13:19). Ibid., 563.

27. Since the name stands for the person, to believe in the name of the only begotten Son of God is to believe in Jesus.

28. Jesus' use of *Egō eimi* ("I Am") is a revelation formula that points to his divine origin from God.

29. The "wrath of God" also plays an important role in Rom. 1:18–32. God's wrath toward sinners will be fully manifested at the end of the ages, but it is already being revealed against all wickedness and impiety, according to Paul.

30. Notice the reference to the future in this text. The believer has eternal life, but a future resurrection still awaits all believers.

31. This is a good example of "absolute faith." The royal official has seen a sign (4:48) and now believes. Included in this faith is faith in Jesus, and faith that Jesus comes from God.

32. This is why Jesus says, "If I have told you about earthly things and you do not believe, how can you believe if I tell you about heavenly things?" (John 3:12). Here the Johannine community speaks through the character of Nicodemus about the mystery of its baptismal experience.

33. On this point, see Brown, *Death of the Messiah,* 2:1265–68. He argues that Nicodemus provides Jesus with a royal burial.

34. On the theme of conversion in the Fourth Gospel, see Witherup, *Conversion,* 74–87. He points to Nicodemus, the Samaritan woman, and the man born blind as examples of people who are converted since they move from darkness to light.

35. On the offense of the incarnation of the Word, see Bultmann, *Theology of the New Testament,* 2:40–49.

36. On Jesus' farewell discourse, see the standard commentaries, especially those of Brown and Schnackenburg. F. F. Segovia, *The Farewell of the Word: The Johannine Call to Abide* (Minneapolis: Fortress, 1991), is especially helpful for a literary analysis of the discourse, and I am indebted to many of his insights.

37. On the genre of the farewell discourse, see Brown, *John,* 2:597–601; and Segovia, *Farewell of the Word,* 1–58.

38. Note that the discourse appears to end at John 14:31, only to resume in 15:1. The present form of the discourse is composed of at least two, if not more, versions of Jesus' farewell discourse (13:31–14:31 and 15:1–16:33). See the chart in Brown (*John,* 2:589–93), which shows the parallels between 13:31–14:31 and 16:4b-33.

39. The punishment of crucifixion was reserved for violent criminals, political rebels, and slaves who attempted to run away from their masters. By assuming the role of a slave when he washes the feet of his disciples, Jesus prefigures the "slave's death" of crucifixion by which he will cleanse them.

40. I am aware that these two interpretations probably represent different levels of tradition, but I am reading the text as a narrative that assigns both interpretations to Jesus.

41. The theme of humble service is a prominent aspect of discipleship in

the Synoptic Gospels. This is the only time, however, that the Johannine Jesus instructs his disciples to be servants to one another.

42. Noticeably absent from the Johannine discussion of love is any exhortation to love God. This omission, however, can be explained by John's theology: hearing and seeing Jesus means hearing and seeing the Father. Therefore, to love Jesus is to love the Father. The theme of loving God, however, does appear in the Johannine epistles.

43. Various forms of the verb *pisteuein* ("to believe") play a prominent role in John 14:1–14.

44. I am indebted to R. F. Collins (*Christian Morality: Biblical Foundations* [Notre Dame, Ind.: Univ. of Notre Dame Press, 1986], 113) for this insight.

45. On this point, see Furnish, *Love Command*, 137.

46. There does not appear to be any significant difference in the use of the singular or plural of *entolē*.

47. When the commandment appears in John 15:12, 17, it is no longer called a new commandment. While other versions of the farewell discourse (15:1–16:33) probably did not speak of the love commandment as new, the present form of the discourse presupposes that readers will recall Jesus' earlier description of this commandment as new. The author of 1 John 2:7–8 insists that he is not writing a new commandment but an old commandment that the community has heard from the beginning. In 2 John 5, the author is more explicit: "But now, dear lady, I ask you, not as though I were writing you a new commandment, but one we have had from the beginning, let us love one another." The old commandment is the new commandment that Jesus gives his disciples in the farewell discourse. For other references to the love commandment see 1 John 3:23; 4:21; and 5:2–3. In 4:21 and 5:2–3, love for one another and love for God are explicitly related in a way that they are not in the Gospel.

48. Lev. 19:34 suggests that the "neighbor" in Lev. 19:18 is one's fellow Israelite.

49. See Furnish, *Love Command*, 138. Brown (*John*, 2:614) suggests that the commandment is new because it is the commandment of the new covenant. He writes: "The newness of the commandment of love is really related to the theme of covenant at the Last Supper—the 'new commandment' of John xiii, 34 is the basic stipulation of the 'new covenant.'" John, however, never mentions covenant or new covenant.

50. Note that the Johannine Jesus does not speak of extending love toward one's enemy.

51. Jesus' words in John 15:25 ("It was to fulfill the word that is written *in their law*, 'They hated me without a cause'") suggest that in this section (15:18–16:4a) the world is viewed as the world of Jewish unbelief.

52. Precisely what is meant by this return (Jesus' resurrection? his parousia?) is not clear.

53. The use of *philein* for "love" instead of *agapein* suggests that there is no essential difference between these two verbs for John. The same verbs are used interchangeably in John 21:15–17.

54. This prayer, in which Jesus prays for future generations of disciples, suggests that the Johannine church did not look for an imminent parousia of its Lord.

Chapter 5: An Ethic of Election

1. (Introduction to Part Two.) I should note, however, that there is an important difference between the Gospels and Paul's own letters. Whereas the Gospels were written decades after Jesus' death, Paul's letters represent his teaching to a particular Christian community at the moment that he gave that instruction.

2. I say "among the earliest" because a number of scholars, especially those who follow a chronology based on Acts, argue that Paul wrote Galatians soon after his first missionary journey, *before* 1 Thessalonians. I, however, would date Galatians later than 1 Thessalonians.

3. See K. P. Donfried and I. H. Marshall, *The Theology of the Shorter Pauline Letters*, NTT (Cambridge: Cambridge Univ. Press, 1993). Donfried and Marshall (9–14) suggest a date as early as A.D. 41–44. I favor a date in the early 50s.

4. Respected conservative commentators F. F. Bruce and I. H. Marshall defend Pauline authorship in their commentaries. R. Jewett (*The Thessalonian Correspondence: Pauline Rhetoric and Millenarian Piety* [Philadelphia: Fortress, 1986]) argues that Paul is the author of 2 Thessalonians, on the basis of the social situation at Thessalonica, which he characterizes as millenarian radicalism. Donfried and Marshall (*Shorter Pauline Letters*, 86) believe that one of the coauthors of 1 Thessalonians, Timothy or Silvanus, may have been the author of 2 Thessalonians. Thus the letter would not be Pauline in the technical sense but written with Paul's knowledge shortly after the first letter.

5. On the paraenetic character of 1 Thessalonians, see A. J. Malherbe, "Exhortation in First Thessalonians," *NovT* 25 (1983) 238–56, and idem, *Paul and the Thessalonians: The Philosophic Tradition of Pastoral Care* (Philadelphia: Fortress, 1987). On the nature of paraenesis, see S. K. Stowers, *Letter Writing in Greco-Roman Antiquity*, Library of Early Christianity (Philadelphia: Westminster, 1986), 91–152. On the election theology of this letter, see J. Becker, *Paul: Apostle to the Gentiles* (Louisville, Ky.: Westminster John Knox, 1993), 130–40; and T. J. Deidun, *New Covenant Morality in Paul*, AnBib 89 (Rome: Biblical Institute Press, 1989), 18–28, 53–63, 86–89.

6. For the sake of convenience, I refer to "Paul" as the author of 2 Thessalonians.

7. This point is made by Becker, *Paul*, 130–40.

8. This distinction is made in an especially pointed way by Schulz, *Ethik*, 290–333. He views the teaching of 1 Thessalonians as an essentially Jewish ethic based upon the Mosaic law, a position Paul supposedly repudiated in his later and more mature letters. A more nuanced position is presented by U. Schnelle, "Die Ethik des 1 Thessalonicherbriefes," in *The Thessalonian Correspondence*, ed. R. F. Collins, BETL 87 (Louvain: Leuven Univ. Press, 1990), 295–305.

9. See K. P. Donfried, "1 Thessalonians, Acts and the Early Paul," in *Thessalonian Correspondence*, ed. Collins, 3–26.

10. This is probably a reference to the affliction that he suffered. See 1 Thess. 2:14–16, where he speaks of the Jews hindering him from speaking to the Gentiles so that they might be saved. Although this is a harsh passage, I do not view it as foreign to Paul's thought as do some who propose that it is a later insertion. It admirably fits the rhetorical strategy of this letter, which presents Paul as a model of one who endures affliction from his own people

in order to encourage the Thessalonians to bear affliction from their fellow countrymen.

11. For a description of the social conflict at Thessalonica and its cause, see J.M.G. Barclay, "Thessalonica and Corinth: Social Contrasts in Pauline Christianity," *JSNT* 47 (1992) 49–74.

12. What is lacking in their faith is a complete understanding of the parousia, a matter that Paul discusses in 1 Thess. 4:12–18.

13. For a careful comparison of the founding of the Thessalonian church as recounted by Paul and Luke, see D. Lührmann, "The Beginnings of the Church at Thessalonica," in *Greeks, Romans, and Christians: Essays in Honor of Abraham J. Malherbe*, ed. D. L. Balch, E. Ferguson, W. A. Meeks (Minneapolis: Fortress, 1990), 237–49.

14. See Malherbe, "Exhortation in First Thessalonians," from which I have taken the examples that follow.

15. Stowers (*Letter Writing*, 91–92) distinguishes between "protrepsis," which urges one to adopt a new and different way of life, and "paraenesis," which encourages or exhorts one to continue a certain way of life. On the basis of this distinction, Paul's original preaching at Thessalonica was protrepsis while this letter is paraenesis.

16. On the effects of conversion and the need for converts to be resocialized into a new community, see Malherbe, *Paul and the Thessalonians*, 34–60, and W. A. Meeks, *The Origins of Christian Morality: The First Two Centuries* (New Haven, Conn.: Yale Univ. Press, 1993), 18–36.

17. The term is used 19 times, most often of the Thessalonians (1 Thess. 1:4; 2:1, 9, 14, 17; 3:2, 7; 4:1, 6, 10, 13; 5:1, 4, 12, 14, 25, 26, 27).

18. On the rhetoric of 1 Thessalonians, see T. H. Olbricht, "An Aristotelian Rhetorical Analysis of 1 Thessalonians," in *Greeks, Romans, and Christians*, ed. Balch, Ferguson, and Meeks, 216–36; B. C. Johanson, *To All the Brethren: A Text-Linguistic and Rhetorical Approach to 1 Thessalonians*, ConBNT 16 (Stockholm: Almqvist & Wiksell International, 1987); F. W. Hughes, "The Rhetoric of First Thessalonians," 94–116, and W. Wuellner, "The Argumentative Structure of 1 Thessalonians as Paradoxical Encomium," 117–36, both in *Thessalonian Correspondence*, ed Collins.

19. I. H. Marshall, "Election and Calling to Salvation in 1 and 2 Thessalonians," in *Thessalonian Correspondence*, ed. Collins, 262.

20. So R. F. Collins, *The Birth of the New Testament: The Origin and Development of the First Christian Generation* (New York: Crossroad, 1993), 73.

21. So Donfried, "1 Thessalonians, Acts and the Early Paul," in *Thessalonian Correspondence*. ed. Collins, 19.

22. So Collins, *Birth*, 74.

23. On the theme of imitation in Thessalonians, see M. A. Getty, "The Imitation of Paul in the Letter to the Thessalonians," in *Thessalonian Correspondence*, ed. Collins, 277–83.

24. Malherbe, "Exhortation in First Thessalonians," 247.

25. *Ibid.*, 246.

26. Malherbe, *Paul and the Thessalonians*, 52–60.

27. Collins, *Birth*, 159–60.

28. On this point, see R. F. Collins, " 'This Is the Will of God: Your Sanctification' (1 Thess 4, 3)," in *Studies on the First Letter to the Thessalonians*, BETL 66

(Louvain: Leuven Univ. Press, 1984), 299–325; and Lührmann, "Beginnings of the Church at Thessalonica," in *Greeks, Romans, and Christians,* ed. Balch, Ferguson, and Meeks, 237–49.

29. The NRSV translates "how you ought to live," but I have attempted to maintain the biblical metaphor, which likens ethical conduct to "walking" in a particular way. See Psalm 1, which contrasts two ways of "walking" or behaving.

30. This biblical metaphor for the moral life occurs throughout the Pauline letters. See its use in Psalm 1.

31. *Greek-English Lexicon of the New Testament Based on Semantic Domains,* 2d ed., ed. J. P. Louw and E. Nida, 2 vols. (New York: United Bible Societies, 1988, 1989), 1:771.

32. The exact meaning of the Greek phrase *to heautou skeuos ktasthai* is a matter of debate. The NRSV translates "that each one of you know how to control your own body" but provides an alternate translation in the footnotes, "how to take a wife for himself." For a strong argument in favor of the latter translation, see Collins, " 'This Is the Will of God,' " 311–14. For an argument for the other translation, see Michael McGehee, "A Rejoinder to Two Recent Studies Dealing with 1 Thess 4:4," *CBQ* 51 (1989) 82–89. I have adopted the translation of the NRSV on the weight of arguments presented in this article, but the matter is not settled.

33. Malherbe (*Paul and the Thessalonians,* 104–5) thinks that Paul may be rejecting the Epicurean notion of being self-taught (*autodidaktos*). J. L. Kloppenborg ("*Philadelphia, Theodidaktos* and the Dioscuri: Rhetorical Engagement in 1 Thessalonians 4:9–12," *NTS* 39 [1993] 265–89) has recently suggested that Paul is alluding to the "nearly proverbial virtue of the Dioscuri, the divine twins, Castor and Polydeuces" (283).

34. Deidun (*New Covenant,* 57–58) understands the term in light of the biblical and rabbinic understanding of *didaskein.* Thus the Thessalonians' love for one another "is the effect of God's immediate and efficacious action at the very source of their moral personality" (58). Drawing upon the writings of Philo, C. J. Roetzel ("*Theodidaktoi* and Handiwork in Philo and 1 Thessalonians," in *L'Apôtre Paul: Personalité, style et conception du ministère,* ed. A. Vanhoye, BETL 73 [Louvain: Leuven Univ. Press, 1986], 324–31) argues that Paul uses the word in the same sense that Philo employs *autodidaktos:* to "refer to the person receiving his wisdom, virtues or knowledge directly from God and therefore needing no human teacher" (328).

35. Roetzel, "*Theodidaktoi* and Handiwork in Philo And 1 Thessalonians," 329–30.

36. On this point, see Malherbe, *Paul and the Thessalonians,* 88–94.

37. While the *ataktoi* ("the disorderly") present a major problem in 2 Thessalonians, that does not appear to be the case here.

38. G. S. Holland, " 'A Letter Supposedly from Us': A Contribution to the Discussion about the Authorship of 2 Thessalonians," in *Thessalonian Correspondence,* ed. Collins, 394–402. Holland himself views the letter as Deutero-Pauline.

39. See, for example, the treatment of this letter in Schulz, *Ethik,* 610–13, and Marxsen, *New Testament Foundations,* 250–55. Both authors treat these letters separately.

40. See B. N. Kaye, "Eschatology and Ethics in 1 and 2 Thessalonians," *NovT* 17 (1975) 47–57; R. Russell, "The Idle in 2 Thess 3.6–12: An Eschatological or a Social Problem?" *NTS* 34 (1988) 105–19; and M. J. J. Menken, "Paradise Regained or Still Lost? Eschatology and Disorderly Behavior in 2 Thessalonians," *NTS* 38 (1992) 271–89. Kaye and Russell maintain that the problem of the *ataktoi* is not related to that of the parousia. In Russell's view, the *ataktoi* are urban poor who were taking advantage of the generosity of their new benefactors within the community by not working. Menken argues on the contrary that the problem of the disorderly is related to that of the parousia. He attributes the behavior of the disorderly to a conviction that the parousia has taken place and paradise is being restored; thus there is no need to work. Jewett (*Thessalonian Correspondence*), who attributes their behavior to millenarian radicalism, has a somewhat similar view.

41. This point is made by Donfried and Marshall, *Shorter Pauline Letters*, 98–99.

42. Donfried and Marshall (*Shorter Pauline Letters*, 98) note that *parakaleō* occurs 8 times (2:12; 3:2, 7; 4:1, 10, 18; 5:11, 14) in the first letter but only 2 times in this letter (2:17; 3:12), whereas *paraggellō* is used only once in the first letter (4:11) but 4 times in the second (3:4, 6, 10, 12).

43. Marxsen, *New Testament Foundations*, 255.

Chapter 6: Ethics for the Sanctified Community

1. According to Acts, Paul went from Thessalonica to Beroea (17:10) to Athens (17:15) to Corinth (18:1), where he stayed for eighteen months (18:11). Since his ministry in Corinth overlapped with the consulship of Gallio (dated about A.D. 51–53), Paul probably established the Corinthian church in the early 50s. He wrote to the Corinthians in the mid-50s during the period of his ministry at Ephesus in Asia Minor (see Acts 18:24–19:41). Luke says nothing about Paul's letter writing.

2. On Paul's moral reasoning, see the stimulating work of J. P. Sampley, *Walking between the Times: Paul's Moral Reasoning* (Minneapolis: Fortress, 1991). Also helpful is R. F. O'Toole, *Who Is a Christian?*: A Study of Pauline Ethics (Collegeville, Minn.: Liturgical Press, 1990).

3. In addition to the works of Sampley and O'Toole, see J. W. Drane, *Paul, Libertine or Legalist? A Study in the Theology of the Major Pauline Epistles* (London: SPCK, 1975); and P. Richardson, *Paul's Ethic of Freedom* (Philadelphia: Westminster, 1979).

4. On this point, see Becker (*Paul*). He defends the unity of 1 Corinthians (187–97) but argues for the composite nature of 2 Corinthians (216–21).

5. Note the frequent occurrence of the expression "now concerning" (7:1; 8:1; 12:1; 16:1), which suggests that Paul is taking up a topic raised by the Corinthians in their letter to him.

6. Here I am summarizing Becker, *Paul*, 216–21.

7. Here I am following V. P. Furnish (*II Corinthians*, AB 32A [Garden City, N.Y.: Doubleday, 1984], 29–55), who argues for a two-letter hypothesis: 2 Corinthians 1—9 followed by 2 Corinthians 10—13. A similar line is taken by J. Murphy-O'Connor, *The Theology of the Second Letter to the Corinthians*, NTT (Cambridge: Cambridge Univ. Press, 1991), 10–17.

8. Romans, Galatians, Philippians, 1 and 2 Thessalonians, Colossians, and Ephesians have more clearly defined sections in which Paul exhorts his readers to live in a particular way, but even in these letters doctrine and ethical teaching are never separated from each other.

9. On this point, see Deidun, *New Covenant,* 12–14 and 28–32, and F. Theilman, *Paul and the Law: A Contextual Approach* (Downers Grove, Ill.: InterVarsity, 1994), 80–99.

10. So Deidun, *New Covenant,* 12.

11. On the theme of *koinōnia,* see J. Reumann, "Koinonia in Scripture: Survey of Biblical Texts," in *On the Way to Fuller Koinonia: Official Report of the Fifth World Conference on Faith and Order,* ed. T. F. Best and G. Gassmann, Faith and Order Paper no. 166 (Geneva: WCC Publications, 1994), 37–69.

12. On the problems that Paul faced, see G. D. Fee, *The First Epistle to the Corinthians,* NICNT (Grand Rapids: Eerdmans, 1987), 4–15. For a discussion of the four factions mentioned in 1 Cor. 1:12, see C. K. Barrett, "Christianity at Corinth," in *Essays on Paul* (Philadelphia: Westminster, 1982), 28–39.

13. This does not mean that the Corinthian community comprised only people from the lower classes of society. There were well-to-do members who housed and supported the church. See A. J. Malherbe, *Social Aspects of Early Christianity,* 2d ed. (Philadelphia: Fortress, 1983), 60–91.

14. On the Christian community as the temple of God, see M. Newton, *The Concept of Purity at Qumran and in the Letters of Paul,* SNTSMS 53 (Cambridge: Cambridge Univ. Press, 1985), esp. 52–78. The theme is also treated by Theilman, *Paul and the Law,* 91–98.

15. On the hardship lists in the Corinthian correspondence, see J. T. Fitzgerald, *Cracks in an Earthen Vessel: An Examination of the Catalogues of Hardships in the Corinthian Correspondence,* SBLDS 99 (Atlanta: Scholars, 1988).

16. This is the implication of Paul's statement, "We have become like the rubbish of the world, the dregs of all things, to this very day" (1 Cor. 4:13).

17. For a study of this section in light of Greco-Roman moral philosophy, see B. Fiore, "Passion in Paul and Plutarch: 1 Corinthians 5—6 and the Polemic against Epicureans," in *Greeks, Romans, and Christians,* ed. Balch, Ferguson, and Meeks, 135–43. For a careful exegesis of the material, see Fee, *Corinthians.*

18. See 1 Cor. 5:6; 6:2, 3, 9, 15, 16, 19.

19. In Deuteronomy the phrase is used in reference to the following: Deut. 13:5 (the false prophet); 17:7 (the idolater); 19:19 (the false witness); 21:21 (the incorrigible son); 22:21 (the unfaithful bride); 24:7 (the kidnapper).

20. That Paul says nothing about the woman may suggest that she was not a Christian.

21. On this passage, see Fee, *Corinthians,* 214–20.

22. On the social setting for this dispute, see A. Mitchell, "Rich and Poor in the Courts of Corinth: Litigiousness and Status in 1 Corinthians 6:1–11," *NTS* 39 (1993) 562–86.

23. On the tradition that God's holy ones will share in the eschatological judgment, see Dan. 7:9, 22; Wisd. Sol. 3:7–8; 5:3; 12:33; Matt. 19:28; Luke 22:38; Rev. 20:4; 1 Enoch 1:9; 38:1; Jub. 23:30; 24:29.

24. The kingdom of God is a major theme in Jesus' preaching but does not occur frequently in the Pauline writings. See Rom. 14:17; 1 Cor. 4:20; 6:9, 10; 15:24, 50; Gal. 5:21; 1 Thess. 2:12; 2 Thess. 1:5; Eph. 5:5; Col. 1:13, 14; 2 Tim. 4:1,

18. In these writings the kingdom is clearly a future reality that has implications for the present ethical life of the believer.

25. The list is not intended to be exhaustive but undoubtedly has in view the kind of conduct Paul wishes to correct. On the difficult phrase *oute malakoi oute arsenokoitai,* which the NRSV translates as "male prostitutes, sodomites," see L. C. Broughton, "Biblical Texts and Homosexuality: A Response to John Boswell," *ITQ* 58 (1992) 121–53; V. Furnish, *The Moral Teaching of Paul: Selected Issues,* 2d ed. (Nashville: Abingdon, 1989), 67–72; and Fee, *Corinthians,* 243–44. I am of the opinion that Paul has adult homosexuals and the young boy prostitutes who service them in view.

26. In 3:16 Paul had already told the Corinthians that they are the temple of God. Here, he seems to have the body of each believer in view. While in tension with each other, the two ideas are not contradictory. The community is God's temple because the Spirit dwells in each believer. The emphasis upon the Spirit dwelling in each believer is especially helpful to Paul's argument against prostitution.

27. This represents a slogan of the Corinthian ascetics that Paul modifies in the first part of this chapter (1 Cor. 7:1–7). Therefore, when he writes, "This I say by way of concession, not of command" (7:6), the concession refers to sexual abstinence rather than to sexual relations. Paul does not view sexuality so negatively as some suppose.

28. The Greek text employs the imperative here, *echetō.* Therefore, 1 Cor. 7:2 could be translated, "let each man *take* his own wife and each woman *take* her own husband."

29. The meaning of Paul's exhortation to slaves (*mallon chrēsai*) is not clear. It could mean "if you can gain your freedom, *make use of your present condition now more than ever,*" or, "*avail yourself of the opportunity.*" In the first instance, Paul would not be encouraging slaves to seek their freedom, in the second he would. On the difficulty of interpreting Paul's attitude in the matter of slavery, see J. Barclay, "Paul, Philemon and the Dilemma of Christian Slave-Ownership," *NTS* 37 (1991) 161–86.

30. On Paul's teaching about divorce, see Collins, *Divorce,* 9–64, and O. L. Yarbrough, *Not Like the Gentiles: Marriage Rules in the Letters of Paul,* SBLDS 80 (Atlanta: Scholars, 1985), 89–122.

31. Holiness here does not refer to an ethical quality. Rather, unbelievers participate in the consecrated status of the community through their spouse.

32. "Stronger" and "weaker" refer to the moral sensitivity of people. Since some members of the community were stronger in their faith convictions, they felt freer in regard to their actions. W. L. Willis (*Idol Meat in Corinth: The Pauline Argument in 1 Corinthians 8 and 10,* SBLDS 68 [Chico, Calif.: Scholars, 1985], 277) writes that the weak in conscience, "had a poor understanding of the Christian faith."

33. Especially helpful for understanding this chapter are Willis, *Idol Meat;* and C. K. Barrett, "Things Sacrificed to Idols," in *Essays on Paul,* 40–59. Also useful is the essay of S. K. Stowers, "Paul on the Use and Abuse of Reason," in *Greeks, Romans, and Christians,* ed. Balch, Ferguson, and Meeks, 253–86.

34. For Paul, conscience (*syneidēsis*) refers to a moral awareness or consciousness of good and evil. See Willis, *Idol Meat,* 89–96.

35. Ibid., 81. He makes a similar point regarding freedom. Paul is not

merely limiting freedom by love. "Rather for Paul love is an act of freedom" (294).

36. On the use of *koinōnia* in this section, see Reumann, "Koinonia in Scripture," 42–44; and Willis, *Idol Meat*, 182–212.

37. C. K. Barrett, *A Commentary on the First Epistle to the Corinthians*, Harper's New Testament Commentaries (New York: Harper & Row, 1968), 299. The same point is made by C. R. Holladay in his stimulating essay "1 Corinthians 13: Paul as Apostolic Paradigm," in *Greeks, Romans, and Christians*, ed. Balch, Ferguson, and Meeks, 80–98, esp. 80–82. My decision to view this passage as paradigmatic for Paul's ministry is indebted to this essay.

38. Barrett (*First Corinthians*, 299–300) suggests that Paul viewed the unintelligible speech called "tongues" as the language of angels.

39. Holladay, "1 Corinthians 13," esp. 88–94.

40. Holladay, "1 Corinthians 13," 89.

41. I have drawn most of these citations from Holladay, "1 Corinthians 13," 89–91. For an argument on behalf of the reading "so that I may boast" in 1 Cor. 13:3, rather than "to be burned," see B. M. Metzger, *A Textual Commentary on the Greek New Testament* (New York: United Bible Societies, 1971), 563–64.

42. Holladay ("1 Corinthians 13," 95) gives a more detailed listing of references.

43. Fitzgerald, *Earthen Vessel*, 147. In this section, I am indebted to many of Fitzgerald's insights about the ethical importance of Paul's apostolic sufferings.

44. As noted in the introduction to this chapter, some view 2 Cor. 1:1–2:13; 7:5–16; 8:1–9:13 as the *last* in a series of letters sent to the Corinthians. I, however, have chosen to read the letter in its canonical order.

45. Paul altered his plans because he had been badly treated at Corinth during his second visit, leading him to write a harsh letter to the community. Since he and the community were not yet reconciled, the time was not opportune for the promised visit (2 Cor. 2:1–4).

46. See C. K. Barrett, "Paul's Opponents in 2 Corinthians," and "PSEUDA-POSTOLOI (2 Cor. 11.13)," in *Essays on Paul*, 60–117.

47. For a discussion of Paul's afflictions in terms of Jewish and Hellenistic background, see S. R. Garrett, "The God of This World and the Affliction of Paul: 2 Cor 4:1–12," in *Greeks, Romans, and Christians*, ed. Balch, Ferguson, and Meeks, 99–117.

48. Murphy-O'Connor (*Second Corinthians*, 45) says that by this image Paul compares himself to a wrestler in the grips of a more skilled opponent.

49. For a detailed discussion of this important term, see Fitzgerald, *Earthen Vessel*, 177–80.

50. The verb *paradidometha* (2 Cor. 4:11) can be taken as passive or middle. Fitzgerald (*Earthen Vessel*, 180) makes a convincing case for taking it as passive.

51. These points are made by Fitzgerald, *Earthen Vessel*, 166 and 171.

52. I am indebted to Fitzgerald (*Earthen Vessel*, 184–201) at this point. In my arrangement of the material, I have slightly altered the translation of the NRSV.

53. On the literary genre of this material, see J. T. Fitzgerald, "Paul, the Ancient Epistolary Theorists, and 2 Corinthians 10—13," in *Greeks, Romans, and Christians*, ed. Balch, Ferguson, and Meeks, 190–200.

54. Whether or not these false apostles are to be equated with the superlative apostles (2 Cor. 11:5; 12:11) is disputed. See the essays of Barrett listed in n. 46.

55. See A. J. Malherbe ("Antisthenes and Odysseus, and Paul at War," in *Paul and the Popular Philosophers* [Minneapolis: Fortress, 1989], 91–119) for a detailed explanation of this imagery.

Chapter 7: Walking by the Spirit

1. "Righteousness" (*dikaiosynē*) occurs in 1 Cor. 1:30; 2 Cor. 3:9; 5:21; 6:7, 14; 9:9, 10; 11:15. The verb "to justify" (*dikaioō*) occurs only in 1 Cor. 4:4; 6:11. Neither word is found in the Thessalonian correspondence. As for "law" (*nomos*), it occurs in 1 Cor. 9:8, 9, 20 (4 times); 14:21, 34; 15:56 but is absent from 2 Corinthians and the Thessalonian correspondence. To be sure, Paul states that he is no longer under the law, but he also emphasizes that he is not free from God's law (1 Cor. 9:20–21). He describes himself as *ennomos Christou* ("under Christ's law"). While maintaining that circumcision and uncircumcision are matters of indifference, he insists that "obeying the commandments of God is everything" (1 Cor. 7:19).

2. The two approaches, of course, are not opposed to each other. As I have already noted in chap. 5, the language of election and sanctification implies justification inasmuch as the sanctified community stands in a right relationship to God on the basis of the Christ event.

3. As B. C. Lategan ("Is Paul Developing a Specifically Christian Ethics in Galatians?" in *Greeks, Romans, and Christians,* ed. Balch, Ferguson, and Meeks, 318–28) notes, Paul is not presenting a systematic Christian ethic here. What he writes in this letter, however, is more theologically developed than what is found in the Thessalonian and Corinthian correspondence.

4. This is the approach of most commentaries. For example F. F. Bruce, *The Epistle to the Galatians: A Commentary on the Greek Text,* NIGTC (Grand Rapids: Eerdmans, 1982), and T. George, *Galatians,* NAC (Nashville: Broadman, 1994). George's commentary is written, in part, as a response to the new perspective. Two important responses to the new perspective are T. R. Schreiner, *The Law and Its Fulfillment: A Pauline Theology of Law* (Grand Rapids: Baker, 1993), and Thielman, *Paul and the Law.*

5. The names most associated with this new perspective are those of E. P. Sanders, *Paul and Palestinian Judaism: A Comparison of Patterns of Religion* (Philadelphia: Fortress, 1977); idem, *Paul, the Law, and the Jewish People* (Philadelphia: Fortress, 1983); and J.D.G. Dunn, *Jesus, Paul, and the Law: Studies in Mark and Galatians* (Louisville, Ky.: Westminster John Knox, 1990); idem, *The Epistle to the Galatians,* BNTC (Peabody, Mass.: Hendrickson, 1993); idem, *The Theology of Paul's Letter to the Galatians,* NTT (Cambridge: Cambridge Univ. Press, 1993). Also important is the recent work of H. Boers, *The Justification of the Gentiles: Paul's Letters to the Galatians and Romans* (Peabody, Mass.: Hendrickson, 1994).

6. J.D.G. Dunn, "The Justice of God: A Renewed Perspective on Justification by Faith," *JTS* 43 (1992) 1–22, p. 15.

7. J.M.G. Barclay, *Obeying the Truth: A Study of Paul's Ethics in Gala-*

tians, Studies of the New Testament and Its World (Edinburgh: T. & T. Clark, 1988), 8.

8. I have already employed this approach in my commentary, *Galatians,* Sacra Pagina 9 (Collegeville, Minn.: Liturgical Press, 1992).

9. There are divergent opinions regarding the date and occasion of Galatians. My own position, as well as a summary of other approaches, is found in *Galatians,* 1–26. In my view, the Galatian churches were the congregations of Antioch in Pisidia, Iconium, Lystra, and Derbe that Paul and Barnabas founded on their first missionary journey, according to the Acts of the Apostles. Although I espouse the South Galatian hypothesis, I think that the letter was written during the period of Paul's Ephesian ministry, near the mid-50s. As for the agitators or Judaizers, I view them as Jewish Christians from Jerusalem, perhaps aligned with the group that confronted Peter at Antioch.

10. In making this statement I am *not* suggesting that the agitators advocated salvation by doing the works of the law.

11. This point is made by Barclay, *Obeying the Truth,* 73.

12. Barclay (*Obeying the Truth,* 9–12) provides a brief review of those who espouse this view. His own work shows the intimate connection between this moral exhortation and the rest of the letter. See his conclusion, 216–17.

13. The traditional interpretation of this text is faith *in* Christ. In recent years, some have suggested that Paul is referring to the faith *of* Christ, that is, the faithfulness toward God that Jesus manifested in his life and death. On the basis of this faith, one believes *in* Christ. The most detailed argument on behalf of this position is made by R. B. Hays, *The Faith of Jesus Christ: An Investigation of the Narrative Substructure of Galatians 3:1–4:11,* SBLDS 56 (Chico, Calif.: Scholars, 1983). I have employed this concept in my commentary; see *Galatians,* esp. 92–104.

14. *Erga nomou* ("works of the law") does not occur in the Old Testament. Recently a parallel has been found in the literature of Qumran. See J. A. Fitzmyer, "Paul's Jewish Background and the Deeds of the Law," in *According to Paul: Studies in the Theology of the Apostle* (New York: Paulist, 1993), 18–35; and M. Abegg, "Paul, 'Works of the Law' and MMT," *BARev* 20 (1994) 52–55. The text of 4QMMT shows that "works of the law" refers to the prescriptions of the Mosaic law. What is not clear is the significance that Paul attached to the works of the law. Does he view them as markers of Jewish identity as the new perspective on Paul maintains, or as attempts to gain one's own righteousness as the traditional Reformation view holds?

15. I do not wish to imply that such an attitude would have been acceptable to Paul; I am simply stating that this was not Paul's primary concern in this letter.

16. So Becker, *Paul,* 278.

17. B. H. Brinsmead, *Galatians—Dialogical Response to Opponents,* SBLDS 65 (Chico, Calif.: Scholars, 1982), 165. Also see Marxsen, *New Testament Foundations,* 142–227.

18. Here, I suspect that "us" refers to the Jewish people who were under this curse. In effect, Paul says, Christ redeemed *us* from the curse, therefore do not put yourselves under the curse from which Christ redeemed us.

19. On the law in Galatians, see Dunn, "Works of the Law and Curse of the Law (Gal. 3.10–14)," in *Jesus, Paul, and the Law,* 215–41; In-Gyu Hong, *The*

Law in Galatians, JSNTSS 81 (Sheffield: Sheffield Academic Press, 1993); Thielman, *Paul and the Law*, 119–44; Sanders, *Paul, the Law, and the Jewish People*, 3–167; and Schreiner, *The Law and Its Fulfillment*.

20. On the image of the *paidagōgos*, see N. H. Young, *"PAIDAGŌGOS:* The Social Setting of a Pauline Metaphor," *NovT* 39 (1987) 150–76.

21. On this point, see R. Jewett, "The Agitators and the Galatian Congregation," *NTS* 17 (1971) 198–212. He argues that Jewish Christians persecuted fellow Christians "to avert the suspicion that they were in communion with lawless Gentiles" (205).

22. Barclay, *Obeying the Truth*, 139.

23. Paul views the law as a totality and does not explicitly make the distinction between its moral and ritual aspects, as most modern Christians do. De facto, however, his approach to the law leads to such a distinction.

24. Other examples of *sarx* used in a neutral sense are Gal. 2:16; 3:3; 4:13; 4:14, 23, 29; 6:12, 13.

25. C. K. Barrett (*Freedom and Obligation: A Study of the Epistle to the Galatians* [Philadelphia: Westminster, 1985], 73) writes, "Flesh, therefore, defined by its opposite, means self-centered existence; egocentric existence; . . . faith looks away from the self and its achievements to God as the centre of its trust; love looks away from the self and its wishes, even its real needs, to the neighbor, and spends its resources on his needs."

26. Hong, *Law in Galatians*, 185.

27. On the law of Christ, see the thorough discussion in Barclay, *Obeying the Truth*, 125–45, and the helpful article by R. B. Hays, "Christology and Ethics in Galatians: The Law of Christ," *CBQ* 49 (1987) 268–90.

28. The closest parallel is 1 Cor. 9:21, where Paul speaks of being under Christ's law (*ennomos Christou*); the Greek phrase in Gal. 6:2 is *ton nomon tou Christou*.

Chapter 8: An Ethic of Imitation and Example

1. On this point, see J. Brant, "The Place of *Memēsis* in Paul's Thought," *SR* 22 (1993) 285–300; Collange, *"De Jésus à Paul,* 197–204; O. Merk, "Nachahmung Christi: Zu ethischen Perspektiven in der paulinischen Theologie," in *Neues Testament und Ethik: Für Rudolf Schnackenburg*, ed. H. Merklein (Freiburg: Herder, 1989), 172–206; and D. Stanley, "Imitation in Paul's Letters: Its Significance for His Relationship to Jesus and to His Own Christian Foundations," in *From Jesus to Paul: Studies in Honor of Francis Wright Beare*, ed. P. Richardson and J. C. Hurd (Waterloo, Ontario, Canada: Wilfrid Laurier University Press, 1984), 127–41.

2. In addition to the standard commentaries on Philippians, see the helpful article of J. T. Fitzgerald, "Philippians, Epistle to the," *ABD*, 5:318–26. Fitzgerald offers a fair presentation of the major positions as well as a helpful bibliography. He sides with those who espouse the literary integrity of the letter and views Philippians as a letter of friendship. As for date and place of origin, the letter was most likely written in either Ephesus (52/53–55/56) or Rome (58–60, the earlier part of Paul's imprisonment, or 60–62, the latter part of the same imprisonment). Fitzgerald favors a Roman origin.

3. Marshall, "The Theology of Philippians," in Donfried and Marshall, *Shorter Pauline Letters*, 119.

4. For example, Becker (*Paul*, 307–15) speaks of two letters: Letter A (1:1–3:1; 4:1–7, 10–23) and Letter B (3:2–21; 4:8–9). Letter A would have been written from prison in Ephesus about 54/55 and Letter B from Greece about 56, shortly before Paul wrote his letter to the Romans. P. Perkins ("Philippians: Theology for the Heavenly Politeuma," in *Pauline Theology, vol. 1, Thessalonians, Philippians, Galatians, Philemon*, ed. J. M. Bassler [Minneapolis: Fortress, 1991], 89) speaks of "a receipt for aid received (4:10–20); a letter on the impending disposition of Paul's case (1:1–3:1; 4:2–7, [8–9]); and a warning against judaizing preachers (3:2–4:1; 8–9)." She does not identity these letters further in terms of time and place.

5. This, of course, raises a further question: Does this new literary setting alter the original meaning of Paul's earlier letters? Given the fact that texts are interpreted within a literary context, I would argue that supposed earlier letters have received a new meaning in their canonical setting.

6. For an argument based upon rhetorical analysis, see D. F. Watson, "A Rhetorical Analysis of Philippians and Its Implications for the Unity Question," *NovT* 30 (1988) 57–88; for studies based on epistolary theology, see L. Alexander, "Hellenistic Letter-Forms and the Structure of Philippians," *JSNT* 37 (1989) 87–101; S. Stowers, "Friends and Enemies in the Politics of Heaven: Reading Theology in Philippians," in *Pauline Theology*, ed. Bassler, 105–21; L. M. White, "Morality between Two Worlds: A Paradigm of Friendship in Philippians," in *Greeks, Romans, Christians*, ed. Balch, Ferguson, and Meeks, 201–15. For arguments based on literary and thematic analysis, see W. J. Dalton, "The Integrity of Philippians," *Bib* 60 (1979) 97–102; D. E. Garland, "The Composition and Unity of Philippians: Some Neglected Factors," *NovT* 27 (1985) 140–73; W. S. Kurz, "Kenotic Imitation of Paul and of Christ in Philippians 2 and 3," in *Discipleship in the New Testament*, ed. F. F. Segovia (Philadelphia: Fortress, 1985); and A. B. Luter and M. V. Lee, "Philippians as Chiasmus: Key to the Structure, Unity and Theme Questions," *NTS* 41 (1995) 89–101.

7. As to date and place, I suppose that the letter was written either from Ephesus during the mid-50s, or from Rome in the late 50s, or even early 60s. I know of no way to adjudicate in a convincing manner between these possibilities.

8. This question must be answered even by those who view Philippians as a composite letter, since the purported editor of our canonical Philippians undoubtedly edited the material with a particular goal in view.

9. The fact that Paul warns the Philippians against Judaizers (3:2–11) indicates the Gentile makeup of this congregation.

10. This does not mean that the Philippians are in prison with Paul. Rather, they have shared in his imprisonment by assisting him.

11. At this point Paul is talking about his situation at Rome or Ephesus, not the situation at Philippi.

12. Paul's attitude toward those who preach from envy and selfishness suggests that, although they preach Christ for the wrong motives, they do not necessarily preach a false gospel as did, for example, the agitators at Galatia.

13. P. T. O'Brien, *The Epistle to the Philippians*, NIGTC (Exeter: Paternoster, 1990), 143.

14. Notice that this section is filled with athletic imagery. The Philippians must contend (*synathlountes*) as one in their struggle (*agōna*) just as athletes must contend in their athletic contests.

15. Note that in Phil. 3:10 Paul seeks to know Christ and the power of his resurrection and the sharing of his sufferings (*koinōnian tōn pathēmatōn*).

16. O'Brien, *Philippians*, 165.

17. Of the 26 occurrences of the verb in the New Testament, 10 are found in Philippians (1:7; 2:2 [twice]; 2:5; 3:15 [twice]; 3:19: 4:2; 4:10 [twice]).

18. This verse presents a problem of translation for all who seek to interpret it, since a verb must be supplied. Translated literally, it reads, "Think this among you which even in Christ Jesus." To make sense of the text, something must be supplied, e.g., "Think this among you which even *was* in Christ Jesus," or "Think this among you that you *have* in Christ Jesus." While the former translation implies that Christ is to be imitated in some fashion, the latter does not. Rather, it suggests that there is an appropriate kind of action for those who are in the realm of Christ. While aware that the debate continues, I have adopted the former translation. See C.F.D. Moule, "Further Reflections on Philippians 2:5–11," in *Apostolic History and the Gospel: Biblical and Historical Essays Presented to F. F. Bruce on His Sixtieth Birthday*, ed. W. W. Gasque and R. P. Martin (Grand Rapids: Eerdmans, 1970), 264–76; and L. W. Hurtado, "Jesus as Lordly Example in Philippians 2:5–11," in *From Jesus to Paul*, ed. Richardson and Hurd, 113–26.

19. Here I am following the translation of *harpagmon* suggested by Moule, "Further Reflections," 266.

20. Note that this section also began with a reference to Paul's absence and presence (Phil. 1:27).

21. On this section and the election theology it contains, see R. P. Martin, *Philippians*, NCB (Grand Rapids: Eerdmans, 1980), 104–6.

22. On the identity of Paul's opponents, see C. L. Mearns, "The Identity of Paul's Opponents at Philippi," *NTS* 33 (1987) 194–204; and M. Tellbe, "The Sociological Factors behind Philippians 3.1–11 and the Conflict at Philippi," *JSNT* 55 (1994) 97–128. For the view that chap. 3 is Deutero-Pauline and that the text is not responding to a real problem at Philippi, see D. J. Doughty, "Citizens of Heaven: Philippians 3.2–21," *NTS* 41 (1995) 102–22. L. T. Johnson (*The Writings of the New Testament* [Philadelphia: Fortress, 1986], 346) makes an interesting point: "The literary function of 3:2–16, which is so often considered a polemic against false teachers, is that of a counterexample, used to highlight the positive model. One reason the historical delineation of Paul's opponents in Philippians is so difficult is that they may not be *his* opponents at all."

23. "The same things," of course, could refer to what Paul has said above, but I have taken it with what follows: Paul's teaching about righteousness based on faith.

24. For a detailed study of the relationship between this chapter and the Christ hymn, see Kurz, "Kenotic Imitation of Paul and Christ." For a study of the theme of imitation in chap. 3 in light of justification by faith, as well as a helpful history of research on the imitation theme in Paul, see Reumann, "Justification and the *Imitatio* Motif in Philippians," in *Promoting Unity: Themes in Lutheran-Catholic Dialogue*, ed. H. George Anderson and James R. Crumley, Jr. (Minneapolis: Augsburg, 1989), 17–28.

25. This is the opinion of Garland ("Composition and Unity of Philippians," 173), who writes: "It is my contention that Paul carefully and covertly wove his argument to lead up to the impassioned summons in 4:2. He wrote primarily to defuse the dispute between these two women that was having disastrous repercussions for the unity of the church."

26. The words of Lategan ("Is Paul Developing a Specifically Christian Ethics in Galatians?" 327) are applicable here: "Paul reaches beyond the constraints of place and time, and in doing so, he demonstrates that it is a message that functions not only in a Palestinian environment but also in a Hellenistic context, giving hope for generations to come."

Chapter 9: The Obedience of Faith

1. J. A. Fitzmyer, *Romans: A New Translation with Introduction and Commentary*, AB 33 (New York: Doubleday, 1993), 87. For a full discussion of the letter's date and place of composition with accompanying bibliography, see pp. 85–88.

2. For example, G. Bornkamm, "The Letter to the Romans as Paul's Last Will and Testament," in *The Romans Debate: Revised and Expanded Edition*, ed. K. P. Donfried (Peabody, Mass.: Hendrickson, 1991), 16–28. The first edition of this book appeared as *The Romans Debate* (Minneapolis: Augsburg, 1977). All references are to the revised and expanded edition, which contains the original articles as well as several new studies.

3. This debate is conveniently chronicled in Donfried, *The Romans Debate*.

4. In speaking of the Roman church, I am not implying that there was a single congregation at Rome. It is more likely that the Roman church consisted of several house churches, not all of which understood the implications of their new faith as did Paul and those who followed him. See the following articles in Donfried, *The Romans Debate*: A.J.M. Wedderburn, "Purpose and Occasion of Romans Again," 195–202; F. Watson, "The Two Roman Congregations: Romans 14:1–15:13," 203–15; and P. Lampe, "The Roman Christians of Romans 16," 216–30.

5. This way of viewing the issue, the distinction between Paul's own concerns and the concerns of the Roman congregation, is made by G. Klein, "Paul's Purpose in Writing the Epistle to the Romans," in *The Romans Debate*, ed. Donfried, 29–43.

6. This particular term is employed by Fitzmyer, *Romans*, 69.

7. H. D. Betz ("The Foundations of Christian Ethics according to Romans 12:1–2," in *Witness and Existence: Essays in Honor of Schubert M. Ogden*, ed. P. E. Devenish and G. L. Goodwin [Chicago: Univ. of Chicago Press, 1989], 55–72) argues that in dealing with criticism, "Paul subjected his entire theology to substantial revision and expansion" (61). Romans, therefore, presents his developed theology, especially as regards ethical matters.

8. In what follows I am indebted, in part, to A.J.M. Wedderburn, *The Reasons for Romans* (Minneapolis: Fortress, 1991).

9. Ibid., 50. On the origins of the Roman church, see Becker, *Paul*, 333–40.

10. Wedderburn, *Reasons for Romans*, 50.

11. One immediately thinks of believers such as Prisca and Aquila (Rom. 16:3; see 1 Cor. 16:19 and Acts 18).

12. This is the thesis of Watson, "Two Roman Congregations."

13. The word "church" appears only in Rom. 16:1, 4, 5, 16, 23. Of these uses, only 16:5 refers to the church at Rome, and in this case the reference is to the church in a particular house ("Greet also the church in their [Prisca and Aquila's] house").

14. The tensions between these groups were probably exacerbated by Claudius's expulsion of the Jews (and Jewish Christians) from Rome in A.D. 49. When Jewish Christians finally returned to Rome, they undoubtedly found a more vibrant and assertive Gentile Christianity.

15. See F. Vouga, "L'épître aux Romains comme document ecclésiologique (RM 12—15)," *ETR* 61 (1986), 485–95. He argues that Paul writes with the hope that the Romans will send him as a delegate to Spain.

16. In my view, when Paul refers to homosexuality, he is not speaking of an orientation toward a particular kind of sexual behavior with which a person is born but a kind of sexual behavior that is freely chosen, whether a person be, by nature, homosexual or heterosexual. Paul, I suspect, would find the contemporary understanding of homosexuality as an orientation quite puzzling.

17. C.E.B. Cranfield (*A Critical and Exegetical Commentary on The Epistle to the Romans,* 2 vols. [Edinburgh: T.& T. Clark, 1975, 1979], 1:151–53) lists, discusses, and evaluates ten proposals for interpreting Rom. 2:6–11. For a recent attempt to solve the problem, see Schreiner, "Did Paul Teach Justification by Works?" in *The Law and Its Fulfillment,* 179–204.

18. On the theme of judgment in Paul's writings, see K. P. Donfried, "Justification and Last Judgement in Paul," *ZNW* 67 (1976) 90–110.

19. Paul exegetes the second part of the text ("and it was reckoned to him as righteousness") in the first half of Romans 4 (4:1–12) and the first part of the text ("Abraham believed God") in the second half of the chapter (4:13–25).

20. See P. J. Achtemeier, *Romans,* Interpretation (Atlanta: John Knox, 1985), 102–3.

21. Here Paul probably has in mind the obedience of Christ, the new Adam, described in 5:12–21, who provides the pattern of obedience for the believer.

22. By this expression Paul understands the whole human person.

23. So Fitzmyer, *Romans,* 458; and J.D.G. Dunn, *Romans,* 2 vols., WBC (Dallas: Word, 1988), vol. 38A:362.

24. Notice that Paul has a more positive view of the law in Romans than in Galatians.

25. On the centrality of God in the letter to the Romans, see L. Morris, "The Theme of Romans," in *Apostolic History and the Gospel,* ed. Gasque and Martin, 249–63.

26. Achtemeier, *Romans,* 193.

27. Dunn, *Romans 9—16,* vol. 38B:705.

28. Fitzmyer, *Romans,* 637.

29. I emphasize that this is my view, since many scholars understand the moral exhortation of Romans rather as general paraenesis. See R. J. Karris, "Romans 14:1–15:13 and the Occasion of Romans," in *The Romans Debate,* ed. Donfried, 65–84; and Vouga, "L'épître aux Romains."

30. This point is forcefully argued by Wedderburn, *Reasons for Romans,* 75–87. Also helpful is J. Moiser, "Rethinking Romans 12—15," *NTS* 36 (1990)

571–82, although I do not agree with the manner in which he has structured the material.

31. My outline is indebted to the work of Wedderburn, *Reasons for Romans*, 75–77. For a general overview of this section, see R. A. Culpepper, "God's Righteousness in the Life of His People: Romans 12—15," *RevExp* 73 (1976) 451–63, as well as the standard commentaries, especially those by Achtemeier, Dunn, and Fitzmyer. For a detailed study, see M. Thompson, *Clothed with Christ: The Example and Teaching of Jesus in Romans 12:1—15:13* JSNTSS 59 (Sheffield: JSOT Press, 1991).

32. On these verses, see Betz, "Foundations of Christian Ethics"; Deidun, *New Covenant*, 93–103; V. P. Furnish, *Theology and Ethics in Paul* (Nashville: Abingdon, 1968), 98–106; G. Therrien, *Le discernement dans les écrits pauliniens*, EBib (Paris: Gabalda, 1973), 139–49.

33. It is possible, of course, to take the phrase "through the mercies of God" with what follows: "by the mercies of God present your bodies . . ." But even in this case, the imperative is founded on the indicative.

34. In what follows, I am indebted to the insights of Furnish, *Theology and Ethics*, 98–106.

35. Note that this text is also related to Rom. 2:17–18, where Paul describes the Jewish person as relying on the law and boasting of his relation to God, knowing God's will and determining what is best (*ginōskeis to thelēma kai dokimaseis to diapheronta*). Paul argues that although the Jews knew God's will, they did not do it. In contrast to them, Paul expects that those whose minds are renewed will both know and do God's will.

36. The same verb is used to describe Jesus' transfiguration (Matt. 17:2; Mark 9:2).

37. This definition is adapted from Bultmann, *Theology of the New Testament*, 1:195.

38. On the concepts of the *sōma* and *nous* in Paul, see ibid, 1:192–203, 211–20.

39. Fitzmyer (*Romans*, 646) writes: "As in 1 Cor 12:12–31, the phrase 'one body' probably does not suggest anything more than a moral union of the members who work together for the common good of the whole, as in the body politic."

40. On the "measure of faith," see Sampley, *Walking*, 46–48, 50–52, 58–60, 63–64.

41. This point is made by Wedderburn in *Reasons for Romans*, 79.

42. Paul's strategy here is similar to that in 1 Corinthians where, after listing various gifts of the Spirit (1 Corinthians 12), he turns to the topic of love (1 Corinthians 13).

43. This point is made by Wedderburn in *Reasons for Romans*, 76.

44. For an interesting approach to the structure of these statements, see D. A. Black, "The Pauline Love Command: Structure, Style, and Ethics in Romans 12:9–21," *FilNeot* (1989) 3–22.

45. On this theme, see Furnish, *Love Command*, 102–11; J. Piper, "*Love Your Enemies," Jesus' Love Command in the Synoptic Gospels and in the Early Christian Paraenesis: A History of the Tradition and Interpretation of Its Uses*, SNTSMS 38 (Cambridge: Cambridge Univ. Press, 1979), 102–119; L. Schottroff, "Non-Violence and the Love of One's Enemies," in *Essays on the Love Commandment*, ed.

L. Schottroff et al. (Philadelphia: Fortress, 1978), 9–39; and G. Zerbe, "Paul's Ethic of Nonretaliation and Peace," in *The Love of Enemy and Nonretaliation in the New Testament,* ed. W. M. Swartley (Louisville, Ky.: Westminster John Knox, 1992), 177–222.

46. Notice that the material is enclosed in a literary bracket: *mēdeni kakon anti kakou apodidontes* (12:17) and *apodote pasin tas opheilas* (13:7). So Wedderburn, *Reasons for Romans,* 76.

47. So Piper, *"Love Your Enemies,"* 111–12, to whom I am indebted for the citations that follow.

48. Ibid., 113.

49. On this difficult phrase, see Fitzmyer, *Romans,* 657–58; Zerbe, "Paul's Ethic," 182–84; and Piper, *"Love Your Enemies,"* 114–19.

50. The literature on the pericope is immense; see the bibliography provided by Fitzmyer, *Romans,* 670–76. A helpful and clear explanation of the text is given by Furnish, *Moral Teaching of Paul,* 115–39.

51. On the historical background to this text, see J. Friedrich, W. Pöhlmann, and P. Stuhlmacher, "Zur historischen Situation und Intention von Röm 13,1–7," *ZTK* 73 (1976) 131–66.

52. The term is used by Dunn, *Romans,* vol. 38B:774.

53. In effect, Paul makes an implicit distinction between the moral and ritual aspects of the law, although he never develops this notion.

54. This is the suggestive title of Sampley's book, *Walking between the Times.*

55. Karris ("Romans 14:1–15:13," 65–84) provides a helpful comparison of Rom. 14:1–15:13 and 1 Cor. 8:1–11:1, but he argues that Paul is only giving general paraenesis in this section rather than addressing a concrete problem in the Roman church.

56. The general manner in which Paul describes the two groups leads some to argue that he is not addressing a specific problem. Others identify the weak as Jewish Christians who continue to observe dietary prescriptions and certain Jewish festivals, and the strong as Gentile believers who do not. With Wedderburn, I do not believe the lines should be drawn so sharply. The weak are believers, be they Gentiles or Jews, whose understanding of the faith requires them to observe certain days and dietary prescriptions, while the strong are believers, be they Gentiles or Jews (like Paul), whose understanding of the faith no longer requires the observance of dietary prescriptions or Jewish festivals.

57. For example, Fitzmyer (*Romans,* 695) translates *pistis* as "conviction" in Rom. 14:23.

Chapter 10: Ethics for a New Creation

1. Nearly all commentators treat the question of authorship, often drawing different conclusions. For example, M. Barth and H. Blanke (*Colossians: A New Translation with Introduction and Commentary,* AB 34B [New York: Doubleday, 1994]) defend the Pauline authorship of Colossians, whereas E. Lohse (*Colossians and Philemon,* Hermeneia [Philadelphia: Fortress, 1971]) argues against it. A reliable survey of the question can be found in R. F. Collins, *Letters That Paul Did Not Write: The Epistle to the Hebrews and the Pauline Pseudepigrapha,*

GNS 28 (Wilmington, Del.: Glazier, 1988), 132–208. For a slightly different view, more favorable to some sort of Pauline authorship of these letters, consult Johnson, *Writings of the New Testament*, 357–80.

2. See Lohse, *Colossians*, 84–91.

3. Ibid., 177–83.

4. Colossians and Ephesians identify the mystery differently. Whereas in Colossians the mystery is Christ, in Ephesians it concerns the Gentiles who have become fellow heirs, members of the same body, sharers in the promises of Christ.

5. For example, Schrage (*Ethics*, 244) writes, "In the fundamental basis and motivation of ethics we find no substantial departure from Paul, at least with respect to the structural relationship between indicative and imperative." In contrast to him, Schulz (*Ethik*, 556–88) views Colossians and Ephesians as legalistic and dependent upon the moral law of the Old Testament.

6. Arguing that Colossians is neither Pauline nor post-Pauline, E. Schweizer (*The Letter to the Colossians: A Commentary* [Minneapolis: Augsburg, 1982], 23) suggests that Timothy composed this letter in his and Paul's name when the conditions of Paul's imprisonment made it impossible for Paul to write or dictate the letter.

7. If the letter is pseudonymous, then Paul's imprisonment is a fiction. If it is not, then his place of imprisonment may be Ephesus as Schweizer believes, or Rome as F. F. Bruce prefers (*The Epistle to the Colossians, to Philemon, and to the Ephesians*, NICNT [Grand Rapids: Eerdmans, 1984], 32).

8. The literature on this topic is voluminous, and the so-called "Colossian heresy" is a central concern in nearly all commentaries. Here, I list only a few resources that I have found helpful: Barth and Blanke, *Colossians*, 373–87; T. J. Sappington, *Revelation and Redemption at Colossae*, JSNTSS 53 (Sheffield: JSOT Press, 1991); R. Yates, "Colossians and Gnosis," *JSNT* 27 (1986) 49–68; idem, "A Reappraisal of Colossians," *ITQ* 58 (1992) 95–117; and A.J.M. Wedderburn, "The Theology of Colossians," in *The Theology of the Later Pauline Letters*, by A.T. Lincoln and A.J.M. Wedderburn, NTT (Cambridge: Cambridge Univ. Press, 1993), esp. 3–22.

9. A number of intriguing questions about this religious philosophy remain unanswered: Were its proponents Christians, Jews, pagans? Was it hostile to faith in Christ, or did it view itself as supplemental to that faith? There are simply not enough data to answer these and related questions.

10. In my view the essay by M. Hooker ("Were There False Teachers in Colossae?" in *Christ and Spirit in the New Testament*, ed. B. Lindars and S. S. Smalley [Cambridge: Cambridge Univ. Press, 1973], 315–32) has much to commend it, even though I do not completely subscribe to her thesis. She contends that Paul was issuing a general warning about spiritual powers other than Christ, but not necessarily opposing a new or specific false teaching.

11. Here, "philosophy" refers to a religious teaching rather than to the rational discourse usually associated with ancient Greek and Roman philosophy.

12. N. A. Dahl ("Christ, Creation, and the Church," in *Jesus in the Memory of the Early Church* [Minneapolis: Augsburg, 1976], 120–40) observes about Paul's ethics: "Its basis can be said to be eschatological, christological and sacramental. But the concrete content of the exhortations is to a considerable extent ethical commonplace, well known also to Judaism and Hellenism" (137).

13. See the stimulating article by G. M. Styler, "The Basis of Obligation in Paul's Christology and Ethics," in *Christ and Spirit in the New Testament*, ed. Lindars and Smalley, 178–88.

14. Whereas Colossians says that the baptized are already raised up, in Romans Paul writes, "For if we have been united with him in a death like his, we *will* certainly be united with him in a resurrection like his" (Rom. 6:5). Ephesians goes further than Colossians, asserting that God "raised us up with him *and seated us with him in the heavenly places* in Christ Jesus" (Eph. 2:6). However, there is no explicit reference to Baptism here.

15. For helpful discussions about this phrase, see Barth and Blanke, *Colossians*, 373–78; Lohse, *Colossians*, 96–99; and Schweizer, *Colossians*, 125–34. The basic issue is the identity of the *stoicheia*. Are they spiritual powers, be they angelic or demonic? The material elements of the world? Rudimentary or elementary teaching? There is no consensus on this point.

16. On the relationship between Ephesians and Colossians, see Barth and Blanke, *Colossians*, 72–114; C. L. Mitton, *Ephesians*, NCB (Grand Rapids: Eerdmans, 1981; first published by Marshall, Morgan & Scott, 1973), 11–20; and R. Schnackenburg, *Ephesians: A Commentary* (Edinburgh: T. & T. Clark, 1991; first published by Benziger Verlag, 1982), 30–33. Note that the commentary of Barth and Blanke favors the Pauline authorship of Colossians and Ephesians. Mitton and Schnackenburg view Ephesians as Deutero-Pauline.

17. Two examples of this are his use of "mystery," which now refers to the union of Gentile and Jew within the church, and the manner in which he presents Paul's teaching on justification by faith (Eph. 2:1–10), which I shall discuss below.

18. Those who view the letter as authentically Pauline usually date it toward the end of the apostle's career, the period of his Roman imprisonment. If the letter is not from Paul, the question is no longer important, although it is possible that the author himself is imprisoned.

19. For the sake of convenience, I refer to this writing as the letter to the Ephesians.

20. All nine references to the church in Ephesians (1:22; 3:10, 21; 5:23, 24, 25, 27, 29, 32) refer to the church universal rather than to the local congregation. See A. T. Lincoln, "The Theology of Ephesians," in *Later Pauline Letters*, ed. Lincoln and Wedderburn, 93.

21. This point is made by E. Best, "Ephesians: Two Types of Existence," *Int* 47 (1993) 39–51. Lincoln ("Theology of Ephesians," 82–83) describes the main problems of the recipients as "powerlessness, instability and a lack of resolve, and these are related to an insufficient sense of identity."

22. For a helpful survey of the literary form of the letter, see Schnackenburg, *Ephesians*, 21–24, and Lincoln, "Theology of Ephesians," 79–83. I am indebted to Lincoln's insight that the first half of the letter is an example of epideictic rhetoric, a letter of congratulations, and the second half an example of deliberative rhetoric, a letter of advice.

23. For a fuller exposition of this, see Therrien, *Le discernement*, 196–200.

24. In fact, Paul alternates between "us" and "you" in this section, and throughout much of the letter. Here, I simply refer to the Ephesians.

25. Schnackenburg (*Ephesians*, 68) writes of this section: "Hence the author, even in praising God, has a practical goal to reach among his addressees:

in looking up to the God and Father of our Lord Jesus Christ, who has blessed us with every spiritual blessing in Christ, he establishes them on the basis fundamental for their self-understanding *and for their consequent behavior in the world*" (emphasis mine).

26. On this point, see A. T. Lincoln, "Ephesians 2:8–10: A Summary of Paul's Gospel?" *CBQ* 45 (1983) 617–30.

27. Paul employs "walking" as a metaphor for conduct several times in Ephesians (2:2, 10; 4:1, 17 [twice]; 5:2, 8, 15). On the background of this metaphor and its use in Ephesians, see Therrien, *Le discernement*, 200–202.

28. Paul usually views justification as a present reality and salvation as something yet to be attained. Thus one is justified but not yet saved. See Rom. 5:9–10.

29. Paradoxically, this updated teaching, which does not employ the language of justification, is closer to the traditional Catholic and Protestant understanding of justification than is the teaching found in Romans and Galatians.

30. The author of Ephesians is more radical than Paul, who never explicitly speaks of Christ "abolishing" the law.

31. On this point, see U. Luz, "Überlegungen zum Epheserbrief und seiner Paränese," in *Neues Testament und Ethik*, ed. Merklein, 376–96.

32. This outline is indebted in large measure to the manner in which Schnackenburg has structured this material in his commentary on Ephesians.

33. One should also note the similarities between this paraenesis and that found in Romans. In both letters the paraenesis begins with the same words (*Parakalō oun hymas*) and makes use of the body-of-Christ imagery for the church, albeit in different ways. See Rom. 12:1–8.

34. These points are made by Therrien, *Le discernement*, 201.

35. In fact, Paul makes a sevenfold appeal to unity here: one body, one Spirit, one hope, one Lord, one faith, one Baptism, one God.

36. This point is made by Schnackenburg, *Ephesians*, 168.

37. Ibid., 192.

38. Ibid., 193.

39. This is the main point of Best, "Ephesians: Two Types of Existence."

40. While there is no explicit reference to the church here (Eph. 4:29), it seems to be implied by the context.

41. On the background for this metaphor, see R. A. Wild, "'Be Imitators of God': Discipleship in the Letter to the Ephesians," in *Discipleship in the New Testament*, ed. Segovia, 127–143.

42. However, one must reckon with 2 Cor. 6:14–7:1, which some see as a later interpolation. In this passage, Paul does draw a sharp distinction between believers and unbelievers.

43. On the background to this text, see R. A. Wild, "The Warrior and the Prisoner: Some Reflections on Ephesians 6:10–20," *CBQ* 46 (1984) 284–98.

44. This point is made by Schnackenburg, *Ephesians*, 285.

45. For a helpful review of the literature, see D. L. Balch, "Household Codes," in *Greco-Roman Literature and the New Testament: Selected Forms and Genres*, ed. D. E. Aune SBLSBS 21 (Atlanta: Scholars, 1988), 25–50. For a thorough study of the household code in Colossians, see J. E. Crouch, *The Origin and Intention of the Colossian Haustafel*, FRLANT 109 (Göttingen: Vandenhoeck &

Ruprecht, 1972). Other helpful studies are R. N. Longenecker, *New Testament Social Ethics for Today* (Grand Rapids: Eerdmans, 1984); C. S. Keener, *Paul, Women, and Wives: Marriage and Women's Ministry in the Letters of Paul* (Peabody, Mass.: Hendrickson, 1992), esp. 139–224; and G. Strecker, "Die neutestamentlichen Haustafeln (Kol 3, 18–4, 1 und Eph 5, 22–6, 9)," in *Neues Testament und Ethik*, ed. Merklein, 349–75.

46. Balch, "Household Codes," 35. Other influences such as the teaching of Greco-Roman moral philosophers and Hellenistic Judaism are not to be excluded.

47. Although the use of direct address, which is also present in the code of 1 Peter but not in the codes of 1 Timothy and Titus, seems to be a minor point, it emphasizes the moral agency and responsibility of those addressed. Thus, while much of the ancient world viewed slaves as mere possessions to be used, the New Testament codes treat them as moral agents.

48. Ephesians employs different imperatives when addressing wives and children. While children are to obey (*hypakouete*), wives are to be submissive or subordinate (*hypotassomenoi*; the imperative in v. 22 is supplied from the imperative in v. 21). The sense of the subordination or submission is to find one's place in the scheme of things.

49. For example, in *The Politics*, Book 1, part 5, Aristotle assumes that the male is superior to the female and therefore rules over her.

50. There is a general tendency in Ephesians to use scripture in its paraenesis, as can be seen in 4:8; 4:25–26; 5:31.

51. For helpful discussions on this point, see Crouch, *Colossian Haustafel*, 152–61; and Keener, *Paul, Women, and Wives*, 184–224.

52. Note that while this phrase is found in the couplet of Gal. 3:28, it is absent from a similar couplet found in Col. 3:11. This suggests to some that Colossians found it necessary to tone down the radical equality expressed in Gal. 3:28.

53. This point is made by Crouch, *Colossian Haustafel*, 120–45, esp. 133–36.

Chapter 11: Reliable Moral Guides

1. A historical survey of the question of authorship is ably presented by Collins, *Letters That Paul Did Not Write*, 88–131.

2. For the pastoral epistles, he is the only apostle. The Pastorals make no reference to other apostles.

3. M. Dibelius and H. Conzelmann, *The Pastoral Epistles: A Commentary on the Pastoral Epistles*, Hermeneia (Philadelphia: Fortress, 1972; first German ed. published in 1955, by J.C.B. Mohr (Siebeck). The English translation is from the 4th rev. ed. by H. Conzelmann, 1966).

4. Ibid., 39–41. The German title of the excursus is "Das Ideal christlicher Bürgerlichkeit."

5. Ibid., 40.

6. Ibid.

7. R. M. Kidd, *Wealth and Beneficence in the Pastoral Epistles*, SBLDS 122 (Atlanta: Scholars, 1990), 11.

8. The most important study is that of Kidd, *Wealth and Beneficence*. Significant contributions have also been made by M. Y. MacDonald, *The Pauline*

Churches: A Socio-historical Study of Institutionalization in the Pauline and Deutero-Pauline Writings, SNTSMS 60 (Cambridge: Cambridge Univ. Press, 1988); and P. H. Towner, *The Goal of Our Instruction: The Structure of Theology and Ethics in the Pastoral Epistles,* JSNTSS 34 (Sheffield: JSOT Press, 1989).

9. This is a major conclusion of Kidd's study.

10. See L. R. Donelson, *Pseudepigraphy and Ethical Argument in the Pastoral Epistles,* HUT 22 (Tübingen: Mohr [Siebeck], 1986); Towner, *Goal of Our Instruction;* and F. Young, *The Theology of the Pastoral Epistles,* NTT (Cambridge: Cambridge Univ. Press, 1994).

11. See Donelson (*Pseudepigraphy and Ethical Argument,* 7–66), who argues that the author employs pseudepigraphy in order to obtain a hearing for his ethical position. There are, however, dissenting voices. For example, Johnson (*Writings of the New Testament,* 381–408) and M. Prior (*Paul the Letter-Writer: And the Second Letter to Timothy,* JSNTSS 23 [Sheffield: JSOT Press, 1989]) have taken issue with the standard position that the Pastorals, especially 2 Timothy, are pseudonymous. G. W. Knight III (*Commentary on the Pastoral Epistles: A Commentary on the Greek Text,* NIGTC [Grand Rapids: Eerdmans, 1992], 3–52) also argues for the Pauline authorship of the letters.

12. Donelson, *Pseudepigraphy and Ethical Argument,* 128.

13. This is the approach of the standard works on New Testament ethics: Schnackenburg (*Die sittliche Botschaft,* 2:95–109), Schrage (*Ethics,* 257–68), and Schulz (*Ethik,* 588–610). Each treats the Pastorals as a homogenous block of material. Johnson (*Writings of the New Testament,* 382) and Prior (*Paul the Letter-Writer,* 168) correctly urge that each letter should be studied on its own merits.

14. This approach was suggested to me by the work of B. Fiore, *The Function of Personal Example in the Socratic and Pastoral Epistles,* AnBib 105 (Rome: Biblical Institute Press, 1986). He maintains that the Pastorals belong to a tradition of hortatory correspondence in which moral teaching is communicated by the use of personal example.

15. This statement about Paul's other correspondence includes the letter to Philemon, which is addressed to Philemon, Apphia, Archippus, and the church in Philemon's house.

16. D. R. MacDonald (*The Legend and the Apostle: The Battle for Paul in Story and Canon* [Philadelphia: Westminster, 1983]) sees the pastoral epistles as attempts to counteract the legends about Paul that underlie such writings as the *Acts of Paul.* One must ask, however, if these legends were known as early as A.D. 80–90.

17. On the genre of the letter, see Fiore, *Function of Personal Example,* 190–236.

18. On the household of God as a controlling metaphor for understanding 1 Timothy, see D. C. Verner, *The Household of God: The Social World of the Pastoral Epistles,* SBLDS 71 (Chico, Calif.: Scholars, 1983).

19. This point is made by R. Karris ("The Background and Significance of the Polemic of the Pastoral Epistles," *JBL* 92 [1973] 549–64), and Fiore (*Function of Personal Example,* 196).

20. Although the vices of this list do not explicitly function as a description of the false teachers, the list suggests that those who follow their teaching will eventually commit such crimes.

21. This point is made by Towner (*Goal of Our Instruction*), who argues that these instructions have the church's mission in view.

22. MacDonald, *Pauline Churches*, 178.

23. It is possible that the whole of 1 Tim. 5:3–16 refers to a single situation: determining who is a real widow in need of help. Others argue that Paul has two kinds of widows in view. In 5:3–8, 16 he is referring to widows who are destitute and in need of assistance. In 5:9–15 he is speaking of an order of widows charged with a ministry of doing good works in which certain widows are enrolled.

24. It is probable that slaves whose masters were believers wanted to be treated with greater equality since they were "brothers and sisters" in Christ. See Col. 4:1 and Eph. 6:9, where masters are reminded that they and their slaves have the same master in heaven.

25. The commandment refers to all that Paul has instructed Timothy in this letter: what Paul has entrusted to him (1 Tim. 6:20).

26. Prior (*Paul the Letter-Writer*, 110–11) dissents from this interpretation, arguing that Paul is not anticipating his death in 1 Tim. 4:6–8. While I have found much of his work helpful, I am not convinced of his position in this regard.

27. Whether or not Timothy is ashamed of Paul's imprisonment and hesitant to suffer with him is not clear from the text. Paul's exhortation that Timothy "rekindle the gift of God" (2 Tim. 1:6) has suggested just such a scenario to Prior, *Paul the Letter-Writer*, 160–64.

28. MacDonald (*Pauline Churches*, 172) believes that the "problem of false teaching in the Pastorals is inseparably linked with the activity of women within the community." Verner (*Household of God*) follows a similar line. While the role of women within the church was an important issue, I am not convinced that it was the central problem the author(s) of these epistles faced.

29. Paul's confidence that the Lord will save him for his heavenly kingdom (2 Tim. 4:18) suggests an eschatological hope rather than confidence that he will be released from his imprisonment.

30. Paul does not appear to make a distinction between the presbyter and the bishop. See Titus 1:5, 7, where "presbyter" and "bishop" are employed almost interchangeably.

31. In 1 Timothy Paul says that he left Timothy in Ephesus to instruct certain people not to teach different doctrines (1 Timothy 3), but in his letter to Titus he writes that he left Titus in Crete for the purpose of appointing elders in every town (Titus 1:5).

32. There are, however, indications that the false teachers are Jewish Christians (Titus 1:10) and that their teaching has something to do with the law (3:9).

33. On *eusebeia*, see the important discussion in Towner, *Goal of Our Instruction*, 147–52.

34. On this point, see Young, *Pastoral Epistles*, 24–46.

35. The Greek, however, could also be punctuated to read, "the great God and our Savior Jesus Christ."

Select Bibliography

The following bibliography is limited to books and articles that deal with, or have an important bearing on, biblical ethics. Other works that have informed my thinking are included in the notes to this work.

Balch, David; Everett Ferguson; and Wayne A. Meeks, eds. *Greeks, Romans, and Christians: Essays in Honor of Abraham Malherbe.* Minneapolis: Fortress, 1990.

Banks, Robert. *Jesus and the Law in the Synoptic Gospels.* SNTSMS 28. Cambridge: Cambridge Univ. Press, 1975.

Barclay, John G. *Obeying the Truth: A Study of Paul's Ethics in Galatians.* Edinburgh: T. & T. Clark, 1988.

Barton, Stephen. *Discipleship and Family Ties in Mark and Matthew.* SNTSMS 80. Cambridge: Cambridge Univ. Press, 1994.

Becker, Jürgen. *Paul: Apostle to the Gentiles.* Louisville, Ky.: Westminster John Knox, 1993.

Best, Ernest. "Ephesians: Two Types of Existence." *Int* 47 (1993) 39–51.

Betz, Hans Dieter. "The Foundations of Christian Ethics according to Romans 12:1–2." In *Witness and Existence: Essays in Honor of Schubert M. Ogden,* edited by Philip E. Devenish and George L. Goodwin, 55–72. Chicago: Univ. of Chicago Press, 1989.

Birch, Bruce C. *Let Justice Roll Down: The Old Testament, Ethics, and Christian Life.* Louisville, Ky.: Westminster John Knox, 1991.

Birch, Bruce, and Larry Rasmussen. *Bible and Ethics in the Christian Life.* Minneapolis: Augsburg, 1976.

Black, David Alan. "The Pauline Love Command: Structure, Style, and Ethics in Romans 12:9–21." *FilNeot* 2 (1989) 3–22.

Boers, Hendrikus. "'We Who Are by Inheritance Jews; Not from the Gentile Sinners.'" *JBL* 111 (1992) 273–81.

Bornkamm, Günther, Gerhard Barth, and Heinz Joachim Held. *Tradition and Interpretation in Matthew.* Philadelphia: Westminster, 1963.

Boughton, Lynne C. "Biblical Texts and Homosexuality: A Response to John Boswell." *ITQ* 58 (1992) 141–53.

Brant, Jo-Ann A. "The Place of *Mimēsis* in Paul's Thought." *SR* 22 (1993) 285–300.

Bultmann, Rudolf. "Das Problem der Ethik bei Paulus." *ZNW* (1924) 123–40.

Byrne, Brendan. "Living Out the Righteousness of God: The Contribution of Rom 6:1–8:13 to an Understanding of Paul's Ethical Presuppositions." *CBQ* 43 (1981) 557–81.

———. "Sinning against One's Own Body: Paul's Understanding of the Sexual Relationship in 1 Corinthians 6:18." *CBQ* 45 (1983) 608–16.

Childress, James F. "Scripture and Christian Ethics: Some Reflections on the Role of Scripture in Moral Deliberation and Justification." *Int* 34 (1980) 371–80.

Childs, Brevard S. *Biblical Theology of the Old and New Testaments: Theological Reflection on the Christian Bible.* Minneapolis: Fortress, 1992.

Chilton, Bruce, and J.I.H. McDonald. *Jesus and the Ethics of the Kingdom.* Grand Rapids: Eerdmans, 1987.

Collange, Jean-François. *De Jésus à Paul: L'Éthique du Nouveau Testament.* Geneva: Labor et Fides, 1980.

Collins, Raymond F. *Christian Morality: Biblical Foundations.* Notre Dame, Ind.: Univ. Notre Dame Press, 1986.

———. *Divorce in the New Testament.* GNS 38. Collegeville, Minn.: Liturgical Press, 1992.

———. " 'This Is the Will of God: Your Sanctification,' (1 Thess 4,3)," and "The Unity of Paul's Paraenesis in 4,3–8: 1 Cor 7, 1–7, a Significant Parallel." *Studies on the First Letter to the Thessalonians.* BETL 66, 299–325, 326–335. Louvain: Leuven Univ. Press, 1985.

Countryman, L. William. *Dirt, Greed and Sex: Sexual Ethics in the New Testament and Their Implications for Today.* Philadelphia: Fortress, 1988.

Crouch, James E. *The Origin and Intention of the Colossian Haustafel.* FRLANT 109. Göttingen: Vandenhoeck & Ruprecht, 1972.

Culpepper, R. Alan. "God's Righteousness in the Life of His People: Romans 12—15." *RevExp* 73 (1976) 541–63.

Daly, Robert, ed. *Christian Biblical Ethics: From Biblical Revelation to Contemporary Christian Praxis: Method and Content.* New York: Paulist, 1984.

Davies, W. D. "Conscience and Its Use in the New Testament," and "The Moral Teaching of the Early Church." In *Jewish and Pauline Studies*, 243–56, 278–88. Philadelphia: Fortress, 1984.

Davies, W. D., and Dale Allison, Jr. "Reflections on the Sermon on the Mount." *Scottish Journal of Theology* 44 (1992) 283–309.

Deidun, T. J. *New Covenant Morality in Paul.* AnBib 89. Rome: Biblical Institute Press, 1981.

Dewar, Lindsay. *An Outline of New Testament Ethics.* London: Univ. of London Press, 1949.

Dodd, C. H. *Gospel and Law: The Relation of Faith and Ethics in Early Christianity.* New York: Columbia Univ. Press, 1951.

Donelson, Lewis R. *Pseudepigraphy and Ethical Argument in the Pastoral Epistles.* HUT 22. Tübingen: J.C.B. Mohr (Paul Siebeck), 1986.

Donfried, Karl Paul. "Justification and Last Judgment in Paul." *ZNW* 67 (1976) 90–110.

Drane, John W. *Paul, Libertine or Legalist? A Study in the Theology of the Major Pauline Epistles.* London: SPCK, 1975.

Dunn, James D. G. *Jesus' Call to Discipleship.* Understanding Jesus Today. Cambridge: Cambridge Univ. Press, 1992.

———. "The Justice of God: A Renewed Perspective on Justification by Faith." *JTS* 43 (1992) 1–22.

———. *The Theology of Paul's Letter to the Galatians.* NTT. Cambridge: Cambridge Univ. Press, 1993.

Enslin, Morton Scott. *The Ethics of Paul.* Nashville: Abingdon, 1962.

Fiore, Benjamin. *The Function of Personal Example in the Socratic and Pastoral Epistles.* AnBib 105. Rome: Biblical Institute Press, 1986.

Fischer, James A. *Looking for Moral Guidance: Dilemma and the Bible.* New York: Paulist, 1992.

Fitzgerald, John T. *Cracks in an Earthen Vessel: An Examination of the Catalogues of Hardships in the Corinthian Correspondence.* SBLDS 99. Atlanta: Scholars, 1984.

Fowl, Stephen. "Receiving the Kingdom of God as a Child: Children and Riches in Luke 18:15ff." *NTS* 39 (1993) 153–58.

Friedrich, Johannes, Wolfgang Pohlmann, and Peter Stuhlmacher. "Zur historischen Situation und Intention von Röm 13,1–7." *ZTK* 73 (1976) 131–66.

Furnish, Victor Paul. "Belonging to Christ: A Paradigm for Ethics in First Corinthians." *Int* 44 (1990) 158–68.

———. *The Moral Teaching of Paul: Selected Issues.* Nashville: Abingdon, 1985.

———. *The Love Commandment in the New Testament.* Nashville: Abingdon, 1972.

———. *Theology and Ethics in Paul.* Nashville: Abingdon, 1968.

Garland, David E. "The Composition and Unity of Philippians: Some Neglected Literary Factors." *NovT* 27 (1985) 140–73.

Gerhardsson, Birger. *The Ethos of the Bible.* Philadelphia: Fortress, 1981.

Gillman, John. *Possessions and the Life of Faith.* Collegeville, Minn.: Liturgical Press, 1991.

Greenfield, G. "The Ethics of the Sermon on the Mount." *SwJT* 35 (1992) 13–19.

Guelich, Robert A. *The Sermon on the Mount: A Foundation for Understanding.* Waco, Tex.: Word, 1982.

Gustafson, James M. "The Place of Scripture in Christian Ethics." *Int* 24 (1970) 430–55.

Harvey, A. E. *Strenuous Commands: The Ethics of Jesus.* Philadelphia: Trinity Press International, 1990.

Hauerwas, Stanley. "The Moral Authority of Scripture." *Int* 34 (1980) 376–70.

Hays, Richard B. "Christology and Ethics in Galatians." *CBQ* 49 (1987) 268–90.

———. "Scripture Shaped Community: The Problem of Method in New Testament Ethics." *Int* 44 (1990) 42–55.

Hiers, Richard H. *Jesus and Ethics: Four Interpretations.* Philadelphia: Westminster, 1968.

Horn, Friedrich Wilhelm. "Ethik des Neuen Testaments 1982–1992." *TRu* 60 (1995) 32–86.

Houlden, James Leslie. *Ethics and the New Testament.* New York: Oxford Univ. Press, 1973.

Hurtado, L. W. "Jesus as Lordly Example in Philippians 2:5–11." In *From Jesus to Paul: Studies in Honor of Francis Wright Beare,* edited by Peter Richardson and John C. Hurd, 113–26. Waterloo, Ontario: Wilfrid Laurier Univ. Press, 1984.

Jacoby, Hermann. *Neutestamentliche Ethik.* Königsberg: Thomas & Oppermann, 1899.

Janzen, Waldemar. *Old Testament Ethics: A Paradigmatic Approach.* Louisville, Ky.: Westminster John Knox, 1994.

Johnson, Luke T. *Sharing Possessions: Mandate and Symbol of Faith.* Philadelphia: Fortress, 1981.

Kaiser, Walter C., Jr. *Toward Old Testament Ethics.* Grand Rapids: Zondervan, 1983.

Keck, Leander. "On the Ethos of Early Christians." *JAAR* 42 (1974) 435–52.

Keener, Craig S. *Paul, Women, Wives: Marriage and Women's Ministry in the Letters of Paul.* Peabody, Mass.: Hendrickson, 1992.

Kertelge, Karl, ed. *Ethik im Neuen Testament.* Questiones Disputatae. Freiburg, Basel, Vienna: Herder, 1984.

Kidd, Reggie M. *Wealth and Beneficence in the Pastoral Epistles: A "Bourgeois" Form of Early Christianity?* SBLDS 122. Atlanta: Scholars, 1990.

Kilner, John F. "A Pauline Approach to Ethical Decision Making." *Int* 43 (1989) 366–79.

Knox, John. *The Ethic of Jesus and the Teaching of the Church.* New York: Abingdon, 1961.

Lazure, Noel. *Le Valeurs morales de la Théologie Johannique (Évangile et épîtres).* EBib. Paris: Gabalda, 1965.

Legasse, Simon. *"Et qui est mon prochain?" Étude sur l'object de l'agapé dans le Nouveau Testament.* LD 136. Paris: Cerf, 1989.

Lehmann, Paul. "The Commandments and the Common Life." *Int* 34 (1980) 341–55.

Lillie, William. *Studies in the New Testament Ethics.* Edinburgh: Oliver & Boyd, 1971.

Lincoln, Andrew T. "Ephesians 2:8–10: A Summary of Paul's Gospel?" *CBQ* 45 (1983) 617–30.

Liu, Peter. "Did the Lucan Jesus Desire Voluntary Poverty of His Followers?" *EQ* 64 (1992) 291–317.

Lohse, Eduard. *Theological Ethics of the New Testament.* Minneapolis: Fortress, 1991.

Long, Edward LeRoy, Jr. "The Use of the Bible in Christian Ethics: A Look at Basic Options." *Int* 19 (1965) 149–62.

Longenecker, Richard N. *New Testament Social Ethics for Today.* Grand Rapids: Eerdmans, 1984.

Malherbe, Abraham. "Exhortation in First Thessalonians." *NovT* 25 (1983) 238–56.

———. *Moral Exhortation, A Greco-Roman Sourcebook.* Philadelphia: Westminster, 1986.

———. *Paul and the Popular Philosopher.* Minneapolis: Fortress, 1989.

———. *Paul and the Thessalonians: The Philosophic Tradition of Pastoral Care.* Philadelphia: Fortress, 1987.

Malina, Bruce J. "Wealth and Poverty in the New Testament and Its World." *Int* 41 (1987) 354–67.

Manson, T. W. *Ethics and the Gospel.* New York: Scribner's, 1960.

Marguerat, D. *Le Jugement dans L'Évangile de Matthieu.* MDB. Geneva: Labor et Fides, 1981.

Marshall, C. D. *Faith as a Theme in Mark's Narrative.* SNTSMS 64. Cambridge: Cambridge Univ. Press, 1989.

Marshall, Laurence Henry. *The Challenge of New Testament Ethics.* London: Macmillan, 1964.

Matera, F. J. "The Culmination of Paul's Argument to the Galatians: Gal 5:1–6:17." *JSNT* 32 (1989) 79–91.

———. "Ethics for the Kingdom of God: The Gospel according to Mark." *LS* 20 (1995) 187–200.

McDonald, Ian. *Biblical Interpretation and Christian Ethics.* Cambridge: Cambridge Univ. Press, 1993.

McEleney, Neil J. "The Beatitudes of the Sermon on the Mount/Plain." *CBQ* 43 (1981) 1–13.

———. "The Principles of the Sermon on the Mount." *CBQ* 41 (1979) 552–70.

Meeks, Wayne A. *The Moral World of the New Testament.* Philadelphia: Westminster, 1986.

———. *The Origins of Christian Morality: The First Two Centuries.* New Haven, Conn.: Yale Univ. Press, 1993.

———. "Understanding Early Christian Ethics." *JBL* 105 (1986) 3–11.

Merk, Otto. *Handeln aus Glauben: Die Motivierungen der Paulinischen Ethik.* MarTS 5. Marburg: Elwert Verlag, 1968.

Merklein, Helmut, ed. *Neues Testament und Ethik: Für Rudolf Schnackenburg.* Freiburg: Herder, 1989.

Mohrlang, Robert. *Matthew and Paul: A Comparison of Ethical Perspectives.* SNTSMS 48. Cambridge: Cambridge Univ. Press, 1984.

O'Hanlon, J. "The Story of Zacchaeus and the Lukan Ethic." *JSNT* 12 (1981) 2–26.

O'Toole, Robert F. *Who Is a Christian? A Study in Pauline Ethics.* ZSNT. Collegeville, Minn.: Liturgical Press, 1990.

Ogletree, Thomas W. *The Use of the Bible in Christian Ethics.* Philadelphia: Fortress, 1983.

Osborne, Eric. *Ethical Patterns in Early Church Thought.* Cambridge: Cambridge Univ. Press, 1976.

Perkins, Pheme. "Ethics (NT)" *ABD,* edited by David Noel Freedman. Vol. 2, 652–65. New York: Doubleday, 1992.

———. *Love Commands in the New Testament.* New York: Paulist, 1982.

———. "New Testament Ethics: Questions and Contexts." *RelStRev* 10 (1984) 321–26.

Pilgrim, Walter. *Good News to the Poor: Wealth and Poverty in Luke-Acts.* Minneapolis: Augsburg, 1981.

Piper, John. *"Love Your Enemies": Jesus' Love Command in the Synoptic Gospels and in the Early Christian Paraenesis: A History of the Tradition and Interpretation of Its Uses.* SNTSMS 38. Cambridge: Cambridge Univ. Press, 1979.

Preisker, Herbert. *Das Ethos des Urchristentums.* Gütersloh: Bertelsmann, 1949.

Przybylski, Benno. *Righteousness in Matthew and His World of Thought.* SNTSMS 41. Cambridge: Cambridge Univ. Press, 1980.

Reumann, John. "Justification and the *Imitatio* Motif in Philippians." In *Promoting Unity: Themes in Lutheran-Catholic Dialogue,* edited by H. George Anderson and James R. Crumley, Jr., 17–28. Minneapolis: Augsburg, 1989.

Richardson, Peter. *Paul's Ethic of Freedom.* Philadelphia: Westminster, 1979.

Ringe, Sharon H. *Jesus, Liberation, and the Biblical Jubilee: Images for Ethics and Christology.* OBT. Philadelphia: Fortress, 1985.

Sampley, J. Paul. *Walking between the Times: Paul's Moral Reasoning.* Minneapolis: Fortress, 1991.

Sanders, Jack T. *Ethics in the New Testament: Change and Development.* Philadelphia: Fortress, 1975.

Schelkle, Karl Hermann. *Theology of the New Testament.* 3 vols. Collegeville, Minn.: Liturgical Press, 1971–1973.

Schnackenburg, Rudolf. *The Moral Teaching of the New Testament.* London: Burns & Oates, 1964.

———. *Die sittliche Botschaft des Neuen Testaments.* 2 vols. HTKNT. Freiburg: Herder, 1986, 1988.

Schottroff, Luise, and Wolfgang Stegemann. *Jesus and the Hope of the Poor.* Maryknoll, N.Y.: Orbis, 1986.

Schottroff, Luise, Christoph Burchard, Reginald H. Fuller, and Jack M. Suggs. *Essays on the Love Commandment.* Philadelphia: Fortress, 1975.

Schrage, Wolfgang. *The Ethics of the New Testament.* Philadelphia: Fortress, 1988.

Schreiner, Thomas R. *The Law and Its Fulfillment: A Pauline Theology of Law.* Grand Rapids: Baker, 1993.

Schulz, Siegfried. *Neutestamentliche Ethik.* Zürcher Grundrisse zur Bibel. Zurich: Theologischer Verlag, 1987.

Schurmann, Heinz, Joseph Cardinal Ratzinger, and Hans Urs von Balthasar. *Principles of Christian Morality.* San Francisco: Ignatius, 1986.

Schweizer, Eduard. "Traditional Ethical Patterns in the Pauline and Post Pauline Letters and Their Development." In *Text and Interpretation,* edited by Ernest Best and R. McL. Wilson. Cambridge: Cambridge Univ. Press, 1979.

Scott, C.A.A. *New Testament Ethics: An Introduction.* 2d ed. Cambridge: Cambridge Univ. Press, 1934.

Segovia, Fernando F., ed. *Discipleship in the New Testament.* Philadelphia: Fortress, 1985.

Sleeper, C. Freeman. "Ethics as a Context for Biblical Interpretation." *Int* 22 (1968) 443–60.

Spicq, Ceslas. *Théologie morale du Nouveau Testament,* 2 vols. EBib. Paris: Lecoffre, 1965.

Stanley, David. "Imitation in Paul's Letters: Its Significance for His Relationship to Jesus and to His Own Christian Foundations." In *From Jesus to Paul: Studies in Honor of Francis Wright Beare,* edited by Peter Richardson and John C. Hurd, 127–42. Waterloo, Ontario: Wilfrid Laurier Univ. Press, 1984.

Stowers, Stanley K. *Letter Writing in Greco-Roman Antiquity.* Library of Early Christianity. Philadelphia: Westminster, 1986.

Strecker, Georg. "Strukturen einer neutestamentlichen Ethik." *ZTK* 75 (1978) 117–46.

———. *Der Weg der Gerechtigkeit: Untersuchung zur Theologie des Matthäus.* 3d rev. ed. FRLANT. Göttingen: Vandenhoeck & Ruprecht, 1971.

Swartley, Willard M., ed. *The Love of Enemy and Nonretaliation in the New Testament.* Louisville, Ky.: Westminster John Knox, 1992.

Sytler, G. M. "The Basis of Obligation in Paul's Christology and Ethics." In *Christ and the Spirit in the New Testament,* edited by Barnabas Lindars and Stephan S. Smalley, 175–88. Cambridge: Cambridge Univ. Press, 1973.

Theilman, Frank. *Paul and the Law: A Contextual Approach.* Downers Grove, Ill.: InterVarsity, 1994.

Therrien, Gérard. *Le Discernement dans les écrits pauliniens.* EBib. Paris: Gabalda, 1973.

Thompson, Michael. *Clothed with Christ: The Example and Teaching of Jesus in Romans 12:1–15:13.* JSNTSS 59. Sheffield: JSOT Press, 1991.

Towner, Philip H. *The Goal of Our Instruction: The Structure of Theology and Ethics in the Pastoral Epistles.* JSNTSS 34. Sheffield: JSOT Press, 1989.

Verhey, Allen. *The Great Reversal: Ethics and the New Testament.* Grand Rapids: Eerdmans, 1984.

———. "The Use of Scripture in Ethics." *RelStRev* 4 (1978) 28–39.

Weber, Kathleen. "The Events of the End of the Age in Matthew." Ph.D. diss., Catholic University of America, Washington, D.C., 1994.

Wendland, Heinz-Dietrich. *Ethik des Neuen Testaments.* Göttingen: Vandenhoeck & Ruprecht, 1970.

White, R.E.O. *Biblical Ethics.* Atlanta: John Knox, 1979.

Wibbing, Siegfried. *Die Tugend- und Lasterkataloge im Neuen Testament: Und ihre Traditionsgeschichte unter besonderer Berücksichtigung der Qumran-Texte.* BZNW 25. Berlin: Töpelmann, 1959.

Wilder, Amos N. *Eschatology and Ethics in the Teaching of Jesus.* Rev. ed. Westport, Conn.: Greenwood, 1978 (first published by Harper & Brothers 1939, 1950).

Willis, Wendell Lee. *Idol Meat in Corinth: The Pauline Argument in 1 Corinthians 8 and 10.* SBLDS 68. Chico, Calif.: Scholars, 1985.

Wilson, S. G. *Luke and the Law.* SNTSMS 50. Cambridge: Cambridge Univ. Press, 1983.

Witherup, Ronald D. *Conversion in the New Testament.* Collegeville, Minn.: Liturgical Press, 1994.

Wright, Christopher J. H. *An Eye for an Eye: The Place of Old Testament Ethics Today.* Downers Grove, Ill.: InterVarsity, 1983.

York, John O. *The Last Shall Be First: The Rhetoric of Reversal in Luke.* JSNTSS 46. Sheffield: JSOT Press, 1991.

Young, Frances. *The Theology of the Pastoral Letters.* NTT. Cambridge: Cambridge Univ. Press, 1994.

Scripture Index

OLD TESTAMENT

Genesis

15:6	189
17	163

Exodus

15:1–18	16
16:7	180
20:12	224

Leviticus

19:2	221–22
19:18	29, 106, 170, 198, 201

Numbers

11:1	180

Deuteronomy

3:13	167
5:13	145
5:16	224
6:4–5	29
21:23	167
24:1–4	28
27:26	167
32:5	180

32:35	198
32:43	205
33:12	135

1 Chronicles

28:5	16

Psalms

17:50	205
22:1	34
29:10	16
31:5	87
34:14	198
47:1–4	17
69:9	204
74:12–13	17
93:1	16
95:3	16
96:10	16
97:1	16
99:1	16
117:1	205

Proverbs

3:4	198
8:15–16	199
25:21–22	198

SCRIPTURE INDEX

Isaiah

6:9–10	21
11:10	205
40:9–10	17
42:6	180
43:15	17
44:6	17
45:1	200
52:7	17

Jeremiah

27:5–6	199

Daniel

2:21	200
2:24–45	18
7:13	18
7:18	18
7:27	18
12:3	180

Hosea

6:6	52

Zechariah

9:9	52

APOCRYPHA

Wisdom of Solomon

10:10	16
13—14	187

NEW TESTAMENT

Matthew

1:1–4:16	38, 50–51
1:21	60
1:23	61
3:1–9	40
3:2	38
3:7–9	38
3:7–12	54, 56
3:10	38
3:13–17	51
3:15	51
3:17	51
4:1–11	51
4:3	51
4:6	51
4:17	37, 38–39, 43
4:18–21	60
4:23–25	43
5—7	57
5:1–2	43
5:3–16	44–45
5:17	48
5:17–20	45–46
5:21–48	46–47
5:44	197, 198
5:48	221
6:1–18	47–48, 55
6:10	39, 49
6:19–7:11	48
6:33	48
7:12	48–49
7:13–14	49
7:15–20	49
7:21	49, 59
7:23	49
7:24–27	49
7:28–29	43
8:1–9:34	43
8:4	52
8:11–12	58
8:17	52
8:18–20	60
8:25	61
9:13	52
9:36	43, 52

10:1–42	43, 57	23	55
10:7	39	23:2	52
11:20–24	58	23:3	54
11:25–27	60	23:16	55
12:1–14	54	24:1–25:46	41, 57–58
12:7	52	24:14	39
12:16–21	52	24:20	53
12:22–32	54	24:31	60
12:28	39	24:37–41	57
12:33–37	54	24:42–44	57
12:34	54	24:45–51	57
12:36–37	58	25:1–13	36, 41, 49, 57
12:41	58	25:14–30	41, 57
12:50	49	25:31–46	36, 41–42, 58
13:1–53	40, 57	26:28	60
13:11	60	26:29	39
13:24–30	40	27:19	50
13:31–33	40	27:39–44	51
13:38	60	27:43	51
13:44	40	28:20	61
13:45–46	40		
13:47–50	40	**Mark**	
14:14	52	1:1–13	15
14:30	61	1:14	21, 23
15:1–20	52, 54–55	1:14–15	15
15:13	58	1:15	18–19, 23, 38, 202
15:17	52	1:16–20	21–22
15:32	52	1:38	21, 32
16:27	58, 59	1:41	34
18:1–35	57	2:1–3:6	26–27
18:20	61	2:2	21
18:23–35	40–41	3:5	34
19:17	53	3:14	116
19:21	53	3:22	24
19:25–30	58	3:29	31
20:1–16	41, 61	3:35	30, 32
20:28	60	4:10–12	19
21:28–30	54	4:12	21
21:28–32	41	4:13–20	19
21:30	49	4:15	25
21:31–32	54	4:17	25
21:32	54	4:26–29	19
21:33–43	41	4:40	24
22:1–14	41, 61	6:1–6	24
22:11–12	41	6:12	21
22:34–40	53	6:30–44	28
22:40	48	6:34	34

Mark (*continued*)

7	27–28
7:18–19	14
7:19	14
8:1–10	28
8:17	24
8:21	24
8:31	25
8:32	32, 34
8:33	22
8:35	22, 23, 31, 33
8:38	30, 31
9:19	24
9:24	24
9:31	25, 32
9:34	25
9:35	22
9:43–48	30
9:47	18, 20
9:48	31
10:1–12	28–29
10:1–31	29
10:2	28
10:3	28
10:4	28–29
10:13–16	29
10:14	34
10:15	20
10:17	30–31
10:17–31	29
10:19	29
10:21	34
10:23	31
10:23–25	18, 20
10:24	31
10:28	22, 24
10:29	23
10:30	31
10:33–34	25, 32
10:33–42	32
10:41	25
10:43–44	22
10:45	34
10:52	24
11:22–23	33
11:28	29
12:13–34	29
12:14	29
12:28	29–30, 201
12:33	30
12:40	31
14:25	20
14:35–36	32
14:36	32
14:41	32
14:50	33
15:29–30	33
15:31–32a	33
15:32	25
15:32b	33
15:34	34
15:43	20

Luke

1:16–17	69
1:47–55	67
3:8	69
3:10	69
3:12	69
3:14	69
4:16–30	68
4:18–19	68
4:21	68
4:43–44	68
5:32	70
6:20–26	75–76
6:20–49	73–79
6:27	198
6:27–36	76–77
6:28	197
6:36	77, 221
6:37–42	77–78
6:43–45	78–79
7:22	68
7:36–50	71
9:51	79
9:51–19:46	79–86
9:57–62	80
10:16	117
10:27	88
10:30–37	88
11:2–13	82–83
11:39–41	83
11:41	88

12:8–9	85	5:24	100
12:13–15	84	5:25	100
12:17	84	5:29	101
12:22–34	84	6:29	97
12:35–40	82	6:47	100
12:41–48	82	6:69	102
13:6–9	70	7:7	95
14:8–10	75	7:28–29	98
14:12–14	76	8:12	95, 99
14:15	66	8:23	95
14:16–24	66, 76	8:31–32	96
14:26–27	81	8:39–47	96
14:28–30	81	9:1–41	96
14:31–32	81	9:39	96
14:33	81	9:41	96
15:1–2	70	10:18	106
15:11–32	71	11:25–26	100
16:1–8	84, 85	12:37–41	103
16:14	83	12:46	95
16:19–31	70, 84	13:1–30	104–5
17:7–10	82	13:1–20:31	94
17:10	82	13:31–14:31	105–7
17:22–38	82	13:31–17:26	104–11
18:1–6	83	13:8	105
18:22	81	13:15	105
19:9	85	13:34	105–7
19:11–27	82	14:6	99
19:12–27	66	15:1–17	107–8
23:34	89	15:5	108
23:40–43	70	15:9–11	108
23:46	86	15:13	107, 108
24:46–48	70	15:18–16:4a	108–9
24:47	71	16:4b–33	109–10
		16:13	99
John		16:16	110
1:5	98	16:28	110
1:10	95	17:1–26	110
1:14	99, 103	17:21	98
1:17	99	18:1–19:42	94
1:19–12:50	94	18:38	99
1:29	95, 96	20:21	98
1:38–39	116	20:31	97, 99
3:14	114		
3:16–17	95	**Acts of the Apostles**	
3:16–21	103	2:38	71
3:17	97	3:19	72
4:23	99	5:31–32	72

Acts of Apostles (*continued*)

11:18	72
11:21	72
13:24	70
14:15	72
15:19	72
15:29	65
17:30	72
19:4	70
26:17–18	72
26:20	72

Romans

1:5	127, 185
1:18–32	187
1:18–2:29	187–88
1:18–3:20	193–94
1:23	187
1:24	194
1:24–25	187
1:25	194
1:26–27	187
1:28	194, 195
1:28–32	187
2:6–8	188
2:6–13	187
2:11	188
2:13	189
3:1–8	187, 189
3:8	169
3:9	189
3:20	188, 189, 201
3:23–24	188
3:27	189
3:31	189
4:1–12	189
4:13–25	189
5:12–21	195
5:20	190
6—7	190–91
6:1	190
6:13	194
6:14	190
6:15	169, 190

6:16	194
6:19	194
7	201
7:1–6	190–91
7:4	191
7:5	191
7:7	191
7:13	191
8:1–4	189
8:4	201
9—11	191–92
9:1–11:36	205
9:14	191
10:4	59, 201, 205
11:11	191
11:28–32	205
11:30–32	193
12:1	194, 204, 205
12:1–2	193–95
12:1–15:13	184–85, 192–204
12:2	194
12:3–16	195–98
12:4–8	207
12:6	196
12:9	196
12:10–13	197
12:14–16	197
12:16	196, 204
12:20	199
13:1–7	185, 199–200
13:6–7	200
13:8	200
13:8–10	200
13:9	201, 204
13:10	201
13:11–14	202
13:12	202
14:1	205
14:1–12	203
14:1–15:13	186, 202–5
14:3	205
14:13–23	203–4
14:23	204
15:1–7	204–5
15:2	204
15:7	193, 205

15:7–13	205	13:8–13	153
16:26	127	16:10	140

1 Corinthians

1:1–2	141–42
1:4–9	141–42
1:10	142
1:10–4:21	142–44
1:11	140
1:26–28	143
1:30	161
2:3	143
4:9–13	143
4:16	142, 144
4:17	140
4:21	144, 151
5:1–13	144–46
5:1–6:20	144–47
5:1–7:40	144–48
5:9	139
5:9–11	222
5:11	146
6:1–11	145
6:1–13	146
6:11	161
6:12–20	146–47, 145
7:1	147
7:1–40	147–48
7:2	148
7:24	148
8:1	151
8:1–13	149–50
8:1–11:1	148, 203
8:3	151
8:11	149
9:1–27	150–51
10:1–33	150
10:12	151
10:24	151, 153
11:1	149
12:12–31	207
13:1–13	151
13:1–3	152
13:4–5	153
13:4–7	152–53

2 Corinthians

1:1–2:13	140
1:3–11	154
1:12–2:13	154–55
2:1–12	154
3:13	155
2:14–6:10	155–57
2:14–7:4	140
3:18	194
4:5	174
4:7–8	155–56
4:13	156
5:10	156
5:21	161
6:4–10	156–57
7:5–16	140
8:1–9:15	140
10:1–18	158
10:1–13:13	140
10:10	158
11:10	158
11:13	157
11:16–12:10	158–59
11:23–29	158–59
12:1–13:10	157–59
12:10	158, 159

Galatians

1:11–2:21	164–66
2:1–5	164
2:5	164
2:11–14	164
2:14	164
2:15–17	164–65
2:16	162
2:17	165–66
2:18–21	166
2:19–20	166
2:21	59, 166
3:1–5:12	167–69
3:8	167
3:10	167

Galatians (*continued*)

3:16	167
3:19	168
3:21	59, 168
3:24	168
3:28	168, 226
4:8	169
4:9	169
4:12–20	168–69
5:1	170
5:3	167
5:4	212
5:11	169
5:13–14	200
5:13–15	169–70
5:14	170
5:16–26	170–72
5:19–21	171
5:22–23	171–72
6:2	172, 204

Ephesians

1:3–14	216
1:3–3:21	215
1:15–23	216–17
1:22–23	207
2:1–10	217
2:8	217
2:11–22	217–18
2:15	217–18
3:1–3	215
3:1–13	218
3:4	218
3:6	218
3:14–21	218
4:1–3	219
4:1–16	219–20
4:1–6:20	215
4:13	220
4:15	220
4:17	220
4:17–24	221
4:17–5:14	220–22
4:17–6:9	218–19
4:25–5:2	221–22
5:1	221–22
5:3–14	222

5:15–6:9	222
5:21	224
5:21–6:9	223–28
6:1–3	224
6:5–8	224–25
6:6	225
6:10–20	222–23
6:12	223
6:21–22	215

Philippians

1:3–11	175–77
1:9	176
1:12–26	177
1:27	177, 183
1:27–2:18	177–80, 182
2:1–4	178
2:5	179, 183
2:5–11	179, 182
2:14–15	180
2:19–30	181
3:1	175, 181
3:1–4:9	182, 181–83
3:9	176, 181
3:10	176
3:10–11	182
3:14	182
3:17	181
4:1	182
4:2–3	182–83
4:4–7	183
4:8	183
4:9	183
4:10–20	175

Colossians

1:1–2:5	210–11
1:15–20	210
1:18	207
1:23	211
1:27	218
1:28	211
2:6–7	212
2:6–23	211–12
2:20	212
3:1–4:6	213–14
3:11	213

3:14	213
3:18	224
3:18–4:1	223–28
3:19	224
3:22–25	224–25
4:7–18	209

1 Thessalonians

1:2–10	126–28
1:2–3:13	125–29
1:3	126, 127
1:9–10	126, 127
2:1–12	128–29
2:13–16	129
2:14–16	120
3:11–13	129
4:1–2	124
4:1–8	130–31
4:1–5:24	126, 130–34
4:5	131
4:9	131–32
4:9–12	131–32
4:13–18	125, 132–33
5:1–11	132–33, 202
5:8	133
5:10	132
5:12–22	133
5:15	198

2 Thessalonians

1:1	135
1:3–12	135
2:1–2	134
2:1–12	134
2:13–14	135
2:15	136
3:1–16	136–37

1 Timothy

1:1	244
1:3–10	233–34
1:4	233
1:5	247
1:15	244
2:1–3:16	234–35

2:2	234, 229, 235
2:4	235, 244
3:16	235
4:1–16	235
4:10	244
5:1–6:2a	235–36
6:2b–21	236
6:3	245
6:11	236
6:14	236
6:18	236

2 Timothy

1:6–2:13	237–38
1:9	238
1:10	244
2:3	237
2:11–12	238
2:14–3:9	238–39
2:22	238, 247
2:24–25	238
3:10–4:8	239–40
3:17	239
4:1	239

Titus

1:5	240
1:5–16	240–21
1:9	240
1:11	241
1:12	241
1:15	246
1:16	240, 241
2:1–10	242
2:1–3:7	241–43
2:2	247
2:11–14	242–43
3:1–2	243
3:3	243
3:4–7	243
3:5–7	246
3:8–15	243

James

2:24	169

Subject Index

afflictions, 135, 154, 155, 156, 157
age
the old and the new, 202
of salvation, 67
this age, 195, 200, 202
almsgiving, 47–48, 83–84, 88
antinomian, 46, 186
antitheses, 46–47, 79
arrogance, 144–47, 149
authorities. *See* state

beatitudes, 44–45, 53, 74–75
blameless, 129, 176, 180, 183, 211,
216, 234, 240–41
body, 144–47

called. *See* election theology
carnal, 149. *See also* flesh
celibacy, 147–48
children
of Abraham, 167–69
of day/light, 132–33
See also parents and children
chosen. *See* election theology
Christ
crucified with, 166
end of the law, 201, 205
example of, 179, 204–5
participation in his sufferings,
155–57, 159
putting on, 202

sufferings of, 159
sufficiency of, 211–12
See also Jesus
circumcision, 148, 164, 165,
167–69, 181, 186–88, 212
communion. *See koinōnia*
community, 133–34, 219–20,
250–52
building up the, 148–53,
177–78, 221
called and sanctified, 141–42
disorderly conduct in, 134,
136
factions and divisions within,
142–44
sanctified, 144–47, 150
conscience, 149, 150, 234, 237, 241.
See also weak and strong
consolation, 154
controversy stories, 26–30
conversion. *See* repentance
creation, 246–47. *See also* world
cross as wisdom, 142–44

discernment, 195
disciples
and the parousia, 57–58
persistence in prayer, 82–83
and possessions, 29, 81, 84–85
as vigilant servants, 82–82
and the world, 108–9

321

discipleship, 104–11, 116–17
   cost of, 80–82
divorce, 28–29, 46, 148
doing good, 76–77, 78–79

election theology, 123–24, 124–34,
   135–36, 141–44, 144–48, 151,
   180, 210, 215, 216–17, 243
entrusted tradition. See parathēkē
eternal life, 31, 99–100, 101–2
ethics and Christology, 209–10,
   213–14, 216

faith, 23–25, 100–103, 115, 127,
   133, 164–66, 166–69, 189,
   203–4, 247, 255
   example of, 102–3
   measure of, 196, 203
false teachers, 223–34, 235,
   238–39, 241
family, 81
fasting, 47–48
flesh, 170–72, 212
   works of, 171–72
food
   laws about, 27–28, 203–4
   sacrificed to idols, 148–51
freedom
   and knowledge, 149–50
   from the law, 170
   and love, 149–50
fruit
   of the ethical life, 107–8
   of the Spirit, 171–72
fulfillment
   of all righteousness, 51
   of the law, 45–46

God
   armor of, 133, 222–23
   commandment of God, 27–28,
      106–7, 201
   faithfulness of, 191–92
   imitation of, 221–22
   impartiality of, 188–89, 225
   kingship of, 15–18

mercy of, 40–41, 193, 205, 244
   taught by, 131–32
   will of, 30, 32–33, 41, 46–49, 56,
      86, 131, 194, 195, 218, 253–54
   wrath of, 56, 101, 126, 129, 186,
      187, 193, 217
Golden Rule, 48, 77
good works, 45, 217, 230, 236,
   241–43, 245–46
grace
   of God, 59–62, 242, 245–46
   and the moral life, 59–62
   saved by, 216–18
   trained by God's, 242–43,
      245–46

hardship lists, 143, 155–56,
   156–57, 158–59
holiness, 130–31
hope, 127, 132–33, 133, 244
household codes, 213, 223–27, 244
human predicament, 94–97,
   187–89, 191
humility, 179
husbands and wives, 147–48, 224,
   246

idolatry, 150, 187
images of the moral life
   armament, 133, 202, 222–23
   clothing, 212, 213, 214
   trees, 38, 49, 78
   walking, 131, 219–20
   warfare, 133, 223
imitation, 127–29, 154. See also
   Paul, imitation of
immorality. See porneia
impurity, 131
incest, 144–45
infancy narrative, 67

Jesus
   abiding in, 107–8
   belief in, 97–103
   compassion of, 34, 52
   faithfulness of, 33–34

farewell discourse, 104–11
and God's will, 32–33, 86
inaugural sermon, 67–68, 74
journey to Jerusalem, 79–85
and the law, 25–30, 45–46,
    52–53, 87–88
and the marginalized, 88–89
prayer of, 86–87, 110–11
merciful and compassionate,
    34, 52–53
model of moral life, 31–34,
    50–53, 86–89
model of righteousness, 50–51
sent by the Father, 97–98,
    249–50
summary of his moral teaching,
    34–35, 62–63, 90–91, 111–
    13
See also Christ; Sermon on the
    Mount; Sermon on the Plain
John and the Synoptics, 92–94,
    113–17
Judaizers, 162–3, 181–2
judging others, 48, 77–78, 203
judgment
    final, 41, 49, 56–59, 96, 101, 110,
        117, 187–88, 203, 222, 249–50
    sober, 195–98
justification, 161–62, 164–66,
    187–89, 217, 243, 246

kingdom of God, 14–15, 18–20,
    37–42, 45–46, 48, 65–69, 97,
    113–14, 171, 204, 222, 248–49
koinōnia ("communion"), 175–77

law, 25–30, 45–46, 166–72, 187–88,
    189, 200–201, 217–18, 253–54
of Christ, 169–72
curse of, 167
as disciplinarian, 168
lawlessness, 56, 63
lawsuits, 145, 14
life, 99–100
light and darkness, 45, 95–96,
    98–99, 101, 222

lists of virtues and vices, 171, 183,
    213, 240–41, 247
living quietly, 132
love, 127, 133, 149–50, 151–53,
    169–70, 176, 196–97, 203–4,
    213, 222, 234, 247, 254–55
and knowledge, 149–50
commandment of, 29–30, 46,
    53, 76–77, 88, 104–11, 112,
    115–16, 170, 200–201
of enemies, 76–77, 88, 197,
    198–99
mutual, 131–32
marriage, 147–48
masters and slaves. See slavery
maturity, 211, 218, 220
mind
    debased, 187, 221
    renewal of, 193–95
models of behavior, 85, 102–3
    religious leaders, 53–56, 83–84
moral exhortation, 125–29, 231–33
moral life
    and community, 250–52
    and doing God's will, 253–54
    and faith, 255
    and judgment, 249–50
    and love, 254–55
    and personal example, 252–53
    and salvation, 248–49
moral philosophers, 1–2, 128, 133,
    153, 245
Mosaic law. See law

narrative and the moral life, 13–14
new commandment, 105–7
new creation, 166, 168, 211, 213,
    214
new man, 217–18
New Testament ethics
    diachronic approach, 2–4
    and the Gospels, 7–8
    and historical reconstruction,
        7–8
    legacy of Jesus and Paul, 8–9
    method of, 1–10, 121–22

New Testament ethics (*continued*)
  and narrative, 13–14
  normative value of, 225–26
  object of, 7
  and Pauline writings, 9, 119–22
  synchronic approach, 5–6
nonretaliation, 46, 76–77, 133,
  198–200

parables and the moral life,
  39–41, 71, 75–76, 78, 82,
  84–85, 107–8
paraenesis, 122, 125, 130, 169–72,
  184–85, 192–205, 207, 213–14,
  215, 218–23
paraenetic letter, 125, 233
parathēkē ("entrusted tradition"),
  229, 232, 236, 237, 245
parents and children, 224
parousia ("coming"), 41, 82, 127,
  129, 130, 132–33, 134, 136,
  180, 183, 202, 230, 242, 249–50
Paul
  afflictions of, 154, 155, 156, 157
  background to his letters,
    123–24, 124–25, 134–35,
    138–41, 162–63, 174–75,
    184–85, 207–10, 214–16,
    229–33, 237, 240
  and boasting, 158–59
  example of his life, 128–29,
    134–37, 152–53, 164, 168–69,
    181–82, 234, 239
  imitation of, 126–28, 136–37,
    144, 149, 150–51, 153–59, 174,
    181–83
  man of integrity, 129, 154–55,
    158
  objections to his gospel, 165–66,
    185–92
  rhetoric of, 129, 210, 215–16,
    236–37
  summary of his moral teaching,
    137, 159–60, 172–73, 183,
    205–6, 227–28, 244–47
perfection, 46–47, 53

persecution, 127, 134
personal example, 237–38, 240,
  244, 252–53
Pharisees and scribes, 53–56
pleasing God, 128–29
porneia ("immorality"), 131,
  144–45, 171, 222
possessions, 28–29, 81, 83–86
power and weakness, 157–59
prayer, 47–48, 82–83
prostitution, 131, 145, 146–47
pseudonymity and Paul's letters,
  120–22, 208–9, 229–33
punishment, 30–31
purity laws, 27–28, 88

reciprocity in the moral life, 76–77
reconciliation, 156–57, 217–18
repentance, 20–23, 38–39, 69–73,
  103, 111–12, 114–15, 127, 238
reversal of fortune, 67, 68–69,
  75–76
reward, 30–31, 56–59
riches, 236
righteousness, 44, 45, 46–48, 110.
  See also justification

Sabbath, 87–88
salvation, 67–69, 231, 244–45,
  248–50
sanctification, 124–34, 130–31,
  141–42
  moral implications of, 144–48
Sermon on the Mount, 7–8, 42–50
Sermon on the Plain, 7–8, 73–79,
  89
sin, 96, 110, 190–91, 204
slavery, 96, 148, 224–25, 236, 242,
  246
social order, 246–47
sound teachers, 240–41, 245
sound teaching, 234, 237, 241–43,
  245
Spirit
  fruit of the, 171–72
  gifts of the, 196

led by the, 171
unity of the, 219–20
walking by the, 170–72
spiritual people, 142
spiritual worship, 193–94
state, 185, 199–200, 243

Torah. *See* law
truth, 99
of the gospel, 163–66

unmarried believers, 147–48

vigilance, 82–83
virtue and vice lists. *See* lists of
virtues and vices
virtuous life, 247

weak and strong, 148–51, 202–05
widows, 235–36, 245–46
woes, 74–75
workers of lawlessness, 49
working out one's salvation, 180
works of the law, 164–66
world, 94–97, 97–98, 108–9, 148,
214, 216, 220–21, 222